Special Tax Zones and EU Law

EUCOTAX Series on European Taxation

VOLUME 66

Introduction

EUCOTAX (European Universities Cooperating on Taxes) is a network of tax institutes currently consisting of eleven universities: WU (Vienna University of Economics and Business) in Austria, Katholieke Universiteit Leuven in Belgium, Corvinus University of Budapest, Hungary, Université Paris-I Panthéon-Sorbonne in France, Universität Osnabrück in Germany, Libera, Università Internazionale di Studi Sociali in Rome (and Università degli Studi di Bologna for the research part), in Italy, Fiscaal Instituut Tilburg at Tilburg University in the Netherlands, Universidad de Barcelona in Spain, Uppsala University in Sweden, Queen Mary and Westfield College at the University of London in the United Kingdom, and Georgetown University in Washington DC, United States of America. The network aims at initiating and coordinating both comparative education in taxation, through the organization of activities such as winter courses and guest lectures, and comparative research in the field, by means of joint research projects, international conferences and exchange of researchers between various countries.

Contents/Subjects

The EUCOTAX series covers a wide range of topics in European tax law. For example tax treaties, EC case law, tax planning, exchange of information and VAT. The series is well-known for its high-quality research and practical solutions.

Objective

The series aims to provide insights on new developments in European taxation.

Readership

Practitioners and academics dealing with European tax law.

Frequency of Publication

2-3 new volumes published each year.

The titles published in this series are listed at the end of this volume.

Special Tax Zones and EU Law

Theory, Implementations, and Future Challenges

Claudio Cipollini

Wolters Kluwer

Published by:
Kluwer Law International B.V.
PO Box 316
2400 AH Alphen aan den Rijn
The Netherlands
E-mail: international-sales@wolterskluwer.com
Website: lrus.wolterskluwer.com

Sold and distributed in North, Central and South America by:
Wolters Kluwer Legal & Regulatory U.S.
7201 McKinney Circle
Frederick, MD 21704
United States of America
Email: customer.service@wolterskluwer.com

Sold and distributed in all other countries by:
Air Business Subscriptions
Rockwood House
Haywards Heath
West Sussex
RH16 3DH
United Kingdom
Email: international-customerservice@wolterskluwer.com

ISBN 978-94-035-1885-5

e-Book: ISBN 978-94-035-1923-4
web-PDF: ISBN 978-94-035-1932-6

Table of Contents

List of Abbreviations xiii

CHAPTER 1
Introduction 1
§1.01 Key Premises 1
§1.02 Historical Background 3
[A] Origin of the Phenomenon 3
[B] Development in the EU Context 5
[1] STZs and Indirect Taxation 5
[2] STZs and Direct Taxation 7
§1.03 The Current Debate on STZs 8
§1.04 Critical Aspects in European Tax Law 9
§1.05 Research Questions 11
§1.06 Objective of the Study 13
§1.07 Limits of the Study 14
§1.08 Definitions 16
§1.09 Outline of the Study 17

CHAPTER 2
The Legal Dimension of STZs 19
§2.01 Introduction 19
§2.02 Definitions 20
[A] The Definition of STZs 20
[B] Other Definitions 21
[1] Free Zones 22
[2] Free Trade Zones 23
[3] Free Ports 24
[4] Special Economic Zones 25
[5] Export Processing Zones 26
§2.03 Classifications 27

§2.04 STZs and Other Figures 28
[A] Tax Havens 28
[B] Customs Warehouses 29
[C] Duty-Free Shops 30
[D] Subsidies 30
§2.05 STZs in the System of Tax Law 31
§2.06 STZs and Objectives of a Social Character 34
[A] General Aspects 34
[B] The Concept of 'Social Tax Incentives' 34
[C] The Role of Social Enterprises 37
§2.07 Final Remarks 40

CHAPTER 3
The EU Law Framework 43
§3.01 Introduction 43
§3.02 STZs and State Aid Law 44
[A] Regional Aid in the TFEU 44
[1] Notion of State aid under Article 107(1) TFEU 44
[a] The Existence of an Undertaking 45
[b] The State Origin 46
[c] Advantage 47
[d] Selectivity 47
[e] Effect on Trade and Competition 49
[2] Exemptions under Article 107(3)(a) TFEU 50
[3] Exemptions under Article 107(3)(c) TFEU 51
[4] The Supervision of the Commission under Article 108 TFEU 51
[5] ECJ Case Law 52
[a] The Juntas Generales Case 53
[b] The Azores Case 54
[c] The UGT-Rioja Case 57
[d] The Gibraltar Case 59
[e] The Sardinia Case 60
[f] The Deufil Case 61
[B] Regional Aid in Secondary Law 63
[1] General Block Exemption Regulation 63
[2] De Minimis Regulation 64
[3] The EU Cohesion Policy: Guidelines on Regional Aid 65
[4] Communications from the Commission on Notified Regional Aid Schemes 69
[C] Social Services of General Interest in the TFEU 69
[1] General Aspects 69
[2] Exemption under Article 106(2) TFEU 70
[3] The Altmark Criteria 72
[D] SSGIs in Secondary Law: The *Almunia* Package 74

[1] Commission Decision 2012/21/EU 74
[2] Commission Communication 2012/C 8/02 75
[3] Commission Regulation (EU) No. 360/2012 (*De Minimis* Regulation) 77
[4] Commission Framework 2012/C8/03 78
[5] Commission Staff Working Document 79
§3.03 STZs and Internal Market Law 81
[A] Fundamental Freedoms in Primary Law 82
[1] General Aspects 82
[2] The Principle of Tax Non-discrimination 83
[3] ECJ Case Law 85
[a] The Sardinia Case 87
[b] The Juntas Generales Case 88
[4] Fundamental Freedoms and SSGIs 89
[B] Harmonization Measures in Secondary Law 90
[1] FZs in the UCC 91
[2] FZs in the Recast VAT Directive 93
[3] FZs in Directive 2008/118/EC (Excise Duty) 94
[4] The Concept of 'Social Advantages' 95
[5] The Concept of 'Social Enterprises' 96
[6] Social Enterprises and Other Soft Law Instruments 98
§3.04 STZs and Harmful Tax Competition 99
[A] General Aspects 99
[B] The Code of Conduct for Business Taxation 100
[1] Main Features 100
[2] STZs and Harmful Tax Measures 102
[3] Guidance on Tax Privileges Related to SEZs 104
§3.05 Final Remarks 105

CHAPTER 4
STZs in the Member States 109
§4.01 Introduction 109
§4.02 STZs Review 111
[A] Bulgaria 111
[1] Bulgarian FZs 111
[B] Croatia 113
[1] Croatian FZs 113
[C] Czech Republic 114
[1] Czech FZs 114
[D] Denmark 114
[1] Copenhagen Free Port 114
[E] Estonia 115
[1] Estonian FZs 115
[F] Finland 116
[1] Finnish FZs 116

[2] Aland Islands 117
[G] France 118
[1] French FZs 118
[2] Urban Tax-Free Zones 119
[3] French Overseas Departments: DOM 120
[4] Saint-Martin 121
[H] Germany 122
[1] German FZs 122
[2] Helgoland and Busingen 123
[I] Greece 124
[1] Greek FZs 124
[2] Mount Athos 124
[J] Hungary 124
[1] Hungarian FZs 124
[K] Italy 125
[1] Italian FZs 125
[2] Urban Tax-Free Zones 126
[3] Special Economic Zones 129
[4] Livigno 130
[5] Campione d'Italia 130
[L] Latvia 131
[1] SEZs in Latvia 131
[M] Lithuania 133
[1] FEZs in Lithuania 133
[N] Luxembourg 135
[1] Luxembourg Free Port 135
[O] Malta 135
[1] Malta Free Port 135
[P] Poland 136
[1] Polish 'Free Customs Duty Areas' 136
[Q] Portugal 137
[1] Madeira 137
[2] Azores 140
[R] Romania 141
[1] Romanian FZs 141
[S] Slovenia 143
[1] Free Port of Koper 143
[T] Spain 143
[1] Spanish FZs 143
[2] Canary Islands 145
[3] Basque Country and Navarra 148
[4] Ceuta and Melilla 150
[U] United Kingdom 151
[1] Gibraltar 151
§4.03 Final Remarks 153

CHAPTER 5
Developing a General Legal Theory of STZs 155
§5.01 Introduction 155
§5.02 The Concept 156
[A] The Territorial Dimension 157
[1] The Geographical Delimitation 157
[2] The Reference Framework 159
[3] The Territorial Connecting Factor 160
[B] The Structural Dimension 163
[1] Exclusion Regimes 164
[2] Subtractive Regimes 164
[C] The Functional Dimension 166
[1] Economic Tax Incentives 167
[2] Social Tax Incentives 170
[D] The Definition 174
§5.03 The Implementing Models 175
[A] The 'FZ' Model 175
[B] The 'State Aid Zone' Model 177
[1] Regional Aid 178
[2] The 'Infra-State Body' 179
[C] The 'Extraterritorial Zone' Model 181
[D] Hybrid Situations 182
§5.04 Summary of the Results 182
§5.05 Final Remarks 184

CHAPTER 6
Towards a New Model for Social Cohesion Policies 185
§6.01 Introduction 185
§6.02 Design of the Model 187
[A] The Territorial Dimension 187
[1] Geographical Delimitation 187
[2] Reference Framework 188
[3] Territorial Connecting Factor 188
[B] The Structural Dimension 189
[1] Tax Allowances and Tax Credits 189
[2] The Focus on Direct Taxation 191
[C] The Functional Dimension 192
[1] The Scope of the Tax Measures 192
[2] Eligible Undertakings 192
[3] Obligations of the Recipient Undertakings 194
[D] The Denomination 195
§6.03 Analysis of the Variables in the EU Law Framework 196
[A] State Aid Rules 196
[1] Social Tax Incentives and SSGIs 198
[2] Outcomes under the Altmark Criteria 199

[3] Outcomes under Article 106(2) TFEU 207
[B] Fundamental Freedoms 210
[1] The Situation of the Recipient Undertakings 211
[2] The Situation of the Employees 213
[3] The Situation of the Suppliers 220
[C] The Code of Conduct for Business Taxation 222
[1] The Code of Conduct Criteria 223
[2] The Guidance on Tax Privileges Related to SEZs 225
§6.04 Summary of the Results 226
§6.05 Synthesis of the Model 229
[A] Territorial Dimension 229
[B] Structural Dimension 229
[C] Functional Dimension 231
§6.06 Final Remarks 232

Chapter 7
Implementation Aspects of the Social Cohesion Zone 233
§7.01 Introduction 233
§7.02 Comparison of the Models under the General Legal Theory of STZs 234
§7.03 The Social Cohesion Zone: An Opportunity for EU Cohesion Policy? 237
[A] General Aspects 237
[B] Legal Background 239
[C] The EU Governance of the Social Cohesion Zone 240
§7.04 The Social Cohesion Zone and the Fiscal Residue 242
§7.05 The Social Cohesion Zone: The Practical Implementation 245
[A] Substantial Aspects 246
[1] Eligibility Conditions 246
[2] Tax Incentive Mechanism 247
[3] Obligations of the Recipient Undertakings 248
[B] Procedural Aspects 249
[1] Selection of the Eligible Areas 249
[2] Public Procurement Procedure 250
[3] Monitoring 251
§7.06 Final Remarks 251

Chapter 8
Conclusions and Recommendations 253
§8.01 Summary of the Research Process 253
§8.02 Answers to the Research Questions and Conclusions 255
[A] The General Legal Theory of STZs 256
[B] The New Model of the Social Cohesion Zone 257
§8.03 Recommendations for Future EU Initiatives 259
§8.04 Areas for Future Research 261

§8.05 Final Conclusions 262

Bibliography 265

Table of Cases 275

Table of Legislation and Policy Documents 281

Index 297

List of Abbreviations

AAE	*Areas Aduaneras Especiales*
AIEM	*Arbitrio sobre las Importaciones y Entregas de Mercancías*
CCC	Community Customs Code
CIT	Corporate Income Tax
COM	*Collectivité d'Outre-Mer* (French Overseas Collectivities)
DOM	*Département et région d'Outre-Mer* (French Overseas Departments)
EAGGF	European Agricultural Guidance and Guarantee Fund
EBIT	Earnings Before Interest and Tax
EBITDA	Earnings Before Interest, Taxes, Depreciation, and Amortization
EC	European Community
ECJ	European Court of Justice
EEC	European Economic Community
EFTA	European Free Trade Association
EPZ	Export Processing Zone
ERDF	European Regional Development Fund
ESF	European Social Fund
EU	European Union
EZ	Enterprise Zone
FEZ	Free Economic Zone
FIFG	Financial Instrument for Fisheries
FTZ	Free Trade Zone
FZ	Free Zone
GBER	General Block Exemption Regulation
GDP	Gross Domestic Product
IGIC	*Impuesto General Indirecto de Canarias*

IRAP	*Imposta Regionale sulle Attività Produttive* (Regional Tax on Productive Activities)
IPSI	*Impuesto sobre la Producción, los Servicios y la Importación*
ITP	*Impuesto sobre Transmisiones Patrimoniales*
NUTS	*Nomenclature des unités territoriales statistiques* (Nomenclature of Territorial Units for Statistics)
OCTs	Overseas Countries and Territories
OECD	Organization for Economic Cooperation and Development
OM	*Octroi de Mer*
OMC	Open Method of Coordination
OMR	*Octroi de Mer Regional*
OR	Outermost Region
PIT	Personal Income Tax
PPS	Purchasing Power Standards
REB	*Registro Especial de Buques y Empresas Navieras* (Special Register for Ships and Shipping Companies)
REF	*Régimen Económico y Fiscal* (Fiscal Economic Regime)
RET	Real Estate Tax
RIC	*Reserva para Inversiones en Canarias* (Reserve for Investments in the Canary Islands)
ROCE	Return on Capital Employed
SEZ	Special Economic Zone
SME	Small and Medium Enterprises
SGEI	Service of General Economic Interest
SGI	Service of General Interest
SSGI	Social Service of General Interest
STZ	Special Tax Zone
TEU	Treaty on the European Union
TFEU	Treaty on the Functioning of the European Union
UCC	Union Customs Code
UK	United Kingdom
UNCTAD	United Nations Conference on Trade and Development
US	United States of America
VAT	Value Added Tax
WISE	Work Integration Social Enterprises
WTO	World Trade Organization
ZEC	*Zona Especial Canaria* (Canary Islands Special Zone)
ZFU	*Zones Franches Urbaines* in France *Zone Franche Urbane* in Italy (Urban Tax-Free Zones)

CHAPTER 1
Introduction

§1.01 KEY PREMISES

The impact of the last economic crisis in Europe has brought severe consequences in most Member States on all levels of the economy, especially for those territories affected by previous development delays.

Within these areas, made more vulnerable by their remoteness and distance, the negative effects have resulted in industrial stagnation and job losses, causing the increase of unprecedented social issues.

Nowadays, European Union (EU) institutions are called upon to provide concrete answers for these situations, through the design and the implementation of effective tax policies in accordance with the fundamental principles of the EU legal framework.

In this context, the starting idea of the present work is that, among the various solutions available, Special Tax Zones (hereinafter also called STZs) can represent a useful instrument for delivering growth and mitigating the state of economic and social emergency of the most disadvantaged areas of the EU.[1]

From a classic perspective, STZs can be identified with a phenomenon belonging to the field of customs law, characterized by the presence of an area of land where the host country's standard customs regimes for import and export are replaced by more liberal rules with the objective of increasing international trade.[2]

As long as this is the case, such measures are exclusively related to indirect taxation with the establishment of a zone where goods can be stored for a prolonged period without the application of custom duties or other indirect taxes.

1. In this sense, *see, ex multis,* UNITED NATIONS – ECONOMIC AND SOCIAL COMMISSION FOR ASIA AND PACIFIC, *Commercial Development of Regional Ports as Logistic Centres,* United Nations Publications, New York, 2002.
2. W. DE JONG, *Establishing Free Zones for Regional Development,* Library of the European Parliament, 2013, available at http://www.europarl.europa.eu/RegData/bibliotheque/briefin-g/2013/130481/LDM_BRI(2013)130481-_REVEN.pdf.

Nevertheless, most recent examples of STZs often offer a broader set of incentives than just customs arrangements, including benefits on income tax.[3]

On these bases, the term 'STZs' can be used – in a first approximation – to encompass under its 'umbrella' all the areas of land where some territorial tax advantages are granted on direct and/or indirect taxation.

Regardless of the type of tax benefits granted by the hosting country, today STZs are common all over the world and, during the last three decades, their presence has multiplied, especially in the United States of America (US) and in many developing countries.[4]

In recent years, even countries within the EU have submitted, with increasing intensity, inquires to the Commission aimed at obtaining authorizations for the establishment of new zones with special tax regimes also related to direct taxation; the main reason under such initiatives is generally associated with the economic idea that the introduction of a level of taxation lower than the one generally applied elsewhere should positively influence, in a more or less relevant way, the choice of location of business activities.[5] In this direction, the stated goal is to create favourable conditions for enterprises and foreign investors, starting a process of economic recovery of those areas that are seriously affected by matters of falling incomes and unemployment.

On these premises, most Member States recently demonstrate a concrete interest towards the theme of STZs, developing some serious initiatives for promoting the same instrument in a set of new strategies for improving the employment rate of the most disadvantaged areas of their national territory.[6]

Nonetheless, STZs have not yet found a systematic framework in the EU legal system; for instance, for what regards the influence of State aid rules and the free movement of persons, these zones are still living moments of great uncertainty.

Moreover, the notion of STZs is still little investigated since it is generally confined to the few experts who deal with customs matters and international tax planning; academic studies on this phenomenon are rare and they usually focus their attention on the economic aspects related to the establishment of a zone, without serious attempts of outlining a legal theory on the topic.[7]

---

3. For example Madeira Free Trade Zone in Portugal and Urban Tax-Free Zones in France and in Italy.
4. In 1970, only a few countries are equipped with such zones, but already in 1996 the Organization for Economic and Cooperative Development (OECD) estimates about 500 industrial Free Zones located in 73 countries, while the international list drawn up in 1997 by the World Economic Processing Zones Association considers more than 800 Export Processing Zones and Commercial Zones throughout the world.
5. For an evaluation of the advantages related to the establishment of an STZ *see* United Nations – Economic and Social Commission for Asia and Pacific, *supra.*, United Nations Publications, New York, 2002.
6. *See* M. Ingrosso, O. Nocerino, F. Roccatagliata, C. Sacchetto, *Le Zone Franche*, Chamber of Commerce of Naples, Naples, 1998, p. 3.
7. The lack of interest on such phenomenon is also linked to the difficulties in defining the border between tax law and customs law. In fact, tax law scholars traditionally confine topics dealing with customs outside the perimeter of tax law studies, assuming that such themes have to be developed and classified under a different area of practice (i.e., customs law). As a predictable consequence of the aforementioned approach, STZs still do not find a systematic framework within the tax law area and no sufficient studies have been made on the topic.

Therefore, the existing literature on STZs generally describes a set of very technical rules about custom administrative procedures, while there is no trace of a systematic approach able to define a comprehensive theory of STZs from a legal perspective.

Given the above, the approach of the present study is first addressed to explore the legal framework and the factual experience of STZs in the EU, with the objective of working out a comprehensive theory on the topic in the field of European tax law.

After the definition of the theoretical background, the second part of this work is aimed at developing a new implementing model of STZs for social cohesion policies; in this direction, the declared objective requires important efforts, as it is necessary to face some critical issues of EU law, such as those dealing with the outer limits of negative integration set by State aid rules and fundamental freedoms.

At the end of the book, STZs are thus presented under a new light both for what concerns their theoretical understanding and the possibility of their practical implementation.

In the first case, in fact, STZs are finally identified as an institute belonging to European tax law, thus providing an innovative reading-key and the proper conceptual categories to deeply understand the factual experience from a legal point of view. In the second case, the outcomes of this study give evidence of the possibility of a practical implementation of the same instrument through the development of a new model in the context of social cohesion policies, approaching the issues related to its compatibility with the variables of EU law.

On the ground of the above premises - and before starting the review of the relevant sources - the present chapter introduces the topic, outlining, among others, not only the historical background and context but also the research questions, the objectives and the limits of this study.

§1.02 HISTORICAL BACKGROUND

[A] Origin of the Phenomenon

The background of STZs is historically related to a system of special rules authorized by the hosting country concerning goods and assets, commercial and industrial activities or transactions made within these territories.

The origin of such zones is closely linked to the need of creating free trade areas, where goods can be stored, handled, and processed without the enforcement of rights, duties, and all the other tax measures normally applicable.[8]

8. *See* M. Ingrosso, O. Nocerino, F. Roccatagliata, C. Sacchetto, *supra.*, Chamber of Commerce of Naples, Naples, 1998, pp. 5-9.

Some authors identify the origins of STZs between the ninth century BC and eighth century BC because of the market development arising from the frequent religious fairs.[9]

Other authors choose to place the origin of STZs a few centuries later, during the Greek Hellenistic period, as part of a system of facilities and tax exemptions that allow to permanently suspend not only indirect taxes on the religious sacrifices and sales, but also customs duties on imports and exports.[10]

Some historical studies identify the 'Port-Ateleia' on the Greek island of Delos as a symbol of the first presence of the same assumptions that characterize these territories nowadays.[11]

Moreover, the so-called *portus immunes* of the Roman period – whose existence is confirmed in the work 'Iugurta' by Sallust – are recognized as the immediate antecedents of STZs,[12] as well as the 'Free Ports' of the late Middle Ages.[13]

However, from a more contemporary and pragmatic perspective, the focus on the topic should be moved to the end of the Second World War, considering the new political and economic framework marked by the primary role of emerging countries.

In that period, in fact, Free Ports become important reference points for new economic initiatives and a crucial tool in international competition as well.

After the Second World War, Germany and Ireland are the first countries – within the territory of the EU – that establish Free Ports and Industrial Zones, such as the best-known cases of the city of Hamburg and the area of Shannon.

In any case, despite the fact that there is not an unanimously recognized 'birthday' of STZs, every kind of contemporary study on the phenomenon should properly start from the end of the Second World War, considering the fact that any attempt to examine previous experiences is relevant only from an historical point of view.

In recent decades, STZs have answered to the needs of international businesses, as industrial countries have realized that they need to maintain their market positions and to expand production and sales structures beyond national borders.

In other words, such areas become the vehicles by which many countries maintain their market position unchanged on the basis of a new policy of minimizing production costs and eliminating any waste.[14]

---

9. S. Finardi, E. Moroni, *Stati d'eccezione, Zone e Porti Franchi nell'economia–mondo*, FrancoAngeli, Milan, 2001, p. 15; N.K. Rauh, *The sacred bonds of commerce: religion, economy, and trade society at Hellenistic Roman Delos, 166-87 B.C.*, J.C. Gieben, Amsterdam, 1993.
10. L. Casson, *The Grain Trade of the Hellenistic World*, in *Ancient Trade and Society*, L. Casson (ed.), Wayne State University Press, Detroit, 1984, p. 76.
11. G. Reger, *Regionalism and Change in the Economy of Independent Delos, 314-167 B.C.*, University of California Press, Berkeley, 1994.
12. *See* L. De Ligt, *Fairs and Markets in the Roman Empire. Economic and Social Aspects of Periodic Trade in a Pre-industrial Society*, J.C. Gieben, Amsterdam, 1993, p. 45.
13. W. Diamond, D. Diamond, *Tax-Free Trade Zones of the World*, M. Bender, New York, 1990; T.H. Lloyd, *England and the German Hanse, 1157-1611: A Study of Their Trade and Commercial Diplomacy*, Cambridge University Press, Cambridge, 1991.
14. G. Vimercati, *Le zone franche industriali nei paesi emergenti. Il sud est asiatico*, FrancoAngeli, Milan 1985.

Furthermore, the same zones have been recently used to pursue other objectives, such as those related to the development delays of the most disadvantaged areas and the social issues linked to job losses and increasing poverty.

Therefore, in recent history, these areas have been often considered as the key tool to manage tax policies aimed not only to favour international competition, but also to create new jobs and to improve the living conditions in the disadvantaged areas affected by serious underdevelopment.

[B] Development in the EU Context

[1] STZs and Indirect Taxation

The historical background of STZs within the EU is characterized by a series of initiatives in the form of directives and regulations essentially aimed at harmonizing national provisions concerning indirect taxation, considering the difficulties in pursuing objectives of harmonization in the field of direct taxation.[15]

Throughout the last decades, in fact, the positive integration of EU law has approached the topic of STZs only for what regards the so called 'Free Zones' (hereinafter named also 'FZs') – characterized by the exclusive presence of tax benefits on indirect taxation – streamlining the related legal framework through a path parallel to the abolition of customs duties between Member States and to the creation of a customs union.

In other terms, the historical development of STZs in the context of EU law generally influences the regulation of the aspect of FZs related to customs duties, Value Added Tax (VAT) and excises, on the ground of the fact that Member States have conferred to the Union the exclusive legislative power only in the field of indirect taxation and not in the area of direct taxation.

On these premises, the notion of FZs evolves over time from the creation of the European Community to the present day, considering that, at the time of its founding, there are zones similar to the current concept of FZs only within the Italian and German territory.[16]

In the first period, the approval of Directive 69/75/EEC[17] establishes the requirement of harmonization between the Member States' rules regarding customs laws and provides a first legal definition of FZs, considered as large areas of land – including cities and villages – that enjoy tax benefits in consideration of their historical, economic, and social background.

15. For some considerations on the initiatives on direct taxation *see* M. Lang, P. Pistone, J. Schuch, C. Staringer, *Introduction to European Tax Law: Direct Taxation*, 3rd Edition, Spiramus Press, Wien, 2013, p. 24.
16. At that time of the European Community founding, Belgium, France, and Luxembourg had no zones, while the Netherlands had only warehouses.
17. Council Directive 69/75/EEC of 4 March 1969 on the harmonization of provisions laid down by law, regulation or administrative action relating to free zones, O.J. 1969, L 58, pp. 11-13.

The Directive represents the legal basis of FZs, containing rules governing not only their functioning but also their establishment.[18] Under Article 10, for instance, every new zone set up with national provisions and in accordance with the principles laid down by the Directive must be notified to the Commission. This notification does not constitute a mere formal act, but a tool that can enable the Commission to verify the full compliance of the provisions enacted by the Member State with the same Directive.

Later, Regulation (EEC) No. 2504/88,[19] based on Article 113 of the EEC Treaty, emphasizes the promotional aspect of FZs for EU trade policy and the important role that such zones play in the redistribution of goods, not only outside, but also inside the perimeter of the Community.

Moreover, the Regulation establishes that Member States may designate parts of the customs territory of the Community as FZs,[20] establishing the area covered by each FZ and ensuring that these areas are enclosed with entry and exit points under the customs supervision (Article 2).

Therefore, in accordance with Regulation (EEC) No. 2504/88, FZs are characterized by the fact that the goods here found are considered, for the purposes of customs duties, as if they were not within the customs territory of the Community.

Later, in 1992, EU institutions put together in a single text – the so-called Community Customs Code (hereinafter also CCC)[21] – all the provisions of customs law issued during a period of twenty-five years and mainly scattered in a multitude of regulations and directives.

The CCC brings back the multiple terms used by Member States to only two concise definitions – FZs and free warehouses – and provides the publication by the Commission of a list of the FZs operating and existing within the territory of the Community.[22] Furthermore, in addition to storage operations, the CCC authorizes to conduct any activity in a FZ of industrial nature (e.g., the production or processing of goods) or commercial nature (e.g., purchase or sale of goods or services as banking and insurance).[23]

---

18. The Directive governs the entrance into the Free Zones of goods of any kind, whatever their number, their country of origin, consignment or destination (Article 2); the loading, unloading, transshipment and storage, the usual forms of handling and operations of destruction (Article 3); the placing on the consumption and use of goods (Article 4); the different treatments that can be used for the same goods (Article 5); the length of time during which goods may remain in Free Zones (Article 6); the divestment thereof (Article 7); the levying of customs duties, taxes having equivalent effect and agricultural levies at the time of release for consumption (Article 8).
19. Council Regulation (EEC) No. 2504/88 of 25 July 1988 on free zones and free warehouses, O.J. 1988, L 225, pp. 8-13.
20. For further information on warehouses and their characteristics, *see* B.J.M. Terra, P.J. Wattel, *European Tax Law*, 6h Edition, Kluwer Law International, Alphen aan den Rijn, 2012, pp. 298 et seq.
21. Council Regulation (EEC) No. 2913/92 of 12 October 1992 establishing the Community Customs Code, O.J. 1992, L 302, pp. 1-50.
22. Communication from the Commission of 23 February 2002 publishing the list of free zones in existence and in operation in the Community, O.J. 2002, C 50, pp. 16-18 (last update 21 August 2019).
23. According to Article 172 of the Community Customs Code, for customs purposes it is sufficient that the exercise of these activities is first notified to the competent authorities.

The last step of the harmonization process coincides with the new Union Customs Code (hereinafter also UCC), approved by Regulation (EU) No. 952/2013[24] that today represents one of the main legal acts dealing with the present topic in the context of EU law; its content is deeply analysed in Chapter 3 which is entirely dedicated to the review of the EU law framework of STZs.

[2] STZs and Direct Taxation

As far as direct taxation is concerned, the historical background of the Union gives evidence of many examples that differ from the FZ regulated by the UCC, with the presence of a broader set of incentives also related to income tax; this clearly means that the past of STZs has not an exclusive value for customs purposes, considering that many areas have been characterized by a set of norms affecting direct taxation.

The Madeira International Business Centre,[25] or the situations of 'Urban Tax-Free Zones' (ZFU) in France (*Zones Franches Urbaines*)[26] and in Italy (*Zone Franche Urbane*)[27] represent clear examples of tax schemes where some benefits have also been granted on direct taxation.

As long as this is the case, the historical development of the phenomenon of STZs in the Union involves some crucial points of analysis concerning the influence of EU law on direct taxation, especially for what regards the evolution in the interpretation of State aid rules and fundamental freedoms.

The basic assumption, in fact, deals with the fact that these types of zones, as they include benefits on direct taxation, may distort competition since some enterprises can take advantages while some others not.

In this regard, the historical development of EU law with reference to STZs finds one of its most important key elements in the progressive evolution of the case law of the European Court of Justice (ECJ) and in some documents issued by the Commission, whose interpretation of State aid rules and fundamental freedoms has contributed significantly to the definition of the current legal framework. Among the most relevant material, it is important to mention a first group of decisions where the ECJ develops its position about the extent of selectivity, being this one of the requirements for the recognition of State aid under the provision of Article 107 TFEU (Treaty on the Functioning of the European Union),[28] with the aim to clearly distinguish the situations in which the tax advantages granted lead to a distortion of competition. Besides such decisions, there is a second group of cases where the ECJ pays attention to the

24. Regulation (EU) No. 952/2013 of the European Parliament and of the Council of 9 October 2013 laying down the Union Customs Code, O.J. 2013, L. 269, pp. 1-101. The Union Customs Code (UCC) has entered into force on 30 October 2013 repealing Regulation (EC) No. 450/2008 of the European Parliament and of the Council of 23 April 2008 laying down the Community Customs Code, O.J. 2008, L 145, pp. 1-64.
25. *See infra* section §4.02[Q][1].
26. *See infra* section §4.02[G][1].
27. *See infra* section §4.02[K][2].
28. Consolidate version of the Treaty on the Functioning of the European Union, O.J. 2012, C 326, pp. 47-390.

interpretation of the exceptions provided under Article 107(3) TFEU, developing some ideas about the limits through which territorial tax advantages – as those provided within STZs – may be granted to a limited area of land without representing an infringement of State aid rules. Moreover, other decisions of the ECJ approach the principle of tax non-discrimination, analysing its related issues with specific references to the phenomenon of STZs.

Finally, the historical background of STZs and direct taxation is also characterized by the content of the Code of Conduct for Business Taxation adopted by the ECOFIN (Economic and Financial Affairs Council) on 1 December 1997.[29]

In all the above sources, it is possible to identify an historical evolution where the EU institutions progressively open a room for studying the implementation of territorial tax benefits on direct taxation; the 'state of the art' of the topic is fully investigated under Chapter 3 where a comprehensive review of the EU law regarding STZs is carried out, including the relevant case law of the ECJ.

§1.03 THE CURRENT DEBATE ON STZS

Today, EU institutions point out the need to promote the growth of competitiveness of regional areas where the standard of living is abnormally low or where there are severe forms of unemployment, searching for tax policies able to facilitate the development of certain regions affected by development delays.

In this context, many studies identify STZs as a valuable tool to carry out regional development policies[30] as they can be used – for example – to fight against undeclared illegal labour,[31] concretely reducing many fees and charges which affect companies and workers.

There are many proponents of the benefits associated with the establishment of STZs who highlight the positive aspects from an economic and political perspective;[32] according to them, STZs can lead to important benefits such as the increase of employment – especially in underdeveloped areas –, the improvement of skills of the local workforce and the creation of new technologies[33] to attract foreign capital or to stimulate local capacity.

29. Conclusions of the ECOFIN Council Meeting on 1 December 1997 concerning taxation policy – Resolution of the Council and the Representatives of the Governments of the Member States, meeting within the Council of 1 December 1997 on conduct for business taxation, O.J. 1998, C 2, pp. 1-6.
30. For an analysis of EU competition policies *see also* F.G. Wishlade, *Regional State Aid and Competition Policy in the European Union*, Kluwer Law International, The Hague, 2003.
31. M. Ingrosso, O. Nocerino, F. Roccatagliata, C. Sacchetto, *supra.*, Chamber of Commerce of Naples, Naples, 1998, p. 40.
32. G.F. Dalla Costa, S. Nardo, M. Menini, *Le zone franche nella globalizzazione. Definizioni, tipologie, percorsi di sviluppo*, CLEUP SC, Padova, 2006, pp. 57 et seq.
33. *See* M. Furlotti, *Le zone franche industriali in una prospettiva di cooperazione tra Europa e America Latina*, in *Economia e politica industriale*, 1986, No. 52, p. 237.

In this sense, the main objective of such zones moves around the economic idea of stimulating a healthy self-propelling regional development,[34] with the creation of new structures and the enhancement of work capacity.

In addition, multinational companies often believe that the interposition of goods in STZs – especially those established in the form of FZs regulated by UCC – allow them to reduce the financial burdens and to increase their cash flow by the suspension of taxation.[35]

According to the same proponents, the activities in STZs usually play a strategic role in the international supply and distribution chains based on the principle of dividing processes, taking advantage from the recent development in the information technology and transportation fields; in this regard, the main products manufactured in STZs are related to industrial sectors – like the textile or the electronic industry – that can produce goods for international markets thanks to relatively unskilled labour force. At the same time, it is worth to mention the recent establishment in such areas of new types of economic activities based on the use of a more qualified labour force,[36] such as in the areas of information technology and finance.

Thus, nowadays in Europe, it is possible to identify a broader framework of different activities attracted by the possibility of using such zones as an opportunity to minimize taxes and to improve their volume of trade.

However, despite any other positive assessment of the phenomenon, these zones are frequently criticized as regimes only able to involve protectionist measures.[37]

It is a topic that, among others, has a lot of credibility with the EU authorities, which do not usually favour the establishment of new zones with benefits on direct taxation.

According to the critics, in fact, tax distortions can affect the free movement of persons, especially when the tax scheme includes benefits related to direct taxation; thus, in such cases, the impediments to the establishment of STZs are generally related to the need of ensuring the full satisfaction of the fundamental freedoms within the internal market.

§1.04 CRITICAL ASPECTS IN EUROPEAN TAX LAW

The background of STZs highlights some relevant gaps in the knowledge, drawing the attention to a series of critical elements that constitute the starting point of the present study.

34. *See* S. Borghi, *Il ruolo delle zone franche industriali nel dialogo nord-sud: il sud-est asiatico*, in *Economia e Politica industriale*, 1985, No. 47, pp. 267 et seq.
35. For a list of such advantages *see* O. Chapman, *Les zones franches dans le monde et aux Etats-Unis*, in *Problemes economiques*, 1986, p. 28. For an interesting economic study *see also* W.R. Mc Daniel, E.W. Kossack, *The Financial Benefits of Users of Foreign-Trade Zones*, in *Columbia Journal of World Business*, 1983, pp. 33 et seq.
36. M. Furlotti, *supra.*, in *Economia e politica industriale*, 1986, No. 52, p. 243.
37. *See*, for instance, D. Spinanger, *Objectives and Impact of Economic Activity Zones – Some Evidence from Asia*, in *Weltwirtschaftliches Archiv*, 1984, Vol. 120, No. 1, pp. 64 et seq.

A first review of the existing literature reveals a general lack of scientific understanding of the phenomenon within the field of tax law; in fact, the most important papers dealing with the theme of STZs represent the results of studies carried out in the field of economics or customs aimed at analysing the effects on business activities and trade.[38]

In this sense, even if some authors make important efforts for determining the reasons for the establishment of such zones,[39] the approach used is exclusively analytical with a focus set on a mere description of the rules governing a specific zone, without properly considering the related legal framework in the light of a systematic view.

The result is that, in the context of law studies, there is no evidence of serious attempts aimed at working out a general theory of STZs, not even by the doctrine active in the field of tax law. In this regard, in fact, the perspective used is essentially based on the description of administrative procedures related to the import/export process, while it is not possible to identify a clear analysis carried out in the light of the main principles of tax law; in particular, the existing literature does not provide a serious approach for deeply understanding the structural and functional variables related to direct and indirect taxation.

Among the main evidences, it is interesting to observe that even the terminology used is the expression of a framework where the tax law variables are poorly understood and investigated; previous studies, in fact, usually identify the same phenomenon using the term 'Free Trade Zones (FTZs)', with various subcategories defined on the basis of the different kinds of benefits granted by the host country.

In this context, many types of zones are mentioned, all characterized by blurred definitional boundaries, such as Commercial FZs, Enterprise Zones (EZs), Export Processing Zones (EPZs),[40] Industrial FZs, Special Economic Zones (SEZs), Free Ports, etc.[41]

---

38. For instance, *see* G.W. Meng, *Evolutionary Model of Free Economic Zones – Different Generations and Structural Features*, in *Chinese Geographical Science*, 2005, Vol. 15, pp. 103-112; I. Soare, D. Nechita, *Free Zones Development in Romania – Premises, Determining Factors and Perspective*, in *Economics and Applied Informatics*, 2010, No. 1, pp. 117-124.
39. For example, *see* C. Xiangming, *The Evolution of Free Economic Zones and the Recent Development of Cross-National Growth Zones*, in *International Journal of Urban and Regional Research*, 1995, Vol. 19, No. 4, pp. 593-621; H.C. Schulze, *Free Trade Zones at the Beginning of the 21st Century*, in *The Comparative and International Law Journal of Southern Africa*, 2002, Vol. 35; W.N. Chang, D.M. Radulescu, *Types of Tax Concessions for Attracting Foreign Direct Investment in Free Economic Zones*, in *CESifo Working Paper Series*, 2004, No. 1175, available at https://papers.ssrn.com/sol3/papers.cfm?abstract_id = 5-34707.
40. R.L. Bolin, *The Global Network of Export Processing Zones*, in *Journal of the Flagstaff Institute*, 1998, Vol. 22, p. 15; A. Basile, D. Germidis, *Investing in Free Export Processing Zones*, OECD Development Centre, Paris, 1984, p. 20; United Nations Conference on Trade and Development, *Export Processing Zones: Role of Foreign Direct Investment and Development Impact, UNCTAD Secretariat Report*, United Nations Publications, Geneva, 1993, p. 5.
41. United Nations: Centre on Transnational Corporations, *The Challenge of Free Economic Zones in Central and Eastern Europe*, United Nations Publications, New York, 1991; United Nations – Economic and Social Commission for Asia and Pacific, *supra.*, United Nations Publications, New York, 2002.

In all the cases, the multitude of wording used focuses the attention on the economic characteristics of each zone, putting in evidence the main aspects related to commercial and industrial dynamics, without providing any specific reference for what concerns the variables of tax law.

Then, there is no evidence of a comprehensive definition of STZs able to encompass all the different situations where a set of territorial tax incentives is granted to a limited area of the hosting State; at the same time, the previous studies neither explore the implementing models nor the key-elements that characterize the concept of STZs.

Furthermore, the coordination between the phenomenon of STZs and EU law is not properly investigated, especially as far as direct taxation is concerned. In this regard, the influence of State aid rules and of free movement of persons is usually explored under a case-by-case analysis on the ground of the decisions issued by the ECJ and the main documents enacted by the Commission; therefore, there is no evidence of a systematic approach for the evaluation of territorial tax incentives under the parameters of EU law.

In summary, the topic of STZs is characterized by the substantial absence of systematic efforts within the tax law literature and, therefore, the first gap of knowledge can be identified in the lack of a general theory of STZs in the context of tax law studies.

The second gap in the knowledge deals with the lack of an implementing model of STZs based on tax incentives of a social character in the area of direct taxation; this study, in fact, starts from the presumption that the existing STZs are not able to face the economic issues of the most disadvantages areas of the Union, with the consequent assumption that a new model of STZs is necessary at the current stage of European integration.

In this regard, the experience of the Member States does not offer examples of tax schemes specifically designed for the development of social cohesion policies, especially when the issues of the most disadvantaged areas of the Union are considered.

In particular, it is not clear whether or not there is still a space left for Member States in consideration of the strict limits set by EU law and the discretionality of the EU institutions in the interpretation of the relevant provisions. Consequently, Member States refrain to assume relevant initiatives in the field, facing many difficulties in setting up a consistent social cohesion policy in favour of the low-income individuals which reside in the most disadvantaged territories.

§1.05 RESEARCH QUESTIONS

As seen above, the phenomenon of STZs has not yet found a final and comprehensive explanation in the context of European tax law; in fact, there are still some unresolved issues concerning, for example, the presence of multiple types of STZs characterized by blurred definitional boundaries.

On these premises, it is necessary to approach the topic from a systematic point of view with an investigation addressed to the development of a general legal theory and to the identification of a common reading-key for the various experiences of territorial tax incentives in the Member States.

Therefore, considering the statement of the problem in the above terms, the first research question in this study can be outlined as follows:

> Research question No. 1
>
> *In the context of European tax law, is it possible to develop a general legal theory of STZs able to explain the different experiences of territorial tax incentives in the Member States?*

This research question is first aimed at identifying the different sides of the concept of STZs starting from the review and the analysis of the relevant resources, including the literature on the topic, the EU law framework for direct and indirect taxation, and the factual experience of the Member States. The development of a general legal theory also involves the formulation of a comprehensive definition of STZs able to encompass all the relevant situations identified in the Member States, both for what regards the areas characterized by tax benefits on direct taxation and the other areas with tax benefits limited to indirect taxation. As the last step, the general legal theory includes the identification of the implementing models as resulting from the analysis of the factual experience of the Member States.

The second research question is defined under a dynamic perspective in relation to the variables of EU law and is formulated in the following terms:

> Research question No. 2
>
> *Is it possible to identify a new implementing model of STZs within the EU law framework addressed to the development of social cohesion policies for the most disadvantaged areas of the European Union?*

In this case, the research question is aimed at promoting an approach to EU law able to support not only the growth of the internal market, but also the harmonious development of welfare and social cohesion in each Member State, especially for what regards the initiatives targeted to the development of the most disadvantaged areas.

For this objective, the study investigates the variables of EU law and verifies the space left for the autonomous initiatives of the Member States; the priority, in fact, is to identify a line of action for the introduction of tax measures, in compliance with EU law, addressed to the low-income groups of individuals which reside in the underdeveloped regions of the EU.

Therefore, to answer the second research question, the following sub-questions are formulated:

2.1 *Can a tax measure of a social character addressed to a limited area of a Member State be considered compatible with the internal market and be exempt from the notification obligation under State aid rules?*
2.2 *Can a tax measure of a social character addressed to a limited area of a Member State, including conditions also based on the residence of the actors involved, be considered compatible with the free movement of persons?*

2.3 *Can a tax measure of a social character addressed to a limited area of a Member State be considered acceptable under the criteria of the Code of Conduct for business taxation?*

The above research sub-questions, which respectively deal with the variables of State aid rules, free movement of persons and harmful tax competition, define the path to be followed to verify the space left for the development of social cohesion policies through the establishment of STZs in the most disadvantaged areas of the Union.

§1.06 OBJECTIVE OF THE STUDY

Research in this area can lead to a deeper understanding of STZs in the context of European tax law, through the development of a general legal theory able to give evidence of the different sides of the phenomenon.

The lack of a systematic framework in the current literature, as well as the multitude of denominations used by the operators, point out the need to develop a theoretical approach to STZs, with a comprehensive concept, a uniform definition, and a set of implementing models as resulting from the analysis of the factual experience.

The importance of this study is also related to the growing need of new useful instruments to tackle the issues of the low-income areas of the Union.

In this sense, it is necessary to carry out the proper initiatives for those territories affected by previous development delays, where the last economic crisis has produced the worst effects in terms of industrial stagnation and job losses.

In this context, some studies already stress the fact that STZs can represent a useful tool for delivering growth and mitigating the state of economic and social emergency in several disadvantaged regions, considering them as an affordable instrument to reduce the gap in the economic development between rich and poor regions of the EU.

Therefore, it is necessary to create a solid theoretical base for an instrument – such as STZs – whose implementation can constitute an important line of action in the context of social cohesion policies addressed to the development of the low-income areas of the EU. In this sense, the urgency of a better understanding of the present phenomenon is strictly connected with the idea of developing the EU as a political union, providing concrete responses against the growing scepticism towards the Union.

One more argument for this study is based on the need to limit the continuous growth of the population in the most developed areas of the EU.

During the last years, in fact, many people coming from the poorest regions of the EU have moved to the richest areas of other Member States on the ground of the free movement of workers granted by EU law.

Consequently, hosting countries are now experiencing new difficulties in consideration of the limited resources of their public infrastructures (such as hospitals and transportations) and the practical impossibility of managing their welfare in case of new arrivals of people from other parts of the EU.

In this regard, the importance of STZs is connected to the possibility of effective measures which could favour a change in behaviour, limiting the significant movement of entire generations of people from the low-income to the high-income areas of the EU.

The challenging route here described first requires serious attempts aimed at the full understanding of STZs, with the definition of solid theoretical bases for a new model suitable for such a purpose.

In summary, the main motivation of the present study is strictly connected to the idea that the future success of the EU depends on the capability of establishing a new balance between rich and poor regions, providing new instruments - such as STZs - that could give response to the serious need of equal opportunities coming from an increasing number of citizens.

On these bases, the scope of this book consists not only in the development of a general legal theory in the context of European tax law, but also in the promotion of a new implementing model of STZs addressed to social cohesion policies for the most disadvantaged areas of the Union. As already said, in fact, the starting presumption is that the existing models of STZs are not able to face the economic hardships of certain underdeveloped areas of the EU, with the consequent assumption that a new model of STZs is now necessary for supporting effective initiatives.

§1.07 LIMITS OF THE STUDY

The limits of the present study can be defined on the ground of four different profiles involving the essential coordinates within which the research process is carried out.

The first limit deals with the scientific field where the general legal theory of STZs is developed; in this case, in fact, the approach exclusively focuses on the area of tax law, while the perspective of other fields of knowledge, such as economics or customs, remains outside the limits of this study. In this regard, the approach here adopted considers not only indirect taxation but also direct taxation, providing the analysis of the broadest spectrum of taxes, with the aim of defining a comprehensive framework.

The second limit regards the sources of law reviewed and analysed during the research process; in this case, in fact, the topic of STZs is explored with exclusive reference to EU law, on one part, and national legislation of the Member States, on the other. This means that any variable deriving from other sources, such as international tax treaties or World Trade Organization (WTO) commercial policies, does not find a space in the context of the present study.

The third limit is related to the recipients of the tax measures considered under the scope of the present research. In this regard, in fact, this study will exclusively cover business taxation, focusing on the tax measures granted in favour of enterprises, namely all the entities engaged in an economic activity, irrespective of their legal form, according to the definition set by Article 1 of Commission recommendation of 6 May 2003;[42] consequently, the tax incentives which are directly granted in favour of

42. Commission Recommendation of 6 May 2003 concerning the definition of micro, small and medium-sized enterprises, O.J. L 124, 2003, pp. 36-41.

individuals not carrying out an economic activity will remain outside the horizon of this research.

The fourth and last limit is linked to the definition of the geographical territory within which the analysis of the factual experience of STZs is carried out. The research, in fact, only considers the territory within which EU law fully applies, on the ground of the objective of the research which is focused on the area of European tax law.

Consequently, the geographical limit is here set according to the provision of Article 52 of the Treaty on the European Union (TEU)[43] that identifies the territory of the EU law application with the boundaries of the Member States.[44]

Nevertheless, it is necessary to clarify this point with reference to the situation of those Member States which include overseas regions and territories enjoying special legal statuses for what regards the EU law application.[45]

A first group of territories, the so-called Outermost Regions (ORs), covers nine specific regions, namely Guadeloupe, French Guiana, Martinique, Réunion, Mayotte,[46] Saint-Martin, the Azores, Madeira and the Canary Islands in accordance with Article 349 TFEU.

The ORs are part of the EU, and therefore are subject to the EU Treaties and secondary Union legislation, since Article 355(1) TFEU indicates that 'common' EU Law is applicable in such territories, without prejudice to Article 349 TFEU.[47]

The second group of territories are the Overseas Countries and Territories (OCTs),[48] which covers countries and territories situated outside mainland Europe

43. Consolidate version of the Treaty on European Union, O.J. 2012, C 236, pp. 13-390.
44. According to Article 52 TEU '*The Treaties shall apply to the Kingdom of Belgium, the Republic of Bulgaria, the Czech Republic, the Kingdom of Denmark, the Federal Republic of Germany, the Republic of Estonia, Ireland, the Hellenic Republic, the Kingdom of Spain, the French Republic, the Italian Republic, the Republic of Cyprus, the Republic of Latvia, the Republic of Lithuania, the Grand Duchy of Luxembourg, the Republic of Hungary, the Republic of Malta, the Kingdom of the Netherlands, the Republic of Austria, the Republic of Poland, the Portuguese Republic, Romania, the Republic of Slovenia, the Slovak Republic, the Republic of Finland, the Kingdom of Sweden and the United Kingdom of Great Britain and Northern Ireland*'. Furthermore, since 1 January 2013 the TEU also applies to Croatia, as stated by the Treaty concerning the accession of the Republic of Croatia to the European Union, O.J. 2012, L 112, p. 10-20.
45. J. Ziller, *Outermost Regions, Overseas Countries and Territories and Others after the Entry into Force of the Lisbon Treaty*, in *EU Law of the Overseas, Outermost Regions, Associated Overseas Countries and Territories, Territories Sui Generis*, D. Kochenov (ed.), Wolters Kluwer, The Hague, 2011, p. 78.
46. By Council Decision 2012/419/EU of 11 July 2012 (O.J. 2012, L 204, p. 131), the European Council has amended the status of Mayotte with regard to the Union with effect from 1 January 2014. Therefore, from that date Mayotte has ceased to be an overseas territory to become an outermost region within the meaning of Articles 349 and 355(1) TFEU.
47. D. Kochenov, *Introducing EU Law of the Overseas*, in *EU Law of the Overseas, Outermost Regions, Associated Overseas Countries and Territories, Territories Sui Generis*, D. Kochenov (ed.), Wolters Kluwer, The Hague, 2011, pp. 3-69.
48. The extensive list of the OCTs is provided by Annex II to the TFEU. Currently, there are twenty-five British, Danish, Dutch, and French countries and territories, associated with the EU. Until the end of 2011, the French overseas community of Saint-Barthélemy has also been an outermost region of the European Union. However, given its remoteness from metropolitan France, specific legal status, close economic relations with partners in the Americas and focus on tourism, France has asked for the status of Saint-Barthélemy to be changed, making it one of the EU overseas countries and territories (OCTs). That change has come into force on 1 January 2012.

with constitutional ties with several EU Member States. These territories are not part of the EU and are not subject to EU law,[49] but are only subject to special association agreements.[50]

The third group includes several territories of the Member States[51] where the degree of implementation of EU law varies from a full non-application[52] to a significant inclusion into the scope of the EU *acquis*.[53]

In this context, the objectives of the present research require to exclude from the analysis all the cases in which EU law is not fully applied. Consequently, while the ORs territories are entirely analysed under this study, the OCTs are not considered because EU law does not fully apply therein. Furthermore, regarding the third group, the scope of the research exclusively covers the situations of the Aland Islands and Gibraltar since they represent the only territories in which EU law applies pursuant to Article 355 TFEU.

In this regard, it is also important to observe that the geographical perimeter of the present research also includes the so-called Extraterritorial Zones that do not belong to the Customs Union territory.[54]

In fact, unless such zones are considered outside the customs line as set by the UCC, they are part of the political territory of the Member States within which EU law is fully applied.

§1.08 DEFINITIONS

The study of STZs faces a first obstacle represented by a plurality of collimating and undefined terminologies.[55]

49. Case C-148/77 *Hansen v Hauptzollamt Flensburg*, [1978] ECR 01787.
50. Taking into consideration these negative characteristics, as well as the fact that these countries and territories are constitutionally related to EU Member States, Article 355(2) TFEU provides that, with regard to the OCTs, special agreements for association set out in Part Four shall apply.
51. D. Kochenov, *The Application of EU Law in the EU's Overseas Regions, Countries and Territories After the Entry Into Force of the Treaty of Lisbon*, in *Journal of International Law and Practice*, 2012, Vol. 20, pp. 669-743.
52. For example Færoe Islands. In detail, according to Article 355 TFEU '*a) the Treaties shall not apply to the Faeroe Islands; (b) the Treaties shall not apply to the United Kingdom Sovereign Base Areas of Akrotiri and Dhekelia in Cyprus except to the extent necessary to ensure the implementation of the arrangements set out in the Protocol on the Sovereign Base Areas of the United Kingdom of Great Britain and Northern Ireland in Cyprus annexed to the Act concerning the conditions of accession of the Czech Republic, the Republic of Estonia, the Republic of Cyprus, the Republic of Latvia, the Republic of Lithuania, the Republic of Hungary, the Republic of Malta, the Republic of Poland, the Republic of Slovenia and the Slovak Republic to the European Union and in accordance with the terms of that Protocol; c) the Treaties shall apply to the Channel Islands and the Isle of Man only to the extent necessary to ensure the implementation of the arrangements for those islands set out in the Treaty concerning the accession of new Member States to the European Economic Community and to the European Atomic Energy Community signed on 22 January 1972*'.
53. For example Aland Island (Article 355 TFEU) and Gibraltar (Annexed declarations, No. 55, TFEU).
54. For example the Island of Helgoland and the territory of Büsingen (Germany), Ceuta and Melilla (Spain), Livigno and Campione d'Italia (Italy). *See* Article 4(1) of the UCC.
55. G.F. Dalla Costa, S. Nardo, M. Menini, *supra.*, CLEUP SC, Padova, 2006, pp. 7 et seq.

For example, the economical literature uses to identify such phenomenon with the general term of 'FTZ', distinguishing various types of zones according to the different economic benefits granted by the host country.

In this context, it is necessary to deal with different denominations like Commercial FZs, EZs, EPZs, Industrial FZs, SEZs, Free Ports, etc.[56]

Such terms reflect not only the various characteristics of every zone, but also the particular perspectives of the field of knowledge in which the study is carried out.

In this sense, it is clear that the terminology used by economic authors differs a lot from the one used within legal studies.

Consequently, the difficulty of framing the issue is enhanced by the fact that such terms are often used to indicate favoured regimes not only related to customs arrangements, but also to different kinds of tax reliefs in the area of direct taxation.

In any case, all the terms above-mentioned result inappropriately for the purpose of the present research because most of them just focus their meaning on the economic peculiarities of every type of zone.

Given the above, the term 'STZs' represents the most favourable option to be adopted in the context of this book; this choice, in fact, results coherent with the idea of developing a comprehensive concept within the tax law field. In other words, with the term 'STZs' it is possible to clearly underline the scope of the present study, highlighting the 'legal side' of the topic and evocating the idea of an institute belonging to the area of tax law.

§1.09 OUTLINE OF THE STUDY

This introduction in Chapter 1 sets out the study's background, its critical aspects, the research questions, and other features of the study, including scope, limitations, and definitions. The overall structure of the book consists of eight chapters, including this introduction.

Chapter 2 deals with the legal dimension of STZs on the ground of the existing literature with the outline of the state of knowledge of the phenomenon among the scholars.

Chapter 3 is focused on the description of the EU law framework of STZs, involving not only the EU treaties provisions and the EU secondary legislation, but also the case law of the ECJ and various documents issued by the Commission in the context of soft law. Here, the EU law framework is reviewed under the variables of State aid law, internal market law, and harmful tax competition.

Chapter 4 is dedicated to the review of the factual experience of the Member States, with the identification of the various examples of STZs and the description of the tax regimes available.

---

56. *See* S. Finardi, E. Moroni, *supra.*, Franco Angeli, Milan, 2001, p. 60, according to which the use of a term rather than another in reference to the various experiences of zone depends on three elements: (1) the name provided by the area; (2) the prevailing character of the activity present within; (3) terms prevailing used in the country where that area is located.

In Chapter 5, the study approaches the research question No. 1 through the analysis of the EU law variables, with the development of a general legal theory of STZs, including a comprehensive concept, a definition, and the identification of a set of implementing models as resulting from the experience of the Member States.

Chapter 6, which is focused on research question No. 2, outlines the basics of a new implementing model of STZs – the 'Social Cohesion Zone' – characterized by the presence of tax advantages in the form of social tax incentives. Also in this case, the process of analysis covers each of the EU law variables starting from an ideal design of STZs addressed to the development of social cohesion policies for the most disadvantaged areas of the EU.

Chapter 7 is dedicated to the discussion of the results achieved with a comparison between the new model of STZs and the other implementing models identified under the general legal theory of STZs; the same chapter includes some considerations on the idea of the Social Cohesion Zone as an innovative instrument for the EU cohesion policy, on the issues related to protectionism and proportionality (with the introduction of the concept of 'fiscal residue'), and on the substantial and procedural aspects in the implementation of the Social Cohesion Zone Model in the EU context.

Finally, in Chapter 8, the conclusions and the recommendations are presented, with overall insights about the results achieved with reference to the research questions.

The cases and all the references contained in this book are updated as of 1 October 2019.

CHAPTER 2

The Legal Dimension of STZs

§2.01 INTRODUCTION

The objective of the present chapter is to explore the legal dimension of STZs on the ground of the existing studies and, at the same time, to define the starting point for the analysis of the research questions.

The review of the literature on the topic, in fact, offers a fundamental opportunity to identify the state of knowledge of STZs with the outline of their basic framework in the context of legal studies.

In the next sections, STZs will be scrutinized considering the work done by the scholars active in the field; the review will approach the definitions and the classifications, including a comparison with similar figures recognizable in the factual experience. Furthermore, the legal literature on tax incentives will assume a fundamental relevance, especially for what regards the relation between the concept of STZs, on the one hand, and the concept of territorial tax advantages, on the other, in order to identify an autonomous framework within the system of tax law.

Finally, the legal dimension will be enriched through the valorization of the functional aspects which are able to drive the initiatives for the establishment of such zones. In this sense, the present chapter will also explore the objectives of social character linked to the introduction of tax incentives in the context of STZs, with a review of the existing literature dealing with 'social tax incentives' and 'social enterprises'. In this way, the literature review will be addressed to the analysis of the research questions; the focus, in fact, will first be set on the contributions on general issues (definitions, classifications, etc.) for the scope of the first research question, which is related to the development of a general legal theory of STZs; then, the review will be extended to the literature on the tax incentives of a social character in order to explore the background of the second research question concerning the development of a new implementing model for social cohesion policies.

§2.02 DEFINITIONS

The literature dealing with STZs is evidently influenced by the characteristics of each legal system and by the use of different denominations at a national level to define the same phenomenon.

The United Nations, in a study of 1991 entitled 'The Challenge of Free Economic Zone',[57] identify twenty-three different definitions of STZs according to the nature of the economic objectives pursued or the type of activity allowed in each jurisdiction.

The same study underlines the fact that these denominations often have strong equivalence, overlapping with each other; in other words, these areas, while presenting some differences in relation to the nature of the economic objectives pursued or to the type of business allowed therein, generally comply with uniform standard model.[58]

On the ground of these findings, Finardi and Moroni conclude in the sense that the use of a specific denomination generally depends on three elements: (1) the name provided by local public authorities; (2) the prevailing character of the activities carried out therein; (3) the wording prevailingly used in the country where the zone is located.[59] In other words, the choice of a specific denomination does not usually assume any substantial legal relevance, being neutral from a systematic point of view.

Given the above, it is now necessary to review the multitude of attempts made by the scholars to provide some definitions of the present phenomenon.

The analysis will start from the case of 'STZs' – since these are assumed as a comprehensive macro-category for the purposes of the present study – and will then be shifted to the most common denominations used in the international context and in the literature active in the field, such as FZs, FTZs, Free Ports, SEZs, and EPZs.

[A] The Definition of STZs

In the context of the present study, the term 'STZs' is associated with the idea of a comprehensive notion able to encompass all the geographic areas characterized by the presence of territorial tax benefits in favour of entities based therein.

The term, in fact, can be associated to the most common situations, including not only the 'tax free zone' within which there is no taxation,[60] but also other zones with a 'special' regime, namely a more favourable regime of taxation than the one generally applied in the rest of the State,[61] such as in the case of partial exemptions or more favouring treatments characterized by the presence of deductions, reductions, or tax credits.

57. U.N. Centre on Transnational Corporations, *The Challenge of Free Economic Zones*, United Nations, New York, 1991, p. 3.
58. *Ibid.*
59. S. Finardi, E. Moroni, *supra.*, FrancoAngeli, 2001, Milan, p. 60.
60. For example the Free Zones established under the EU customs legislation where no custom duties and other charges are applied.
61. For example the Canary Islands Economic and Fiscal Regime (REF) characterized by the presence of a lower taxation (*see infra* section §4.02[T][2]).

On these premises, by the term 'STZs' it is possible to easily trace the boundaries of a general macro-category able to include different implementing models of territorial tax benefits in the most comprehensive form.

Among the classic approaches to the topic, it is important to note that the use of the term 'STZs' is rare,[62] while previous studies, in most of the cases, merely underline the presence of a multitude of relevant situations characterized by different and more specific denominations, such as 'FZs', 'FTZs' or 'Free Ports', without the outline of a valuable definition for a comprehensive macro-category.

Only recently, it is possible to find out some occasional examples of studies where the term 'STZs' is scientifically used to identify the same phenomenon in the most comprehensive form.

In 2015, an important step has been made by an international group of legal scholars, who undertake a research project on STZs with the aim of obtaining a structured view on their tax incentives and practices.[63] In the context of the mentioned project, Laukkanen identifies 'STZs' as 'areas where tax regulations are more beneficial than in the generally applicable tax system of the surrounding jurisdiction or country'.[64] This definition can include various situations and is relevant because it focuses on the tax variable of the zone regime.

Furthermore, in a recent paper published in 2017 by the University of Michigan Law School, Avi-Yonah and Vallespinos define an 'STZ' as a 'preferential tax regime that is ring-fenced', specifying that 'a preferential tax regime is "ring fenced" when the sponsoring country effectively protects its domestic economy from the harmful effects of its own tax breaks'.[65]

[B] Other Definitions

Apart from the examples of the previous section, the existing literature does not offer more valuable definitions of the term 'STZs'.

Otherwise, more interesting definitions can only be found moving the focus to other denominations which are often recognized in the factual experience at the international level.

---

62. *See* the EU Parliamentary written question E-3120/07 of 21 June 2007 (O.J. 2008, C 45, pp. 1-226) where the same terminology is used. Outside Europe, in 2001 the Australian Tax Office (ATO) classified King Island and Furneaux Island as a 'Special Tax Zone', qualifying its residents for a higher tax rebate.
63. The International Bureau of Fiscal Documentation (IBFD), which is based in Amsterdam (The Netherlands), is the organization that provides the scope, framework and control of this research project aimed '*to obtain a structured view on selected STZs, their tax incentives and practices, their acceptability, possibly classify the zones, and provide recommendations on the practices and tax issues for the STZ residence countries as well as for multinational enterprises, the OECD and the European Union*' (more information available at https://www.ibfd.org/Academic/Academic-Research).
64. A. Laukkanen, *The Development Aspects of Special Tax Zones*, in *Bulletin for International Taxation*, 2016, Vol. 70, No. 3, pp. 152-162. *See also* A. Laukkanen, P. Pistone, J. de Goede, *Special Tax Zones in the Era of International Tax Coordination*, IBFD, 2019, p. 3.
65. R.S. Avi-Yonah, M. Vallespinos, *Special Tax Zones and the WTO*, University of Michigan Public Law Research Paper No. 545, 2017, available at https://ssrn.com/abstract=2928644.

Among these denominations, the most common are 'FZ', 'FTZ', 'Free Port', 'SEZ', and 'EPZ', given that they are not only widely spread all over the world under general schemes introduced by national legislators, but also frequently reviewed by the literature on this topic.

For this reason, it is necessary to complete the present review referring to the definitions which are provided for each of these different denominations.

[1] Free Zones

FZs certainly represent the most common denomination recognizable in the international experience, especially within the field of customs where they are considered as a standard for benefits granted in the area of indirect taxation.

In the EU context, for example, an interesting definition has been provided under Article 1(2) of Directive 69/75/EEC[66] according to which FZ means 'whatever the expression used in Member States, any territorial enclave established by the competent authorities of Member States in order that goods therein may be considered as being outside the customs territory of the Community for the purposes of applying customs duties, agricultural levies, quantitative restrictions or any charges or measures having equivalent effect'.

In the International Convention on the simplification and harmonization of customs systems, signed in Kyoto on 18 May 1973, the definition of FZ is developed from a broader perspective in the following terms: a part of the territory of a State where any good introduced is regarded as being outside the customs territory with reference to the customs duties and is not subject to the usual controls of the customs authorities.[67]

Moreover, Mercosur – the organization of the internal market of Argentina, Brazil, Uruguay, and Paraguay – provides for two different terms: '*Areas Aduaneras Especiales*' (AAE) and '*Zonas Francas*', which are both characterized by being an enclave inside the customs territory of a country where different rules apply with respect to the general customs regime.[68]

In the experience of the Member States, Bulgaria and France offer other interesting definitions; in the first case, a FZ is defined as 'a delimited part of the territory of the People's Republic of Bulgaria, where the pursued economic activities shall be exempted from taxation with custom duties',[69] while in the case of France, Article 286 of the French Customs Code states that a FZ corresponds to any territorial enclave established for the purpose of making the goods in the customs territory considered as not being in the customs territory for the purposes of customs duties, taxes or other quantitative restrictions.

---

66. Council Directive 69/75/EEC of 4 March 1969 on harmonization of legal action, regulatory and administrative arrangements for the free zones regimes, no longer in force, O.J. 1969, L 58, pp. 11-13.
67. *See* S. Finardi, E. Moroni, *supra.*, FrancoAngeli, Milan, 2001, p. 60.
68. *See* S. Finardi, E. Moroni, *supra.*, FrancoAngeli, Milan, 2001, p. 62.
69. Article 3 of Decree of 14 July 1987, No. 2242, O.J. of Bulgaria No. 55 of 17 July 1987.

Among the scholars, Udina and Conetti (1994) define a FZ as an area where 'foreign goods are stored, handled and processed, excluded from the custom territory of a State or, exceptionally, of two neighbouring States and at whose outer limits customs duties (on imported goods) are not collected ... in order to mostly promote international trade and sometimes the industrial and agricultural development of these spaces and indirectly of those surrounding'.[70]

Other authors consider a FZ as a well-defined area, access to which is controlled by tax and customs authorities, and where foreign goods of all origins and nature may be introduced and re-exported without being subject to customs duties or import restrictions,[71] or as an area where the application of customs laws and other related regulations – that the state or other institutions apply elsewhere to businesses and workers – are suspended.[72]

Moreover, some scholars try to cover very heterogeneous situations, identifying the FZ as a geographically or administratively limited area within which the commercial and/or industrial activities benefit from a special treatment in tax matters.[73]

For example, Wall emphasizes the derogation from the system of common rules of the national territory and defines the FZ as 'an area in which domestic policies are not in place and, as a result, foreign companies are induced to profitably invest on the basis of comparative advantages of the country'.[74]

In the same direction, one more definition is provided in a paper of Ana T. Romero according to which a FZ is considered a well-defined geographical area or an area where manufactured goods are produced only for the exportation or a service area deployed in any part of the country, that benefits from special investment incentives or from promotion of investment incentives such as exemption from payment of customs duties and privileged tax and financial treatment.[75]

On the ground of the above definitions, it is evident that the term 'FZs' is mainly related to the establishment of an area where special benefits are granted for customs duties and other indirect taxes; nevertheless, at the same time, it is possible to conclude that the term is sometimes used in the literature as a synonymous of 'STZs' with a broader meaning able to encompass all the territorial situations where some forms of tax benefits are granted, including tax measures in the field of direct taxation.

[2] Free Trade Zones

One more denomination widely spread in the international community is represented by the FTZ.

---

70. *See* M. Udina, G. Conetti, *Zone Franche,* in *Enc. Giuridica Treccani,* Rome, 1994.
71. P. Lorot, T. Scwob, *Les Zones franches dans le monde,* in *La Documentation francaise,* 1987, pp. 11 et seq.
72. K.W. Shatz, D. Spinanger, *Zone Franche e prospettive nella Repubblica Federale di Germania,* in *Economia e Banca,* 1986, pp. 250 et seq.
73. M. Ingrosso, O. Nocerino, F. Roccatagliata, C. Sacchetto, *supra.,* Chamber of Commerce of Naples, Naples, 1998, pp. 9 et seq.
74. D. Wall, *Export Processing Zones,* in *Journal of World Law,* No. 10, 1976, pp. 478-489.
75. A.T. Romero, *ILO's World Labour Report of 1996,* International Labour Organization (ILO), 1996.

In US literature, Lomax defines FTZs as areas with a specific definition in or near a port, which are considered external to the customs territory.[76] In this regard, it is also worth to remember the definition provided by the US legislator in the Foreign Trade Zone Act of 1934 according to which the Foreign Trade Zone is 'a defined area, closed and controlled under the supervision of a special office of federal official, conducted by a company within a regime of public service, in or adjacent to a port customs, without any resident population, with facilities for loading and unloading, the storage of goods, for their rapprochement by land or water; an area where the goods can be taken, stored and subjected to certain specific handling. If re-exported to foreign locations, the goods may leave the zone without paying customs duties and without the intervention of the customs officers, except for certain conditions ...'.[77]

A more recent definition is provided by Ingrosso, Nocerino, Roccatagliata, and Sacchetto according to which FTZs are areas where transhipment, storage, and handling are carried out and where goods, introduced while waiting to be reimported or imported, may be subjected to manipulation to improve their presentation or commercial quality.[78]

By the review of the above sources, it is clear that FTZs are essentially related to customs operations with tax benefits granted on customs duties; in this sense, it is possible to conclude that they generally have a strong equivalence with the notion of FZs developed in the context of customs law.[79]

[3] Free Ports

Furthermore, it is interesting to remember the case of the 'Free Port' to be intended as the set of port facilities (pool of water, dropped, docks, warehouses) which are outside the line of the custom border.

One of the first definitions is given by MacElwee who defines the modern Free Port as 'an area of a port separated from the national customs territory through a barrier. Ships can enter in this port, download, upload and leave without customs formalities. The goods are stored, repackaged, manufactured and re-exported without any customs formalities. Only when the goods pass through customs to reach consumers in the country they are subject to customs investigation and pay the tariff required. A Free Port is a duty-free area within the political boundaries of a nation'.[80]

In more recent times, Finardi and Moroni define a Free Port or a Free Point as a port or a part of a port where some privileges are granted, especially for what concerns

76. A.L. Lomax, *The Foreign Trade Zone*, School of Business Administration, University of Oregon, Eugene (Oregon), 1947, p. 5.
77. *See* A. Isaacs, *International Trade Tariff and Commercial Policies*, Richard D. Irwin Inc., Chicago (Illinois), 1948, pp. 753 et seq.
78. M. Ingrosso, O. Nocerino, F. Roccatagliata, C. Sacchetto, *supra.*, Chamber of Commerce of Naples, Naples, 1998, p. 12.
79. In this sense *see also* A. Laukkanen, P. Pistone, J. de Goede, *supra.*, IBFD, 2019, p. 17, where FTZs are defined as '*areas within the territory of a state where goods from third countries can enter without satisfying customs duties until the importer decides the fate of those goods*'.
80. R.S. Mac Elwee, *Port Development*, McGraw Hill, 1926, New York, p. 381. *See also* R.S. Thoman, *Free Ports and Foreign-Trade Zones*, Cornell Maritime Press, Cambridge, 1956.

taxation, in order to stimulate commercial traffic for economic operators based within the boundaries of the port, as well as for those of third countries.[81]

Therefore, the free port can be considered as an STZ, considering that 'it aims to provide economic growth in the country where it is located, promote the creation of jobs and increase employment, as well as foster the improvement of industrial, financial, trade and technology markets through the granting of tax benefits to the companies and individuals located therein'.[82]

[4] Special Economic Zones

The definition of SEZs is determined individually by each country. In the legislation of EU Member States, for example, it is worth to note that Poland offers a specific definition of SEZs, considered as a part of the Polish territory administered separately for the running of businesses, with tax exemptions involving direct taxation on preferential terms defined under the Act on SEZs of 20 October 1994.[83]

Following a recent initiative, also Italian legislation offers its own definition of an SEZ intended as 'a geographically delimited and clearly identified area, located within the borders of the State, also consisting of non-territorially adjacent areas provided that they present a functional economic link, and that include at least a port area [...] For the business of economic and entrepreneurial activities, the companies already operational and those that will set up in the SEZ can benefit from special conditions, in relation to the incremental nature of investments and business development activities'.[84]

According to Akinci and Crittle,[85] the SEZ typically includes: a geographically limited area (usually fenced), single management/administration, eligibility for benefits based upon the physical location within the zone, separate customs area (duty-free benefits), and streamlined procedures.

In literature, Italian scholars try to use such a terminology in a broader sense to identify the main features of a macro-category encompassing all the different situations relevant under the present study.[86] In this sense, in fact, Finardi and Moroni define SEZs as areas or zones characterized by the presence of a regulation of the economic activities that differ, totally or in part, from the one of the hosting State, in particular for what concerns the regulation of international trade.[87]

81. S. Finardi, E. Moroni, *supra.*, FrancoAngeli, 2001, Milan, p. 63.
82. A. Laukkanen, P. Pistone, J. de Goede, *supra.*, IBFD, 2019, p. 38.
83. Article 2 of Act of 20 October 1994 on Special Economic Zones, O.J. of Poland No. 123/1994, item 600. Special Economic Zones in Poland have been abolished from 30 June 2018.
84. Article 4(2) Law Decree of 20 June 2017, No. 91, O.J. of Italy No. 141 of 20 June 2017.
85. G. Akinci, J. Crittle, *Special Economic Zone: Performance, Lessons Learned, and Implication for Zone Development (English)*. Foreign Investment Advisory Service (FIAS) occasional paper. Washington, DC: World Bank, 2008, p. 9, available at http://documents.worldbank.org/curated/en/343901468330977533/Special-economic-zone-performance-lessons-learned-and-implication-for-zone-development.
86. S. Finardi, E. Moroni, *supra.*, FrancoAngeli, 2001, Milan, p. 15.
87. S. Finardi, E. Moroni, *supra.*, FrancoAngeli, 2001, Milan, p. 59. For more definitions of 'Special Economic Zones' *see also* T. Farole, *Special Economic Zones in Africa: Comparing Performance*

[5] Export Processing Zones

The last relevant example for the purposes of the present review is the one of 'EPZs' which is widely spread in the world, especially in developing countries.

Basile and Germidis define the EPZ as 'an area that is administratively or geographically defined, which enjoys a special status that allows the free importation of instrumentation and different materials destined for the manufacture of goods for export. The special status usually implies favourable legal provisions and regulations generally related to taxation and which constitute incentives for foreign investment'.[88]

In 1993, the United Nations Conference on Trade and Development (UNCTAD), in a work entitled 'Export Processing Zones: Role of Foreign Direct Investment and Developmental Impact', defines the EPZs as '*a well-defined geographical area that enjoys customs privileges and other incentives and in which primary activity is the manipulation of goods for export [...] a modern adaptation of free port or special economic zone*'.[89]

Warr summarizes the characteristics of a typical EPZ in four points: (1) tax free import offer of raw materials and subsidies for the purchase of raw materials or semifinished products available on the domestic market of the host country; (2) granting of temporary exemption from taxation of income in favour of companies; (3) offer to companies to reduce or cancel paperwork and customs, with a relative reduction in administrative costs and delays; possibility of setting up companies controlled entirely by foreign capital; possibility of total repatriation of profits; possibility of employing skilled labour and foreign management; possibility to avoid the process of preventive approvals for the importation of foreign instruments; possibility to use the import quotas assigned to the host country by certain commercial blocks such as the EU; (4) offer to companies of generally lower rates than outside the EPZ for renting buildings and spaces and for the use of electricity.[90]

One more definition is given by Bolin, according to which a EPZ is '*a duty-free centre for attracting and supporting foreign investment in export-oriented productions, through the careful provision of broad-spectrum services able to adapt to the constant change in production and distribution on a world scale*'.[91]

---

and Learning from Global Experiences, The World Bank Ed., 2011, p. 23; J. Chaisse, J. Hu, *International Economic Law and the Challenges of the Free Zones*, Kluwer Law International, 2019, p. 2; L. Moberg, *The Political Economy of Special Economic Zones: Concentrating Economic*, Routledge, 2017, p. 1.

88. A. Basile, D. Germidis, *Investing in Free Export Processing Zones*, OECD Development Centre Studies, Paris, 1984, p. 20.
89. UNCTAD, *Export Processing Zones: Role of Foreign Direct Investment and Development Impact*, UNCTAD Secretariat, Geneva, 1993, p. 5.
90. P. Warr, *Export Processing Zones*, in *Export Promotion Strategies; Theory and Evidence from Developing Countries* C. Milner (ed.), New York University Press, New York, 1990, pp. 135 et seq.
91. R.L. Bolin, *The Global Network of Export Processing Zones*, in *The Global Network of Free Zones in the 21st Century*, Flagstaff Institute, Flagstaff, 1998, p. 15.

Because of the above definitions, it is evident that EPZs mainly assume a relevance in the context of import/export operations, being generally intended as a tool for companies involved in the international trade of goods.

§2.03 CLASSIFICATIONS

The multitude of denominations and definitions mentioned in the previous sections contributes to outline a complex and differentiated framework which is influenced by the factual experience of each jurisdiction.

Nonetheless, the legal background of the topic can also offer some interesting points of view for a classification of the various forms of STZs according to the specific rules involved and the tax benefits granted.

The first attempt for a valuable classification has been made in the field of customs and dates back to the seventies, with a focus set on the typologies of economic operations authorized within each regime.

According to the International Convention of Kyoto of 1973, in fact, a distinction may be made in the context of customs between two broad categories of STZs, namely the 'commercial free zones' and the 'industrial free zones'.[92]

In commercial FZs, the permitted operations are generally limited to those necessary for the preservation of the goods and the usual forms of handling to improve their packaging or marketable quality or to prepare them for shipment, while processing or manufacturing operations are normally prohibited. In this case, goods admitted to a zone shall also be allowed to undergo operations necessary for the preservation and for the shipment, such as grouping of packages, sorting and grading, and repacking.[93]

Differently, in industrial FZs, also processing and manufacturing operations are permitted, with the increase of the value of goods in the context of the authorized process.[94]

In more recent times, Ingrosso, Nocerino, Roccatagliata, and Sacchetto have approached the classification issue from a different point of view, with the development of a categorization system which is more focused on the legal perspective.

These authors analyse STZs, grouping them into two broad categories: the so-called classic FZs, on one part, and the 'free zones of exception', on the other.[95]

The first category essentially includes situations characterized by the presence of tax advantages on customs duties and sometimes on other indirect taxes. In this sense, FZs, FTZs, EPZs, Free Ports, are evident examples of 'classic free zones', corresponding to areas where goods, which are introduced therein, enjoy an exemption from customs duties regardless of the length of their stay. Furthermore, in the same areas, if goods are

92. World Customs Organization, *International Convention on the Simplification and Harmonization of Customs Procedures*, Kyoto, 18 May, 1973, Annex F.1.
93. *Ibid.*
94. *Ibid.*
95. M. Ingrosso, O. Nocerino, F. Roccatagliata, C. Sacchetto, *supra.*, Chamber of Commerce of Naples, Naples, 1998, pp. 11-12.

processed or assembled, they can be re-exported without any tax burden; this basically means that, until the goods are stored within these areas, all the operations of transshipment, embarkation, storage, handling can be carried out without any restriction of a customs nature, while the payment of customs duties becomes due only when the goods are eventually introduced in the customs territory of the hosting State.[96]

Differently, in the 'free zones of exception' other types of tax advantages may be granted, dealing also with direct taxation. In particular, such areas are associated not only to import and export operations, but also to commercial and productive activities, stimulating the development of foreign industrial facilities through the introduction of advantages on direct taxation and the subsequent reduction of the overall tax burden on companies and individual entrepreneurs.[97]

This classification of STZs, which distinguishes between 'classic free zones', on one part, and 'free zones of exception', on the other, represents still today a fundamental point of reference within the literature on the topic, being able to highlight some of the substantial aspects which are relevant from the tax law perspective. In this sense, in fact, the same classification finally results in a distinction between areas where benefits are only granted for indirect taxes and areas where tax benefits also involve the field of direct taxation.

§2.04 STZs AND OTHER FIGURES

The legal dimension of STZs also entails the identification of the boundaries between the present phenomenon and other similar figures, such as tax havens, customs warehouses, duty-free shops, and subsidies.

In the factual experience, in fact, such terminology is often used in an undefined way, without the proper understanding of the limits of the various concepts.

Nevertheless, thanks to a careful review of the main literature on the topic, it is still possible to trace a line of division between STZs and such similar figures.

[A] Tax Havens

A tax haven is generally defined as a low-tax independent jurisdiction with a goal of attracting capital, or simply a jurisdiction that has low or non-existent taxes. According to Gravelle, tax havens are limited to those countries that also have such other characteristics as the lack of transparency, bank secrecy, the lack of information sharing, and requiring little or no economic activity for an entity to obtain a legal status.[98]

96. *Ibid.*
97. *Ibid.*
98. J.G. Gravelle, *Tax Havens: International Tax Avoidance and Evasion*, Congressional Research Service, 2010, Washington DC, p. 2.

In this case, the tax legislation is especially designed to attract the formation of branches and subsidiaries of parent companies based in heavily taxed industrial countries.[99]

Given the above, it is clear that tax havens cannot be classified as STZs for the following reasons.

First, tax havens are independent jurisdictions, always corresponding to a territory of full sovereignty, while, in the case of STZs, the area concerned is a limited part of a hosting country where a more favourable tax regime applies compared to the standard one applied in the rest of the same hosting country.

Second, tax havens are generally characterized by the lack of exchange of information, thus representing tools for tax evasion with a scope that is different from the aims set under the establishment of STZs.[100]

Therefore, the present research is strictly focused on the topic of STZs, while the different figure of tax havens is excluded from the field of investigation.

[B] Customs Warehouses

Customs warehousing is a procedure under the UCC that allows storage in a customs warehouse of: (i) non-Union goods, without such goods being subject to import duties or commercial policy measures or (ii) Union goods, where EU legislation governing specific fields provides that their being placed in a customs warehouse shall attract the application of measures normally attached to the export of such goods.[101]

The resulting framework determines that customs warehouses (public or private) are specially designated locations – a building or other secured area – authorized by the customs authority and under its control where goods may be stored or manipulated without the payment of duties or other indirect taxes.[102]

Thus, the difference between STZs, on one part, and customs warehouses, on the other, is essentially based on two specific elements. First, it is necessary to put in evidence the different geographical delimitation of the area that, in case of customs warehouses, remains limited to a building, a shed, or an enclosure of a minimum surface.[103] Second, customs warehouses are a figure exclusively related to customs and, thus, they only deal with indirect taxation.

On the contrary, STZs are always areas of land of important dimensions and often offer a broader and more complex set of tax benefits also related to direct taxation.

99. A. Starchild, *Tax Havens for International Business*, Macmillan Press, London, 1994, p. 1.
100. In this sense *see* A. Laukkanen, P. Pistone, J. de Goede, *supra.*, IBFD, 2019, p. 24.
101. *See* Article 240 of Council Regulation (EU) No. 952/2013 of 9 October 2013 laying down the Union Customs Code (UCC), O.J. 2013, L. 269, pp. 1-101.
102. *See* Article 240(2) UCC.
103. In this sense, *see* M. Ingrosso, O. Nocerino, F. Roccatagliata, C. Sacchetto, *supra.*, Chamber of Commerce of Naples, Naples, 1998, p. 13. *See also* A. Laukkanen, P. Pistone, J. de Goede, *supra.*, IBFD, 2019, p. 20, where the idea is expressed that *'an FTZ is obviously an area, whereas a customs warehouse is a place'*.

[C] Duty-Free Shops

Duty-free shops are exempt from the payment of certain indirect taxes and duties, provided that the goods are sold to travelers with a final destination out of the hosting State.

The list of products that can be sold duty-free varies by jurisdiction, as well as how they can be sold and the process of calculating the duty to be refunded.

Duty-free shops are usually based in the international zone of airports, sea ports, and train stations, while, more rarely, they can be found on the roadway beside the entry or exit points of the national border.[104]

Within the EU context, these shops have been abolished for intra-EU travellers in 1999,[105] but they are retained for travellers whose final destination is outside the EU.

It is evident that such figure does not correspond to the instrument of STZs, considering its different design by the structural and functional point of view. A duty-free shop, in fact, is always identified with one or more business entities aimed at the selling of goods to final consumers with tax incentives limited to indirect taxation; differently, STZs are limited areas of land of a certain dimension established for promoting a well-defined tax policy, which offer a broader and more complex set of tax incentives on direct and/or on indirect taxation for enterprises based therein.

[D] Subsidies

In this context, it is also important to explore the relation between the concept of STZs and the concept of subsidies.

In general, an advantage able to improve the economic and financial situation of the recipient may assume the form of a positive aid or a negative aid.

Positive aid includes direct payments, state guarantees, and other positive financial measures of any kind.

Negative aid, also defined as 'fiscal aid', assumes the form of tax advantages with the reduction of the tax burden normally payable by the beneficiary under the relevant standard tax legislation.[106]

Within this conceptual framework, subsidies represent an example of positive aid, as they consist of financial grants reserved to enterprises, provided that certain conditions are fulfilled.[107]

---

104. M. Ingrosso, O. Nocerino, F. Roccatagliata, C. Sacchetto, *supra.*, Chamber of Commerce of Naples, Naples, 1998, p. 16.
105. On the topic *see* A. Gebauer, N. Chang Woon, R. Parsche, *Lessons of the 1999 Abolition of Intra-EU Duty Free Sales for the New EU Member States*, in *CESifo Economic Studies*, Oxford, 2005, Vol. 51.1., pp. 133-157.
106. For the distinction between the categories of 'positive aid' and 'negative aid', *see* M. Lang, P. Pistone, J. Schuch, C. Staringer, *Introduction to European Tax Law: Direct Taxation*, 3rd Edition, Spiramus Press, Wien, 2013, p. 103; P. Boria, *Taxation in European Union*, 2nd Edition, Springer International Publishing, Cham, 2017, p. 153.
107. For the purposes of the present study, the term 'subsidy' is used in a strict sense (as an antonym to a tax) in order to define a sum of money granted from public funds to help an industry or a business in a particular economic sector. Nevertheless, it is important to note that, in many

Differently, in the case of STZs, the advantages provided always assume the form of negative aid, considering that they correspond to tax benefits in a technical sense, with the reduction of the tax burden through various mechanisms, such as deductions, tax credits, tax rebates, tax deferrals, etc.

On these premises, it is evident that the distinction usually made between positive and negative aid offers an interesting point of view to trace and separate the boundaries of the conceptual categories of STZs and subsidies.

Nevertheless, it is not possible to conclude that subsidies are completely irrelevant for the topic of STZs. The theme of subsidies, in fact, might assume a relevance for the purposes of the present research as far as the corresponding amount would be exempted from income tax according to a specific provision; in such a case, the tax measure would exclude the amount of subsidies from the calculation of the taxable base for income tax, determining a more favourable tax treatment for the recipient of the same subsidies.

In summary, it is correct to assume that subsidies are not tax advantages in a strict sense and, therefore, they do not directly involve STZs which are always characterized by the provision of a certain benefit in the form of a negative aid, with the reduction of the standard tax burden. Nonetheless, at the same time, it is not possible to completely exclude the theme of subsidies from the field of the present investigation, considering that they might assume, at least indirectly, a relevance for the determination of the taxable base within the tax scheme introduced in an STZ.

§2.05 STZs IN THE SYSTEM OF TAX LAW

The previous studies on the topic are not limited to the mere provision of a series of definitions or the outline of a general classification of STZs.

By the review of the main literature, in fact, it is also possible to recognize some more steps done for a deeper comprehension of the phenomenon from the legal point of view.

In this sense, Ingrosso, Nocerino, Roccatagliata, and Sacchetto, driven by the aim of evaluating such zones under the tax law perspective, set the focus of their analysis on the effects deriving from the introduction of more favourable provisions, identifying the core of the phenomenon of STZs in the legal category of 'tax advantages'.[108]

Following this path, in fact, it seems possible to set the topic in the context of tax law studies, with a systematic approach able to highlight the substance of STZs from the legal point of view.

---

other studies, the term 'subsidy' is used in a broader sense to cover not only financial grants from public resources, but also tax concessions granted in form of subsidization. For these considerations *see* World Trade Organization, *World Trade Report 2006*, pp. 47 et seq., available at https://www.wto.org/english/res_e/booksp_e/anrep-_e/wtr06-2b_e.pdf.

108. M. Ingrosso, O. Nocerino, F. Roccatagliata, C. Sacchetto, *supra.*, Chamber of Commerce of Naples, Naples, 1998, p. 85. For the same conclusions *see also* A. Laukkanen, P. Pistone, J. de Goede, *supra.*, IBFD, 2019, p. 69.

This step is fundamental to set the basics for an autonomous life of STZs within the world of legal studies and to identify their placement with reference to the *summa divisio* between the general part and the specific part of tax law.

From a comparative perspective, in fact, tax law is generally accepted in each jurisdiction as an independent branch of law structured according to the level of concretization of tax law norms; in this sense, the discipline is usually divided into a general part, on one hand, concerning institutional lines of the national tax system, including constitutional principles and the implementation of tax law, and a specific part, on the other hand, regarding the rules relevant under the various typologies of taxes.[109]

The general part of tax law is made up of general information about tax law and its object, norms and relationships. It includes legal norms concerning the tax system in general, such as the assessment and the collection of taxes, the structure of tax administrators and their rights and obligations, forms, procedures, methods of tax control, penalties, and litigation.

Differently, the specific part of tax law contains the substantive and procedural rules of the various typologies of taxes which are split between many different legal sources.

Given the above, from a systematic point of view and according to the approach of the scholars, it is possible to place the phenomenon of STZs within the general part of tax law. It is evident, in fact, that the main features of STZs can be reviewed only according to a level of concretization that usually corresponds to the approach of the general part of tax law; in this regard, in fact, STZs concern the tax system in general, involving the study of a general instrument and not the analysis of a set of norms enacted for the regulation of a specific tax.

Within the general part of tax law, Ingrosso, Nocerino, Roccatagliata, and Sacchetto usually place STZs under the topic of tax advantages, as they represent one of the various instruments for introducing a set of favouring norms aimed at the achievement of objectives of economic or social policy.[110] In this regard, in fact, the phenomenon of tax advantages is characterized by a certain level of autonomy from the point of view of the functional analysis, considering that it includes a real subsystem of norms through which each State is intended to implement the values and principles of the Constitution and realize the goals and objectives marked and protected therein.

It follows that tax advantages are not used as a tool for the achievement of revenue targets, but they are related to objectives of an extra fiscal nature (i.e., economic and social policies). In other words, beside tax norms appointed to solve the problem of securing the withdrawal, there are other norms pursuing further goals of social and economic nature. On the same bases, it is thus possible to identify a series of logical connections between the promotional principles and constitutional values of

---

109. M. Radvan, *System of Financial Law: System of Tax Law: Conference Proceedings. 1*, Masaryk University, Faculty of Law, Brno, 2015. pp. 18-28.
110. M. Ingrosso, O. Nocerino, F. Roccatagliata, C. Sacchetto, *supra.*, Chamber of Commerce of Naples, Naples, 1998, p. 85. For a deep analysis of the instrument of tax advantages *see* P. Boria, *Il Sistema tributario*, Wolters Kluwer Italia, Milan, 2008, pp. 1029 et seq.

a State, on one hand, and the tax norms issued by the same State for achieving the related goals, on the other hand.[111]

In this context, even STZs can represent an expression of the same subsystem of norms related to the phenomenon of tax advantages in general, considering their strict focus on the dialectic between the values directly belonging to the system of tax law (e.g., the ability to pay) and other general values protected by different rules and constitutional principles (e.g., social protection for the most disadvantaged people).

At the same time, STZs assume a specific position within that subsystem of tax advantages on the ground of the fact that, in this case, tax benefits are granted by a State through an instrument which is always characterized by an essential territorial dimension.

In this regard, STZs generally consist of a package of tax benefits granted to a limited area of the hosting State, while all the other types of tax advantages are generally granted on the basis of objective and/or subjective elements that do not involve a territorial dimension; according to Dagnino, in fact, within the field of tax advantages and its subsystem of norms, it is possible to identify not only the category of territorial tax benefits – corresponding to the theoretical concept of STZs developed in the present research – but also the categories of objective tax benefits and subjective tax benefits.[112] Objective tax benefits are identified any time the favouring treatment is provided with reference to a specific event or a material fact,[113] while subjective tax benefits are those for which the preferential treatment is linked to the personal condition of the taxpayer.[114] Nevertheless, such categorization should not be strictly intended since the factual experience offers various examples of territorial tax benefits where the territorial element is associated with additional requirements involving the material facts and/or the subjective condition of the taxpayer.[115]

In summary, on the ground of the literature review, STZs can be placed in the general part of tax law and, more precisely, in the area dealing with the subsystem of norms which regulate the phenomenon of tax advantages.

Here, STZs assume an autonomous position besides the categories of objective and subjective tax benefits, considering the presence of tax policy goals that are always pursued on a territorial basis.

In other words, within the same subsystem of norms, the territorial dimension is able to distinguish the concept of STZs from other types of tax advantages (i.e., objective tax advantages and subjective tax advantages), highlighting its main features from the systematic point of view and identifying its placement in the context of tax law.

111. P. Boria, *supra.*, Wolters Kluwer Italia, Milan, 2008, p. 1049.
112. A. Dagnino, *Agevolazioni fiscali e potestà normativa*, CEDAM, Padova, 2008, p. 10.
113. A relevant example of an objective tax benefit is represented by the introduction of rules aimed to favour an activity irrespective of the nature of the managing entity (e. g. charity or assistance activity).
114. For instance, a tax benefit reserved to specific categories of beneficiaries (e.g., agricultural enterprises) without any requirement for what concerns the performance of specific activities.
115. That is the case of tax benefits reserved to entrepreneurs investing in R&D activities, where both the subjective and the objective requirements are provided by law. In this sense, *see* A. Dagnino, *supra.*, CEDAM, Padova, 2008, p. 40.

§2.06 STZs AND OBJECTIVES OF A SOCIAL CHARACTER

[A] General Aspects

As already seen, the phenomenon of STZs can be framed setting a strong parallelism with the category of 'tax advantages', giving evidence of various substantial aspects under the tax law perspective.

In this direction, the understanding of STZs also requires an investigation on the different aims pursued by the governments through the introduction of tax advantages, with an approach more focused on the functional aspects and on the objectives of extra-fiscal nature which evidently differ from the mere collection of public revenue.

Among these objectives, the social character of a tax measure introduced in an STZ certainly assumes a fundamental role for the purposes of the present study; in fact, as the second research question is related to the possibility of a new model of STZs for the development of social cohesion policies, the research process must first be oriented to an investigation on the main results of the literature dealing with the social character of a tax measure.

On these bases, the literature review, from now onwards, must be driven by the substance of the same research question and the associated aspects, with the description of the studies on the so-called hidden welfare and the outline of the views of the scholars related to the introduction of tax incentives of a social character.

From this perspective, Traversa offers the possibility of tracing the perimeter of the category of 'social tax incentives' - also defined as 'not-income related tax incentives' - within which the introduction of favouring norms is aimed at achieving objectives of social policy and is targeted at groups of individuals needing more social protection.[116]

These benefits represent a common tool for the development of welfare, such as in the case of tax incentives aimed at solving the issues of unemployment, with the consequent introduction of deductions, exemptions or reduced tax rates.[117]

Given the above, it is now necessary to review the literature focused on the study of social tax incentives and social enterprises, outlining the general framework where the second research question can be developed.

[B] The Concept of 'Social Tax Incentives'

The theory of the 'hidden welfare state'[118] represents the main background in literature able to offer some instruments to explore the possible introduction of tax incentives of a social character in the context of STZs.

---

116. E. Traversa, *Tax Incentives and Territoriality Within the European Union: Balancing the Internal Market with the Tax Sovereignty of Member States*, in *World Tax Journal*, 2014, p. 339.
117. European Commission - Employment Social Affairs and Inclusion, *The relationship between social security coordination and tax law, Analytical report 2014*, European Commission Publications, 2014, p. 17.
118. *See* C. Howard, *The Hidden Welfare State: Tax Expenditure and Social Policy in the United States*, Princeton University Press, Princeton, 1997.

In this sense, in fact, the same theory is useful to define what a social policy entails and, at the same time, to provide a content for the notion of social tax incentives.

In the US, the idea of tax incentives of a social character is associated to the concept of tax expenditures with social welfare objectives, such as those for income security, healthcare, employment and training, housing, social services, education and veterans' benefits.

These studies start from the idea that the social policies pursued by a State may be achieved not only thanks to the so-called visible welfare state (the State providing social security benefits), but also through the 'hidden welfare state'[119] whose main scope is to compensate the taxpayer for losses, reduced income or extra costs, thanks to the introduction of new tax benefits.

Among the most relevant studies, Howard focuses on the connection between the category of social tax incentives and the concept of the 'hidden welfare state'.[120] According to the author, in fact, such incentives are considered to be equivalent to direct expenditures programmes and can be viewed as alternative ways of accomplishing similar policy objectives.[121] Therefore, tax expenditures constitute a system of 'fiscal welfare' that is conceptually distinct from the social welfare system of direct public spending and the occupational welfare system of fringe benefits;[122] in this sense, tax expenditures constitute '*the third and often neglected method*' of providing welfare benefits, along with transfer payments and in-kind services.[123]

On these premises, Howard suggests a path directed to achieve a rewarding definition of the notion of 'social policy' - which is evidently instrumental to better identify the category of 'social tax incentives' - setting out a double step process for the recognition of the perimeter of the same concept.[124]

The first step deals with the identification of the substantial beneficiaries of the tax incentives. According to the author, in fact, social policy programmes - such as those that guarantee a minimum standard of living and protect citizens against losses of income beyond their control, especially losses caused by retirement, sickness, disability, or unemployment - are not only targeted at the poor class, but also to the middle class, considering that most of the tax expenditures benefit individuals whose income is above the poverty line.[125]

---

119. J.P. Owens, *Tax Expenditures and Direct Expenditures as Instruments of Social Policy*, S. Cnossen, (ed.), Comparative Tax Studies, Amsterdam, 1983, p. 171. *See also* C. Howard, *supra.*, Princeton University Press, Princeton, 1997; B. Greve, *The Hidden Welfare State, Tax Expenditure and Social Policy*, in *Scandinavian Journal of Social Welfare*, 1994, p. 206.
120. C. Howard, *supra.*, Princeton University Press, Princeton, 1997, p. 3.
121. US Congress - Joint Committee on Taxation, *Estimates of Federal Tax Expenditures for Fiscal Years 1992-1996*, Government Printing Office, Washington D.C.,1991, p. 3.
122. R. Titmuss, *Essays on the Welfare State*, Yale University Press, New Haven, 1959, pp. 17-30.
123. P. Flora, A. Heidenheimer, *The Historical Core and Changing Boundaries of the Welfare State*, in *The Development of Welfare States in Europe and America*, P. Flora, A. Heidenheimer (eds), Transaction Bookis, New Brunswick, 1981, p. 26.
124. C. Howard, *supra.*, Princeton University Press, Princeton, 1997, pp. 18 et seq.
125. *Ibid.* For a similar approach *see also* T.R. Marmor, J.L. Marshaw, P.L. Harvey, *America's Misunderstood Welfare State*, Basic Books, New York, 1990; F.C. Pampel, J.B. Williamson, *Age, Class, Politics, and the Welfare State*, Cambridge, University Press, Cambridge, 1989.

The second step involves the identification of social welfare as the primary objective of the policy programme, taking as point of reference a specific list of government functions. In this regard, certain government functions must be immediately excluded from the concept of social tax incentives since they pursue objectives not related with the management of social policy programmes (e.g., national defence, energy, commerce, and transportation[126]). Differently, there are other government functions that certainly belong to the social welfare domain, such as income security, health, housing, education, employment, training, social services, and veterans' programmes.

Academic studies generally accept this framework and sometimes distinguish between functions at the core and the periphery.[127] Core functions usually include income security, health, employment, and job training. Housing, social services, education, and veterans' programmes usually occupy the periphery.

On the ground of the above ideas, the Joint Committee on Taxation of the US Congress has realized a comprehensive list of tax expenditures with social welfare objectives, where tax benefits are grouped using the traditional categories of income security, health, employment and training, housing, education, social services, and veterans' benefits and services.[128]

According to Howard, the same list represents a fundamental point of reference for setting the limits of the concept of 'social policy'; in this regard, in fact, it is possible to conclude that the category of social tax incentives, as an instrument of social policy, includes all the tax benefits that are not only targeted to individuals belonging to the poor and middle class (as substantial beneficiaries), but also defined in the context of one or more of the functions mentioned in the same list of tax expenditures.[129]

In summary, the review of the above literature offers the possibility to define the boundaries of the category of social tax incentives on the basis of two different conditions: first, there is the need of limiting the benefits to individuals belonging to the low and middle-income class; second, it is always necessary to set the tax measure within a well-defined government function, with a transparent and clear definition of the scope of the tax benefits.

In conclusion, the category of social tax incentives, as defined thanks to the support of the above literature, can assume a fundamental relevance in the context of STZs, highlighting the functional perspective of the related tax measures.

126. Nevertheless, under certain circumstances, also public transportation could be included in a policy programme with social welfare as the primary objective. In some cases, in fact, government functions, such as education and other social services, require the possibility for disadvantaged categories of individuals to use the public transportation network at a reduced fare.
127. P. Flora, A. Heidenheimer, *supra.*, in P. Flora, A. Heidenheimer, *The Development of Welfare States in Europe and America*, Transaction Bookis, New Brunswick, 1981, pp. 17-34.
128. US Congress – Joint Committee on Taxation, *supra.*, Government Printing Office, Washington D.C., 1991; US Congress – Office of Management and Budget (OMB), *Analytical Perspectives, Budget of the United States Government, Fiscal Year 1996*, Government Printing Office, Washington, D.C., 1995.
129. C. Howard, *supra.*, Princeton University Press, Princeton, 1997, pp. 18 et seq.

[C] The Role of Social Enterprises

Social tax incentives have been defined through a set of fundamental coordinates including the income of the individuals towards which the same measure is targeted, on one part, and the specific government functions developed through the tax measure, on the other.

In this sense, employment, training, housing, income security, and education represent the main examples of the government functions involved by the introduction of social tax incentives, while the improvement of the living conditions of the individuals belonging to the low and the middle-income class – and not carrying out a business activity – is the ultimate target of such initiatives.

In this framework, social tax incentives may be granted in various forms which are not limited to the direct provision of tax advantages in favour of the targeted individuals, but also include the introduction of a differentiated tax treatment in favour of third entities carrying out, even occasionally, activities of a social character.

While in the first case the tax liability of the individuals belonging to the low and middle income class is lowered through the introduction of a tax exemption or a tax rate reduction which is directly applied to their income, in the second case, otherwise, the advantages are granted in favour of entities which are active in the social field, such as charities or non-profit organizations. Therefore, in the latter situations, the government function is concretely pursued in consideration of the indirect effects of the same tax measures, with a focus on the link between the behaviour of the third entities directly interested by the more favourable tax treatment and the corresponding effects on the disadvantaged groups of individuals which are the ultimate target of such initiatives.

In other words, third entities may become the vehicle through which a social objective is concretely achieved in favour of the targeted individuals; in this sense, in fact, the targeted individuals, even if they are not directly interested by these tax measures, can benefit from the strongest position acquired by the third entities which are involved in activities of a social character, for example through more job positions in the local market or through a wider set of social services available.

On these premises, it is then possible to identify situations where enterprises are used as a filter between public finance and groups of individuals who require more protection, being a sort of vehicle through which the State may improve the living conditions of specific categories of disadvantaged individuals; therefore, enterprises are used as a selective tool for the identification of the substantial beneficiaries of such measures, according to a set of requirements provided by law.

In this context, the phenomenon of social enterprises can assume a fundamental relevance for the purposes of the present study, opening a new room for the development of social cohesion policies through the instrument of STZs.

Therefore, it is necessary to offer a brief overview of the main literature on the topic, with a focus set on the views of the scholars on the possible relationship between social enterprises and social tax incentives

According to Barrett and Veal, the concept of social enterprise is notoriously difficult to categorically define, given the many goals of the different entities operating in the field, and the diverse contexts in which the term is used across jurisdictions.[130]

In a report which dates back to 1999, the Organization for Economic Cooperation and Development (OECD) underlines the fact that there is no universal, commonly accepted definition of social enterprises as the concept has not yet been widely institutionalized, thus stressing the difficulty of giving a legal definition.[131] However, while the forms of social enterprises are highly diverse – as they arise spontaneously within civil society in response to current changes to the welfare – they all have a similar practical implementation and ethical approach. In this sense, since the concept of social enterprise does not correspond to a precise legal form, definitions tend to describe the functions of social enterprises; the functional approach, in fact, seems to be an appropriate analytical tool, given the wide variety of legal forms in the different countries covered by the concept.

On the ground of the above considerations, the OECD concludes that, in any case, the expression 'social enterprise' can refer to 'any private activity conducted in the public interest, organized with an entrepreneurial strategy but whose main purpose is not the maximization of profit but the attainment of certain economic and social goals, and which has a capacity for bringing innovative solutions to the problems of social exclusion and unemployment'.[132]

More recently, Defourny and Nyssen define social enterprises as 'not-for-profit organizations providing goods or services directly related to their explicit aim of benefiting the community [...] They rely on a dynamic involving various types of stakeholders in their governing bodies'.[133]

Social enterprises may be active in a wide spectrum of activities, as the 'social purpose' may refer to many different fields. Nowadays, 'Work Integration Social Enterprises' (WISE) represent the dominant form of social enterprises whose main objective is to help low qualified unemployed people.[134] In several countries, the development of specific public schemes targeted to this type of social enterprises has even led to associate the concept of social enterprise with employment creation initiatives.[135]

WISE activities are widespread throughout the EU with strongly identifiable organizational forms such as Italy's 'type B' or 'working integration' social cooperatives, French enterprises for the reintegration of economic activity, Finnish social enterprises, and Poland's social cooperatives.[136]

130. J. Barrett, J. Veal, *Social Enterprise: Some Tax Policy Considerations*, in *Journal of the Australasian Tax Teachers Association*, 2013, p. 154.
131. OECD, *Social Enterprises*, OECD publications, Paris, 1999, p. 9.
132. *Ibid.*
133. J. Defourny, M. Nyssens, *Social Enterprise in Europe: Recent Trends and Developments*, in *Social Enterprise Journal*, 2008, p. 5.
134. M. Nyssen, *Social Enterprise – At the Crossroads of Market, Public Policies and Civil Society*, Routledge, London and New York, 2006.
135. J. Defourny, M. Nyssens, *supra.*, in *Social Enterprise Journal*, 2008, p. 8.
136. European Commission, *A map of social enterprises and their eco-systems in Europe. Synthesis Report*, European Commission Publications, 2014, p. 8.

Beyond work integration itself, several social enterprises are to be found across the full spectrum of social welfare services (long-term care for the elderly and for people with disabilities; early education and childcare; employment and training services; social housing; social integration of disadvantaged individuals such as ex-offenders, migrants, drug addicts, etc.; healthcare and medical services).[137]

In any case, the most visible efforts in the study of the relation between social enterprises and social tax incentives are due to the United Kingdom (UK) experience where scholars investigate the possibility and the legal issues related to the introduction of innovative tax schemes, such as in the case of social investment tax reliefs designed to encourage individuals to support social enterprises and to simplify the access to new sources of finance.[138]

In particular, Heaney examines tax incentive schemes in the UK, focusing the analysis on the case of tax incentives for social enterprises investors. According to the author, tax incentives have a role to play in the promotion of investment flows, but the range of UK enterprise incentive schemes is ill-suited to the legal forms most commonly adopted by social enterprises. In this sense, in fact, tax reliefs are available for equity investment, but social entrepreneurs usually choose legal forms limited by guarantee, which do not allow equity issuance. The end result is that many social enterprises are shut off from potential sources of growth capital and are restricted to a grant-dependent/loan financing mentality;[139] in conclusion, according to Heaney, the specific legal form adopted by a social enterprise is crucial to its ability to benefit from different tax incentive schemes.[140]

Also Carpenter and Keller Lauritzen make a reference to the possibility of tax incentives for social enterprise investors; according to them, in fact, national governments can relieve the tax burden of private investors (including even private citizens) investing in social enterprises.[141] In such cases, reliefs can be given on the amount invested or on interests and dividends earned through investments.[142]

---

137. Further common situations belonging to the same phenomenon are recognizable in the following areas: land-based industries and the environment (e.g., agriculture, horticulture, food processing, environmental services, and environmental protection) in countries like the Czech Republic, Malta, and Romania; serving community interest needs in countries like the UK, Germany, and the Netherlands (e.g., housing, transportation, and energy) and cultural, sport and recreational activities (e.g., arts, crafts, music, and tourism) in Croatia, Estonia, Finland, Greece, Hungary, Malta, and Sweden. Therefore, it is worth to note that the main activity fields of work integration and welfare service provision have been recently expanded to sectors of general interest other than welfare in a strict sense, such as the provision of educational, cultural, environmental, and public utility services.
138. A recent implementation of such tax schemes can be found in the UK legislation giving effect to social investment tax reliefs (SITR) corresponding to schedules 11 and 12 of the Finance Act 2014, amending the Income Act 2007. Pursuant to the SITR rules, individuals making an eligible investment can deduct 30% of the cost of their investment from their income tax due. The investment must be held for a minimum period of three years for the relief to be retained.
139. V. Heaney, *Investing in Social Enterprise: The Role of Tax Incentives*, Centre for the Study of Financial Innovation (CSFI), London, 2010, p. 52.
140. *Ibid.*, p. 4.
141. G. Carpenter, J.R. Keller Lauritzen, *Promoting Social Enterprise Financing* (Discussion paper), Danish Technological Institute, Centre for Policy and Business Analysis, Taastrup (Denmark), 2016, p. 9.
142. *Ibid.*, p. 10.

One more interesting document is represented by the report commissioned by the City of London Corporation and Big Society Capital in order to examine the case for providing tax incentives for wealthy individuals in case of social investments.[143] In particular, the report aims at providing practical guidance on how the relief could be created by adapting existing structures. The intention of a tax relief would be to see greater social investments from wealthy individuals into distinctive schemes for public benefit; moreover, according to the same report, the implementation of such a scheme requires the establishment of a framework with the identification of the types of target organizations. For tax purposes, however, the same report underlines again the fact that it is always appropriate to focus on the legal form of a social enterprise, as this is the key factor for determining what type of capital can be raised.[144]

Given the above, the literature on social enterprises offers an interesting perspective for the purposes of the present study; among the social tax incentives for STZs, in fact, the possibility should be explored of introducing tax advantages granted in favour of social enterprises based therein, with eligibility subject to the achievement of social impact targets.

In other words, the review of the previous studies highlights a new room where social enterprises might be used as a strategic instrument in the context of STZs, namely as a powerful vehicle to grant tax incentives of a social character for improving the living conditions of the individuals which reside in the disadvantaged areas of the Union.

§2.07 FINAL REMARKS

The review of the multitude of studies presented in this chapter offers the opportunity to trace a first framework of the legal dimension of STZs.

As already seen, there are different views regarding not only the definitions, but also the denominations used to identify the phenomenon; it is clear, in fact, that the use of a specific denomination usually depends on the name provided by local public authorities and the wording which is prevalent in the country where the zone is located.[145]

The distinction between 'classic free zones', on one part, and 'free zones of exception', on the other, represents still today a fundamental classification and a reference point for any legal approach to the topic, being the logical result of the essential distinction between the categories of indirect taxes and direct taxes in the context of tax law studies.

At the same time, the recognition of STZs within the general phenomenon of tax advantages constitutes one more step for the definition of the legal dimension, providing an important contribution in the identification of the substantial nature of such zones.

143. Worthstone, Wragge & Co LLP, *The Role of Tax Incentives in Encouraging Social Investment*, City of London Economic Development, London, 2013.
144. *Ibid.*, p. 3.
145. S. Finardi, E. Moroni, *supra.*, FrancoAngeli, 2001, Milan, p. 60.

Nevertheless, it is evident that the various aspects regarding STZs have always been approached in a disorganic form, without the outline of a solid and comprehensive general legal theory. This phenomenon, in fact, is still little investigated from the systematic perspective, especially when the analysis is carried out within the area of tax law.

Furthermore, as far as the focus is shifted to the possible introduction of tax incentives of a social character within the perimeter of an STZ, the previous studies present many weak points, considering that today it is still not possible to recognize important efforts addressed to the understanding of the relationship between STZs and social tax incentives.

The work already done by the scholars, in fact, is limited to provide a general overview on social tax incentives, without the study of their possible implementations in the context of STZs.

The issue is even more serious with respect to the fact that the same category of social tax incentives is only marginally investigated in literature and, apart from the studies made by Howard, there are no relevant efforts in the identification of clear examples of what social tax incentives really entail.

In conclusion, previous studies are insufficient as they are not focused on the territorial dimension of social tax incentives and their possible implementation in the context of STZs; social enterprises and the related tax incentives, in fact, are analysed only through a very general perspective which is not able to highlight the connections with the topic of STZs.

In any case, on the ground of the above considerations, it is possible to lay down the track which will drive the next stages of the research process.

First of all, it seems necessary to deepen – under the first research question – the legal substance of the phenomenon in order to trace the basics of a general legal theory, filling the systematic gap identified in the existing literature.

Then, on the same basis, it is important to move the study towards the relation between STZs, social tax incentives and social enterprises, approaching the second research question outlined in the introduction of the present book; in this sense, in fact, social enterprises, as far as they are based within the territory of an STZ, might become a fundamental vehicle to grant social tax incentives in favour of disadvantaged groups of individuals residing in the same zones.

CHAPTER 3

The EU Law Framework

§3.01 INTRODUCTION

The EU law framework of STZs involves a complex set of different legal sources, including not only the provisions of the TFEU and the related case law, but also a multitude of regulations, directives, decisions, and other soft law instruments adopted by the Commission.

The objective of the present chapter is to identify these sources and to define the coordinates at the EU level able to influence the phenomenon of STZs with the creation of a solid background for the analysis of the research questions.

In this direction, the research process is targeted towards a careful review of the relevant sources, both for what regards the text of the provisions in force and the statements contained in the relevant case law; the focus is set on the legal variables that influence the phenomenon of STZs, outlining a comprehensive overview of the relevant EU legal framework.

From the systematic point of view, the review is structured on the ground of the distinction between the three macro-areas of State aid law, internal market law, and harmful tax competition.

The selection of the sources is driven by the object of the research questions; in this sense, the review is not limited to the phenomenon of territorial tax advantages in a strict sense, but it is also extended to the world of social tax incentives and social enterprises with particular reference to the so-called social services of general interest (hereinafter also SSGIs).

The main scope is to explore a wider framework where the phenomenon of STZs can interact with the legal aspects related to the introduction of tax incentives of a social character at the sub-State level. By this approach, it is finally possible to set a bridge between STZs and tax incentives of a social character for the purposes of the research question No. 2 which is essentially focused on the development of a new model of STZs based on the introduction of tax incentives of a social character.

Therefore, the first part of the analysis involves the aspects of State aid law with a description of the common framework of regional aid and SSGIs which is relevant for the phenomenon of STZs; the second part deals with internal market law and, in particular, with the issues deriving from the implementation of the fundamental freedoms both in the TFEU and in secondary law; finally, the third part is dedicated to the relation between STZs and the phenomenon of harmful tax competition with a focus on the content of the Code of Conduct for Business Taxation and its specific measures.[146]

§3.02 STZs AND STATE AID LAW

State aid law assumes a fundamental role for the definition of the legal framework of STZs in the EU context.

State aid provisions, in fact, ensure that domestic support for business entities, including negative aid in the form of tax advantages, does not distort competition with a negative effect on the trade between Member States; in other words, it is evident that such rules often interact with STZs,[147] outlining a set of conditions which are relevant for the purposes of the present research.

For this reason, the following sections are dedicated to the discipline of State aid with particular reference to the phenomenon of regional aid, both for what regards the rules set by the TFEU, on one part, and the sources of secondary law, on the other, with a review of the main legal instruments adopted by the EU institutions.

The same review also includes social services of general interest, opening a different perspective for the analysis of the research question No. 2, especially for what regards the relation between STZs and social cohesion policies; in this sense, the EU rules for social services of general interest represent a fundamental field of investigation to evaluate in which terms tax incentives of a social character may be designed in the context of a new model of STZs.

[A] Regional Aid in the TFEU

[1] Notion of State aid under Article 107(1) TFEU

According to Article 107(1) TFEU a measure constitutes State aid if an economic advantage is granted by a transfer of State resources favouring certain undertakings, and if the aid has a potential effect on competition and trade between Member States.

This principle is associated with the idea that goods, services, and capital have to be freely exchanged between economic operators based within the EU territory,

146. For an explanation regarding the status and the role of the Code of Conduct for Business Taxation *see infra* section §3.04[B][1].
147. In this sense *see* A. Laukkanen, P. Pistone, J. de Goede, *supra.*, IBFD, 2019, p. 87.

neutralizing the tax variable by the harmonization of rules affecting production and trade.[148]

The Commission specifically focuses on the notion of State aid in its Notice of 19 July 2016,[149] clarifying the different qualifying elements, namely: the existence of an undertaking, the State origin of the measure, the granting of an advantage, the selectivity of the measure and its effect on competition and trade between Member States.

[a] The Existence of an Undertaking

State aid rules only apply when the measure is granted to an undertaking, either directly or indirectly.[150]

According to the position held by the ECJ, undertakings are entities engaged in an economic activity, regardless of their legal status and the way in which they are financed.[151] Thus, the classification of a particular entity as an undertaking entirely depends on the nature of its activities;[152] the ECJ, in fact, has consistently held that any activity consisting in offering goods and services on a market is an economic activity and that the existence of a market for certain services depends on the way those services are organized in the Member State concerned. Accordingly, the same distinction between economic and non-economic activities is based on the ground of political choices and economic developments in a given Member State and, therefore, it is not possible to define an exhaustive list of economic or non-economic activities.[153]

In this context, the mere fact that an undertaking might engage in an activity that has a social element does not prevent it from being considered as carrying on an economic activity.[154] In particular, whilst benefits granted by the State to employees are normally not regarded as State aid, payments made through public funds or tax exemptions for certain employees might have the result of reducing or substituting the

148. For a comprehensive analysis of State aid rules *see* M. Lang, P. Pistone, J. Schuch, C. Staringer, *supra*, 3rd Edition, Spiramus Press, Wien, 2013, pp. 93 et seq.; B.J.M. Terra, P. J. Wattel, *supra.*, 6th Edition, Kluwer Law International, Alphen aan den Rijn, 2012, p. 242 et seq. For a specific analysis of the relation between State aid rules and tax benefits *see* C. Fontana, *Gli aiuti di Stato di natura fiscale*, G. Giappichelli (ed.), Turin, 2012.

149. Commission notice on the notion of State aid as referred to in Article 107(1) TFEU, O.J. 2016, C 262, pp. 1-50. For a comprehensive overview of the notion of State aid based on the Commission 2016 Notice *see* R. Luja, *Do State Aid Rules Still Allow European Union Member States to Claim Fiscal Sovereignty?*, in *EC Tax Review*, 2016, No. 5-6, pp. 312-324.

150. Case T-52/12 *Greece v Commission*, [2014] ECRII-0000, paragraph 41.

151. Case C-41/90 *Klaus Höfner and Fritz Elser v Macrotron GmbH*, [1991] ECR I-01979, paragraph 21. *See also* Case C-118/85 *Commission v Italy*, [1987] ECR 2599.

152. Commission notice on the notion of State aid as referred to in Article 107(1) TFEU, O.J. 2016, C 262, pp. 1-50, paragraph 7.

153. *Ibid.*, paragraph 15.

154. Case T-81/07 *KG Holding NV v Commission*, [2009] ECR II-2411, paragraph 179. In this case, a subsidiary company, whose principal activity consisted in the provision of services of finding employment for jobseekers, integrating people living with disabilities into the labour market as well as general staff placement services, was regarded as being engaged in an economic activity.

employment costs and, thus, might be viewed as being an aid to the same undertaking.[155]

[b] The State Origin

The imputability of the measure to the State and the granting of an advantage directly or indirectly through State resources are two separate and cumulative conditions both referring to the public origin of the same measure.[156]

For what regards imputability, the measure is considered as imputable to the State any time a public authority grants an advantage to a beneficiary, even if the same public authority enjoys legal autonomy from the State. According to the Commission, the imputability to the State of a measure taken by a public undertaking may be recognized from a set of indicators based on the circumstances of the case and on the context in which the measure is taken.[157]

Then, only advantages granted directly or indirectly through State resources can constitute State aid pursuant to Article 107(1) TFEU; in this sense, State resources also include resources of intra-State bodies and, under certain circumstances, resources of private bodies.[158]

In this context, the transfer of State resources may take the form of a 'positive aid', such as in the case of direct grants, loans, guarantees, and direct investments in the capital of companies.

Nevertheless, according to the Commission, the category of State aid includes not only grants and performance of a positive content, but also public measures reducing burdens on business in the form of 'negative aid';[159] thus, territorial tax benefits, resulting in a favourable treatment to beneficiaries, such as those granted in the case of an STZ, are generally considered as prohibited State aid - or better as prohibited regional aid - since they use to reduce the burdens on undertakings in various forms including, for example, a total or partial exemption, a tax credit, or a deferral.[160]

155. Case C-30/59, *Steenkolenmijnen v High Authority*, [1961] ECR 1, p. 29.
156. Commission notice on the notion of State aid as referred to in Article 107(1) TFEU, O.J. 2016, C 262, pp. 1-50, paragraph 38.
157. *Ibid.*, paragraph 42.
158. *Ibid.*, paragraph 48.
159. *Ibid.*, paragraph 51. In this sense, *see also* Case C-387/92 *Banco de Credito Industrial SA, now Banco Exterior de Espana SA v Ayuntamiento de Valencia*, [1994] ECR I-00877, in which the problem is investigated for the first time; *see also* Case C-328/99 *Italian Republic and SIM 2 Multimedia S.p.A. v Commission of the European Communities*, [2003] ECR I-04035; Case C-276/02 *Spain v Commission of the European Communities*, [2004] ECR I-08091.
160. C. Bucicco, *Compatibilità europea degli interventi a sostegno delle aree colpite da calamità naturali*, in M. Basilavecchia - L. Del Federico - A. Pace - C. Verrigni, *Interventi finanziari e tributari per le aree colpite da calamità, tra norme interne e principi europei*, G. Giappichelli (ed.), Turin, 2016, p. 154. For an interesting source deepening the State aid topic within the tax law field *see* W. Schoen, *Taxation and State aid law in the European Union*, in *Internal market Law Review*, Kluwer Law International, The Hague, 1999, Vol. 36, No. 5, pp. 911-936; D. Collie, *State Aid in the European Union: The Prohibition of Subsidies in an Integrated Market*, in *International Journal of Industrial Organization*, 2000, pp. 867-884; D. Brautigam, O. Fjeldstad, M. Moore, *Taxation and State-Building in Developing Countries: Capacity and Consent*, Cambridge University Press, Cambridge, 2008; K. Bacon, *Differential Taxes, State Aids and the*

[c] Advantage

The Commission also specifies that an advantage, within the meaning of Article 107(1) TFEU, is any economic benefit which an undertaking could not have obtained under normal market conditions;[161] in other words, an advantage is present any time the financial situation of an undertaking is improved as a result of State intervention on terms differing from normal market conditions.

In its Communication, the Commission refers to the 'market economy operator' test as the relevant method to assess whether the State has granted an advantage to an undertaking by not acting like a market economy operator with regard to a certain transaction.[162] In that respect, according to the Commission, it is not relevant whether the intervention is aimed at pursuing public policy objectives; in fact, only the effect of the measure on the undertaking is relevant, and not the cause or the objective of the State intervention.[163]

For the purposes of STZs, the advantage generally consists in a reduction of the tax burden in favour of the beneficiaries provided through the introduction of allowances, tax credits, exemptions, or a mere deferral of the tax burden.

[d] Selectivity

To fall within the scope of Article 107(1) TFEU, the measure must be specific or selective in the sense that it favours only '*certain undertakings or the production of certain goods*'. Hence, not all measures which favour economic operators fall under the notion of aid, but only those which grant an advantage in a selective way to certain undertakings or categories of undertakings or to certain economic sectors.[164] According to the Commission, the selectivity of the measures should normally be assessed through a three-step analysis.

First, the reference system must be identified focusing on a consistent set of rules that generally apply to all undertakings falling within its scope. In the case of taxes, the reference system is based on such elements as the tax base, the taxable persons, the taxable event, and the tax rates.

Second, it should be determined whether a given measure constitutes a derogation from the reference system, with the introduction of a differentiated treatment between economic operators which are in a comparable factual and legal situation.

Third, it is necessary to establish whether such a derogation is justified by the nature or the general scheme of the reference system; in fact, if a derogation measure

---

Lunn Poly Case, in *European Competition Law Review*, 1999, p. 384; P. Nicolaides, *Fiscal State Aid in the EU: The Limits of Tax Autonomy*, in *World Competition*, 2004, p. 365.

161. Commission notice on the notion of State aid as referred to in Article 107(1) TFEU, O.J. 2016, C 262, pp. 1-50, paragraph 66.
162. *Ibid.*, paragraph 75.
163. *Ibid.*, paragraph 67.
164. *Ibid.*, paragraph 117.

is justified by the nature or the general scheme of the system, it will not be considered selective and will thus fall outside the scope of Article 107(1) TFEU.[165]

The Commission also distinguishes between material and regional selectivity.

The material selectivity usually implies that the measure applies only to certain undertakings or certain sectors of the economy in a Member State.[166]

In any case, in order to establish the material selectivity of a tax measure, it is not necessary to identify certain specific features that are characteristic of and common to the undertakings that are the recipients of the tax advantage; in other words, the same measure could be selective even if the tax benefits are not limited to a particular category of undertakings. According to the ECJ, in fact, the appropriate criterion to establish the selectivity of a general measure is merely whether the recipient undertakings are placed in a position that is more favourable than that of other undertakings which, in the light of the objective pursued by the general tax system concerned, are in a comparable factual and legal situation.[167]

The regional selectivity – or territorial selectivity – generally refers to all measures that apply only to certain parts of the territory of a Member State. In this sense, in fact, tax measures which are implemented at a local level in the form of regional aid – such as in the case of STZs – are normally considered as being able to favour certain undertakings as long as the individual Member State's territory is assumed as the reference system.[168] However, the reference system is not always identified with the entire territory of the Member State; as stated by the ECJ, in fact, measures with a regional or local scope of application may not be selective if certain requirements are fulfilled.

In this regard, the Commission identifies three different scenarios.

In the first scenario, the central government of a Member State unilaterally decides to apply a lower level of taxation within a defined geographical area; in such a case, it is evident that the related measures are territorial selective.

The second scenario corresponds to a form of symmetrical devolution of tax powers in which all infra-State authorities at a particular level (e.g., regions) of a Member State have the same autonomous power to establish the applicable tax rate within their territory, independently of the central government. In this case, the measures adopted by the infra-State authorities are not selective since it is impossible to determine a normal tax rate capable of representing the reference framework.

In the third scenario, which corresponds to the asymmetrical devolution of tax powers, only certain regional or local authorities can adopt tax measures applicable within their territory. In this case, the assessment of the selective nature of the measure

165. *Ibid.*, paragraph 128.
166. *Ibid.*, paragraph 120.
167. In this sense, *see* Joined cases C-20/15 P and C-21/15 P *Commission v World Duty Free Group SA, formerly Autogrill España SA, Banco Santander SA, Santusa Holding SL*, [2016] ECR I-0000, paragraphs 77, 78, regarding the Spanish goodwill amortization regime which has been considered as unlawful State aid by the Commission (on the assumption that the related provisions treated foreign transactions more favourably than domestic transactions without any objective reason).
168. A. Dagnino, *supra.*, CEDAM, 2008, p. 146.

depends on whether the authority concerned is sufficiently autonomous from the central government of the Member State, namely when the criteria of the institutional, procedural and economic, and financial autonomy are fulfilled.[169] If all of these criteria of autonomy are present, the region in question, not the Member State, becomes the only geographical reference framework for the assessment of the selectivity of a tax measure.[170]

[e] Effect on Trade and Competition

Within the meaning of Article 107(1) TFEU, a measure granted by the State is considered to distort or threaten to distort competition when it is liable to improve the competitive position of the recipient compared to other undertakings with which it competes.[171]

In particular, a distortion of competition can be found when the State grants a financial advantage to an undertaking in a liberalized sector where there is competition. Furthermore, public support to undertakings only constitutes State aid under Article 107(1) TFEU when it affects trade between Member States. In this regard, it is not necessary to establish that the aid has an actual effect on trade between Member States but only whether the aid is liable to affect such trade.[172]

For example, the relatively small amount of aid or the relatively small size of the undertaking does not automatically exclude the possibility that trade between Member States might be affected. According to the Commission, in fact, a public subsidy granted to an undertaking which provides only local or regional services and does not provide any services outside its State of origin may nonetheless have an effect on trade between Member States where undertakings from other Member States could provide such services.[173]

On these premises, it is evident that STZs may include prohibited State aid – in the form of regional aid – as far as Member States decide to introduce tax benefits targeted only at undertakings based therein, conferring a selective advantage with respect to other undertakings which are based out of the perimeter of such zones.

In this sense, in fact, STZs may produce negative effects on competition and evolve into prohibited State aid; the general idea is that the disparity of taxes on commercial transactions and trade between Member States – and, thus, even territorial tax advantages in the form of regional aid – may potentially lead to distortions of competition in the EU internal market. Given the above, it is evident that also the tax benefits granted to the entities based in STZs must be deeply analysed under State aid rules.

---

169. For the review of the criteria of institutional, procedural and economic and financial autonomy *see infra* section §3.02[A][5] (the *Azores* case).
170. Commission notice on the notion of State aid as referred to in Article 107(1) TFEU, O.J. 2016, C 262, pp. 1-50, paragraphs 142-144.
171. *Ibid.*, paragraph 187.
172. *Ibid.*, paragraph 190.
173. *Ibid.*, paragraph 192.

[2] Exemptions under Article 107(3)(a) TFEU

Beside the conditions set by Article 107(1) TFEU to consider a measure as a prohibited State aid, it is important to note that some exemptions to the same prohibition are identified for regional aid under Article 107(3) TFEU.[174]

In particular, as far as the phenomenon of STZs is concerned, Article 107(3)(a) and (c) TFEU[175] identifies two relevant categories of aid where the measure may be declared compatible with the internal market after the assessment of the Commission.

In this sense, Article 107(3)(a) TFEU provides that aid may be granted to promote the economic development of areas where the standard of living is abnormally low or where there is serious underemployment, and of the 'ORs' referred to in Article 349 TFEU,[176] in view of their structural, economic and social situation. This first category of aid concerns only those regions where the economic situation is extremely unfavourable in relation to the EU as a whole, so that the assessment of these factors must not be made with reference to the national average in the Member State concerned, but in relation to the EU level.[177]

For the assessment of such aid, the Commission may take account of many different elements, such as the geographical remoteness of the region from the principal business centres and all the other factors which are able to increase the costs of transports and infrastructures. In this regard, the planned aid must be necessary for the development of less favoured areas since, otherwise, the same aid would not be compatible with the internal market.

In any case, the relevance of such category of exempted aid for the phenomenon of STZs is evident; the related tax incentives, in fact, can be in principle designed according to the exemption of Article 107(3)(a) TFEU as long as the same area is affected by a serious underdevelopment in comparison to the EU average.

---

174. Communication from the Commission – Guidelines on regional State aid for 2014-2020, O.J. 2013, C 209, pp. 1-45 (*see infra* section §3.02[B][3]).
175. According to Article 107(3) TFEU '*the following may be considered to be compatible with the internal market: (a) aid to promote the economic development of areas where the standard of living is abnormally low or where there is serious underemployment, and of the regions referred to in Article 349, in view of their structural, economic and social situation; (b) aid to promote the execution of an important project of common European interest or to remedy a serious disturbance in the economy of a Member State; (c) aid to facilitate the development of certain economic activities or of certain economic areas, where such aid does not adversely affect trading conditions to an extent contrary to the common interest; (d) aid to promote culture and heritage conservation where such aid does not affect trading conditions and competition in the Union to an extent that is contrary to the common interest; (e) such other categories of aid as may be specified by decision of the Council on a proposal from the Commission*'.
176. In accordance with Article 349 TFEU, the so-called outermost regions include nine specific regions: Guadeloupe, French Guiana, Martinique, Réunion, Mayotte, Saint-Martin, the Azores, Madeira, and the Canary Islands.
177. Case C-248/84 *Germany v Commission*, [1987] ECR 4013, paragraph 19; Case C-310/99 *Italy v Commission*, [2002] ECR I-2289, paragraph 77.

[3] Exemptions under Article 107(3)(c) TFEU

Article 107(3)(c) TFEU allows for the approval of aid to facilitate the development of certain economic activities or of certain economic areas.

In relation to regional aid, this category of exemptions is wider in scope than that available under Article 107(3)(a) TFEU; in this second case, in fact, the development of certain areas is not restricted by the economic conditions necessary for the application of the first category of exemptions, allowing regional aid intended to favour the economic development of areas of a Member State which are disadvantaged in relation to the national average and not necessary with reference to the EU level.

Such category of exempted aid is permissible only to the extent that it does not adversely affect trading conditions contrary to the common interest; accordingly, aid should be limited to the minimum necessary.[178]

In this case, the Commission has the responsibility, under a system of prior authorizations, to ensure that every Member State only conceives and designs aid measures useful to help companies in producing goods and services that would not otherwise be provided in the internal market, avoiding measures that distort competition. In this sense, the Commission, while moving within a large discretion to declare aid compatible, always needs to take account of the provisions of the treaties as interpreted by the ECJ[179] and, thus, has to verify if such aid can be aimed at some other objectives set out by the treaties.

[4] The Supervision of the Commission under Article 108 TFEU

The measures constituting State aid are covered by a system of prior authorization by the Commission according to Article 108 TFEU and to the procedural rules set by Regulation (EU) No. 2015/1589.[180]

In particular, a measure constituting State aid must be notified to the Commission,[181] while Member States may not implement the same measure before a formal approval by the Commission (so-called standstill clause[182]). If the measure has been already implemented in violation of such procedural rules, the Commission, any time it considers the aid incompatible with the internal market, may decide that the Member

178. Case T-349/03 *Corsica Ferries France sas v Commission*, [2005] ECR II-2197, paragraph 317.
179. Case C-42/02 *Diana Elisabeth Lindman*, [2003] ECR I-13519, in which the ECJ has decided that certain grounds may also justify indirect discrimination. *See also* the case *Rewe-Zentral AG v Bundesmonopolverwaltung fur Branntwein* by which the ECJ decides that the infringement of the fundamental freedoms may also be justified by general grounds of public interest (Case C-120/78 *Rewe-Zentral AG v Bundesmonopolverwaltung für Branntwein*, [1979] ECR 649).
180. Council Regulation (EU) No. 2015/1589 of 13 July 2015 laying down detailed rules for the application of Article 108 TFEU,Council Regulation (EU) 2015/1589 of 13 July 2015 laying down detailed rules for the application of Article 108 of the Treaty on the Functioning of the European Union (Text with EEA relevance) O.J. 2015, L 248, pp. 9-29.
181. *Ibid.*, Article 2.
182. *Ibid.*, Article 3.

State must amend or abolish it;[183] this suppression implies, in principle, that the Member State must recover the aid from the beneficiary or beneficiaries.[184]

Therefore, the Commission assumes a fundamental role for any initiative aimed at the establishment of an STZ being able to influence and limiting the actions of the Member States on the ground of the procedural rules set by Regulation No. 2015/1589.[185]

In this sense, in fact, the establishment of STZs under the exempted categories of aid remains, in principle, subject to the supervision activity of the Commission and to a prior scrutiny which must be carried out before the implementation of the related measures. Nevertheless, according to Article 108(4) TFEU, the Commission may always adopt specific regulations when the Council, pursuant to Article 109 TFEU, has previously determined that some categories of State aid may be exempted from the procedural rules above described, including the notification requirement. The issue will be further described *infra* in the section dedicated to the review of regional aid in the secondary law with particular reference to the content of the General Block Exemption Regulation (GBER).[186]

[5] ECJ Case Law

The ECJ has a fundamental role in the interpretation of State aid rules with the development of a series of principles that are relevant for the purposes of the present study.

Therefore, the focus must be set on the review of the ECJ case law, with a selection limited to the most significant cases where the Court directly intervenes on the topic of STZs, outlining the essential boundaries under which State aid rules shall be applied.

As it will be shown below, there are some interesting cases where the Court investigates the extent of selectivity in the context of an STZ, this being one of the conditions for the recognition of prohibited State aid under the provision of Article 107 TFEU.

In particular, the selectivity is sometimes analysed as 'territorial selectivity' (*see Juntas Generales*, *Azores*, *UGT-Rioja*, *Gibraltar*) with reference to common situations where tax benefits are granted to all the entities based in a limited area of the Member State, without a differential treatment according to the material features of such entities and their activities.

In other cases, the selectivity is otherwise represented as 'material selectivity' (*Gibraltar* and *Sardinia*), being this a further field of investigation where the Court points out the situations where the favouring tax treatment is reserved only to entities

183. *Ibid.*, Article 22.
184. *Ibid.*, Article 16. *See also* P. Craig, G. De Búrca, *EU Law: Text, Cases, and Materials*, 6th Edition, Oxford University Press, New York, 2015, pp. 1145 et seq.
185. The procedural rules of Regulation (EU) No. 2015/1589, including the notification obligation, also apply in case of aid for the so-called Social Services of General Interest (SSGIs) granted according to the regime of exemption set by Article 106(2) TFEU (*see infra* section §3.02[C]).
186. *See infra* section §3.02[B][1].

with some specific material features and not to all the entities based in the same zone, working out further criteria through which it is possible to detect the selective nature of the related measures.

Beside such case law dealing with the subject of selectivity, both territorial or material, it is worth remembering one more case (*Deufil*) where the ECJ clarifies the perspective from which it is necessary to evaluate territorial tax incentives under State aid rules, setting the focus on the potential effects of the same measures and not on the original aims pursued.

[a] The Juntas Generales Case

In the *Juntas Generales* case (*Administración General del Estado v Juntas Generales de Guipúzcoa and Diputación Foral de Guipúzcoa*)[187] the focus must be set on the opinion delivered by Advocate General Saggio,[188] considering the absence of a final decision from the ECJ.[189]

In his Opinion, Advocate General Saggio deeply analyses the requirement of territorial selectivity in the context of State aid rules with an assessment formulated on a set of tax measures introduced by the Autonomous Community of the Spanish Basque Country.

The case is relevant for the present research since the characteristics of the Basque Country clearly correspond to the legal dimension of an STZ; in this sense, in fact, the authorities of this territory have regulatory powers in the area of direct taxation with an autonomous system of income tax which differs from the standard one generally applied in the rest of Spain.

In details, the Court is here asked to rule on the compatibility, among others, between State aid rules and the provincial laws - the so-called *normas forales* - adopted by three authorities belonging to the Autonomous Community of the Basque Country, containing urgent fiscal measures. These laws establish a series of fiscal advantages in relation to corporate and personal income tax (PIT) and in favour of both legal persons and individuals based in this STZ, provided that some requirements are fulfilled.

In this case, the Advocate General Saggio points out the difficulty of determining which circumstances, linked to the nature and scheme of the system, can justify the difference of treatment which arises from the Basque laws in respect of the national legislation in force. According to his opinion, in fact, the fiscal autonomy of the Basque Territories does not reflect any specificity of the territory in question - in terms of

187. Joined cases C-400/97, C-401/97 and C-402/97 *Administración General del Estado v Juntas Generales de Guipúzcoa and Diputación Foral de Guipúzcoa, Juntas Generales d'Alava and Diputación Foral d'Alava and Juntas Generales de Vizcaya*, [2000] ECR I-01073.
188. Opinion of Advocate General Saggio delivered on 1 July 1999 in Joined cases C-400/97, C-401/97 and C-402/97 *Administración General del Estado v Juntas Generales de Guipúzcoa and Diputación Foral de Guipúzcoa, Juntas Generales d'Alava and Diputación Foral d'Alava and Juntas Generales de Vizcaya, ibid.*
189. Since by letters of 8 February 2000, received at the Court Registry on 14 February 2000, the Tribunal Superior de Justicia del País Vasco informed the Court that, as a result of the discontinuance of the applicant in the cases in the main proceedings, it is withdrawing its requests of 30 July 1997 for preliminary rulings.

economic conditions such as level of employment, production costs, infrastructures, labour cost – which would require, indirectly, fiscal treatment different from that in force in the reference framework (in this case corresponding to the rest of the Spanish territory). In other words, the scheme which results from these provisions satisfies only the desire to favour investments in the Basque territories and to improve the competitiveness of the companies. Therefore, the same scheme is characterized by the exceptional nature of the measures which derogates from the standard tax legislation, being thus not in compliance with Article 107 TFEU.[190]

In summary, in this case, the condition of territorial selectivity, with reference to the measures adopted in an STZ, is essentially associated to the circumstance that in the area concerned it is not possible to recognize any disadvantaged economic situation. In such cases, according to the Opinion of Advocate General Saggio, the tax measures cannot be justified and, thus, they have to be considered as territorial selective, representing an infringement of State aid rules.

[b] The Azores Case

More recently, the Court has changed the direction followed in the *Juntas Generales* case, opening the doors to a new flexible approach to territorial selectivity within the context of STZs and regional autonomy. In this sense, in fact, the *Azores* case (*Portuguese Republic v Commission*[191]) focuses on the analysis of situations in which an infra-State body, such as a region or a municipality, enjoys sufficient institutional, procedural, and economic autonomy to be able to determine its own tax system, defining the political and economic environment in which undertakings operate.

In the new context, the fulfilment of the conditions of institutional, procedural, and financial autonomy is sufficient to exclude, in principle, the territorial selectivity of a tax measure.

Azores are characterized by a favouring tax regime for the undertakings based therein compared to the standard tax regime applied at the national level in Portugal. For these reasons, they can be considered as an STZ to be reviewed for the scope of the present study, being a limited territory where some specific tax advantages are granted in favour of enterprises.

In this case, the Portuguese Republic seeks the annulment of Commission Decision 2003/442/EC[192] on the part of a new tax scheme adapting the national tax

190. Joined cases C-400/97, C-401/97 and C-402/97 *Administración General del Estado v Juntas Generales de Guipúzcoa and Diputación Foral de Guipúzcoa, Juntas Generales d'Alava and Diputación Foral d'Alava and Juntas Generales de Vizcaya*, [2000] ECR I-01073, paragraph 38.
191. Case C-88/03 *Portugal v Commission*, [2006] ECR I-7115. For a comprehensive analysis of the case *see* G. Bizioli, *L'autonomia finanziaria e tributaria regionale*, G. Giappichelli (ed.), Turin, 2012, pp.123-127; G. Melis, *La delega sul federalismo fiscale e la cosiddetta 'fiscalità di vantaggio': profili comunitari*, in *Rassegna Tributaria*, 2009, No. 4, pp. 1003 et seq.; A. Carinci, *Autonomia impositiva degli enti sub-statali e divieto di aiuti di Stato*, in *Rassegna Tributaria*, 2006, No. 5, pp. 1783 et seq.; V. Ficari, *Aiuti fiscali regionali, selettività e 'insularità': dalle Azzorre agli enti locali italiani*, in *Diritto e pratica tributaria internazionale*, 2007, pp. 319 et seq.
192. O.J. 2003, L 150, pp. 52-63.

system to the specific characteristics of the Autonomous Region of the Azores which concerns reductions in the rates of income tax.

The case is interesting given the fact that the Court - unless the measure taken by the government of Azores has been finally considered as selective and not general - clearly identifies the conditions under which territorial tax advantages - such as those granted to STZs - do not have to be considered selective for the purposes of State aid rules.[193]

The starting point of the analysis is the legislative measure adopted by the local government of the Azores Region[194] through which the national tax system has been adapted to the region's specific characteristics, including a section concerning reductions in the rates of income tax applied automatically to all economic operators.

According to Portuguese authorities, such tax benefits, which consist in a reduction in the rates of income tax, are intended to allow undertakings in the Azores to overcome the structural handicaps resulting from their location in an insular region in the periphery of the Union.

In order to determine the selective nature of the measure at issue, the ECJ examines whether, within the context of the same legal system, that measure constitutes an advantage for certain undertakings in comparison with others which are in a comparable legal and factual situation. Thus, the identification of the reference framework has a particular importance in this case, since the existence of an advantage may be established only when compared with standard taxation.[195]

Here, for the first time, the Court states that the reference framework does not necessarily correspond to the entire national territory of the Member State concerned. In fact, it is possible that an infra-State body enjoys a legal and factual status which makes it sufficiently autonomous in relation to the central government of a Member State, with the result that, by the measures it adopts, it is that body and not the central government which plays a fundamental role in the definition of the political and economic environment in which undertakings operate. In such a case, it is the area in which the infra-State body exercises its powers, and not the country as a whole, that constitutes the relevant context for the assessment of whether a measure adopted by such a body favours certain undertakings in comparison with others in a comparable legal and factual situation.[196]

In particular, according to the position of the ECJ, three conditions must be fulfilled in order to obtain the requirement of regional autonomy[197] under which tax benefits introduced therein may not be considered as selective.

193. For a critical review of this approach *see* P. Nicolaides, *Developments in Fiscal Aid: New Interpretations and New Problems with the Concept of Selectivity*, in *European State Aid Law Quarterly*, 2007, I, pp. 43 et seq.
194. By Regional Legislative Decree of 20 January 1999, No. 2/99/A, as amended by Regional Legislative Decree of 30 December 1999, No. 33/99/A.
195. Case C-88/03 *Portugal v Commission*, [2006] ECR I-7115, paragraph 56.
196. *Ibid.*, paragraph 58.
197. *Ibid.*, paragraph 67.

First, from a constitutional point of view, the regional authority needs to have a separate political and administrative status from the national government (institutional autonomy).

Second, the measure must be adopted with no central government authorized to directly affect the decision (procedural autonomy).

Finally, the financial consequences of the beneficial treatment given to undertakings in the region must not be offset by aid or subsidies from other regions or from the central government (economic and financial autonomy).

In conclusion, according to the above conditions, it is always necessary to verify if the region plays a key role in the definition of a '*political and economic environment*' not constrained by decisions taken by the general economic policy of the Member State.[198]

In other words, the regional authority must assume the responsibility for the political and financial consequences of the tax reduction measures implemented.

On these premises, the Court finally states that in this case the decision of the government of the Autonomous Region of the Azores to exercise its power to reduce the rates of national tax on revenue has not been adopted in accordance with all the conditions set out above.

In this regard, the Court observes that, under the Constitution of the Portuguese Republic, the Azores form an autonomous region with its own political and administrative status and its own self-government institutions which have the power to exercise their own fiscal competence and adapt national fiscal provisions to regional specificities.[199]

Nevertheless, as far as the condition of economic autonomy is concerned, it must be observed that, in the context of the adaptation of the national tax system to regional specificities, the constitutional principle of national solidarity is stated to mean that the central State contributes, with the autonomous regional authorities, to the achievement of economic development and the correction of inequalities deriving from insularity and to economic and social convergence with the rest of the national territory. Thus, the application of that principle of solidarity provided by the Portuguese Constitution gives rise to a duty incumbent on both the central and regional authorities to promote the correction of inequalities arising from insularity by reducing the local tax burden and by an obligation to ensure an appropriate level of public services and private activities. Therefore, although the reduction in tax revenue for the Azores region is clearly aimed at the correction of inequalities in economic development, such measure is in any event offset by a financing mechanism which is centrally managed in the form of budgetary transfers.[200]

Accordingly, because of the lack of the third condition of economic and financial autonomy, the relevant legal framework for determining the selectivity of the tax measures adopted by the local government cannot be defined exclusively within the geographical limits of the Azores region. Given the above, the Court concludes that

198. *Ibid.*, paragraph 58.
199. *Ibid.*, paragraph 70.
200. *Ibid.*, paragraph 75.

those measures must be assessed in relation to the whole of the Portuguese territory, in the context of which they appear to be selective.

In conclusion, the Azores case represents a fundamental point of reference for understanding the approach of the EU institutions in the application of State aid rules to the phenomenon of STZs. In this sense, in fact, this case offers a comprehensive view from the ECJ concerning the requirement of selectivity, with the identification of the various conditions under which a territorial tax measure shall be scrutinized with respect to its reference framework.

[c] The UGT-Rioja Case

In the case *Unión General de Trabajadores de La Rioja (UGT-Rioja) and Others v Juntas Generales del Territorio Histórico de Vizcaya and Others*[201] the Court confirms the position previously held in *Portuguese Republic v Commission* and specifies that the conditions of institutional autonomy, procedural autonomy and economic and financial autonomy are the only conditions which must be satisfied for the territory of an infra-State body in order to be the relevant framework for assessing the selective nature of a tax measure.

In this case, the actions for annulment brought in the main proceedings concern a provision contained in the so-called *normas forales*of the *Juntas Generales de Vizcaya* (i.e., one of the three provinces forming part of the Autonomous Community of the Basque Country) which sets a corporate tax rate at 32.5% which is under the standard national rate of 35% and introduces a new deduction for investments not provided under Spanish tax law. For this reason, the issue of this case assumes a direct relevance in the context of the review, since it deals with an evident example of a territorial tax advantage granted in the form of a rate reduction for corporate income tax (CIT); in other words, the tax advantage under the scrutiny of the ECJ, being reserved to the entities established in a limited area of the Spanish territory, is able to qualify the entire territory of the Autonomous Community of the Basque Country as an STZ for the scope of the present research.

In details, the national court refers a question on the interpretation of Article 107(1) TFEU to the ECJ, asking whether tax legislation which is adopted with a general application and which does not confer an advantage on certain undertakings or the production of certain goods, is to be regarded as 'selective' and subject to the provisions of State aid rules, solely on the ground of the fact that the effects of that legislation are exclusively limited to the territorial jurisdiction of an infra-State authority with autonomy in tax matters.

It is evident that, even in this case, the point under the scrutiny of the ECJ is strictly connected with the topic of STZs, considering that the application of State aid rules to such zones always involves the identification of the geographical reference framework for the purposes of the verification of the selectivity requirement.

201. Joined cases C-428/06 to C-434/06 *Unión General de Trabajadores de La Rioja (UGT-Rioja) and Others v Juntas Generales del Territorio Histórico de Vizcaya and Others*, [2008] I-06747.

On these bases, the Court identifies the infra-State body to be taken as the reference framework, considering that the Autonomous Community of the Basque Country is made up of three provinces: Alava, Vizcaya, and Guipuzcoa. The boundaries of those provinces coincide with those of the Historical Territories, bodies which enjoy rights of ancient origin called '*fueros*', entitling them to levy and collect tax. According to the Court, it is both to the Historical Territories and to the Autonomous Community of the Basque Country that reference must be made for the purpose of determining whether the infra-State body made of those Historical Territories and that Community enjoy sufficient autonomy to constitute the reference framework in the light of which the selectivity of a measure should be assessed.[202]

In particular, for what concerns the first condition of institutional autonomy, the Court states that infra-State bodies, such as the Historical Territories and the Autonomous Community of the Basque Country – to be considered as an STZ for the purposes of the present study – fully satisfy the institutional autonomy criterion considering their political and administrative status which is distinct from that of the central government.[203]

Then, for what regards the procedural autonomy, the Court states that, according to provisions of the Economic Agreement between the Autonomous Community of the Basque Country and the Kingdom of Spain adopted by Law No. 12/2002,[204] a committee set by the central government may examine draft local laws (*normas forales*) in the area of taxation and seek, by negotiation, to eliminate any divergences between those draft laws and the tax legislation applicable in the rest of the Spanish territory. However, considering that, in the absence of an agreement within the committee, the central government is not able to impose the adoption of laws with a particular content, the committee merely represents a consultation and conciliation body rather than a mechanism by which the central government could impose its own decision. Thus, in this case, the central government is not able to directly intervene in the process of adopting local laws (*normas forales*) and, consequently, the procedural criterion seems to be fully fulfilled.[205]

In the same case, the ECJ also analyses the third criterion of financial autonomy making a further step towards a clear interpretation of the conditions under which a tax measure introduced in an STZ may not be considered as territorial selective. In this regard, according to the Advocate General Kokott, the mere fact that it appears from a general examination of the financial relations between the central State and its infra-State bodies that there are financial transfers between the former and the latter, cannot, in itself, suffice to demonstrate that those bodies do not assume the financial consequences of the tax measures which they adopt and, accordingly, that they do not enjoy financial autonomy, since such transfers may take place for reasons unconnected

202. *Ibid.*, paragraph 75.
203. *Ibid.*, paragraph 87.
204. *Ley 12/2002, de 23 de mayo, por la que se aprueba el Concierto Económico con la Comunidad Autónoma del País Vasco*, O.J. of Spain No. 124 of 24 May 2002, pp. 18617-18636.
205. Joined cases C-428/06 to C-434/06 *Unión General de Trabajadores de La Rioja (UGT-Rioja) and Others v Juntas Generales del Territorio Histórico de Vizcaya and Others*, [2008] I-06747, paragraph 108.

with the tax measures. Consequently, it is necessary to examine whether the local laws adopted by the Historical Territories may result in hidden compensation in sectors such as social security or in the functioning of an inter-territorial compensation fund.[206]

Nevertheless, the Court concludes stating that it is reserved to the national court, which alone has jurisdiction to identify the national law applicable and to interpret it, to determine whether the Historical Territories and the Autonomous Community of the Basque Country have such autonomy, which, if so, would have the result that the laws adopted within the limits of the areas of competence granted to those infra-State bodies by the Constitution and the other provisions of Spanish law are not of a selective nature within the meaning of the concept of State aid as referred to in Article 107(1) TFEU.[207]

Therefore, in this case, the reasoning of the ECJ assumes an important relevance in the context of the present study, as it clearly defines the conditions of the institutional, procedural and financial autonomy, opening an interpretative approach to Article 107(1) TFEU which is able to influence the phenomenon of STZs.

[d] The Gibraltar Case

The issue of territorial selectivity with reference to a tax measure is further analysed in the Gibraltar case (*Commission and Spain v Government of Gibraltar and United Kingdom*[208]).

The case deals with a Commission decision finding that some new tax measures introduced in Gibraltar constitute State aid because of a system of corporate taxation under which companies in Gibraltar are taxed, in general, at a lower rate than those in the UK. Therefore, the favouring tax treatment reserved to the companies based in this territory – and, in particular, the lower rate for the CIT compared to the standard one applied in the UK – constitutes the key aspect which is able to qualify Gibraltar as an STZ for the purposes of the present research.

In contrast with the Commission, the General Court here states that the applicable reference framework corresponds exclusively to the geographical limits of the territory of Gibraltar, which means that no comparison can be made between the tax regime applicable to companies established in Gibraltar and that applicable to companies established in the UK.

In this case, the requirement of institutional autonomy is easily presumed by the General Court,[209] while the procedural autonomy is identified by the fact that no UK law in respect of tax matters has ever been applied to Gibraltar.[210] Finally, for what concerns the financial autonomy, the General Court states that the UK's financial

206. *Ibid.*, paragraph 137.
207. *Ibid.*, paragraph 144.
208. Joined Cases T-211/04 to T-215/04 *Commission and Spain v Government of Gibraltar and United Kingdom*, [2008] II-03745.
209. *Ibid.*, paragraph 89.
210. *Ibid.*, paragraph 99.

assistance to Gibraltar is only linked to specific circumstances and has no causal link with the tax reform.[211]

The same case offers the opportunity to analyse the position taken by the ECJ with reference to the different aspect of material selectivity, namely a situation where the favouring tax treatment is reserved only to entities with some specific material features and not to all the entities based in an STZ. Following the appeal against the judgement of first instance, in fact, the Commission stresses again the fact that the tax measures introduced by the tax reform in Gibraltar are able to favour only offshore companies without any real economic activity carried out in the same territory. In this regard, the Grand Chamber of the ECJ finally states that, in this case, offshore companies avoid taxation precisely on account of their specific features and, thus, the proposed tax reform is materially selective in that it confers selective advantages on offshore companies.[212]

In summary, while territorial selectivity cannot be recognized in the present case under the reasoning of the ECJ – since only the territory of Gibraltar has to be considered as the reference framework for the assessment of the related tax measures – on the contrary, as far as the focus is set on material selectivity, the ECJ finally concludes that such tax advantages are able to favour only offshore companies and not all business entities based in that territory. Therefore, the same tax advantages cannot be considered as a general measure within Gibraltar, but they assume a material selective nature since they favour only certain undertakings based in that territory.[213]

[e] The Sardinia Case

The issue of material selectivity is further analysed in the Sardinia case (*Presidente del Consiglio dei Ministri v Regione Sardegna*[214]) with more elements able to clarify the position of the ECJ.

The judgment refers to a preliminary ruling on the interpretation of Article 107 TFEU in the context of a proceedings between the President of the Italian Council of Ministers and the Region of Sardinia regarding the establishment by that region of a tax on stopovers for tourist purposes by aircraft used for the private transportation of persons, or by recreational craft, to be imposed only on operators whose tax domicile is outside the territory of that region.

The referring court asks whether Article 107 TFEU must be interpreted as meaning that tax legislation, adopted by a regional authority, which establishes a

211. *Ibid.*, paragraph 107.
212. Case C-106/09 P & C-107/09 P *Commission and Spain v Government of Gibraltar and United Kingdom*, [2011] I-11113, paragraph 184. For a deep analysis of the case *see* R. Luja, *The Selectivity Test: The Concept of Sectorial Aid*, in *State Aid and Tax Law* A. Rust, C. Micheau (eds), Wolters Kluwer International, The Hague, 2013, pp. 110-112, where the author criticizes the conclusions of the ECJ because of the lack of a benchmark test in the evaluation of the selective nature of the tax regime for off-shore companies.
213. For the last developments of the ECJ case law regarding material selectivity *see also* Joined cases C-20/15 P and C-21/15 P *Commission v World Duty Free Group SA, formerly Autogrill España SA, Banco Santander SA, Santusa Holding SL*, [2016] ECR I-0000.
214. Case C-169/08 *Presidente del Consiglio dei Ministri v Regione Sardegna*, [2009] I-10821.

regional tax on stopovers, such as those provided for under Article 4 of Regional Law of 11 May 2006, No. 4,[215] to be imposed only on operators whose tax domicile is outside the territory of the region, constitutes a State aid measure in favour of undertakings established in that territory.

The Court here states that, in the light of the nature and objectives of that tax, all the natural and legal persons who receive stopover services in Sardinia are in an objectively comparable situation, irrespective of their place of residence or the place where they are established. Consequently, the measure cannot be regarded as general, since it does not apply to all operators of aircraft or pleasure boats which make a stopover in Sardinia and, thus, such measure is material selective representing a State aid in favour of specific undertakings established in Sardinia.[216]

In this case, the assessment of comparability between natural and legal persons who receive stopover services in Sardinia assumes a fundamental relevance for the final judgement about the compliance of such tax measure with State aid rules. In this sense, according to the position held by the ECJ, the measure cannot be considered as general in its reference framework (Sardinia) since it assumes a material selective nature as far as it is targeted to favour only operators with a domicile in the territory of that region.

The reasoning of the ECJ directly influences the same approach to STZs; in this regard, in fact, it is evident that territorial tax incentives must always be designed as general measures for all the entities in a comparable situation which are based in the territory of an STZ, without assuming a material selective nature in the terms above described.

[f] The Deufil Case

In the case *Deufil GmbH & Co. KG v Commission*[217] the ECJ evaluates the introduction of investment subsidies aimed at promoting the economic development of the Bergkamen area in Germany where, according to the claimant, the standard of living is abnormally low because of serious unemployment.

The case is interesting for the purposes of STZs since it deals with an initiative clearly aimed at the introduction of a set of incentives for a limited territory of a Member State, involving the criteria under which investment subsidies may be granted in consideration of the level of development of the area.

215. O.J. of Region of Sardinia 2006, No. 15.
216. Case C-169/08 *Presidente del Consiglio dei Ministri v Regione Sardegna*, [2009] I-10821, paragraph 63. For a comprehensive review of the case *see* R. Luja, *Revisiting the Balance Between Aid, Selectivity and Selective Aid in Respect of Taxes and Special Levies*, in *European State Aid Law Quarterly*, 2010, No. 1, pp. 161-168, where the author focuses on the comparability analysis related to selectivity and on the identification of the proper benchmark by looking at the nature and structure of tax system as a whole.
217. Case C-310/85 *Deufil GmbH & Co. KG v Commission*, [1987] 00901.

The Court stresses again the principle under which the Commission has a discretion involving economic and social assessments to be made in the EU context.[218] In this case, according to the ECJ, the Commission does not exceed the limits of its discretion by considering an aid for investments – which increases production capacity in a sector where there is already considerable overproduction – as contrary to the common interest.[219]

Apart from the statements on the extent of the Commission competence, the same case offers further elements of analysis, considering that the Court here specifies that Article 107 TFEU does not distinguish between the measures of State intervention concerned by reference to their causes or their aims but defines them in relation to their effects.[220] In other words, the general objectives pursued by the Member State with reference to the territorial benefits introduced in an area are not in themselves sufficient to put them outside the scope of Article 107 TFEU.[221] Accordingly, measures that fulfil the criteria of State aid do not fall outside the scope of Article 107(1) TFEU merely because they might seek to achieve some other social or economic objectives.[222]

The position here held by the ECJ clearly influences the approach to the phenomenon of STZs in the EU context. In particular, it finally recognizes that the judgement on such initiatives under State aid rules cannot be limited to the original aims and the social and economic objectives pursed by the tax measures adopted in an STZ; therefore, it is always necessary to carry out an evaluation focused on the potential effects of territorial tax incentives, paying attention to a set of economic indicators able to influence the internal market and the trade between Member States.

In summary, on the ground of the above case law, it is evident that the ECJ has a fundamental role in the interpretation of State aid rules with reference to the phenomenon of STZs; the positions held by the ECJ, in fact, – especially for what concerns the requirement of selectivity – provide the essential coordinates for the initiatives aimed at the establishment of an STZ, better defining the limits of their legitimacy in the context of the present study.

218. *See also* Case C-169/95 *Spain v Commission*, [1997] I-00135 where it is clearly expressed the principle according to which the Courts, '*when examining the lawfulness of the exercise of such freedom, cannot substitute their own assessment of the matter for that of the competent authority but must restrict themselves to examining whether the assessment of the competent authority contains a manifest error or constitutes a misuse of power*'.

219. Case C-310/85 *Deufil GmbH & Co. KG v Commission*, [1987] 00901, paragraph 18.

220. Case C-173/73 *Italy v Commission*, [1974] ECR 709, paragraph 13; Case C-241/94 *France v Commission*, [1996] ECR I-4551, paragraph 20; Case C-75/97 *Belgium v Commission*, [1999] ECR I-3671, paragraph 20.

221. The same principle is expressed in the Joined Cases C-278/92, C-279/92 and C-280/92 *Kingdom of Spain v Commission*, [1994] I-04103, where the Court states that, '*as regards the application of Article 92(3) of the Treaty, the Commission enjoys a wide discretion, the exercise of which involves assessment of an economic and social nature which must be made within a Community context*'.

222. Case C-487/06 *British Aggregates Association v Commission*, [2008] ECR I-10515, paragraph 84.

[B] Regional Aid in Secondary Law

[1] General Block Exemption Regulation

The framework of State aid rules that are relevant for the purposes of the present research is completed by the secondary legislation developed on the ground of Article 109 TFEU according to which the Council may enact regulations for the application of Articles 107 and 108 TFEU at its own political discretion.[223] Under this rule, the Council has adopted Regulation (EC) No. 994/98,[224] replaced by Regulation (EU) No. 1588/2015,[225] allowing the Commission to exempt from the notification not only aid for small and medium-sized enterprises, research and development, aid concerning the environment, employment and training, but also investment aid and operating aid in compliance with the map for regional aid approved by the Commission for each Member State. Accordingly, the Commission has declared certain categories of aid compatible with the internal market, enacting Regulation (EU) No. 651/2014[226] (the so-called GBER), amended by Regulation (EU) No. 1084/2017.[227]

Under this Regulation, regional investment aid measures are considered as compatible with the internal market within the meaning of Article 107(3) TFEU and are exempted from the notification requirement of Article 108(3) TFEU,[228] provided that a set of conditions are fulfilled concerning the eligible costs in tangible and intangible assets and the estimated wage costs arising from job creation as a result of an initial investment.[229]

In any case, the aid intensity in gross grant equivalent shall not exceed the maximum aid intensity established in the regional aid map which is in force at the time the aid is granted in the area concerned.[230]

The GBER also provides that operating aid schemes in ORs, sparsely populated areas, and very sparsely populated areas are compatible with the internal market

223. *See* L. Del Federico, *Introduzione allo studio della finanza pubblica per le aree colpite da calamità*, in *supra.*, M. Basilavecchia, L. Del Federico, A. Pace, C. Verrigni, G. Giappichelli (eds), Turin, 2016, pp. 16-18.
224. Council Regulation (EC) No. 994/98 of 7 May 1998 on the application of Articles 92 and 93 (now 87 and 88 respectively) of the Treaty establishing the European Community to certain categories of horizontal State aid, O.J. 1998, L 142, pp. 1-4.
225. Council Regulation (EU) No. 1588/2015 of 13 July 2015 on the application of Articles 107 and 108 of the Treaty on the Functioning of the European Union to certain categories of horizontal State aid, O.J. 2015, L 248, pp. 1-8, which replaces as of 14 October 2015 Council Regulation (EC) No. 994/98 of 7 May 1998.
226. Commission Regulation (EU) No. 651/2014 of 17 June 2014 declaring certain categories of aid compatible with the internal market in application of Articles 107 and 108 of the Treaty, O.J. 2014, L 187, pp. 1-78.
227. Commission Regulation (EU) No. 1084/2017 of 14 June 2017, amending Commission Regulation (EU) No. 651/2014 of 17 June 2014, as regards aid for port and airport infrastructure, notification thresholds for aid for culture and heritage conservation and for aid for sport and multifunctional recreational infrastructures, and regional operating aid schemes for outermost regions and amending Regulation (EU) No. 702/2014 as regards the calculation of eligible costs, O.J. 2017, L 156, pp. 1-18.
228. Commission Regulation (EU) No. 651/2014 of 17 June 2014, Article 14(1).
229. *Ibid.*, Article 14(4).
230. *Ibid.*, Article 14(12).

within the meaning of Article 107(3) TFEU and are exempted from the notification requirement of Article 108(3) TFEU, as far as some specific conditions are fulfilled.[231]

In particular, for what regards sparsely populated areas, the regional operating aid schemes must compensate for the additional transport costs of goods which have been produced in areas eligible for operating aid, as well as additional transport costs of goods that are further processed in those areas.[232]

Otherwise, in ORs, the operating aid schemes must compensate for the additional operating costs incurred in those regions as a direct result of one or several of the permanent handicaps referred to in Article 349 TFEU, provided that the annual aid amount per beneficiary under all operating aid schemes implemented under this Regulation does not exceed a certain percentage.[233]

Given the above, the GBER offers an interesting support for the initiatives aimed at the establishment of an STZ; in this sense, in fact, the introduction of territorial tax incentives – in the form of investment and operating aid – can be exempted from the notification obligation, provided that the same measures are granted in compliance with a series of conditions and according to the regional aid map approved by the Commission for each Member State.

[2] De Minimis Regulation

In quantitative terms, the rule of Article 107 TFEU represents a '*de minimis* rule' in the sense that State aid below certain thresholds of intensity cannot negatively influence EU trade. In this regard, the regulatory framework is represented by the Commission Regulation (EU) No. 1407/2013[234] (also defined as '*de minimis* Regulation'), adopted on the basis of Council Regulation (EC) No. 994/1998.[235] The Regulation provides an exemption from the notification requirement, provided that the measure is in compliance with specific conditions, such as the total amount of the aid (not exceeding EUR 200,000 for each enterprise over a period of three fiscal years), the method of calculation and the methods of control.[236]

231. *Ibid.*, Article 15(1).
232. *Ibid.*, Article 15(2).
233. *Ibid.*, Article 15(4).
234. Commission Regulation (EU) No. 1407/2013 of 18 December 2013 on the application of Articles 107 and 108 of the Treaty on the Functioning of the European Union to *de minimis* aid, O.J. 2013, L 352, pp. 1-8 (replacing Commission Regulation (EC) No. 1998/2006 of 15 December 2006 on the application of Articles 87 and 88 of the Treaty to *de minimis* aid, O.J. 2006, L 379, pp. 5-10).
235. Council Regulation (EC) No. 994/98 of 7 May 1998 on the application of Articles 92 and 93 of the Treaty establishing the European Community to certain categories of horizontal State aid, O.J. 1998, L 142, pp. 1-4, replaced by Council Regulation (EU) No. 1588/2015 of 13 July 2015 on the application of Articles 107 and 108 of the Treaty on the Functioning of the European Union to certain categories of horizontal State aid, O.J. 2015, L 248, pp. 1-8.
236. Commission Regulation (EU) No. 1407/2013 of 18 December 2013 on the application of Articles 107 and 108 of the Treaty on the Functioning of the European Union to *de minimis* ad, O.J. 2013, L 352, pp. 1-8; C. Fontana, *supra.*, G. Giappichelli (ed.), Turin, 2012, pp. 196 et seq.

In this regard, the *de minimis* Regulation only applies to transparent aid, namely aid in respect of which it is possible to calculate precisely the gross equivalent of the aid *ex ante* without any need to undertake a risk assessment.[237]

On these bases, the *de minimis* Regulation can assume a specific relevance for allowing the establishment of an STZ under State aid rules; in this sense, the introduction of a set of tax incentives in a limited territory assumes a legitimate form under State aid rules as far as the related thresholds - in terms of gross equivalent of the aid - do not exceed the same limits set by the *de minimis* Regulation, corresponding to EUR 200,000 for each enterprise in a period of three fiscal years.

[3] The EU Cohesion Policy: Guidelines on Regional Aid

In the context of secondary law, the Commission has also been able to develop its own vision of 'good' State aid policy with reference to all the other measures not covered by the GBER or by the *de minimis* Regulation.

As already seen, regional aid, as defined under Article 107(3)(a) and (c) TFEU, represent an exception to the general State aid prohibition, considering that the distortion of competition resulting from their application is justified in presence of certain conditions. The first condition is based on the exceptional nature of regional aid; pursuant to the provision of Article 107(3)(a) TFEU, in fact, State aid may be declared acceptable by the Commission when the rules in question are settled to promote the economic development of areas where the standard of living is abnormally low or where there is serious unemployment. Furthermore, according to Article 107(3)(c) TFEU, State aid may also be declared acceptable when they facilitate the development of certain economic areas without adversely affecting trade between Member States to an extent contrary to the common interest.

On these bases, the Commission sets its focus on the harmonization of national policies through a soft law approach in the context of the EU cohesion policy, with the definition of a common framework of non-binding rules for the interpretation of the exemptions provided under Article 107(3)(a) and (c) TFEU.[238]

The first step is the adoption of the guidelines on regional aid covering the period 2000-2006,[239] then replaced by new guidelines for the period 2007-2013.[240]

A review process was launched in 2010 to adapt the same guidelines to the overall reduction in regional disparities in the EU over the last years, to the effects of the

237. *Ibid.*, Article 4(1).
238. For an interesting deepening of the concept of 'Regional aid' *see* E. TRAVERSA, *The Selectivity Test: The Concept of Regional Aid*, in *State Aid and Tax Law*, A. RUST, C. MICHEAU (eds), Wolters Kluwer International, Alphen aan den Rijn, 2013, pp. 119 et seq.
239. Communication from the Commission - Guidelines on national regional aid, O.J. 1998, C 74, pp. 9-18.
240. Communication from the Commission - Guidelines on national regional aid for 2007-2013, O.J. 2006, C 54, pp. 13-44.

economic crisis and to the objectives of State aid modernization in the context of EU cohesion policy.[241]

On these bases, the Commission has adopted new guidelines for the period 2014-2020[242] highlighting the basic criteria under which Member States may grant aid to companies in order to support the development of disadvantaged regions in the Union.

The new document also involves the study and the development of the fiscal policies related to regional aid, offering an important point of reference for the definition of the legal framework of STZs.

These guidelines are part of a broader strategy aimed at the modernization of State aid control, through the use of more effective aid measures targeted at cases with the most relevant impact on competition.

According to the Commission,[243] the primary objective of State aid control in the field of regional aid is to ensure a level playing field between Member States, promoting the implementation of various measures in accordance with regional development strategies defined in the context of the European Regional Development Fund (ERDF), the European Social Fund (ESF), the Cohesion Fund, the European Agricultural Fund for Rural Development or the European Maritime and Fisheries Fund.

In these guidelines, the Commission sets out the conditions under which regional aid may be considered compatible with the internal market under the system of exemptions defined by Article 107(3)(a) and (c) TFEU.

In detail, an aid measure is considered compatible with EU law only if it satisfies each of the following criteria:

(a) contribution to a well-defined objective of common interest: a State aid measure must be aimed at an objective of common interest in accordance with Article 107(3) TFEU;
(b) need for state intervention: a State aid measure must be targeted towards a situation where aid can lead to a material improvement that the market cannot deliver itself, for example by remedying a market failure;
(c) appropriateness of the aid measure: the proposed aid measure must be an appropriate policy instrument to address the objective of common interest;
(d) incentive effect: the aid must change the behaviour of the undertaking concerned supporting an additional activity which would not be carried out without the aid or would be carried out in a restricted or different manner or location;
(e) proportionality of the aid (aid to the minimum): the aid amount must be limited to the minimum necessary to induce the additional investment or activity in the area concerned;

241. *See also* F.G. Wishlade, *Regional State Aid and Competition Policy in the European Union*, Kluwer Law International, The Hague, 2003.
242. Communication from the Commission – Guidelines on regional State aid for 2014-2020, O.J. 2013, C 209, pp. 1-45.
243. *Ibid.*, paragraph 3.

(f) avoidance of undue negative effects on competition and trade between Member States: the negative effects of aid must be sufficiently limited, so that the overall balance of the measure is positive;
(g) transparency of the aid: Member States, the Commission, economic operators, and the public must have easy access to all relevant acts and to pertinent information about the aid awarded.

Moreover, in the same guidelines, the Commission establishes the criteria for identifying the areas that fulfil the conditions of Article 107(3) (a) and (c) TFEU. Accordingly, Member States can designate the areas that fulfil these conditions as 'A' or 'C' areas; the resulting regional aid map must be notified and approved by the Commission before regional aid can be awarded to undertakings located in the same areas.

In this regard, the Commission considers that the combined population of 'A' and 'C' areas in the Union must be lower than that of the non-designated areas; thus, the total coverage of those designated areas must be less than 50% of the EU population.

In detail, the Commission considers that the conditions of Article 107(3)(a) TFEU are fulfilled in NUTS 2[244] regions that have a gross domestic product (GDP) per capital below or equal to 75% of the Union's average. Accordingly, a Member State may designate the following areas as 'A' areas:

(a) NUTS 2 regions whose GDP per capital in purchasing power standards (PPS) is below or equal to 75% of the EU average (based on the average of the last three years for which Eurostat data are available);
(b) the ORs.

Then, the Commission identifies two categories of 'C' areas:

(1) areas that fulfil certain pre-established conditions and that a Member State may therefore designate as 'C' areas without any further justification (predefined 'C' areas);[245]

244. The current NUTS 2013 classification is valid from 1 January 2015 and lists 98 regions at NUTS 1 (major socio-economic regions), 276 regions at NUTS 2 (basic regions for the application of regional policies) and 1342 regions at NUTS 3 level (small regions for specific diagnoses). The NUTS classification (Nomenclature of territorial units for statistics) is a hierarchical system for dividing up the economic territory of the EU for the purpose of the collection, development and harmonization of European regional statistics (available at http://ec.europa.eu/eurostat/web/nuts/overview).

245. There are two sub-categories of predefined Article 107(3)(c) areas: former Article 107(3)(a) areas and sparsely populated areas. The former are NUTS II regions that are designated as (a) areas during the period 2011-2013 but which no longer fall within that category. The latter are NUTS II regions with less than eight inhabitants per km2 or NUTS III regions with less than 12.5 inhabitants per km2.

(2) areas that a Member State may, at its own discretion, designate as 'C' areas, provided that the Member State demonstrates that such areas fulfil certain socioeconomic criteria (non-predefined 'C' areas).[246]

According to the same guidelines, regional aid aimed at reducing the current expenses of an undertaking constitute operating aid and are not to be regarded as compatible with the internal market. Nevertheless, such aid may be considered compatible if it is aimed at tackling specific or permanent handicaps faced by undertakings in disadvantaged areas falling within the scope of Article 107(3)(a) TFEU, or to compensate for additional costs to carry out an economic activity in an OR or to prevent or reduce depopulation in very sparsely populated areas.

Given the above, the guidelines of the Commission assume a primary role in the review of the legal framework of STZs; in this sense, in fact, they define not only the conditions for considering a measure compatible with the internal market, but also the criteria for identifying the eligible areas under Article 107(3)(a) and (c) TFEU.

In this regard, the establishment of STZs is clearly influenced by the regional aid map and the identification of the 'A' and 'C' areas, especially when the related tax benefits are introduced to support the development of the most disadvantaged areas of the Union in accordance with the objectives set by Article 107(3)(a) and (c) TFEU.

As it will be shown in the next Chapter 4, ZFU in Italy offer an interesting example regarding the application of the guidelines to STZs; in that case, in fact, the Commission identifies the tax benefits there granted as measures falling within the exception provided by Article 107(3)(c) TFEU (aid of social and economic policy), considering them proportionate to the objectives pursued and, therefore, not able to distort competition and trade between Member States.[247]

246. A Member State may designate non-predefined Article 107(3)(c) areas on the basis of a number of criteria: Criterion 1: contiguous areas of at least 100,000 inhabitants located in NUTS 2 or NUTS 3 regions that have: (i) a GDP below or equal to the EU-28 average, or (ii) an unemployment rate above or equal to 115% of the national average. Criterion 2: NUTS 3 regions of less than 100,000 inhabitants that have: (i) a GDP below or equal to the EU-28 average, or (ii) an unemployment rate above or equal to 115% of the national average. Criterion 3: islands or contiguous areas characterised by similar geographical isolation (e.g., peninsulas or mountain areas) that have: (i) a GDP below or equal to the EU-28 average, or (ii) an unemployment rate above or equal to 115% of the national average, or (iii) less than 5,000 inhabitants. Criterion 4: NUTS 3 regions, or parts of NUTS 3 regions that form contiguous areas, that are adjacent to an 'a' area or that share a land border with a country outside the European Economic Area (EEA) or the European Free Trade Association (EFTA). Criterion 5: contiguous areas of at least 50,000 inhabitants that are undergoing major structural change or are in serious relative decline, provided that such areas are not located in NUTS 3 regions or contiguous areas that fulfil the conditions to be designated as predefined areas or under Criteria 1 to 4.

247. Communication from the Commission of 28 October 2009, COM (2009) No. 8126 final.

[4] Communications from the Commission on Notified Regional Aid Schemes

For the purposes of the present research, it is also necessary to approach the study of the various communications issued by the Commission with reference to the evaluation process of the regional aid schemes notified by the Member States pursuant to Article 108 TFEU.

In fact, when an initiative is not covered by the GBER or by the *de minimis* Regulation, the Member State concerned must notify the relevant tax scheme to the Commission in order to allow a prior assessment based on the criteria set by Article 107(3) TFEU (according to the principles of the guidelines on regional aid).

The communications from the Commission, any time they authorize the introduction of a tax scheme in the context of an STZ, assume a fundamental relevance, offering a view on the practical implementation of the principles set within the guidelines on regional aid and contributing to clarify the approach of the Commission to the phenomenon of STZs.

In particular, according to the general structure of these communications, the assessment of the Commission is first focused on the existence of the aid with the identification of the conditions required under Article 107(1) TFEU. Then, under this methodology, the second step is generally aimed at verifying the compatibility of the measure with reference to the necessity and proportionality, the avoidance of undue negative effects on competition, and the transparency.[248]

This material will be reviewed in detail in the next Chapter 4 where each STZ established under Article 107(3) TFEU is scrutinized not only with reference to the set of tax incentives there provided, but also with reference to the content of the specific authorization issued by the Commission.

[C] Social Services of General Interest in the TFEU

[1] General Aspects

In the context of the present study, the review of the EU legal framework and the selection of the relevant sources must be driven according to the object of the research questions which includes, under the scope of research question No. 2, the development of a new model of STZs based on the introduction of tax incentives of a social character.

Accordingly, as far as State aid law is concerned, the so-called Social Services of General Interest (SSGIs) assume a fundamental role for the purposes of this research, considering the possible introduction of tax incentives of a social character for the undertakings involved in the provision of such services within the perimeter of an STZ.

SSGIs, in fact, cover a wide set of services which are aimed at countering possible market failures and enhancing citizens' protection, in particular for disadvantaged

248. For a recent example of this methodology in the assessment of a tax measure see Communication from the Commission of 6 April 2018 (State aid No. 48571), COM (2018) No. 1661 final, O.J. 2018, C 180, pp. 1-8.

groups of people. The pursued objective is mainly to improve citizens' welfare by providing accessible services; in this sense, SSGIs are generally aimed at achieving high levels of employment, high levels of human health protection, social and territorial cohesion, etc.

Therefore, EU rules for SSGIs, including the case law of the ECJ and the soft law instruments developed by the Commission, represent an important field of investigation, as they are able to set a bridge between STZs and tax incentives of a social character in the context of State aid law.

The result is the definition of a wider framework for the possible implementation of social tax incentives in the context of STZs, with the outline of a fundamental background for the development of a new model of STZs within the scope of research question No. 2.

[2] Exemption under Article 106(2) TFEU

The review must first be focused on the provisions of the Treaty able to identify the discipline of SSGIs in the context of State aid rules.

SSGIs are generally considered, together with the so-called Services of General Economic Interest (SGEIs), as a subset of what is referred to as 'Services of General Interest' (SGIs).[249]

In this regard, it is important to observe that SSGIs, as they generally correspond to an activity of an economic nature,[250] are subject to the same SGEI regime, including the related State aid rules. Therefore, in the context of the present review, the legal framework of SSGIs will be outlined with a direct reference to the discipline provided for SGEIs, considering that a strict distinction between the two categories is not necessary for such a purpose.

On these premises, according to Article 106(2) TFEU,[251] SGEIs are defined as an exception to the general State aid prohibition set by Article 107(1) TFEU, becoming compatible with the internal market any time a specific set of conditions is fulfilled.[252]

249. For the concept of SGI see Commission staff working document, Guide to the application of the European Union rules on state aid, public procurement, and the internal market to services of general economic interest, and in particular to social services of general interest, Brussels, 2013, SWD(2013) 53 final/2, p. 21.
250. *See* Communication from the Commission of 26 April 2006, *Implementing the Community Lisbon programme: Social services of general interest in the European Union*, COM (2006) No. 177 final.
251. For a general overview of Article 106(2) TFEU *see* P. Craig, G. De Búrca, *supra.*, New York, 2015, pp. 1155 et seq.
252. Article 106(2) TFEU: '*Undertakings entrusted with the operation of services of general economic interest or having the character of a revenue-producing monopoly shall be subject to the rules contained in the Treaties, in particular to the rules on competition, in so far as the application of such rules does not obstruct the performance, in law or in fact, of the particular tasks assigned to them. The development of trade must not be affected to such an extent as would be contrary to the interests of the Union*'.

The first condition requires the existence of an SGEI; in other words, aid falling under Article 106(2) TFEU must be granted to an undertaking for a 'genuine and correctly defined' SGEI.[253]

Article 106(2) TFEU does not contain a clear-cut definition of SGEI and, therefore, Member States enjoy a wide discretion in determining what they consider to be an SGEI.[254] Nevertheless, important limits to this discretion are imposed by EU law and in case of a manifest error of assessment;[255] for example, some conceptual limits to the notion of SGEIs can be identified under Article 14 TFEU where the role of SGEIs is underlined 'in promoting social and territorial cohesion'. Therefore, although Member States have a wide margin of discretion, according to the position held by the ECJ, it is necessary that the service designated as an SGEI satisfies certain minimum criteria. For example, the ECJ states that an SGEI must be universal and compulsory in nature, even though an SGEI does not need to be a service that meets the need of the whole population since it is sufficient that a limited group of people enjoys the same service.[256]

One more characteristic of SGEIs is the need for such services to be undertaken in the public interest or to be addressed to citizens.

In this regard, an undertaking may have an exclusive or special right to provide the service in question; however, even in absence of such rights, the existence of an SGEI can finally be established by concluding that the service needs to be offered to every citizen requesting the service.[257]

According to the second condition, the responsibility to provide an SGEI must have been entrusted to an undertaking by a public authority.[258] The undertaking can be either private or public in order to fall under Article 106(2) of the TFEU.

In this regard, the national hierarchical level at which the entrustment takes place is irrelevant in order to meet this requirement (municipality, regions, government, etc.). Nonetheless a vertical relation is necessary between the contracting authority and the undertaking and an act of entrustment must always be established.[259]

The third and last condition involves determining whether or not the Treaty rules obstruct the performance of the service obligation assigned to the undertaking. This assessment is done by reviewing whether the advantage given to the beneficiary

253. Case T-125/12 *Viasat Broadcasting UK v Commission*, O.J. 2015, C 389, paragraph 61.
254. Communication from the Commission of 19 January 2001, *Services of general interest in Europe*, O.J. 2001 C 17; Case T-289/03 *BUPA and others v Commission*, [2008] ECR II-00081, paragraph 167; Case T-17/02 *Fred Olsen, SA v Commission*, [2005] ECR II-02031, paragraph 216.
255. Case T-289/03 *BUPA and others v Commission*, [2008] ECR II-00081, paragraph 166; Case T-17/02 *Fred Olsen, SA v Commission*, [2005] ECR II-02031, paragraph 216. In this sense, *see also* A. Koukiadaki, *EU Governance and Social Services of General Interest: When Even the UK Is Concerned*, in *EU Law, Governance and Social Policy European Integration online Papers*, J.C. Barbier (ed.), 2012, Special Mini-Issue 1, Vol. 16, Article 5, available at http://eiop.or.at/eiop/texte/2012-005a.htm.
256. Case T-289/03 *BUPA and others v Commission*, [2008] ECR II-00081, paragraphs 186-187.
257. *Ibid.*, paragraphs 188-190.
258. Case T-125/12 *Viasat Broadcasting UK v Commission*, O.J. 2015, C 389, paragraph 61.
259. Commission Decision 82/371/EEC of 17 December 1981 relating to a proceeding under Article 85 of the EEC Treaty (IV/29.995 – NAVEWA-ANSEAU), O.J. 1982, L 167, pp 39-52.

undertaking is necessary in order for the SGEI to be carried out by the undertaking under economically acceptable conditions. In other words, assessment under Article 106(2) of the TFEU involves a necessity test.[260]

In summary, if a compensation measure addressed to an SGEI (or to an SSGI) - such as a specific set of social tax incentives - is considered to be State aid pursuant to Article 107(1) TFEU, it can still fall under Article 106(2) of the TFEU and be declared compatible with the internal market if the Member State is able to demonstrate that the same measure meets all the three conditions above described.

[3] The Altmark Criteria

The *Altmark* case[261] represents a fundamental step for the interpretation of State aid rules with reference to SGEIs and SSGIs.

In this case, the ECJ identifies under what circumstances a State measure relevant for an SGEI or an SSGI, such as a public service compensation, is not considered a State aid.

For what regards the facts, *Altmark Trans GmbH* is a local bus company benefiting from State aid by the German government; one of its competitors asks for the annulment of the licences granted to *Altmark Trans* on the basis that the financial solvency of this company cannot be guaranteed as it needs subsidies for operating the service. The same competitor also claims that the subsidies are not compatible with EU law, representing prohibited State aid under Article 107 TFEU.[262]

The German court refers questions to the ECJ for a preliminary ruling, asking whether subsidies intended to compensate a public transport service always fall under the general State aid prohibition or whether, having regard to the service provided and the significance of the field of the activity concerned, the same subsidies are not liable to affect trade between Member States.[263]

The ECJ reasoning starts from the basic assumption that, when assessing whether a State aid measure is compatible with the internal market, only the effects of such measures must be taken into consideration.[264]

On these premises, the ECJ identifies four cumulative criteria to be fulfilled in order for such measure to fall outside the definition of State aid which is relevant for the purposes of Article 107(1) TFEU.

---

260. Case T-125/12 *Viasat Broadcasting UK v Commission*, O.J. 2015, C 389, paragraph 61.
261. Case C-280/00 *Altmark Trans GmbH and Regierungspräsidium Magdeburg v Nahverkehrsgesellschaft Altmark GmbH, and Oberbundesanwalt beim Bundesverwaltungsgericht*, [2003] ECR I-07747. For a detailed review of the case *see inter alia*, M. Klasse, *The Impact of Altmark: The European Commission Case Law Responses*, in *Financing Services of General Economic Interest*, E. Szyzyczak, J.W. van de Gronden (eds), TMC Asser Press, The Hague, 2013, p. 36.
262. Case C-280/00 *Altmark Trans GmbH and Regierungspräsidium Magdeburg v Nahverkehrsgesellschaft Altmark GmbH, and Oberbundesanwalt beim Bundesverwaltungsgericht*, [2003] ECR I-07747, paragraphs 19-29.
263. *Ibid.*, paragraphs 30-31.
264. *Ibid.*, paragraph 77.

First, the beneficiary must have a clearly defined public service obligation to discharge.[265] In particular, the public service obligation in question must be external to the operator concerned and, thus, not including measures in the interest of the undertaking (such as improvement of employee relations).[266]

Second, the parameters on which compensation is calculated must be established in advance in an objective and transparent manner, to avoid overcompensation which may confer economic advantages to the recipient.[267]

Third, the compensation cannot exceed what is necessary to cover all costs incurred in the discharge of the public service in question, taking into account the relevant expenses and a reasonable profit for the undertaking.[268]

Fourth, the undertaking must be selected pursuant to a public procurement procedure or, in alternative, the compensation to the beneficiary must be determined on the basis of an analysis of the costs of a typical well-run undertaking which meets all the necessary public service requirements, considering the relevant receipts and a reasonable profit for discharging the obligations.[269]

Given the above, from the *Altmark* case onwards the cumulative criteria defined by the ECJ become a testing tool to verify whether or not a compensation measure for a public service, corresponding to an SGEI or an SSGI, constitutes State aid for the purpose of Article 107(1) TFEU.[270]

Accordingly, any time the above four criteria are fulfilled, the measure falls outside the scope of State aid law and, therefore, it is not necessary to provide evidence of the conditions set by Article 106(2) TFEU in order to make the same measure compatible with the internal market. At the same time, as the four criteria are all met, Member States are no longer bound by the obligation to notify their measure to the Commission according to the procedural rules of Article 108 TFEU.[271]

Differently, if a Member State fails to fulfil even one of the *Altmark* criteria, the compensation constitutes State aid and is subject to the notification requirement and the standstill obligation laid down in Article 108 TFEU. In this case, the aid measure can still be declared compatible with the internal market as far as the conditions set by Article 106(2) TFEU are fulfilled or when they fall under the exemptions provided by Article 107(3) TFEU.[272]

In conclusion, the *Altmark* test, which is based on the four criteria above described, assumes a fundamental role for the assessment of any measure specifically

---

265. *Ibid.*, paragraph 89.
266. *See* Case C-251/97 *France v Commission of the European Communities* [1999] ECR I-6639, Opinion of Advocate General G. Fennelly, paragraph 20.
267. Case C-280/00 *Altmark Trans GmbH and Regierungspräsidium Magdeburg v Nahverkehrsgesellschaft Altmark GmbH, and Oberbundesanwalt beim Bundesverwaltungsgericht*, [2003] ECR I-07747, paragraph 90.
268. *Ibid.*, paragraph 92.
269. *Ibid.*, paragraph 93.
270. K. Bacon, *European Union Law of State Aid*, 3rd Edition, Oxford University Press, Oxford, 2017, pp. 54-55.
271. P. Craig, G. De Búrca, *supra.*, New York, 2015, p. 1136.
272. For the relation between the Altmark test and Article 106(2) TFEU *see* P. Nicolaides, *Altmark Requires Efficiency; Article 106(2) TFEU Does Not!*, 2017, available at http://www.sipotra.it/wp-content/uploads/2017/03/Altmark-Requires-Efficiency.pdf.

targeted at an SGEI or at an SSGI. Therefore, for the scope of the present research, as far as a set of tax incentives is granted within a limited part of a Member State only in favour of enterprises providing an SGEI or an SSGI, the application of the *Altmark* criteria finally outlines the dimension of State aid rules and, in particular, whether or not the tax measure at issue has to be scrutinized under the general State aid prohibition set by Article 107(1) TFEU and the related system of exemptions.

[D] SSGIs in Secondary Law: The *Almunia* Package

The *Almunia* package, consisting of a Decision, a Communication, a *de minimis* Regulation, a framework, and a working document, represents an essential source of secondary law in the context of SSGIs.

The main scope of the *Almunia* package is to provide guidance for Member States in the identification of the requirements to fulfil in order to introduce measures compatible with the internal market, better defining not only the concepts of SGEI and SSGI, but also the circumstances under which the grant of compensation does not entail an infringement of State aid law.

Therefore, these instruments are adopted with the purpose of clarifying State aid principles and to simplify the application of State aid rules by national governments, limiting the focus of the Commission to larger cases involving serious negative effects on the internal market.

[1] Commission Decision 2012/21/EU

Commission Decision 2012/21/EU[273] clarifies under which conditions a public service compensation measure, constituting State aid under Article 107(1) TFEU (therefore, not fulfilling the four *Altmark* criteria), may be compatible with the internal market and exempt from the notification obligation laid down in Article 108(3) TFEU.[274]

In particular, Article 2(1)(c) of the Decision provides an exhaustive list of services constituting SSGIs which are exempted from the notification requirement, no matter the size of the compensation, namely '*health and long term care, childcare, access to and reintegration into the labour market, social housing and the care and social inclusion of vulnerable groups*'.

Therefore, the decision does not exempt all services constituting SSGIs, but merely provides the mentioned list which is held to be exhaustive. Nonetheless, it is evident that the concept of 'inclusion of vulnerable groups' puts emphasis on the possibility for Member States to include various types of social services within the concept and, by this way, to benefit from the exemption of the notification requirement.

273. Commission Decision 2012/21/EU of 20 December 2011 on the application of Article 106(2) of the Treaty on the Functioning of the European Union to State aid in the form of public service compensation granted to certain undertakings entrusted with the operation of services of general economic interest, O.J. 2012, L 7, p. 3-10.
274. *Ibid.*, Article 1.

Differently, in case of public services not included in the aforementioned list, the related measures can eventually fall under Article 2(1)(a) of the decision, according to which only compensation that does not exceed EUR 15 million a year is exempt from the notification requirement. In the views of the Commission, in fact, such amounts of aid are exempt because they are not considered to affect EU trade and competition.

In any case, the applicability of the decision is subject to the condition of entrustment, namely whether the beneficiary undertaking has been specifically entrusted, by way of one or more acts, with the provision of a particular public service. According to the decision, the entrustment act should include the content and duration of the public service obligation, the undertaking and, where applicable, the territory concerned, the nature of any exclusive or special rights assigned to the undertaking by the granting authority, a description of the compensation mechanism, the parameters for calculating, controlling and reviewing the compensation, and a specific reference to the same decision.[275]

The decision outlines a few more important conditions for its applicability, such as the time limit of ten years in regard of the period of time a public service is entrusted to an undertaking[276] and the prohibition of overcompensation with reference to the public service obligation.[277]

Furthermore, the decision provides a number of provisions with the purpose of monitoring the fulfilment of the conditions laid down in Article 106(2) TFEU. Among such provisions, it is worth to remember the regular control from the Member States on the risk of overcompensation for public service obligations,[278] and an obligation for Member States to submit reports on the application of the decision.[279]

[2] Commission Communication 2012/C 8/02

The main scope of the Communication of the *Almunia* package[280] is to clarify the various aspects of the *Altmark* judgement with particular reference to concepts of State aid rules such as economic activity, undertaking, State resources, and SGEI.

In the first section of the Communication, the Commission underlines the basic principle according to which Member States are generally free to determine the content of an SGEI - and, thus, also of an SSGI - the organization and the financing mechanism.[281]

In any case, the same discretion is counterbalanced by the need to comply with the EU rules on public procurement, and, where these are not applicable, with the

275. *Ibid.*, Article 4.
276. *Ibid.*, Article 2(2).
277. According to Article 5(1) of the Decision '*the amount of compensation shall not exceed what is necessary to cover the net cost incurred in discharging the public service obligations, including a reasonable profit*'.
278. *Ibid.*, Article 6.
279. *Ibid.*, Article 9.
280. Communication from the Commission of 11 January 2012 on the application of the European Union State aid rules to compensation granted for the provision of services of general economic interest, O.J. 2012, C 8, pp. 4-14.
281. *Ibid.*, paragraph 2.

principles of the Treaty, namely non-discrimination and the basic standards of transparency, equality in treatment, proportionality, and mutual recognition.[282]

In the second section, the Commission clarifies the meaning of many provisions relating to State aid in general. For what regards the concept of undertaking, for example, the Commission underlines the distinction between economic and non-economic activities, limiting the application of State aid rules to the situations where a certain activity consists in offering goods and services in a market environment.[283]

Moreover, according to the Communication, the concept of 'State resources' is associated not only to direct grants and payments from the State or other public bodies, but also to tax benefits of any kind.[284] In this sense, it is clear that under the perspective of the Commission, also a compensation for an SSGI granted in the form of a tax benefit can assume relevance for the purposes of the *Altmark* test; accordingly, the phenomenon of STZs can be linked to the topic of SSGIs as far as the compensation is granted from the State through the use of tax incentives in favour of the enterprises which are entrusted with the provision of a specific public service in a limited territory of the Member State.

Then, concerning the concept 'effect on trade', the Commission emphasizes that in an open and competitive market the entrustment of an SGEI 'by methods other than through a public procurement procedure' may lead to preventing the entry to the market for competitors and therefore to a market distortion.[285]

The third section of the Communication is dedicated to the discussion of the *Altmark* criteria under which compensation for SGEIs - and, thus, for SSGIs - does not constitute State aid.

With reference to the first criterion, namely the existence of an SGEI, the Commission clarifies that Member States have a wide margin of discretion in defining a given service as an SGEI and in granting compensation to the service provider. The Commission's competence in this respect is limited to checking whether the Member State has made a manifest error when defining the service as an SGEI and to the assessment of any State aid involved in the compensation.[286]

For what regards the second criterion (entrustment), the Commission focuses on the content of the entrustment act, specifying a set of requirements which essentially reproduce those described under the Commission Decision 2012/21/EU.[287]

The Commission then clarifies the concept of 'reasonable profit' with respect to the third *Altmark* criterion (avoidance of overcompensation), making reference to '*the rate of return on capital that would be required by a typical company considering*

282. *Ibid.*, paragraph 5.
283. *Ibid.*, paragraph 12.
284. *Ibid.*, paragraph 32.
285. *Ibid.*, paragraph 37.
286. *Ibid.*, paragraph 46.
287. According to paragraph 52 of the Communication '*Based on the approach taken by the Commission in such cases, the act or series of acts must at least specify: (a) the content and duration of the public service obligations; (b) the undertaking and, where applicable, the territory concerned; (c) the nature of any exclusive or special rights assigned to the undertaking by the authority in question; (d) the parameters for calculating, controlling and reviewing the compensation; and (e) the arrangements for avoiding and recovering any overcompensation*'.

whether or not to provide the service of general economic interest for the whole duration of the period of entrustment, taking into account the level of risk'.[288]

Furthermore, with reference to the fourth *Altmark* criterion, the Commission recommends the adoption of an open, transparent and non-discriminatory public procurement procedure. In this sense, the Commission recommends the use of the open procedure as the one which ensures the best conditions, allowing the participation of the greatest number of competitors. Nonetheless, also the restricted procedure is considered acceptable in the views of the Commission, especially where the contracting authority selects the economic operators from a range of previous candidates, making the whole process more manageable and less costly. Otherwise, the competitive dialogue can be 'acceptable' only in 'exceptional cases', such as where the authority is not able to accurately define the technical means of the contract in advance. This is due to the fact that this procedure confers a wider discretion in the hands of the contracting authority restricting the participation of interested operators. Finally, in the case of the negotiated procedure, only the negotiated procedure with prior publication can satisfy the *Altmark* criterion, while the negotiated procedure without prior publication has to be excluded from this field of application.[289]

Then, the Communication clarifies the award criteria for a tender in the context of SGEIs. In this regard, the 'lowest price' in every case fulfils the *Altmark's* fourth criterion, while the 'most economically advantageous tender' is deemed sufficient only where 'the award criteria are closely related to the subject-matter [...] and allow for the most economically advantageous offer to match the value of the market'.[290]

Given the above, it is evident that the main scope of the Communication is not only to clarify the *Altmark* criteria, but also to achieve more use of a public procurement procedure, more enforcement of transparency and non-discrimination in these procedures and eventually more competition for the awarding of SGEI and SSGI contracts.

*[3] Commission Regulation (EU) No. 360/2012 (***De Minimis** *Regulation)*

One more instrument of the *Almunia* package for simplifying the application of SGEI rules is the SGEI *de minimis* Regulation.[291]

288. *Ibid.*, paragraph 61.
289. Communication from the Commission on the application of the European Union State aid rules to compensation granted for the provision of services of general economic interest, O.J. 2012, C 8, pp. 4-14, paragraph 66.
290. *Ibid.*, paragraph 67.
291. Commission Regulation (EU) No. 360/2012 of 25 April 2012 on the application of Articles 107 and 108 of the Treaty on the Functioning of the European Union to *de minimis* aid granted to undertakings providing services of general economic interest, O.J. L 114, pp. 8-13.

According to this Regulation, public service compensation that does not exceed EUR 500,000 over a period of three years[292] should be deemed not to distort competition in the internal market and the trade between Member States; therefore, such aid is exempt from the notification requirement set by Article 108(3) of the TFEU.[293]

In the views of the Commission, the need of a separate *de minimis* Regulation for SGEI - whose effects can be extended to SSGIs not covered by the general exemption set by Article 2(1)(c) of the decision - is associated to the idea that the ceiling below which public service compensation does not have an effect on trade or competition usually differs from that established under the general *de minimis* Regulation. On these premises, the ceiling for SGEIs is raised from the amount of EUR 200,000, which is provided in the general *de minimis* Regulation, to the amount of EUR 500,000.

In any case, under the SGEI *de minimis* Regulation, there are some important requirements in order for a compensation measure to avoid scrutiny by the Commission. In this sense, in fact, Member States are always required to inform the beneficiary undertaking under which service obligation the advantage is granted for, and the undertaking has to be entrusted with the SGEI in writing.[294] In addition, the entrustment act must contain a reference to the SGEI *de minimis* Regulation and the measure in question has to be specifically granted for the purpose of an SGEI.[295]

Furthermore, it is required that the beneficiary undertaking is not in difficulty;[296] in this regard, the Commission does not consider it appropriate for beneficiary undertakings to receive aid when they are insolvent, unless such aid is part of a restructuring concept.

[4] Commission Framework 2012/C8/03

The Framework[297] is applicable to aid which is not covered by the Decision or by the SGEI *de minimis* Regulation and, therefore, not exempted from the notification obligation.

In these situations, in fact, the public service compensation constitutes State aid under Article 107(1) TFEU and, therefore, is subject to the notification requirement pursuant to Article 108(3) TFEU.[298]

Being this the case, the Framework represents the basis on which the Commission verifies the fulfilment of the criteria set out in Article 106(2) TFEU in order to consider the same State aid measure as an aid compatible with the internal market.

292. *Ibid.*, Article 2(2).
293. *Ibid.*, Article 2(1).
294. *Ibid.*, Article 3(1).
295. *Ibid.*, Recital 6.
296. *Ibid.*, Article 1(2)(h).
297. Communication from the Commission, *European Union framework for State aid in the form of public service compensation*, O.J. 2012, C 8, p. 15-22.
298. *Ibid.*, paragraph 3.

First, according to the Framework, aid for SGEIs is considered compatible with the internal market when it is granted for a genuine and correctly defined SGEI as referred to in Article 106(2) TFEI.[299]

Furthermore, the same aid is compatible only where the public authority complies with the EU rules on public procurement;[300] this is the most important condition of compliance under the Framework according to which the use of public procurement procedures is always necessary in case of entrustment of a public service obligation in SGEIs.

According to the Framework, the Commission, while fully respecting the Member State's wide margin of discretion to define the content of an SGEI, may require amendments in the related scheme, for instance in the allocation of the aid, where it can reasonably show that it would be possible to provide the same SGEI at equivalent conditions for the users, in a less distortive manner and at lower cost for the State.[301]

[5] Commission Staff Working Document

The content of the staff working document attached to the *Almunia* Package[302] is aimed at clarifying certain issues concerning the application of EU rules, notably those on State aid, public procurement, and fundamental freedoms.

For the purposes of the present study, this document assumes a specific relevance in the parts dedicated to the concepts of Service of General Interest (SGI), Service of General Economic Interest (SGEI), and Social Service of General Interest (SSGI), with an important contribution to the clarification of the terminology used in the resulting legal framework.

The concept of SGI is linked to a general macro-category including those services that public authorities of the Member States at national, regional or local level classify as being of general interest and, therefore, subject to specific public service obligations. According to the document, although the term covers both economic activities and non-economic services, only economic activities are subject to specific EU legislation and are influenced by the internal market and competition rules of the Treaty.[303]

SGEIs, to be intended as a subset of SGIs, are defined as 'economic activities which deliver outcomes in the overall public good that would not be supplied (or would be supplied under different conditions in terms of objective quality, safety, affordability, equal treatment or universal access) by the market without public intervention'.[304] In such cases, a public service obligation is imposed on the provider by way of an entrustment and on the basis of a general interest criterion. This definition is thus able to highlight one of the main purposes of SGEIs, namely to bring consumer

299. *Ibid.*, paragraph 12.
300. *Ibid.*, paragraph 19.
301. *Ibid.*, paragraph 56.
302. Commission staff working document, *Guide to the application of the European Union rules on state aid, public procurement and the internal market to services of general economic interest, and in particular to social services of general interest*, Brussels, 2013, SWD(2013) 53 final/2.
303. *Ibid.*, p. 21.
304. *Ibid.*

welfare by providing services that, if left to market forces alone, would not have been provided or not under similar conditions.

Finally, the concept of SSGIs corresponds to one more subset of SGIs including two main groups of services in addition to health services, namely: (1) statutory and complementary social security schemes, organized in various ways (mutual or occupational organizations), covering the main risks of life, such as those linked to health, ageing, occupational accidents, unemployment, retirement, and disability; (2) other essential services provided directly to the person playing a prevention and social cohesion role with customized assistance to facilitate social inclusion and safeguard fundamental rights.[305]

One more characteristic of SSGIs is related to their necessary nature; in this sense, in fact, SSGIs are essential, being specifically addressed to disadvantaged groups of people and not to citizens as a whole as in the case of SGEIs (e.g., electricity, water supply, waste management, etc.).[306]

In principle, SSGIs may be of an economic or non-economic nature, depending on the activity involved; in this regard, the working document points out that, according to the ECJ, the economic nature of an activity neither depends on the legal status of the operator or of the organization (which may be a public body or not for-profit[307]), nor

305. *Ibid.*, p. 22. In particular, according to the Commission staff working document, in the first place such services '*offer assistance to persons faced by personal challenges or crises (such as debt, unemployment, drug addiction or family breakdown). Secondly, they include activities to ensure that the people concerned are able to completely reintegrate into society (rehabilitation, language training for immigrants) and, in particular, return to the labour market (occupational training and reintegration). These services complement and support the role of families in caring for the youngest and oldest members of society in particular. Thirdly, these services include activities to integrate people with long-term health or disability problems. Fourthly, they also include social housing, which provides housing for disadvantaged citizens or socially less advantaged groups*'.For a definition of SSGI *see also* H. Wollmann, G. Marcou, The *Provision of Public Services in Europe: Between State, Local Government and Market*, Edward Elgar Publishing, Cheltenham, 2010. According to these authors '*Social services are services for people and families. They include child care, long-term care for the elderly and frail, and health services; and they can include basic education, basic cultural amenities (e.g. public libraries) and sports facilities (e.g. swimming pools). Such services are usually financed by budgetary appropriations or social security contributions and only to a limited extent by user contributions*'.

306. For the identification and recognition of SSGIs *see also* Communication from the Commission of 26 April 2006, *Implementing the Community Lisbon programme: Social services of general interest in the European Union*, COM (2006) No. 177 final, paragraph 1.1, where it is specified that general characteristics of these kinds of services are: (i) '*to operate on the basis of the solidarity principle, which is required, in particular by the non-selection of risks or the absence, on an individual basis, of equivalence between contributions and benefits'; (ii) to be a 'comprehensive and personalized integrating the response to differing needs in order to guarantee fundamental human rights and protect the most vulnerable'; (iii) not to be 'for profit and in particular to address the most difficult situations and are often part of a historical legacy'; (iv) to 'include the participation of voluntary workers, expression of citizenship capacity; they are strongly rooted in (local) cultural traditions'; (vi) 'this often finds its expression in the proximity between the provider of the service and the beneficiary, enabling the taking into account of the specific needs of the latter'; and, (vi) to highlight 'an asymmetric relationship between providers and beneficiaries that cannot be assimilated with a "normal" supplier/consumer relationship and requires the participation of a financing third party*'.

307. Case C-172/98 *Commission of the European Communities v Kingdom of Belgium*, [1999] ECR I-03999.

on the nature of the service (e.g., social security or health service[308]); furthermore, the economic nature of an activity does not depend on how it is classified in national law. Differently, in order to determine whether a given service constitutes an economic activity, a case-by-case examination must be made of all the characteristics of the activity in question, particularly of the way the service is provided, organized and financed in the Member State concerned.[309]

In this sense, according to ECJ case law, activities that are performed by the State - or on behalf of the State - as part of its duties in the social field, for example, do not constitute an economic activity,[310] such as in the case of services provided by an organization as part of an obligatory insurance scheme,[311] or courses provided under the national education system.[312]

Despite the above case law from the ECJ, the Commission usually adopts a narrow position according to which every social service is deemed to be economic in nature[313] and, therefore, subject to the same SGEI regime, including the related State aid rules.

Given the above, although SGEIs and SSGIs are two distinct categories within the general macro-category of SGIs, it is possible to conclude that they usually overlap, at least partially, in the context of the *Almunia* package; in this sense, in fact, measures constituting SSGIs are generally subject to the same rules applicable to SGEIs since they both are deemed to be economic in nature according to the position held by the Commission.

§3.03 STZs AND INTERNAL MARKET LAW

The internal market has always been the core of the European integration process.

In this respect, the fundamental freedoms are defined in the context of internal market law, also influencing the initiatives aimed at the establishment of territorial tax incentives.

Therefore, it is necessary to focus the present review on the aspects of internal market law which are able to influence and characterize the phenomenon of STZs at the EU level, including the aspects associated with social tax incentives.

---

308. Case C-157/99 B.S.M. *Geraets-Smits v Stichting Ziekenfonds VGZ and H.T.M. Peerbooms v Stichting CZ Groep Zorgverzekeringen*, [2001] ECR I-05473, paragraph 50.
309. Commission staff working document, *Guide to the application of the European Union rules on state aid, public procurement and the internal market to services of general economic interest, and in particular to social services of general interest*, Brussels, 2013, SWD(2013) 53 final/2, p. 21, p. 103.
310. Case C-109/92 *Stephan Max Wirth v Landeshauptstadt Hannover*, [1993] ECR I-06447.
311. Case C-355/00 *Freskot AE v Elliniko Dimosio*, [2003] ECR I-05264.
312. Case C-263/86 *Belgian State v René Humbel and Marie-Thérèse Edel*, [1988] ECR 05365.
313. *See* Communication from the Commission of 26 April 2006, *Implementing the Community Lisbon programme: Social services of general interest in the European Union*, COM (2006) No. 177 final, paragraph 2.1, where, according to the Commission '*almost all services offered in the social field can be considered "economic activities" within the meaning of Articles 43 and 49 of the EC Treaty*'.

The review will first approach the provisions of primary law dealing with the fundamental freedoms, including an overview on the main decisions issued by the ECJ based on the implementation of the principle of tax non-discrimination.

Afterwards, secondary law will represent a further step of the same review with the description of the harmonization measures adopted by the EU legislator for what regards the discipline of indirect taxes (customs duties, VAT, and excise duties) and the concepts of social advantages and social enterprises.

[A] Fundamental Freedoms in Primary Law

[1] General Aspects

The fundamental freedoms are aimed at ensuring the effective pursuit of the basic goals of the European internal market, promoting a reduction of physical barriers and legal restrictions imposed by the various Member States.[314]

The fundamental freedoms have a specific relevance for the phenomenon of STZs, as they involve a prohibition for the Member States to adopt protectionist tax policies able to obstruct or restrict the free movement of goods, persons, services or capital.

In particular, the principle of free movement of goods is fixed by Article 28(1) TFEU, where the establishment of customs duties or charges with equivalent effect which can obstruct or limit the circulation of the goods in the trade between the Member States is forbidden. The free movement of goods has already found a detailed layout in secondary EU law, with a series of initiatives aimed at providing a detailed discipline in the field. Given the above, in the ECJ case law there are no relevant cases dealing with the restriction of the free movement of goods; the principle of the free movement of goods, in fact, is not questioned in the tax jurisdiction of the Member States precisely because of the incisiveness and the accuracy of the rules contained in EU secondary legislation, such as the UCC, the Recast VAT Directive and the Excise Duty Directive.

The free movement of services is basically ensured through a policy of harmonization of indirect taxes; even in this case, secondary legislation represents the instrument used for the implementation of the free movement of services, considering the importance of the Recast VAT Directive in the context of VAT.

The free movement of capital is ensured by Article 63 TFEU according to which all restrictions on the movement of capital between Member States and between Member States and third countries are prohibited. Finally, the principle of free movement of persons is defined by Article 21 TFEU with the right of every citizen of the EU to move and reside freely within the territory of the Member States. Consequently, this general rule results in a prohibition of any restrictions and discrimination which may hinder nationals to move within the EU.

314. For a comprehensive overview of the free movement of persons in EU law *see* P. Craig, G. De Búrca, *EU Law: Text, Cases, and Materials*, 6h Edition, Oxford University Press, New York, 2015, pp. 1136.

The principle of free movement of persons gives birth to two different rights. First, there is the right of workers to move freely within the EU (free movement of workers); in this regard, Article 45 TFEU provides the abolition of all restrictions based on nationality or residence of the employee in relation to remuneration and all the other conditions of employment. Second, there is the right to establish a self-employed activity (i.e., a business or a professional activity) within the EU (freedom of establishment); on the basis of the freedom of establishment the non-resident has the right to access to the self-employed activities and the right to establish enterprises in the Member State concerned under the same conditions defined for residents. Within this context, it is evident that the establishment of STZs with a set of territorial tax incentives may determine a differentiated tax treatment for the undertakings which are based in a limited area of the Member State, with a restriction of the freedom of establishment for all the other economic operators out of the perimeter of the zone.

[2] The Principle of Tax Non-discrimination

The protection of fundamental freedoms through the prohibition of restrictions is inherent to the principle of tax non-discrimination; in this sense, for instance, the violation of the free movement of persons is mostly found in the presence of national measures which introduce a disadvantage for residents of other Member States and, therefore, produce a discriminatory effect.

From the systematic point of view, the principle of tax non-discrimination is instrumental to the pursuit and the defence of the internal market and, therefore, it can be considered as a species of the broader genus of the fundamental freedoms.[315]

In particular, the principle of tax non-discrimination focuses on the legality of a national rule with respect to the EU order with particular reference to the discriminatory effect produced in the treatment of non-residents compared to residents.[316]

In this context, the ECJ assumes a fundamental role in the interpretation of the prohibitions set by the TFEU, tracing the limits of the initiatives of the Member States aimed at the introduction of restrictive measures, including those generally provided with the establishment of an STZ.

In this sense, the fundamental freedoms, as far as they are interpreted in the light of the principle of tax non-discrimination, become relevant in the reasoning of the ECJ in order to prevent nationality-based tax discrimination, namely in a situation where a Member State, for example, uses its tax system to discriminate against nationals of other Member States who enter its territory to work.[317]

315. For these views *see* P. Boria, *Taxation in European Union*, 2nd Edition, Springer International Publishing, Cham, 2017, p. 111.
316. *Ibid.*, p. 112.
317. *See* Case C-204/90 *Hanns-Martin Bachmann v Belgian State*, [1992] ECR I-00249.

Furthermore, the ECJ uses the same approach to forbid not only nationality-based tax discrimination, but also residence-based tax discrimination, thus highlighting the relevance of the principle of non-discrimination in the context of STZs.[318]

Today, the principle of non-discrimination, which is mainly based on differences in treatment on the ground of nationality or on the residence of the persons involved, usually refers to the eventual presence of a less favourable treatment clause for citizens or residents of other Member States, while the introduction of a more favourable treatment is generally permitted. The ECJ, in fact, excludes the application of this principle to the so-called reverse discrimination, which is realized any time a Member State reserves to its own citizens a less favourable treatment than the one granted to citizens of other Member States.[319]

As far as STZs are concerned, the relevance of the principle of tax non-discrimination is essentially associated to the possibility of a differentiated tax treatment between the residents of an STZ and all the other residents of the hosting State; in such cases, in fact, there are still important doubts of legitimacy about the introduction of a more favourable treatment for the residents of an STZ, considering that the situations of residents and non-residents could be considered as comparable in the eyes of the EU institutions. In this sense, territorial tax incentives are generally considered by the ECJ as violating the free movement of persons or the freedom to provide services and, therefore, as producing a discriminatory effect; the case law, in fact, is generally focused on cases where such incentives are seen as discriminatory on the basis of nationality or assimilated criteria based on the residence of the taxpayer benefiting from the tax advantage.[320]

Given the above, it is clear that the principle of tax non-discrimination plays a relevant role for the implementation of the fundamental freedoms within STZs, especially with regard to the linking criteria through which an individual or an enterprise may finally be considered based within the territory of a zone; these criteria, in fact, may be defined according to the nationality, the residence, or, in the case of enterprises, also through the criterion of the 'permanent establishment'.

In summary, on the ground of the specific linking criteria adopted by the national legislator, the principle of tax non-discrimination represents an essential tool for the assessment of the compliance of an STZ with the fundamental freedoms.[321]

This is true not only with reference to the field of indirect taxation where the legislative competence has already been turned over to the EU, but also in the case of direct taxation. In the latter case, in fact, the ECJ always states that, even though direct taxation does not fall within the EU competence, nevertheless Member States are

318. *See*, Case C-279/93 *Finanzamt Köln-Altstadt v Roland Schumacker*, [1995] ECR I-225, paragraphs 27-29.
319. P. Adonnino, *Non-discrimination Rules in International Taxation, General Report*, in *Cahiers de droit fiscal international*, IFA, Periodicals Service Company, Vol. 78b, Deventer, 1993, pp. 26 et seq.
320. *See* Case C-169/08 *Presidente del Consiglio dei Ministri v Regione Sardegna*, [2009] I-10821.
321. A. Dagnino, *supra.*, CEDAM, 2008, p. 173.

required to exercise their legislative powers in compliance with EU law.[322] Therefore, the principle of tax non-discrimination is considered as the benchmark for assessing the implementation of the fundamental freedoms and to define the limits of the initiatives at the national level aimed at the establishment of restrictive measures, including those usually applied in the context of an STZ.[323]

[3] ECJ Case Law

The review of the case law on the topic offers the opportunity to identify some relevant decisions where STZs are scrutinized under the perspective of the fundamental freedoms and with reference to discrimination in the tax treatment between residents and non-residents.

In this regard, the work of the ECJ is focused on the implementation of the principle of tax non-discrimination, in particular through the identification of a valid cause of justification within the provisions of the TFEU.

In these cases, the Court carries out the so-called rule of reason test with a careful evaluation of the relevance of the interests involved through a process usually split into four steps:[324]

(1) assessment of the comparability of a situation involving a non-resident with the situation of a resident (comparability test);
(2) verification of the existence of a national rule with a discriminatory content, with a differential treatment of the two comparable situations (discrimination test);
(3) existence of a reasonable cause of justification of the discriminatory national rule (justification test);
(4) when a cause of justification exists, verification of the proportionality of the national discriminatory rule (proportionality test).

Therefore, the rule of reason test is crucial to verify the limits of the Member State's competence in the establishment of STZs, being essentially aimed at identifying the proper balance between fundamental freedoms, on one part, and the national interests invoked as justifications, on the other.

322. Case C-279/93 *Finanzamt Köln-Altstadt v Roland Schumacker*, [1995] ECR I-225; Case C-80/94 *H. E. J.* Wielockx v. *Inspecteur der Directe Belastingen*, [1995] ECR I-2493; Case C-107/94 *P. H. Asscher v Staatssecretaris van Financiën*, [1996] ECR I-03089; Case C-250/95 *Futura Participations SA and Singer v Administration des contributions*, [1997] ECR I-02471; Case C-118/96 *Jessica Safir v Skattemyndigheten i Dalarnas Län, formerly Skattemyndigheten i Kopparbergs Län*, [1998] ECR I-01897.
323. A. Dagnino, *supra.*, CEDAM, 2008, p. 176.
324. For an overview of the four steps of the rule of reason test *see* M. Lang, P. Pistone, J. Schuch, C. Staringer, *Introduction to European Tax Law: Direct Taxation*, 3rd Edition, Spiramus Press, Wien, 2013, pp. 56 et seq.

Among such interests, the Court sometimes accepts not only those related to the cohesion of the tax system[325] or the effective implementation of tax controls aimed to combat tax avoidance and evasion,[326] but also those associated to objectives of social policy.[327] In any case, such measures - pursuant to the test of proportionality representing the fourth step of the ECJ determination process - must be suitable for guaranteeing the achievement of one or more legitimate objectives invoked by that Member State and must not go beyond what is necessary to achieve those objectives.

In more details, the proportionality test involves three stages concerning the suitability, the necessity, and the proportionality *strictu sensu* of a tax measure.[328] The suitability of the tax measure deals with the relationship between the means and the end: the question asked is whether the chosen measure is suitable or appropriate to achieve the given aim proposed.[329] In the second stage the measure's proportionality is assessed under the profile of its necessity. In particular, the 'least restrictive alternative' usually represents the basic concept around which such interpretation is carried out; therefore, if there are several different measures a Member State can adopt for achieving the given objective, it must choose that measure which is the least restrictive with regard to the fundamental freedoms.[330] Finally, the test of proportionality involves the so-called proportionality *stricto sensu*, meaning that a measure is disproportionate if it imposes an excessive burden on the individual.[331]

Given the above, the following case law review does not cover the multitude of cases where the ECJ implements the various steps of the rule of reason with reference to the use of tax incentives in general; in this sense, in fact, the selection is strictly limited to the cases where the ECJ directly approaches a situation specifically involving an STZ, issuing a final decision on the compatibility between the preferential tax treatment there granted and the fundamental freedoms.

---

325. *See* Case C-204/90 *Hanns-Martin Bachmann v Belgian State*, [1992] ECR I-00249.
326. Case C-264/96 *Imperial Chemical Industries plc (ICI) v Kenneth Hall Colmer*, [1998] ECR I-04695; Case C-270/83 *Commission of the European Communities v French Republic (Avoir fiscal)*, [1986] ECR 273.
327. *See* joined Cases C-447/08 and C-448/08 *Criminal proceedings against Otto Sjöberg (C-447/08) and Anders Gerdin (C-448/08)*, [2010] ECR I-06921, paragraph 43 where according to the Court '*considerations of a cultural, moral or religious nature can justify restrictions on the freedom of gambling operators to provide services, in particular in so far as it might be considered unacceptable to allow private profit to be drawn from the exploitation of a social evil or the weakness of players and their misfortune. According to the scale of values held by each of the Member States and having regard to the discretion available to them, a Member State may restrict the operation of gambling by entrusting it to public or charitable bodies*'.
328. T.I. Harbo, *The Function of the Proportionality Principle in EU Law*, in *European Law Journal*, 2010, Vol. 16, No. 2, p. 165.
329. *See* in this regard Case C-145/88 *Torfaen Borough Council v B&Q plc*, [1989] ECR I-3815; Case C-169/91 *Stoke-on-Trent CC v B&Q plc*, [1992] ECR I-6457.
330. D. Weber, *Tax Avoidance and the EC Treaty Freedoms: A Study of the Limitations under European Law to the Prevention of Tax Avoidance*, in *Eucotax Series on European Taxation 11*, The Hague, Kluwer law international, 2005, p. 209. *See* Case C-101/94 *Commission of the European Communities v Italian Republic*, [1996] ECR I-02691.
331. T.I. Harbo, *supra.*, in *European Law Journal*, 2010, Vol. 16, No. 2, p. 165.

Based on such methodology, the resulting framework focuses only on two relevant decisions issued by the ECJ where important statements are made concerning the implementation of the fundamental freedoms in the context of an STZ.

[a] The Sardinia Case

The case *Presidente del Consiglio dei Ministri v Regione Sardegna*[332] – already mentioned in relation to State aid rules[333] – is an important example of the position held by the ECJ on the differences in the tax treatment between resident and non-resident companies with reference to a limited territory of a Member State (the region of Sardinia in Italy). Here, the analysis of the Court approaches a situation where the non-resident company is affected by a less favourable tax treatment, with the final identification of a form of discrimination based on the application of different rules to comparable situations. Among the relevant number of cases on the topic, this judgement assumes a specific value as it focuses on the compatibility of a tax measure adopted by a regional authority which is specifically targeted at the undertakings based in the region of Sardinia.

In detail, the preliminary ruling concerns the interpretation, among others, of Article 56 TFEU (ex Article 49 EC) on the freedom of providing services in the context of a proceeding between the President of the Italian Council of Ministers and the Region of Sardinia regarding the establishment by that region of a tax on stopovers for tourist purposes. In this case, the referring court asks whether Article 56 TFEU must be interpreted as precluding tax legislation, adopted by a regional authority, such as Article 4 of Regional Law of 11 May 2006, No. 4, which provides the imposition of a regional tax in the event of stopovers for tourist purposes by aircraft used for the private transport of persons, or by recreational craft, where that tax is imposed only on undertakings which have their tax domicile outside the territory of the region. The ECJ confirms that the situation of residents and the situation of non-residents in a given Member State are not generally comparable, since there are objective differences between them, both from the point of view of the source of the income and from the point of view of the ability to pay tax.[334] Nevertheless, the Court makes a further step on the ground of the principle of tax non-discrimination, stating that also the specific characteristics of the relevant tax must be taken into account in the comparison of the situation of the taxpayers; accordingly, a difference in treatment between residents and non-residents may constitute a restriction on the freedom to provide services prohibited by Article 56 TFEU where, as in this case, there is no objective difference in the situation which would justify different treatment between various categories of taxpayers. In this specific situation, in fact, in terms of the consequences for the environment, all natural and legal persons who receive the services in question are in an objectively comparable situation with regard to that tax, irrespective of the place

332. Case C-169/08 *Presidente del Consiglio dei Ministri v Regione Sardegna*, [2009] I-10821.
333. *See supra* section §3.02[A][5].
334. *See* Case C-527/06 *Renneberg*, [2008] ECR I-7735, paragraph 59.

where they reside or are established.[335] In particular, as the Advocate General Kokott states, even if it is accepted that private aircraft and recreational craft making stopovers in Sardinia constitute a source of pollution, that pollution is caused regardless of where those aircraft and boats come from and, in particular, it is not linked to the tax domicile of those operators. Therefore, the restriction on the freedom to provide services set by the tax legislation at issue cannot be justified on grounds relating to environmental protection since the basis for applying the regional tax on stopovers introduced by that legislation is a distinction between persons which is unrelated to that environmental objective.[336] Therefore, the tax legislation at issue constitutes a form of discrimination and a restriction on the freedom to provide services since it taxes only operators of aircraft used for the private transport of persons, or of pleasure boats, who have their tax domicile outside the territory of the region, without imposing the same tax on the operators established in that territory.

In summary, a difference in treatment between residents and non-residents of the zone is permitted - in the light of the above decision of the ECJ - only if the non-resident taxpayer is not in an objectively comparable situation to the one of the resident, considering the specific characteristics of the relevant tax measure.

[b] The Juntas Generales Case

In the case of companies, the terms of comparison are generally between a non-resident company with a permanent establishment in the STZ territory, on one part, and a resident company based in the same STZ, on the other; here, it is evident that the permanent establishment of the non-resident company is in a comparable situation with the resident company and, thus, both situations have to be treated in the same manner.[337]

Consequently, the linking criteria to define if a company is based in an STZ cannot be identified with the residence of the company, but with the place in which its permanent establishment is based, since any other solution could lead to a violation of the principle of tax non-discrimination.

In this regard, the case *Administración General del Estado v Juntas Generales de Guipúzcoa and Diputación Foral de Guipúzcoa, Juntas Generales d'Alava and Diputación Foral d'Alava and Juntas Generales de Vizcaya,*[338] even in the absence of a final

335. Case C-169/08 *Presidente del Consiglio dei Ministri v Regione Sardegna*, [2009] I-10821, paragraph 37.
336. *Ibid.*, paragraph 45.
337. K. Dziurdz, C. Marchgraber, *Non-discrimination in European and Tax Treaty Law*, Series on International Tax Law, M. Lang (ed.), Wien, Linde, 2015, p. 52.
338. Joined cases C-400/97, C-401/97 and C-402/97 *Administración General del Estado v Juntas Generales de Guipúzcoa and Diputación Foral de Guipúzcoa, Juntas Generales d'Alava and Diputación Foral d'Alava and Juntas Generales de Vizcaya*, [2000] ECR I-01073.

decision from the ECJ,[339] offers an interesting perspective for the evaluation of the linking criteria in the light of the Opinion here issued by Advocate General Saggio.[340]

In this case, the Court is asked for a preliminary ruling concerning the interpretation of Article 49 TFEU (ex Article 52 EC) on the freedom of establishment and, in particular, whether it precludes the Basque legislation on urgent fiscal measures to stimulate investment and the development of economic activities.[341] Such legislation, in fact, makes the grant of tax benefits conditional on residence or on a considerable percentage of the total volume of transactions in the Basque territory. According to such provisions, a company from another Member State which wishes to open a branch, agency, or establishment in the Basque Country while maintaining its own business (and therefore its residence for tax purposes) in the State of origin cannot benefit from this tax benefit.[342] According to the Opinion of Advocate General Saggio, the conditions imposed by the Basque legislation for entitlement to fiscal advantages constitute a discriminatory measure for the purposes of Article 49 TFEU and, thus, the same principle of tax non-discrimination precludes such legislation.[343] In conclusion, according to the same Opinion, a permanent establishment of a non-resident company cannot be excluded from tax benefits in such a situation, since, otherwise, a discriminatory treatment would be unlawfully imposed.

[4] Fundamental Freedoms and SSGIs

As already seen for State aid law, Social Services of General Interest (SSGIs) assume a fundamental role in the context of the present research, considering the possible introduction of territorial tax incentives in an STZ for the undertakings involved in services of a social character.

SSGIs, where they constitute an economic activity in the terms defined by the ECJ,[344] are covered by the freedom of establishment (Article 49) and the free movement of services (Article 56).[345]

In this context, the freedom of establishment for SSGIs is ensured through the application of the principle of tax non-discrimination, with the prohibition of any restriction able to produce a discriminatory effect in the treatment of non-residents compared to residents.

339. *See supra* note 189.

340. Opinion of Advocate General Saggio delivered on 1 July 1999 in Joined cases C-400/97, C-401/97 and C-402/97 *Administración General del Estado v Juntas Generales de Guipúzcoa and Diputación Foral de Guipúzcoa, Juntas Generales d'Alava and Diputación Foral d'Alava and Juntas Generales de Vizcaya*, [2000] ECR I-01073.

341. *Ibid.*, paragraph 16.

342. *Ibid.*, paragraph 19.

343. *Ibid.*, paragraph 25.

344. Commission staff working document, *Guide to the application of the European Union rules on state aid, public procurement and the internal market to services of general economic interest, and in particular to social services of general interest*, Brussels, 2013, SWD(2013) 53 final/2, p. 103. In particular, according to this document, non-economic activities are not covered by any of these rules.

345. *Ibid.*

For this purpose, the ECJ carries out the 'rule of reason test' where the eventual existence of a reasonable cause of justification assumes a specific role in the assessment of the discriminatory national rule (third step of the rule of reason).

In particular, in the case of SSGIs, a discriminatory rule can be justified by the Member State when the objectives pursued may be qualified as 'overriding reasons of public interest' under the rule of reason test; in this sense, in fact, according to the ECJ, considerations of social policy may justify restrictions on the fundamental freedoms,[346] as far as they are suitable for guaranteeing the achievement of one or more legitimate objectives invoked by that Member State and do not go beyond what is necessary to achieve those objectives.

For example, the ECJ states that overriding reasons relating to the public interest capable of justifying a restriction on the freedom to provide services include the protection of workers,[347] the fight against undeclared work, as well as the protection of the financial balance of social security systems.[348]

At the same time, it is important to observe that the case law of the ECJ does not provide a comprehensive definition of public interest, limiting its decisions to the description of a series of examples of situations that are relevant under such notion.

Therefore, the ECJ always leaves open the list of public interests, on the ground of the fact that the choice of public interests which a Member State wishes to promote by granting tax incentives is a matter of its own discretion.[349]

According to this flexible approach to the concept of public interest, it is possible to conclude that also the social policy objectives pursued in the context of an SSGI may constitute 'overriding reasons of general interest' able to justify the application of discriminatory measures under the rule of reason test, provided that the said measures are proportionate to the objectives pursued.[350]

[B] Harmonization Measures in Secondary Law

In the context of internal market law, the review of the sources of secondary law includes a set of legislative measures adopted at the EU level for the harmonization of indirect taxation with particular reference to customs duties, VAT and excise duties, in consideration of the aspects related to the phenomenon of STZs.

346. Joined Cases C-447/08 and C-448/08 *Criminal Proceedings Against Otto Sjöberg (C-447/08) and Anders Gerdin (C-448/08)*, [2010] ECR I-06921, paragraph 43.
347. Case C-515/08 *Dos Santos Palhota and Others*, [2010] ECR I-09133, paragraph 47.
348. *See*, to that effect, Case C–346/06 *Dirk Rüffert v Land Niedersachsen*, [2008] ECR I-01989, paragraph 42.
349. *See* E. Traversa, *Tax Incentives and Territoriality within the European Union: Balancing the Internal Market with the Tax Sovereignty of Member States*, in *World Tax Journal*, 2014, p. 339. *See also* G. Bizioli, *Impact of the Freedom of Establishment on Tax Law*, in *EC Tax Review*, 1998, No. 4, pp. 239-247, where the author stresses the relativity of concepts such as public policy or public security (often used by the ECJ to refer to the general concept of public interest) '*because they change in time, national usage, and geographic location*'.
350. Commission staff working document, *Guide to the application of the European Union rules on state aid, public procurement and the internal market to services of general economic interest, and in particular to social services of general interest*, Brussels, 2013, SWD(2013) 53 final/2, p. 105.

Furthermore, secondary law in this field includes the various sources dealing with the concepts of social advantages and social enterprises; the analysis of the research question No. 2, in fact, requires the definition of a comprehensive background for the discipline of social tax incentives, including such relevant concepts belonging to the EU law framework.

[1] FZs in the UCC

The UCC, approved by Regulation (EU) No. 952/2013,[351] represents an essential source of norms for ensuring the free movement of Union goods in the customs territory of the Union and a common customs treatment of non-Union goods brought into that territory.

In the UCC - as well as in the Recast VAT Directive and in the Excise Duty Directive - the phenomenon of STZs is essentially associated to the so-called FZs, according to a terminology traditionally in use in the context of customs operations and indirect taxation.

In other words, FZs are here identified as a subcategory of STZs and, in this regard, the UCC offers a fundamental support in the definition of the related EU legal framework, with a set of norms aimed at regulating the tax benefits there provided through the suspension of custom duties and other charges in the context of indirect taxation.

The review of title VII of the UCC deals with special procedures and, in particular, with a situation corresponding to a delimited area of land that is characterized by the presence of territorial tax benefits. According to Article 210 UCC, in fact, FZs are considered as a special procedure of storage under which Union or non-Union goods may be placed. More precisely, a FZ, under the scope defined by Article 237 UCC, is a part of the customs territory of the Union limited from the rest of it, in which non-EU goods introduced therein are considered, both for the customs duties and for trade policy measures, as not situated in the territory of the Union, provided that they are not released for free circulation or placed under another customs procedure or used or consumed under conditions other than those provided by customs regulations.

Compared to previous sources,[352] the new regulatory context set by the UCC is characterized not only by the cancellation of the distinction between warehouses and FZs, but also by the inclusion of the latter zones within the so-called special customs regimes for storage and by the abolition of FZs 'not landlocked'.

In a first period, in fact, according to Regulation (EC) No. 2700/2000[353] two different types of zones have been established:

351. Council Regulation (EU) No. 952/2013 of 9 October 2013 laying down the Union Customs Code, O.J. 2013, L. 269, pp. 1-101.
352. Council Regulation (EEC) No. 2913/92 of 12 October 1992 establishing the Community Customs Code, O.J. 1992, L 302, pp. 1-50.
353. Council Regulation (EC) No. 2700/2000 of 16 November 2000 amending Council Regulation (EEC) No. 2913/92 establishing the Community Customs Code, O.J. 2000, L 311, pp. 17-20.

(1) 'Control type I Free Zones' that have a perimeter fence supervised by customs, so that goods placed there are automatically under this regime.[354]
(2) 'Control type II Free Zones' that are regulated by a set of norms similar to those governing customs warehouses. Consequently, unlike traditional-style FZs, physical control does not take place at entry and exit points, while the goods are subjected to a declaration in order to be able to benefit from the regime.[355]

Nevertheless, today, according to Article 243 UCC, the FZ may only be set in a landlocked mode, confirming an approach already announced by Regulation (EC) No. 450/2008.[356]

Then, Articles 243 and 244 UCC recognize the possibility for Member States to designate parts of the customs territory of the Union as FZs; Member States shall also determine the area covered and the entry and exit points of each FZ, which are subjected to customs supervision.

The tax benefits of the FZ generally consist in the suspension of the levy of customs duties through a deferral regime for goods introduced into the area; in this regard, in fact, Article 237(1)(a) UCC provides that under a storage procedure – such as the FZ – non-Union goods may be stored in the customs territory of the Union without being subject to import duties.

Furthermore, pursuant to Article 237(1)(b) UCC, the same tax benefits are extended to other charges '*as provided for under other relevant provisions in force*', considering that, beside customs duties, these are other charges usually applied as non-Union goods are introduced into the territory of the Union.

The goods introduced in a FZ may be stored without time limit,[357] with the suspension of import customs duties and other charges, until they are not assigned to the final exportation to non-EU countries (without satisfying the customs duties imposed on goods at the time of import) or to the release for free circulation in the Union (with the consequent payment of custom duties on importation).

In exceptional circumstances, the customs authorities may set a time-limit by which a storage procedure must be discharged, in particular where the type and nature of the goods may, in the case of long-term storage, pose a threat to human, animal or plant health or to the environment.[358]

From the functional point of view, the tax benefits granted in a FZ – essentially represented by the suspension of custom duties – are the result of economic policies

354. Article 799(1)(a) of Council Regulation (EEC) No. 2454/93 of 2 July 1993 laying down provisions for the implementation of Council Regulation (EEC) No. 2913/92 establishing the Community Customs Code, O.J. 1993, L 253, pp. 1-766.
355. *Ibid.*, Article 799(1)(b). In this regard, *see* W. De Jong, *Establishing Free Zones for Regional Development*, Library of the European Parliament, 2013, available at http://www.europarl.europa.eu/RegData/bibliotheque/br-iefing/2013/130481/LDM_BRI(20-13)130481REVEN.pdf.
356. Council Regulation (EC) No. 450/2008 of 23 April 2008 laying down the Community Customs Code (Modernized Customs Code), O.J. 2008, L 145, pp. 1-64.
357. Article 238(1) UCC.
358. Article 238(2) UCC.

carried out by the Member States and, therefore, it is not possible to identify any kind of influence related to social policies and welfare.

In the territory of a FZ it is possible to carry out any industrial or commercial activity and any type of provision of services, even if the exercise of such activities must be previously notified to the customs authorities which may apply certain prohibitions or limitations (Article 244 UCC).

In particular, the use of a FZ is not confined to a mere storage function. Under Article 220 UCC, in fact, it is expected that during their stay goods within the FZ may (i) be subjected to usual forms of handling, even without prior authorization; (ii) be placed under the inward processing arrangements; (iii) be placed under the transform processing under customs control; (iv) be placed under the temporary admission regime; (v) be abandoned; (vi) be destroyed; (vii) be used or consumed on the sole condition that such goods, in the case of release for free circulation or temporary admission, would not be subject to import duties or to the common agricultural policy or commercial policy measures.

The regulatory framework of FZs is completed by a series of further provisions that define the administrative aspects relevant for their establishment and their supervision by the customs authorities.

For example, according to Article 214 UCC, all persons carrying on an activity involving the storage, working, or processing of goods, or the sale or purchase of goods in FZs, must keep appropriate records in a form approved by the customs authorities. The records must contain the information which enable the customs authorities to supervise the procedure concerned, in particular with regard to identification of the goods placed under that procedure, their customs status and their movements.

Finally, it is worth to note that Member States must communicate to the Commission information on their FZs which are in operation;[359] accordingly, the Commission has released a list of the FZs in operation in the customs territory of the Union, which is periodically updated following new communications from the Member States.[360]

[2] FZs in the Recast VAT Directive

The Directive 2006/112/EC[361] – also named 'Recast VAT Directive' – provides relevant norms that contribute to define the regulatory framework of STZs for ensuring the free movement of goods and services.

In this case, the terminology used by the EU legislator is the same already found in the UCC and, therefore, the notion of FZ provided in the latter – defined as a special procedure of storage – represents the fundamental model of reference even for any aspect linked to the application of VAT.

359. Article 243(2) UCC.
360. *See supra* note 22.
361. Council Directive 2006/112/EC of 28 November 2006 on the common system of value added tax, O.J. 2006, L 347, pp. 1-118.

The Recast VAT Directive allows the Member States to exempt from VAT the supply of goods and services carried out in a FZ, giving them the possibility of introducing national norms aimed at providing such exemption.

According to Article 156 of the same Directive, in fact, Member States are able to exempt from VAT, among others, the supply of goods that are intended to be placed in a FZ, while the following Article 159 specifies that the same Member States may also exempt the supply of services related to the supply of goods referred to in Article 156.

In this regard, it is important to note that the tax incentive is generally related to the supplies of goods and services made between entities based within the territory of a FZ. Otherwise, in the case of a supply between a non-EU operator and an operator based in a FZ, the exemption from VAT is already determined pursuant to Article 237 UCC according to which under a FZ, '*non-Union goods may be stored in the customs territory of the Union without being subject to other charges as provided for under other relevant provisions in force*'.

In any case, the Directive provides an exemption from VAT which is merely temporary, consisting in a suspension of the taxation; it is evident, in fact, that the same goods brought into the FZ regime are to be subjected to charge of VAT once they exit the zone to enter the Union territory or are released for consumption.

In this sense, Article 71 of the Recast Vat Directive provides that '*where, on entry into the Community, goods are placed under one of the arrangements or situations referred to in Articles 156, 276 and 277,* [including the Free Zone[362]] *or under temporary importation arrangements with total exemption from import duty, or under external transit arrangements, the chargeable event shall occur and VAT shall become chargeable only when the goods cease to be covered by those arrangements or situations*'.

In other words, any time goods are introduced into a FZ, the chargeable event is delayed until such goods are covered by the FZ regime.

These conclusions are also confirmed by Article 202 of the Recast VAT Directive according to which '*VAT shall be payable by any person who causes goods to cease to be covered by the arrangements or situations listed in Articles 156, 157, 160 and 161*'.

Finally, from the functional point of view, it is interesting to observe that, also in this case, the tax incentives provided through the Recast VAT Directive are generally related to the development of economic policies in the context of international trade, without any implication concerning social policy objectives and welfare in general.

[3] FZs in Directive 2008/118/EC (Excise Duty)

The main scope of Directive 2008/118/EC[363] (hereinafter also Excise Duty Directive) is to ensure the free movement of excise goods in the territory of the Union.

362. In this sense *see* Case C-571/15, *Wallenborn Transports SA v Hauptzollamt GießenCase*, published in the electronic Report of Cases (Court Reports -general).
363. Council Directive 2008/118/EC of 16 December 2008 concerning the general arrangements for excise duty and repealing Directive 92/12/EEC, O.J. 2009, L 9, pp. 12-30.

In this case, the tax benefits on excise duty are designed in the same form used for customs duties and VAT, with a structure of the tax norm founded on the delay of the chargeable event for the goods introduced in the territory of a FZ.

The set of these provisions is very complex and it is based on the coordination of different norms, whose final result is the suspension of excise duty until goods are placed under the FZ procedure.

In detail, pursuant to Article 7 of Directive 2008/118/EC, excise duty becomes chargeable at the time of release for consumption, assuming that '*release for consumption shall mean, among others, the importation of excise goods, including irregular importation, unless the excise goods are placed, immediately upon importation, under a duty suspension arrangement*'. Moreover, Article 4 defines '*importation of excise goods*' as the entry into the territory of the Union of excise goods unless the goods upon their entry into the Union are placed under a customs suspensive procedure or arrangement, as well as their release from a customs suspensive procedure or arrangement. And, finally, the same Article 4 clarifies that '*customs suspensive procedure or arrangement*' means any one of the special procedures provided under Regulation (EEC) No. 2913/92,[364] among which it is possible to identify the same FZ.

By the above set of norms, it is clear that the chargeable event for what concerns excise duty is excluded any time the goods are placed within the FZ, since the placement of goods in such zones is not considered as importation and, consequently, as a form of release for consumption.

Also in the case of excise duty, from the functional point of view, the tax benefits that characterize the FZ are clearly targeted to objectives of economic policy, while the pursuit of a specific social aim is generally excluded.

[4] The Concept of 'Social Advantages'

In the context of internal market law, the review of the discipline of 'social advantages' assumes a specific relevance for the purposes of research question No. 2, which is focused on the possibility of a new model of STZs based on social tax incentives.

The concept of 'social advantages', in fact, as used in Article 7(2) of Regulation (EU) No. 492/2011,[365] can be associated with the category of social tax incentives, since they both share the same objectives and the same functional perspective.

Regulation (EU) No. 492/2011 aims to ensure the achievement of the free movement of workers as enshrined in primary law (Article 45 TFEU), guaranteeing equal treatment for what regards any conditions of employment and also access to social advantages within the internal market.

Nonetheless, it is neither possible to identify a uniform definition of 'social advantages' in the text of this Regulation nor in other EU legislative sources. The concept of social advantages, in fact, is only defined in the case law of the ECJ in a very

364. Council Regulation (EEC) No. 2913/92 establishing the Community Customs Code, O.J. 1992, L 302.
365. Regulation (EU) No. 492/2011 of 5 April 2011 on freedom of movement for workers within the Union, O.J. 2011, L 141, p. 1-12.

broad and general way,[366] simply referring to all the advantages which, '*whether or not linked to a contract of employment, are generally granted to national workers primarily because of their objective status as workers or by virtue of the mere fact of their residence on the national territory and the extension of which to workers who are nationals of other Member States therefore seems suitable to facilitate their mobility within the Union*'.[367]

On the ground of such a broad concept, today social advantages also include financial benefits and non-financial benefits which are not traditionally perceived as social advantages, such as in the case of public transport fare reductions for large families,[368] child raising allowances,[369] funeral payments,[370] minimum subsistence payments,[371] and study grants.[372]

In this context, it is then important to observe that a strict definition of the concept of social advantages at the EU level would probably interfere with the legislative competence of Member States;[373] thus, a broad and flexible concept of social advantages seems to represent the only feasible option at the current stage of the European integration process.

In conclusion, even if the notion of social advantages can easily be associated with the category of social tax incentives – at least from the conceptual point of view – the review of EU law does not offer a useful path for better defining the limits of the same category for the purposes of the present research. In this sense, in fact, the broad concept of social advantages resulting from the ECJ case law, on one part, and the absence of a clear definition in the related Regulation, on the other, do not allow the identification of relevant elements for the purposes of the present research.

[5] The Concept of 'Social Enterprises'

As already said in the previous Chapter 2, social enterprises may assume a fundamental role in the context of the present study, considering their possible use as an instrument to introduce social tax incentives within the territory of STZs.

Therefore, in the light of the scope of research question No. 2, which is aimed at the development of a new model of STZs based on social tax incentives, it is now

366. A. Czekay-Dancewicz, *Access to Social Benefits and Advantages for EU Migrant Workers, Members of Their Families and Other Categories of Migrating EU Citizens*, 2013, p. 1, available at http://ec.europa.eu/social/BlobServlet?d ocId = 11714&langId = en.
367. Case C-207/78 *Criminal Proceedings Against Gilbert Even and Office National des pensions pour travailleurs salariés*, [1979] ECR I-02019, paragraph 22; Case C-85/96 *María Martínez Sala v Freistaat Bayern*, [1998] ECR I–2691.
368. Case C-32/75 *Cristini v SNCF*, [1975] ECR 1085.
369. Case C-85/96 *María Martínez Sala v Freistaat Bayern*, [1998] ECR I–2691.
370. Case C-237/94 *O'Flynn v Adjudication Officer*, [1996] ECR I-2617.
371. Case C-75/63 *Hoekstra v Bestuur der Bedrijfsvereniging voor detailhandel en Ambachten*, [1964], ECR 987.
372. Case C-237/87 *Volvo AB v Erik Veng (UK) Ltd.*, [1988] ECR 6211; Case C-3/90 *Bernini (MJE) v Netherlands Ministry of Education and Science*, [1992] ECR I-1071; Case C-542/09 *Commission v Netherlands*, published in the electronic Reports of Cases (Court Reports – general).
373. *Ibid.*

necessary to review the sources of internal market law dealing with the phenomenon of social enterprises.

The notion of social enterprises is defined under Regulation (EU) No. 1296/2013[374] establishing a EU Programme for Employment and Social Innovation for the period 2014-2020. Under this Programme, social enterprises are established with the aim to (i) increase the availability of finance for vulnerable persons, microenterprises, and social enterprises; and (ii) build up the institutional capacity of microcredit providers and support the development of the social investment market.[375] The final objective is to consolidate the social dimension of the Union and to ensure the free movement of persons in the context of internal market law.[376]

According to Article 2(1) of this Regulation 'social enterprise' is an undertaking, regardless of its legal form, which:

(a) in accordance with its articles of association, statutes or with any other legal document, has as its primary objective the achievement of measurable, positive social impacts rather than generating profit for its owners, members, and shareholders, and which: (i) provides services or goods able to generate a social return and/or (ii) employs a method of production of goods or services that embodies its social objective;
(b) uses its profits first and foremost to achieve its primary objective and has predefined procedures and rules covering any distribution of profits to shareholders and owners which ensure that such distribution does not undermine the primary objective; and
(c) is managed in an entrepreneurial, accountable, and transparent way, in particular by involving workers, customers, and stakeholders affected by its business activities.

Therefore, according to the above definition, the notion of social enterprise entails organizational forms which are characterized by governance criteria, economic criteria, and social criteria.

First, for what concerns the governance criteria, social enterprises always benefit from a certain degree of autonomy since they are voluntarily established, independent, and private legal entities; in particular, even when they heavily depend on public subsidies, they are not managed, directly or indirectly, by public authorities. Moreover, their decision-making power is not usually based on the founders/members' stake in the share capital of the organization, but is rather democratic with one member corresponding to one vote. However, also private companies (e.g., limited liability companies) may be considered social enterprises, insofar as they are established to pursue social goals, rather than generate profit.

374. Regulation (EU) No. 1296/2013 of the European Parliament and of the Council of 11 December 2013 on a European Union Programme for Employment and Social Innovation ('EaSI') and amending Decision No. 283/2010/EU establishing a European Progress Microfinance Facility for employment and social inclusion, O.J. 2013, L 347, p. 238-252.
375. *Ibid.*, Article 26.
376. *Ibid.*, Recital 9.

Second, for the economic criteria, it is important to note that social enterprises are usually based on the exercise of an economic activity producing and selling goods and/or services and they must have at least one employee to be considered a social enterprise.

Third, the social criteria are associated to the existence of an explicit social purpose, such as to benefit the community or a specific group of people, for example; the primary goal of a social enterprise, in fact, is to pursue social goals, rather than generate profit. In this regard, it is worth to remember the fact that social enterprises must reinvest the majority of profit or surplus to pursue their main statutory goals.[377]

In summary, today the concept of social enterprises is part of the internal market law where it is defined under Regulation (EU) No. 1296/2013. In the same context, social enterprises may influence the approach to STZs any time a set of territorial tax incentives is designed with a clear objective of a social character; this basically means that, in such cases, social enterprises may become a vehicle and an instrument to be used for the achievement of the objectives pursued through the establishment of an STZ.

[6] Social Enterprises and Other Soft Law Instruments

Within soft law it is possible to identify one more definition of social enterprise at the EU level aimed at avoiding unqualified or abusive practices.

According to a Communication of 2011 from the Commission, in fact, a social enterprise is 'an operator in the social economy whose main objective is to have a social impact rather than make a profit for their owners or shareholders. It operates by providing goods and services for the market in an entrepreneurial and innovative fashion and uses its profits primarily to achieve social objectives. It is managed in an open and responsible manner and, in particular, involves employees, consumers, and stakeholders affected by its commercial activities'.[378]

The idea of 'social economy', which is included in the above definition, relies on democratic decision-making processes able to control the effective achievement of the organization's goals. Many types of organizations can be associated to the idea of social economy, such as associations, cooperatives, foundations, and social enterprises.[379]

In this regard, the same Communication underlines the following defining features of social economy organizations: (i) the primacy of the social objective over capital; (ii) voluntary and open membership; (iii) democratic control by membership;

---

377. UNDP, *Legal Framework for Social Economy and Social Enterprises: A Comparative Report*, European Center for Not-for-Profit Law, 2012, p. 5, available at http://ecnl.org/dindocuments/442_ECNL%20UNDP%20Social%20Economy%20Report.pdf.
378. Communication from the Commission to the European Parliament, the Council, the European Economic and Social Committee and the Committee of Regions, *Social business initiative creating a favourable climate for social enterprises, key stakeholders in the social economy and innovation*, COM(2011) No. 0682 final, paragraph 1.
379. European Commission – Directorate-General for Internal Market, Industry, Entrepreneurship and SMEs, *Social enterprises and the social economy going forward. A call for action from the Commission Expert Group on Social Entrepreneurship (GECES)*, 2016, p. 51, available at http://ec.europa.eu/growth/sectors/social-economy/enterprises/expert-groups.

(iv) the combination of the interests of members/users and/or the general interest; (v) the defence and application of the principle of solidarity and responsibility; (vi) autonomous management and independence from public authorities; (vii) most of the surpluses are used in pursuit of sustainable development objectives, services of interest to members or the general interest.[380]

Furthermore, in the context of social enterprises, there are two additional terms that are usually brought into the discussion for defining the same phenomenon, namely, 'solidarity economy' and 'third sector'. The former term refers to those economic activities in which social relations of solidarity have priority over individual interests or material profit; thus, these organizations emphasize the social dimension involved in any economic activity. Differently, the term 'third sector' is mainly used in literature to refer to organizations other than those publicly owned and the private for-profit ones, thus emphasizing their hybrid nature.[381]

§3.04 STZs AND HARMFUL TAX COMPETITION

[A] General Aspects

From the point of view of the EU institutions, the promotion of policies with an emphasis on the use of territorial tax incentives, aimed in particular at promoting the localization of economic activities or capital investment in a limited area of a Member State, is generally considered as harmful for the process of European integration and, therefore, as an element to counteract.

According to this perspective, in fact, the Commission promotes the integration at the EU level of national tax policies in order to reduce the phenomenon of tax competition between the Member States.

In this context, the so-called harmful tax competition is identified with the adoption of fiscal policies by a Member State through a set of measures which lead to the excessive lowering of the domestic tax burden in order to provide an attractive tax system; an example is the introduction of tax incentives that induce the economic operators to relocate from the State of residence to a zone in a different State on the ground of strategic choices which are not in line with the natural development of a business.[382]

In this sense, the use of territorial tax incentives is sometimes a deviation from the standard tax policies adopted by other States, representing an interference with respect to the allocation decisions of economic operators; such a situation could lead to a form of harmful tax competition when attracting capital and enterprises from the territory of residence to a different territory.

In the case of STZs, harmful tax competition may arise as far as tax benefits are there reserved exclusively for non-residents and when the same advantages do not

380. *Ibid.*
381. *Ibid.*, p. 52.
382. For these considerations *see* P. Boria, *Taxation in European Union*, 2nd Edition, Springer International Publishing, Cham, 2017, p. 166.

result as proportionate and transparent, and do not refer to genuine economic activities.

On these bases, harmful tax competition becomes a serious issue, especially when the measures adopted within an STZ are able to affect in a significant way the location of business activities in the EU territory, providing a significantly lower level of taxation than that applied out of the territory of the zone.

Given the above, the initiatives at the EU level aimed at fighting against harmful tax competition assume a specific relevance for the purposes of the present research; therefore, it is now necessary to approach the same issue from the perspective of STZs, identifying the limits of legitimacy of territorial tax incentives according to the soft law instruments adopted by the EU institutions to counteract the negative effects of harmful tax competition.

[B] The Code of Conduct for Business Taxation

[1] Main Features

Beside the relevant provisions of State aid law and internal market law, the framework of STZs at the EU level is completed by the Code of Conduct for Business Taxation adopted by the ECOFIN Council on 1 December 1997.[383]

The document is a legally non-binding political commitment between Member States and represents a very important point of reference in the planning activity aimed at the establishment of STZs.

The Code embodies a soft law process strategy designed to circumvent the Member States' propensity to disagree about taxation.[384] In particular, the Code defines harmful tax measures as measures (including administrative practices) which affect or may affect in a significant way the location of business activities in the EU territory and which provide for a significantly lower level of taxation, including zero taxation, than that generally applied in the Member State concerned.

In this context, the fight against harmful tax competition is aimed not only at a more effective use of State aid rules, but also at the elimination of general tax measures which lure foreign capital and other investments away from their source country, by offering lower tax rates or different tax bases. Thus, from an economic point of view, the Code of Conduct intervenes when the foreign investor is influenced to invest capital in a country at a preferential lower tax charge.

For the assessment of national tax measures, the Code lists the following characteristics as relevant and harmful: (a) availability of the tax advantage only for non-residents or for domestic goods, or for transactions with non-residents; (b)

383. Conclusions of the ECOFIN Council Meeting on 1 December 1997 concerning taxation policy – Resolution of the Council and the Representatives of the Governments of the Member States, meeting within the Council of 1 December 1997, O.J. 1998, C 2, pp. 1-6.

384. W.W. Bratton, J. Mc Cahery, *Tax Coordination and Tax Competition in the European Union: Evaluating the Code of Conduct on Business Taxation*, in *Internal Market Law Review*, 2001, Vol. 38, No. 2, p. 677.

ring-fencing: protection of the domestic market against the tax advantage, so that the measure does not erode the domestic tax base of the State concerned (but only other States' tax bases); (c) lack of substance: granting of the tax advantage irrespective of any real economic activity; (d) lack of arm's-length dealing; (e) non-transparency: unpublished advance ruling and negotiability of the tax burden.[385]

The Code of Conduct, which belongs to the genus of soft law, provides the blocking of new measures of direct taxation favouring some activities in a country and producing competitive situations related to a particular territory (so-called standstill clause). Accordingly, there is a sort of freezing of such tax regulations in Member States since the introduction of the Code of Conduct, preventing them to grow in quantity and quality.

Furthermore, the Code of Conduct provides the gradual dismantling of the tax measures producing harmful tax competition (so-called rollback clause).[386]

Since the Code of Conduct has no binding force, it is crucial for the Commission's practice to identify the line between general and selective tax incentives, as only the latter category is under the control of State aid rules.[387] In this regard, it is important to note that a measure previously authorized by the Commission under the State aid rules might not be acceptable under the Code of Conduct criteria for harmful tax competition, as the State aid rules (especially for what concerns the requirement of selectivity) may partly overlap with those for harmful tax competition, but they are not identical.[388]

The group implementing the Code of Conduct - also named 'Code of Conduct Group' - consists of high representatives of the Member States and is chaired by one of them rotating every two years. The Commission is a mere observer and adviser, while the group directly reports to the Council.

In order to achieve the objectives of the Code, the aforementioned working group is in charge of the assessment of the tax measures that may fall within the scope of the Code of Conduct and of the supervision of the information regarding such measures.

Since the year 2003, the Code of Conduct Group is an institutionalized part of EU direct tax policy. Its assessment of national measures has become an ongoing process, the scope of which has been extended considerably upon the accession of new Member States. The group mainly checks that no new harmful tax measures are introduced and that previously rolled-back measures are not reintroduced in any form.[389]

Given the above, the Code of Conduct represents one more element to be considered in the establishment of STZs. In fact, even though it is true that this document is not binding for the Member States - belonging to the genus of soft law - it is clear that the political strength resulting from its approval and implementation

385. For an in-depth analysis of the Code of Conduct, *see also* B.J.M. Terra, P.J. Wattel, *supra.*, 6th Edition, Kluwer Law International, Alphen aan den Rijn, 2012, p. 236; W.W. Bratton, J. Mc Cahery, *supra.*, in *38 Internal market Law Review*, 2001, No. 2, pp. 677-718.

386. P. Boria, *Diritto tributario europeo*, A. Giuffrè (ed.), Milan, 2010, pp. 245 et seq.

387. W. Schon, *supra.*, in *Internal market Law Review*, 1999, Vol. 36, No. 5, pp. 911-936.

388. P. Boria, *supra.*, A. Giuffrè, (ed.) Milan 2010, pp. 247 et seq.

389. B.J.M. Terra, P.J. Wattel, *supra.*, 6th Edition, Kluwer Law International, Alphen aan den Rijn, 2012, pp. 236 et seq.

clearly influences any initiative of a single Member State aimed at introducing territorial tax benefits in the context of an STZ.

Therefore, each STZ should be set in compliance with the prohibitions set by the Code, without any form of tax benefit reserved exclusively for non-residents or for domestic goods, and provided that the same benefits are proportionate, transparent, and only granted to genuine economic activities.

Nevertheless, it is worth to note that there is no scientific consensus on the theoretical definition of harmful tax competition and even the factual evidence is somewhat disputed by both economists and political scientists.[390] This is because the criteria identified by the Code of Conduct Group do not derive from a list on which a representative panel of economists has previously agreed; according to some economists, in fact, it would be nonsense to discriminate between harmful and non-harmful competition[391] and, therefore, the same Code would not seem to score well in terms of transparency and legitimacy.[392]

[2] STZs and Harmful Tax Measures

In the so-called Primarolo report,[393] which is written on the ground of paragraph G of the Code, the Code of Conduct Group identifies sixty-six tax measures considered as harmful, including various examples of territorial tax benefits granted in the territory of STZs.

The first situation considered as harmful in the context of an STZ corresponds to the Captive Insurance regime of Aland Islands where tax benefits are granted to captive insurance companies – even to non-residents – with a reduced CIT rate.[394]

Then, the group identifies as harmful the tax measure applied in the Shannon Airport Zone to income for certified trading operations of companies based therein, both residents and non-residents. In this case, in fact, income from certified operations is taxed at a reduced CIT rate, provided that the companies are engaged in the repair or maintenance of aircraft or in trading operations, including financial service activities able to contribute to the use or development of the airport.[395]

In the case of Trieste Financial Services and Insurance Centre, authorized financial services, subject to a number of conditions and offered to Eastern European countries, benefit from the CIT exemption and from the 50% reduction in local income tax. However, ceilings are put on the total amount of tax concessions and on the total

390. *See, inter alia*, S.J. Basinger, M. Hallerberg, *Remodeling the Competition for Capital: How Domestic Politics Erase the Race to Bottom*, in *American Political Science Review*, 2004, Vol. 98, No. 2, pp. 261-276.
391. C.M. Radaelli, *The Code of Conduct Against Harmful Tax Competition: Open Method of Coordination in Disguise?* in *Public Administration*, 2003, Vol. 81, No. 3, p. 522.
392. *Ibid.*, p. 528.
393. *See* Report from the Code of Conduct Group (Business Taxation) to ECOFIN Council of 23 November 1999, Council of European Union, SN(1999) 4901, Annex A, p. 72, available at: https://ec.europa.eu/taxation_customs/sites/taxation/files/docs/body/primarolo_en.pdf. The measure has been abolished as of 1 January 2003.
394. *Ibid.*
395. *See Ibid.*, p. 162.

amount of investments and loans. The above scheme – considered as harmful according to the Code of Conduct Group – is open to Italian residents and there are limits on the amounts of loans or investments that can be made and on the amount of tax benefits available, as well as control procedures to ensure that funds are invested in Eastern Europe.[396]

Furthermore, tax benefits granted to Madeira and Sta. Maria (Azores) FZs are considered harmful by the Primarolo report since they are available to authorized financial activities carried out principally with non-residents of Portugal. Some of these activities, in fact, are exempted from CIT. Equally, exemption is provided from municipal and local taxes as well as from taxes on income from patents and royalties. Interests on foreign loans and securities are not subject to withholding tax if those loans are used for investments in the same FZs.[397]

One more example of a regime considered as harmful under the work of the Code of Conduct Group is the one related to the Basque Country and Navarra coordination centres, being these entities whose activities consist of management, direction, supervision, and centralization of transactions and services within an international group of companies. At the time of the investigation, the tax rate is lower than the standard CIT in Spain and the tax base is calculated in accordance with two alternative methods to be chosen by the taxpayer; the normal method (accounting profit) or the simplified method (25% of all operating expenses, except financial expenses), provided that at least 25% of the equity is related to shareholders non-resident in Spain.[398]

Then, for what concerns the STZ of Gibraltar, three different measures are considered as potentially harmful. The first measure is the Gibraltar 1992 Companies regime reserved to the companies registered in Gibraltar whose principal object is to hold 5% or more participations in other companies, provided that, in any year of assessment, 51% or more of the company's income derives from investments and no Gibraltar resident owns a beneficial interest in any share of the company. According to such regime, a 1992 company that is a parent company of a subsidiary (minimum share of 25%) is exempt from tax in respect of the income of the subsidiary.[399]

The second harmful measure adopted in Gibraltar is the exempt (Offshore) Companies and Captive Insurance regime according to which benefits are available to companies incorporated in Gibraltar, or to registered branches of non-resident companies in Gibraltar. The main requirements are that no Gibraltar resident must have any beneficial interest in the shares of the company, and that the company must not trade (or carry on a business) with Gibraltarian resident individuals or resident corporate entities. A Gibraltar incorporated company may apply for a tax exempt status; such registration entitles the company and the beneficial owner to exemption from all income tax and estate duty for twenty-five years. Accordingly, no tax is payable on profits, dividends, interests, payable to non-residents of Gibraltar.[400]

396. *See Ibid.*, p. 63.
397. *See Ibid.*, p. 70.
398. *See Ibid.*, p. 34.
399. *See Ibid.*, p. 256.
400. *See Ibid.*, p. 258.

The third and last tax measure in Gibraltar identified as potentially harmful is the Qualifying (offshore) Companies and Captive Insurance regime according to which Qualifying Companies are either companies incorporated in Gibraltar or registered in Gibraltar as branches of foreign companies, provided that they do not trade or carry on business operations in Gibraltar unless income arises from outside Gibraltar and no Gibraltarian or resident of Gibraltar has a beneficial interest in the Qualifying Company. In this case, the tax rate, charged on profits at a rate between 2% and 18%, is determined by the Financial and Development Secretary and is valid for twenty-five years.[401]

In case of Poland, the SEZs regime has been scrutinized and classified as harmful by the Code of Conduct Group, especially for what concerns the possibility of granting export aid in the Mielec SEZ.[402] The consequent amendments adopted by Poland have been considered adequate by the group, even though two enterprises have been allowed to benefit from the export aid for a transitional period granted by the Accession Treaty until 31 December 2011.[403]

In conclusion, all the tax measures above described, since they are considered as harmful according to the principles of the Code of Conduct, have been strongly revised or even gradually dismantled pursuant to the so-called rollback clause, with the aim to avoid any further production of the effects of harmful tax competition.

Nevertheless, such measures still represent an interesting example of the implementation of the criteria set out by the Code, providing a further field of study for the definition of the legal framework of STZs.

[3] Guidance on Tax Privileges Related to SEZs

The Code of Conduct Group has recently issued a specific guidance on tax privileges related to the phenomenon of STZs.[404]

This document, which has been endorsed by the Council (ECOFIN) on 16 June 2017, is literally dedicated to 'SEZs', intended as a special geographic area of a Member State,[405] and it is aimed at counteracting harmful tax competition, with specific reference to the use of territorial tax incentives.

According to the document, business tax privileges available for STZs have to be particularly scrutinized by the Code of Conduct Group when one or more of the following circumstances are met:

401. *See Ibid.*, p. 259.
402. Report from the Code of Conduct Group (Business Taxation) to the ECOFIN Council of 25 May 2010, Council of the European Union, document No. 10033/10, p. 4.
403. *Ibid.*
404. Guidance of the Code of Conduct Group (Business Taxation) on tax privileges related to special economic zones of 19 June 2017, Council of the European Union, Brussels, Document No. 10487/17.
405. The term 'special economic zones' is here used in a very broad and comprehensive way; therefore, the content of this document can assume a general relevance in all the situations included within the general category of Special Tax Zones.

a. access to the zone, either *de jure* or *de facto*, specifically favours foreign investors or discriminates against domestic investors or the tax benefits available to companies operating in the zone specifically favour transactions with non-residents or discriminate against domestic transactions;
b. the regulations for the zone place restrictions on activities that require a substantial economic presence;
c. the regulations do not require a definite *de jure* and *de facto* link between real economic activity carried on within the zone (such as distribution and manufacturing activities and activities that generate employment, assets and investments) and the profits for which the tax privilege is granted;
d. tax privileges are also available for the highly mobile activities (for example, activities typical of the banking or insurance industry, intra-group services or activities consisting only of the holding of equity participations and earning only dividends and capital gains) that are permitted in the zone;
e. there is a lack of regular tax audits verifying that the profits accruing in the zone and allocated to the activities to which tax privileges are available are commensurate with those activities;
f. the terms and conditions for establishing a zone, for being allowed to operate in the zone and for the benefits available for companies operating in a zone are not clearly defined in public legislation or are not limited in time, or permission to establish a zone or to be active in a zone is subject to discretionary powers.[406]

Given the above, according to this document, the main elements which suggest the existence of a harmful tax measure are essentially associated with the presence of tax incentives specifically targeted at non-residents, with the absence of a substantial economic activity within the zone, and with the lack of transparency in the granting of the same measure.

Therefore, as far as at least one of the above conditions is met, the measures adopted in an STZ must be assessed under the principles of the Code of Conduct for business taxation in order to determine whether or not they can finally be considered as harmful.

In any case, this initiative of the Code of Conduct Group represents an important point of reference for the definition of the EU legal framework which is relevant for STZs; the above-mentioned conditions, in fact, contribute to clarify the views of the EU institutions around the phenomenon of STZs in the context of harmful tax competition, with a better definition of the conditions under which the tax measures there granted may be considered as harmful.

§3.05 FINAL REMARKS

The review of the legal sources made in this chapter offers the opportunity to evaluate the current stage of development of the discipline of STZs within the EU law framework.

---

406. Guidance of the Code of Conduct Group (Business Taxation) on tax privileges related to special economic zones of 19 June 2017, Council of the European Union, Brussels, document No. 10487/17, Annex.

As seen, the approach of the EU institutions is based on multiple instruments with the use of hard law and soft law in the context of State aid rules, fundamental freedoms, and harmful tax competition.

In any case, the perspective changes as far as indirect taxation and direct taxation are separately considered for the purposes of STZs.

In the first situation, customs duties, VAT, and excise duties are fully harmonized at the EU level through a set of regulations and directives which replace national legislation; this basically means that the discipline of the tax incentives granted in STZs for the purposes of indirect taxation is already defined at the EU level, while national norms only assume a marginal role which is generally limited to the clarification of some implementing aspects.

Differently, in the case of direct taxation, there is a lack of substantial harmonization, considering that the use of hard law is limited to the regulations dealing with the general block exemption[407] and to the *de minimis* exemption[408] in the context of State aid rules. In this sense, soft law actually represents the preferred option in the field, especially when it is necessary to identify non-binding instruments for the adoption of a common approach to regional aid and the related policies;[409] furthermore, here the ECJ case law becomes an essential point of reference for the interpretation of State aid rules and fundamental freedoms as stated in the TFEU.

Soft law is also the approach used for counteracting harmful tax competition; the Code of Conduct for business taxation, in fact, is a non-binding instrument which exclusively assumes a political value in the relations between the Member States and the EU institutions.

These differences between indirect and direct taxation strongly influence the current framework of STZs: for example, while in the case of customs duties it is possible to identify a harmonized instrument at the EU level for granting tax incentives in the territory of an STZ – namely the FZ intended as a customs procedure under the UCC – on the contrary, in the case of income tax, it is not possible to immediately recognize a uniform EU model applied to the tax incentives granted within such zones.

In conclusion, despite the various instruments used within hard law and soft law, the current stage of development of the discipline of STZs still presents some important limits which contribute to create uncertainty in the EU law framework in a continuous tension between the opposite thrusts of tax harmonization and tax sovereignty; in this

407. Commission Regulation (EU) No. 651/2014 of 17 June 2014 declaring certain categories of aid compatible with the internal market in application of Articles 107 and 108 of the Treaty, O.J. 2014, L 187, pp. 1-78.
408. Commission Regulation (EU) No. 1407/2013 of 18 December 2013 on the application of Articles 107 and 108 of the Treaty on the Functioning of the European Union to *de minimis* aid, O.J. 2013, L 352, pp. 1-8 (replacing Commission Regulation (EC) No. 1998/2006 of 15 December 2006 on the application of Articles 87 and 88 of the Treaty to *de minimis* aid, O.J. 2006, L 379, pp. 5-10).
409. Communication from the Commission – Guidelines on regional State aid for 2014-2020, O.J. 2013, C 209, pp. 1-45.

sense, in fact, the main issues are still today the absence of harmonization in the field of direct taxation and the important differences in the various Member States in the approach to some basic concepts and notions (e.g., SSGIs, social advantages, social enterprises).

CHAPTER 4

STZs in the Member States

§4.01 INTRODUCTION

Beside the literature and the legal framework already examined in the previous chapters, this study must also include the factual experience of STZs in the EU context, with a focus on the different situations where a set of territorial tax advantages is granted to the entities based in a limited area of a Member State.

On these premises, the content of this chapter deals with the experience of each Member State, providing a comprehensive description of the various examples of STZs with a review of the national legislation in force.

The selection of the relevant situations is based on the coordinates defined under the previous chapters; in this sense, the literature on the topic, with the definitions of STZs, and other similar figures, on one part, and the relevant legislation at the EU level, on the other, offer an essential instrument for the identification of each STZ in the factual experience.

For example, the UCC is here used to recognize the FZs in existence in the Member States, assuming that the same areas can be defined under the macro-category of STZs, according to the legal dimension already explored in the context of Chapter 2.

Then, State aid rules represent one more useful tool for the identification of many other STZs in the Member States, not only considering the position of the ECJ in the Azores case, but also in the light of the exemptions for regional aid provided under Article 107(3)(a) and (c) TFEU. In such cases, the attention is focused on tax law provisions able to introduce a special regime within a limited part of the national territory, assuming as the reference framework the standard tax regime applied in the rest of the Member State.

Furthermore, other situations derive from the mere exclusion of an area of a Member State from the territorial scope of one or more taxes already harmonized at the EU level; therefore, in these situations, EU secondary law, as far as it provides the limits of the territorial scope of taxation, becomes the parameter to measure and verify the existence of an STZ in such terms.

In any case, the incentives that are considered for the identification of an STZ are only those provided under tax law provisions, while other types of incentives of a merely economical nature – such as those related to the use of simplified administration procedures[410] – are not considered for the purposes of the present investigation.

Furthermore, the present review exclusively covers the situations where tax incentives concern business taxation, focusing on the tax measures granted in favour of enterprises, namely all the entities engaged in an economic activity, irrespective of their legal form, according to the definition set by Article 1 of Commission Recommendation of 6 May 2003.[411] Accordingly, as far as direct taxation is concerned, STZs generally involve income tax – both in the form of CIT and PIT when related to self-employed activities – dividend withholding tax, capital gains tax, and real estate tax (RET) for the aspects associated to business taxation.[412] Otherwise, under indirect taxation, many examples of STZs mainly include tax incentives for what regards VAT, custom duties, and excise duty.

Various resources are used to support the research process on the ground of the above parameters, such as the list of FZs in existence and in operation in the EU, communicated to the Commission by the customs authorities of the Member States according to Article 243(2) UCC.[413] Among other relevant sources, it is also important to mention the data base of the Export Helpdesk of the EU Commission,[414] the database in the search engine for State aid cases provided by the EU Commission,[415] and the Investment Climate Statement Reports of the Bureau of Economic and Business Affairs of the US Department of State.[416] Furthermore, the legal texts of the relevant national legislation represent one more instrument used to identify the territorial tax incentives in force in each Member State.

The final result of the research confirms the existence of situations corresponding to an STZ within most of the Member States (twenty-one over a total of twenty-eight Member States), with the sole exclusion of Austria,[417] Belgium, Cyprus, Ireland, Netherlands, Slovakia, and Sweden.

410. For instance, Bulgaria industrial zones cannot be considered STZs as they offer modern infrastructures and attractive conditions for establishing production, warehousing, logistics and other activities, without grating any kind of specific tax advantage.
411. Commission Recommendation of 6 May 2003 concerning the definition of micro, small and medium-sized enterprises, O.J. 2003, L 124, pp. 36-41.
412. In Italy, it is possible to identify one more type of direct tax: the Regional Tax on Productive Activities (IRAP).
413. *See supra* note 22.
414. Available at http://exporthelp.europa.eu.
415. Available at http://ec.europa.eu/competition/state_aid/register.
416. Available at https://www.state.gov/e/eb/rls/othr/ics/index.htm.
417. In the case of Austria, the territories of Jungholz and Mittelberg cannot be regarded as STZs, considering that they are excluded from the application of the Austrian VAT but the German VAT is applied therein. Consequently, it is not possible to identify any tax advantage granted to entities based in these zones.

In this context, some Member States have a dedicated legislation on STZs,[418] at least for the aspects of direct taxation not already harmonized at the EU level, while other Member States do not have an organic approach to the phenomenon since the relevant provisions are set within various legal sources of a more general content.[419]

Given the above, the following review is organized in a series of sections dedicated to each single Member State, with the description of the relevant situations corresponding to the basic scheme of an STZ.

Accordingly, the review will include all the relevant situations which can be set under the legal dimension of STZs, including not only the FZs regulated by the UCC, but also 'Free Ports' (Denmark, Luxembourg, Malta, Slovenia), 'ZFUs' (France, Italy), 'Overseas Departments' (France), 'SEZs' (Italy, Latvia), 'Free Economic Zones (FEZs)' (Lithuania), 'Free Customs Duty Areas' (Poland), as well as other single zones characterized by the presence of a specific set of tax advantages (Aland Islands in Finland, Saint-Martin in France, Helgoland and Busingen in Germany, Mount Athos in Greece, Livigno and Campione d'Italia in Italy, Madeira and Azores in Portugal, Canary Islands, Basque Country, Navarra, Ceuta and Melilla in Spain, Gibraltar in the UK).

§4.02 STZs REVIEW

[A] Bulgaria

[1] Bulgarian FZs

FZs in Bulgaria are expressly mentioned in the comprehensive list[420] of the Commission including all the FZs in existence in the customs territory of the Union; they are established under the harmonized rules set at the EU level by the UCC and, for this reason, they assume a specific relevance for the purposes of the present research, being a form of implementation of the EU law framework for STZs, as already reviewed in the context of the previous chapter.

Therefore, such zones consist in a special storage procedure under a suspension arrangement,[421] with tax benefits limited to indirect taxation (i.e., deferral of customs duties, VAT, and excise duty), and are characterized by the presence of a perimeter fence with control at entry and exit points.

For what regards national legislation, an interesting definition of FZs is contained in Decree of 14 July 1987, No. 2242,[422] according to which '*a Free Zone shall be a delimited part of the territory of the People's Republic of Bulgaria, where the pursued economic activities shall be exempted from taxation with custom duties*'.[423]

418. The main examples are Bulgaria, Croatia, Latvia, Lithuania, Malta, Poland, Romania, Slovenia.
419. Such in the case of the following Member States: Czech Republic, Denmark, Estonia, Finland, France, Germany, Greece, Italy, Luxembourg, Portugal, and Spain.
420. *See supra* note 22.
421. According to Article 210 of UCC the storage is a special customs procedure which includes Free Zones.
422. Decree of 14 July 1987, No. 2242, O.J. of Bulgaria No. 55 of 17 July 1987.
423. *Ibid.*, Article 3.

In Bulgaria, there are actually six FZs which are located on strategic transport routes close to the ports of Vidin and Rousse and to the cities of Dragoman, Svilengrad, Plovdiv, and Bourgas.[424]

In line with the provisions of the UCC, the national legislation provides for the suspension of the levy of customs duties for goods introduced in such zones; in this sense, according to Decree of 14 July 1987, No. 2242, '*imported and exported goods services rendered, from and to foreign countries, subject to manufacturing, commercial and other economic activities in the zones, shall be exempted from customs duties*'.[425] The same national norm specifies that such advantage '*shall also apply to exchange of goods and services between Free Zones on the territory of this country*'.[426]

Also the other indirect taxes, namely VAT and excise duty, are applied according to the principles stated, respectively, by the Recast VAT Directive and the Excise Duty Directive.

In particular, the application of VAT[427] is suspended as non-Union goods enter the zone and, until they leave the zone, they remain under the customs regime of a FZ regulated by the UCC. According to the Bulgarian VAT Act,[428] in fact, when the goods are placed in an FZ, the import (i.e., the chargeable event) is considered as implemented only when the goods are no longer under the FZ procedure on the territory of the State.

In the same way, excise duty is not applied in case of transaction of goods in a FZ pursuant to the Excises and Tax Warehouses Act according to which the goods are subject to excise duty '*at the time of their import in the territory of the country*'.[429]

---

424. *See* US Department of State, Bureau of Economic and Business Affairs, *2014 Investment Climate Statement*, June 2014, available at www.state.gov.
425. Article 13(2) Decree of 14 July 1987, No. 2242, O.J. of Bulgaria No. 55 of 17 July 1987.
426. Furthermore, Article 166 of the Bulgarian Customs Act of 1998 (O.J. of Bulgaria No. 15 of 6 February 1998) confirms the exemption from custom duties, stating that '*for the purpose of import customs duties and trade policy importation measures foreign goods are considered as being outside the customs territory of the Republic of Bulgaria provided they have not been placed under import regime or another customs regime and have not been used or consumed in contravention to the customs regulations*'. On these premises, the exemption from customs duties is granted by national law in compliance with Article 237 UCC according to which non-Union goods placed under a storage procedure – as a Free Zone – are not subject to import duties or other charges.
427. The Bulgarian standard VAT rate is 20%.
428. O.J. of Bulgaria No. 63 of 4 August 2006, effective as from the date of entry into force of the Treaty concerning the Accession of the Republic of Bulgaria to the European Union (1 January 2007).
429. *See* Article 19 Law on Excises and Tax Warehouses Act, O.J. of Bulgaria No. 91 of 15 November 2005.

[B] Croatia

[1] Croatian FZs

In Croatia there are eleven operating FZs ranging from sea port-based zones located at Pula, Rijeka, Split, Ploče, and in the Splitsko-dalmatinska area, to other strategically located zones in Krapina, Kukuljanovo, Osijek, Vukovar, Skrljevo, and Zagreb.[430]

Croatian FZs are all mentioned in the list of FZs in operation in the customs territory of the Union[431] and they essentially consist in a special storage procedure with a fully harmonized discipline under the provisions of the UCC – as already reviewed in Chapter 3 – and tax benefits limited to indirect taxation (i.e., deferral of customs duties, VAT, and excise duty).

Nonetheless, it is possible to identify some national norms which expressly deal with the phenomenon of FZs.

In this regard, according to national legislation, FZs[432] are defined as a *'part of the territory of the Republic of Croatia, enclosed and marked, in which the economic activities are carried out according to some specific conditions'*.[433] Furthermore, Article 172 of the Croatian Customs Law[434] identifies these zones as *'a part of the customs territory that is separated from the rest of the customs territory, where: a) foreign goods are not considered to be within the customs territory of the Republic of Croatia for the purpose of paying the import duty and commercial policy import measures, on condition that the goods are not released for free circulation or placed under some other customs procedure or use, or that they are not consumed or used otherwise than provided for in the conditions regulated by the customs rules, and b) on the Croatian goods intended for export, that are regulated by special rules based on their placing in a free zone or free warehouse, are to be applied measures which would have been applied when exporting those goods'*.

More provisions in the national legislation are then aimed at implementing the harmonized EU discipline for indirect taxes; first, entities based in Croatian FZs join the suspension of the levy of custom duties according to Article 27(a) of the Act on FZs; second, according to Article 37(b) of the Act on FZs, the supply of goods to a FZ and the supply of goods within a FZ are exempt from VAT until the same goods are not imported into the national territory; third, goods introduced in Croatian FZs are exempt

430. For further information on Croatian STZs *see* D. Borozan, *Free zone – the Source of Socio-Economic Benefit*, in *Interdisciplinary Management Research Journal*, Osijek, 2007, Vol. 3, pp. 75-91; I. Kireta, *Tax Incentive Regimes in Croatia, Macedonia (FYR) and Serbia – Should They Compete?*, in *European Taxation*, 2013, pp. 215 et seq.

431. *See supra* note 22.

432. In some cases, the Croatian legislator also uses the term 'Free Trade Zone'.

433. Article 2 of the Croatian Act on Free Zones, O.J. of Croatia Nos 44/96, 92/05, 85/08, 148/13.

434. O.J. of Croatia Nos 78/99, 94/99, 117/99, 73/00, 92/01.

from excise duties under a suspension arrangement pursuant to Article 6, paragraph 2 of the Excise Duties Act.[435]

[C] Czech Republic

[1] Czech FZs

In the Czech Republic there are currently seven FZs in the following areas: Kralove, Mosnov, Pardubice, Praha 1 (Graddo), Praha 4 (Spedquick), Praha 10 (Esces Spol.), Veverskè Kninice (B.F.C.W. Logistic).

Also in the case of the Czech Republic, FZs assume relevance for the purposes of this study since they are established under the harmonized rules of the UCC and, thus, under the same EU legal framework of STZs; they are included in the list of FZs in operation in the customs territory of the Union as communicated by the Member States to the Commission;[436] they are enclosed areas with entry and exit points subject to customs supervision where a special procedure of storage applies with tax benefits limited to indirect taxation (i.e., deferral of customs duties, VAT, and excise duty).

Within national legislation it is possible to identify some provisions which merely implement the EU harmonized rules concerning the application of VAT in an FZ; in particular, according to Act No. 235/2004,[437] when non-Union goods are stored into such zones, VAT is suspended until the goods are imported into the EU (where they become 'Union goods') or consumed within the zone,[438] while Union goods introduced into the FZ territory are considered as already exported outside the EU.[439]

Similar rules are provided for what regards excise duty; according to Act No. 353/2003,[440] in fact, when non-Union goods are imported into Czech STZs from outside the EU territory, excise duties are suspended until the goods are exported out of the zone into the EU (where they become 'Union goods') or are consumed within the zone.

[D] Denmark

[1] Copenhagen Free Port

Denmark has one FZ corresponding to the Copenhagen Free Port, whose tax regime is defined under the harmonized EU framework.

The Copenhagen Freeport regime, in fact, is set according to the FZ regime provided under Article 237 of the UCC, consisting of a special procedure of storage with

---

435. O.J. of Croatia No. 83/09. Pursuant to Article 6, paragraph 2 of the Excise Duties Act '*the payment of excise duty shall be suspended in respect of the excise products which been placed, immediately after their import, under a custom suspension procedure or brought into a free zones or a free warehouse*'.
436. *See supra* note 22.
437. VAT Act No. 235/2004, available at https://www.mzv.cz/jnp/.
438. *Ibid.*, Article 12.
439. *Ibid.*, Article 66.
440. Excise Tax Act No. 353/2003, available at https://www.mzv.cz/jnp/.

benefits limited to indirect taxation (i.e., deferral of customs duties and other charges, such as VAT and excise duty).

As all the other FZs which are relevant for the present review, the Copenhagen Free Port is mentioned in the list of FZs in operation in the customs territory of the Union.[441]

The same area, which is totally enclosed with customs control at entry and exit points, is actually managed by the Port Authority represented by the Copenhagen Malmo Port AB (CMP). In this regard, manufacturing operations can be established in the Freeport area provided that a special permission is granted by customs authorities.[442]

[E] Estonia

[1] Estonian FZs

FZs in Estonia are established in the ports of Paldiski, Muuga, and Sillamae and are all regulated under the harmonized framework of the UCC, with benefits limited to indirect taxation (deferral of customs duties and other charges, such as VAT and excise duty).

Paldiski Port and Muuga Port are both located in Northern Estonia, while Sillamae Port is located in the Eastern part of Estonia, being thus the closest EU port to Russia.[443]

These FZs are totally enclosed areas with entry and exit points under the customs supervision and are all mentioned in the list of FZs as communicated by the Member States to the Commission.[444]

Also in this case, there are some national provisions which implement the set of rules already harmonized at the EU level under the common framework described within Chapter 3. In this sense, the deferral of customs duties is provided under Article 54 of the Estonian Customs Act in compliance with the rules set out by Article 237 of the UCC.

Then, Article 15(3) of the Estonian VAT Act[445] states that VAT is not charged when non-Union goods are placed in an FZ and such goods have not been consumed or used under conditions other than those prescribed by the customs rules. The same benefit is applied to Union goods transferred and placed in a FZ for export purposes.

Furthermore, Estonian FZs benefit from the suspension of the levy of excise duties according to the provisions set out by the Estonian Alcohol, Tobacco, Fuel and

441. *See supra* note 22.
442. *See* US Department of State, Bureau of Economic and Business Affairs, *2013 Investment Climate Statement – Denmark*, April 2013, Report, available at http://www.state.gov/e/eb/rls/othr/ics/2013/204630.htm.
443. For further information on Estonian Free Zones *see* O. Pavuk, T. Narushevich, G. Pilaitis, T. Merkulova, *Free Zones on the Fence*, in *The Baltic Course*, No. 2(5) 2002.
444. *See supra* note 22.
445. O.J. of Estonia, I, 2003, 82, 554.

Electricity Excise Duty Act[446] in line with the content of the Excise Duty Directive. In detail, in fact, Article 24 of the mentioned act establishes that the tax liability arises only upon release for consumption of excise goods or '*bringing them into Estonia from another Member State outside an excise suspension arrangement*'.[447]

[F] Finland

[1] Finnish FZs

Finland has two FZs, the Hanko Free Port and the Oulu Free Port, whose operations are subject to the supervision of the National Board of Customs.

The Finnish Customs Act of 2004[448] outlines the essential elements of FZs according to the fundamentals of the UCC specifying that the National Board of Customs of the Ministry of Finance may grant permission to establish such zones.[449]

These FZs, whose benefits are limited to indirect taxation (i.e., deferral of customs duties and other charges, such as VAT and excise duty), have a perimeter fence with entry and exit points under the customs supervision and are mentioned in the list of FZs in operation in the Union, as communicated by the Member States to the Commission.[450]

Beside the deferral of custom duties provided by Article 237 UCC, it is possible to identify some national provisions implementing the EU Directives on VAT and excise duties.

In the case of VAT, under Article 72(3) of the Finnish VAT Act,[451] tax is neither payable on sales of goods, which are transferred to an FZ or already situated in an FZ, nor on sales of services performed therein. This is in line with the provision set out by Article 156 of the Council Directive 2006/112/EC according to which Member States are able to exempt, among the others, the supply of goods that are intended to be placed in an FZ.

Then, for what regards excise duties, the regime set out by the Finnish Act on Excise Duty[452] provides for the exemption from excise duty of the goods introduced in the perimeter of FZs until such goods are realized for consumption or moved outside the zone and imported into the EU.

446. O.J. of Estonia, I, 2003, 2, 17.
447. *Ibid.*, Article 24.
448. Customs Act No. 1466 of 29 December 1994, available at http://www.wipo.int/wipolex/en/details.jsp?id=1499.
449. *Ibid.*, Section 8.
450. *See supra* note 22.
451. Valued Added Tax Act No. 1501 of 30 December 1993, available at https://www.finlex.fi/.
452. *See* Article 17 of the Act on Excise Duty No. 182/2010 of 19 March 2010, available at https://www.alko.fi/.

[2] Aland Islands

The territory of the Aland Islands is excluded from EU rules on VAT and excise duties pursuant to Article 2(a) of the Protocol No. 2 of the Treaty for the Accession of Finland in the EU;[453] as a result of this regulatory framework, this territory falls outside the EU fiscal area of VAT and excise duties, while, at the same time, it is part of the EU Customs Union.

The exclusion from the territorial scope of the EU VAT system and excise duty system is then confirmed respectively by Article 6 of the Recast VAT Directive and by Article 5 of the Excise Duty Directive.

In this case, the tax benefits applied within the Aland Islands are wider in their scope than the corresponding advantages granted to the FZs regulated by the UCC; while in the latter case, there is a mere suspension of the levy of VAT and excise duty under a customs suspension arrangement, otherwise, in the former case, the tax advantage is the result of a territorial exclusion and, thus, it is granted for any relevant operation, including the release for consumption.

Apart from the above benefits on indirect taxation (in this case limited to VAT and excise duty), it is important to observe that the taxation system of this zone – falling within the competence of Finland[454] – is characterized by a certain level of fiscal autonomy under Finnish constitutional law mainly based on the Act on the Autonomy of Aland.[455] According to these norms, in fact, '*Aland Islands shall have legislative powers in respect of* [...] *the additional tax on income for Aland and the provisional extra income tax, as well as the trade and amusement taxes, the bases of the dues levied for Aland and the municipal tax*'.[456] Nevertheless, the autonomy of the Aland Islands does not only rely on its own resources, but also comes from the central government through the use of State funds whose amount is calculated on the basis of the 'equalization' principle.[457]

In summary, the Aland Islands are a relevant situation for the scope the present review in the light of their exclusion from the territorial scope of indirect taxes harmonized at the EU level; in this regard, the provisions of the Recast VAT Directive and of the Excise Duty Directive, as far as they set the territorial limit of their application, become the parameter used to qualify the Aland Islands as an STZ in the context of the present research.

453. Act concerning the conditions of accession of the Kingdom of Norway, the Republic of Austria, the Republic of Finland and the Kingdom of Sweden and the adjustments to the treaties on which the European Union is founded, O.J. 1994, C 241, pp. 9-404.
454. F. Murray, *The European Union and Member State Territories: A New Legal Framework under the EU Treaties*, Springer, The Hague, 2012, pp. 131 et seq.
455. Act of 16 August 1991, No. 1144, available at http://www.finlex.fi/fi/laki/kaannokset/19-91/en19911144.pdf.
456. *Ibid.*, Section 18.
457. *Ibid.*, Section 46.

[G] France

[1] French FZs

The list of FZs published by the Commission[458] includes two FZs based in the French territory: the FZ of Le Verdon at the Port of Bordeaux and the FZ of French Guyana.

The FZ of Le Verdon, managed by the Port of Bordeaux Authority, is based in a strategic area for agricultural and industrial trade in southwest France; otherwise, the FZ of French Guyana is based in a strategical position in South America and is managed by the local chamber of commerce and industry.

French FZs, which are also defined under Article 286 of the French Customs Code,[459] are set in accordance with the harmonized framework of the UCC, with benefits which are limited to indirect taxation (i.e., deferral of customs duties and other charges, such as VAT and excise duty).

Apart from the deferral of customs duties provided under Article 237 UCC, as far as the focus is set on the national legislation, it is possible to identify some norms regarding VAT and excise duty which implement the legislation adopted at the EU level (i.e., Recast VAT Directive and Excise Duty Directive); for example, according to Article 277A of the French Tax Code,[460] VAT is not charged within the perimeter of a FZ until goods introduced therein are released for consumption;[461] the same deferral is provided for excise duty under Article 302G of the French Tax Code.[462]

However, it is worth noting that the entire territory of French Guyana is already excluded from the application of VAT according to the territorial limitation of the scope of the VAT directive.

---

458. *See supra* note 22.
459. *See* Article 286 of the French Customs Code (*Code des douanes*) according to which '*on entend par zone franche toute enclave territoriale instituée en vue de faire considérer les marchandises qui s'y trouvent comme n'étant pas sur le territoire douanier pour l'application des droits de douane et des taxes dont elles sont passibles à raison de l'importation, ainsi que des restrictions quantitatives*'.
460. *See* Article 277A *Code General des Impotes* according to which '*Sont effectuées en suspension du paiement de la taxe sur la valeur ajoutée les opérations ci-après:[...] Les livraisons de biens destinés à être placés sous l'un des régimes suivants: Le régime fiscal suspensif*' (e.g., Free Zone).
461. *See* Article 291 *Code General des Impotes*: '*Les importations de biens sont soumises à la taxe sur la valeur ajoutée [...] Est considérée comme importation d'un bien: [...] b. la mise à la consommation en France d'un bien placé, lors de son entrée sur le territoire sous l'un des régimes suivants prévus par les règlements communautaires en vigueur: conduite en douane, magasins et aires de dépôt temporaire, zone franche, entrepôt franc, entrepôt d'importation, perfectionnement actif, admission temporaire en exonération totale des droits à l'importation, transit externe ou sous le régime du transit communautaire interne*'.
462. *See* Article 302G *Code général des impôts*: '*Sont également considérés comme se trouvant en régime suspensif des droits d'accises, les alcools, les boissons alcooliques et les tabacs manufacturés placés ou destinés à être placés sous l'un des régimes suivants prévus par les règlements communautaires en vigueur: magasins et aires de dépôt temporaire, entrepôt d'importation, zone franche, entrepôt franc, perfectionnement actif, admission*'.

[2] Urban Tax-Free Zones

ZFUs[463] have been introduced in France by the Law of 14 November 1996, No. 96-987,[464] with the aim to develop economic activities and to create social integration and employment for local residents.

The Commission has authorized the French ZFUs,[465] considering the same tax scheme as an exemption to State aid rules under Article 107(3)(c) TFEU, referring to the category of aid to facilitate the development of certain economic activities or of certain economic areas.

In particular, the Commission, in its authorizing communication, has considered the tax measures at issue as necessary and proportionate with respect to the objective pursued (social and economic cohesion) and, therefore, compatible with the internal market.[466]

Nowadays, more than one hundred of ZFUs are based in various part of the French territory,[467] all characterized by the fact that the tax advantages granted only concern direct taxes and are finalized to contribute to objectives of social policy.

According to the Law of 14 November 1996, No. 96-987, enterprises established in the ZFU territory and meeting a certain number of criteria enjoy the exemption from income tax due on profits derived from activities in the ZFU, limited to EUR 50,000 per taxpayer per twelve-month period. The ceiling is increased by EUR 5,000 per every new employee hired as of 1 January 2006 resident in a ZFU and employed full-time for a period of at least six months. The exemption is for the total amount during the first five years, while there is a partial and digressive exemption during the next three years.[468]

Some conditions must be respected in order to benefit from the ZFU regime; enterprises, in fact, must have no more than 50 employees and must realize a turnover or total assets of less than EUR 10 million, while the capital or voting rights must not be held directly or indirectly (25% or more) by companies whose workforce exceeds 250 employees and whose annual turnover before tax exceeds EUR 50 million or whose total annual balance sheet exceeds EUR 43 million.[469]

---

463. In 2014 the French Parliament (*Assemblee Nationale*) has adopted an amendment modifying the denomination of '*Zones Franches Urbaines*', adding the term '*territoires entrepreneurs*' (*see* Amending Finance Law of 29 December 2014, No. 1655, O.J. of France of 30 December 2014, Article 48).
464. *Loi No. 96-987 du 14 novembre 1996 relative à la mise en oeuvre du pacte de relance pour la ville*, available at https://www.legifrance.gouv.fr/affichTexte.do?cidTexte=JORFTE-XT000000196 404.
465. *See* Communication from the Commission of 22 June 2006 (State aid No. 70/A/2006), COM (2006) No. 2329 final, O.J. 2006, C 242, pp. 18.
466. *Ibid.*, paragraph 3.4.
467. The complete list of French ZFUs is available at http://sig.ville.gouv.fr/atlas/ZFU/.
468. In this case 60% exemption for the sixth year, 40% exemption for the seventh year, and 20% exemption for the eighth year.
469. In non-fixed activities (e.g., building trades, street trading, taxis), the enterprise benefits from the tax exemption since it has an effective implementation in the area (e.g., office or workshop) and one of the following conditions is met: (i) it employs at least one full-time employee sedentary who operates in areas assigned to the activity: (ii) it achieves at least 25% of its revenue from customers located in the ZFU territory.

The exemption is not applicable to entities that are active in the areas of automotive, shipbuilding, manufacture of handmade textile fibres, steel or road transport of goods and furniture leasing, leasing of non-commercial buildings, agriculture, and construction-sale.

According to the Law of 29 December 2014, No. 1655,[470] the ZFU regime with its tax benefits is extended until 31 December 2020, but the enterprises established from 1 January 2015 onwards, must comply with the following further conditions. First, the number of employees living in a ZFU territory with a permanent employment contract or with a contract of at least twelve months must be equal to at least half of the total employees. Second, the number of employees hired after the fulfilment of the same conditions of contract and residence must be at least half of all employees hired during the same period.

Given the above, ZFUs in France represent relevant examples of STZs in the context of the present research; the set of tax advantages provided under their regime, in fact, is granted according to the EU law framework of STZs and, in particular, according to an exemption to the general State aid prohibition which is stated by Article 107(3)(c).

[3] French Overseas Departments: DOM

The French Overseas Departments – *Département et région d'Outre-Mer* (DOM), which include the territories of Guadaloupe, French Guyana, Martinique, Reunion, and Mayotte, can be considered as STZs in the light of a complex set of tax advantages granted according to the EU law framework described in the previous Chapter 3; in this sense, in fact, the related tax advantages derive not only from the exclusion of such zones from the territorial scope of EU directives on VAT and excise duty, but also from the introduction of a favouring tax regime on direct taxation under State aid rules.

The Commission, in fact, has authorized the tax schemes there granted through a series of communications issued in the context of State aid rules; in a first time, the Commission states that such measures are compatible with the internal market in the light of Article 107(3)(a), considering that French Overseas Departments are defined as ORs in the terms set by Article 349 TFEU;[471] then, more recently, the authorization is otherwise granted according to the exemption set under Article 107(3)(c) TFEU with a final evaluation from the Commission essentially based on the proportionality and the transparency of the aid.[472]

470. Amending Finance Law of 29 December 2014, No. 1655, O.J. of France of 30 December 2014, Article 48. For further information about ZFUs *see* C. Bucicco, *Il fondamento giuridico delle zone franche urbane e l'equivoco con le zone franche di diritto doganale*, in *Diritto e Pratica Tributaria*, 2008, I, pp. 105 et seq.

471. *See, inter alia*, Communication from the Commission of 23 October 2007 (State aid No. 21502), COM (2007) No. 5115, O.J. 2008, C 14, p. 10.

472. *See* Communication from the Commission of 15 May 2019 (State aid No. 50299), COM (2019) No. 3592 final, O.J. 2019, C 221, pp. 1-5; Communication from the Commission of 19 July 2018

On these bases, the French government has introduced a set of tax advantages in the French Overseas Departments in order to encourage investments therein and to support their industrial and economic development.

According to Girardin Law,[473] individuals investing in a new building enjoy a full deduction from their taxable income of the total amount paid in the year of acquisition – taxes and fees excluded – provided that the building acquired has to be rented for six years as a principal residence; if the total amount exceeds the net taxable income of the year of acquisition, the surplus can be carried forward to the following taxable income. Girardin Law also permits the deduction of rental charges and loan interests.

Furthermore, taxpayers domiciled in DOM territories benefit from a tax credit on income tax to be paid as specified in Article 197 of the French Tax Code. The amount of the tax credit granted starts from 30% (Guadaloupe, Martinique and Reunion, with a maximum of EUR 5,100 of tax credit) to 40% of the total amount due (Guyana and Mayotte, with a maximum of EUR 6,700 of tax credit).

The benefit is applied for taxpayers domiciled in a DOM territory on the 31 December of the tax year and is calculated on the tax due on the income earned through the same year.

As far as indirect taxation is concerned, French overseas departments are excluded from the territorial scope of the Recast VAT Directive and, therefore, from the application of the common EU VAT system. Nevertheless, some DOM territories enjoy a special VAT system that sensibly differs from the common EU VAT system; for example, according to Article 296 of the French Tax Code, in Guadaloupe, Martinique, and Reunion the standard VAT rate for importing items is 8.5%, with certain products eligible at a reduced VAT rate of 2.1%.

French overseas departments are also excluded from the territorial scope of Directive 2008/118/EC concerning the general arrangements for excise duty;[474] therefore, instead of the common EU excise system, these territories have their own excise system, with a sea excise (*Octroi de Mer* – OM) and a regional sea excise (*Octroi de Mer Regional* – OMR) charged on various goods at different rates.[475]

[4] Saint-Martin

Saint-Martin in the Caribbean Sea is an OR of the French Overseas Collectivities – *Collectivité d'Outre-Mer* (COM) characterized by a composite framework of territorial tax benefits

(State aid No. 50370), COM (2018) No. 4545 final, O.J. 2018, C 317, pp. 1-10; Communication from the Commission of 10 December 2014 (State aid No. 38566), COM (2014) No. 9316 final, O.J. 2015, C 44, pp. 1-12.

473. Law of 21 July 2003, No. 2003-660, amending Article 199-*undecies* of the French Tax Code, available at https://www.legifrance.gouv.fr/affichTexte.do?cidTexte=JORFTEXT000-000605 656.

474. *See* Article 5(2) of Council Directive 2008/118/EC of 16 December 2008.

475. *See* Article 37 of Law of 2 July 2004, No. 2004-639, available at https://www.legifrance-.gouv .fr/affichTexte.Do?cidTexte=JORFTEXT000000253374&cateo-rieLien=id.

According to the Commission,[476] the tax advantages on direct taxation which are available in Saint-Martin do not constitute State aid, considering that such zone enjoys sufficient institutional, procedural, and economic autonomy to determine its own tax system in line with the position held by the ECJ from the Azores case onwards.[477]

On these premises, Saint-Martin assumes a relevance in the context of this review, representing an important example of STZs where a substate body establishes a favouring tax regime with respect to the standard one applied in the mainland France.

In details, business entities based in Saint-Martin join reduced CIT rates; for example, while in case of large companies a standard rate of 20% is applied, small and medium businesses (SMEs) benefit from a reduced corporate tax rate of 10% up to EUR 40,000 of profits;[478] furthermore, gains derived from certain intangible fees (sale, concession, sub-concession) or from financial securities giving access to capital enjoy a tax rate of 10%.[479]

Then, under the provisions of Girardin Law,[480] entities investing in a new building join a full deduction from their taxable income of the total amount paid in the year of acquisition – taxes and fees excluded – at the same conditions already seen for the French Overseas Departments (DOM).

For what concerns indirect taxation, the *Collectivité of Saint-Martin*, although formally part of the customs territory of the EU, has a special 'Free Port' status granted in 1939; accordingly, goods imported into the territory are not subject to customs duties or import tariffs, with the sole exception of a special import tariff on gasoline applied according to local laws.

Furthermore, Saint-Martin is excluded from the territorial scope of Directive 2006/112/EC; thus, instead of VAT, a general tax on turnover is applied in the island with a rate of 4%.[481]

The territory of Saint-Martin is also excluded from the territorial scope of the EU Excise Directive and, therefore, from the common EU excise duty system.

[H] Germany

[1] German FZs

In Germany there are currently two FZs (Freeport of Cuxhaven and Freeport Bremerhaven) which are set as a special procedure of storage under the provisions of the UCC.

476. Communication from the Commission of 3 June 2009 (State aid No. 326/08 *Réduction des taux d'imposition à Saint-Martin*), COM (2009) No. 4026 final, O.J. 2009, C 264, p. 3.
477. Case C-88/03 *Portugal v Commission*, [2006] ECR I-7115.
478. *See* Article 219 of *Code General des Impots de la Collectivite de Saint-Martin*, available at http://www.com-saint-martin.fr/ressources/CGI_SM-1er-janvier-2016-v.1.1.pdf.
479. *Ibid.*, Article 200A(2).
480. The Commission has approved the related tax scheme in 2010 as an aid compatible with the internal market pursuant to Article 107(3)(a) TFEU. *See* Communication from the Commission of 29 September 2010 (State aid No. 325/08 *Aide fiscale à l'investissement à Saint-Martin*), COM (2010) No. 6471 final, O.J. 2011, C 181, p. 31.
481. *See* Article 259 *Code General des Impots de la Collectivite de Saint-Martin.*

Such zones, both mentioned in the list of FZs periodically updated by the Commission,[482] have a perimeter fence with entry and exit points under the customs supervision and provide a set of tax benefits limited to indirect taxation according to the harmonized EU law framework described in Chapter 3 (i.e., deferral of customs duties and other charges, such as VAT and excise duty).

The deferral of customs duties is granted according to Article 237 of the UCC, while, for excise duty, the same deferral is provided under the relevant national legislation[483] in line with Article 7 of the Directive 2008/118/EC.

Then, Article 5 of the Turnover Tax Act (UStG)[484] provides that VAT is not charged where non-Union goods are introduced in German FZs until the same goods are not moved outside the zone and imported in the EU territory.

[2] Helgoland and Busingen

The island of Helgoland and the zone of Busingen enjoy a tax-exempt status, as they are part of the political territory of Germany and the EU, but at the same time excluded from the common VAT area,[485] from the common excise duty area[486] and from the Customs Union.[487]

Therefore, customs duties, VAT, and excise duties are not applied within these STZs, considering their exclusion from the territorial scope of the relevant EU legislation.

On these bases, it is interesting to observe that the tax-exempt status of these territories is very different from the situation of the FZs regulated under the UCC; while in the latter case, in fact, there is a mere deferral of indirect taxes until the goods are moved out of the zone and imported into the EU or realized for consumption, otherwise, in the case of Helgoland and Busingen, the exclusion from the territorial scope of the EU legislation produces definitive effects covering not only the import/export operations, but also the release for consumption.

In summary, Helgoland and Busingen can be qualified as STZs because their territories are excluded from the scope of the EU legislation on indirect taxation, with the establishment of an exceptional situation in comparison to the standard tax regime applied in the rest of Germany for customs duties, VAT, and excise duties.

---

482. *See supra* note 22.
483. For instance, *see* Article 19 of Tobacco Tax Law (TabStG) of 15 July 2009, O.J. of Germany, I S. 1870.
484. Value Added Tax Act (UStG) of 26 November 1979, available at http://www.gesetze-im-internet.de/ustg_1980/BJNR119530979.html.
485. Article 6(2) of the Council Directive 2006/112/EC of 28 November 2006 on the common system of value added tax, O.J. 2006, L 347, pp. 1-118.
486. Article 5(3) of the Council Directive 2008/118/EC of 16 December 2008 concerning the general arrangements for excise duty and repealing Directive 92/12/EEC, O.J. 2009, L 9, pp. 12-30.
487. Article 4(1) UCC.

[I] Greece

[1] Greek FZs

In Greece, there are four FZs located in the port areas of Piraeus, Thessaloniki, Heraklion, and Astakos (Platigiali), which are all set as a special procedure of storage under the harmonized framework of the UCC with benefits limited to indirect taxation.

These zones are mentioned in the list of FZs in operation in the customs territory of the Union, as communicated by the Member States to the Commission;[488] they have a perimeter fence with entry and exit points under the supervision of customs authorities.

Within the national legislation, FZs are identified – in accordance with the provisions of the UCC – as parts of the territory where non-Union goods are considered, for the application of import duties, taxes, and other commercial policy measures, as not being within the customs territory, while Union goods introduced therein are considered as already exported outside the EU.[489]

Accordingly, national provisions provide that VAT and excise duty are not charged on non-Union goods imported into an FZ until the goods are transferred out of the zone into the EU (where they become 'Union goods') or consumed within the zone.[490]

[2] Mount Athos

The territory of Mount Athos is excluded from the VAT area according to Article 6 of Directive 2006/112/EC and, therefore, constitutes an STZ with respect to the rest of Greece where VAT is fully applied according to a set of rules harmonized at the EU level.

The exclusion, which is provided on the basis of the specific status of Mount Athos granted by Article 105 of the Greek Constitution, is definitive and general, producing effects which are relevant for all the types of operations, including the release for consumption.

[J] Hungary

[1] Hungarian FZs

In Hungary there is only one FZ in the area of Záhony which is included in the updated version of the list of FZs provided by the Commission.[491]

488. *See supra* note 22.
489. *See* Article 39(1) of the Greek Customs Code (Law No. 2960 of 22 November 2001, O.J. of Greece No. 265/A/2001).
490. *See* Article 25 of the Greek VAT Code (Law No. 2859/2000, O.J. of Greece No. 248/A/2000).
491. *See supra* note 22.

This area, established in 2017, is regulated by the same harmonized rules of the UCC as a special procedure of storage with a perimeter fence under the control of customs authorities.

The set of benefits available is the same as provided for all the FZs under the UCC, with the deferral of customs duties, VAT, and excise duties until the goods are moved out of the zone and imported into the EU or realized for consumption.

In the context of national legislation, the deferral of VAT is confirmed under the Act on VAT of 2007 where it is expressly stated that '*exemption shall be granted for the supply of goods and the intra-Community acquisition of goods which are intended to be placed in a free zone or in a free warehouse*'.[492]

[K] Italy

[1] Italian FZs

The Italian peninsula is characterized by the presence of two FZs in operation based in the Port of Trieste and in Venice.[493]

The Port of Trieste represents the first FZ established in the Italian territory, considering that it has always enjoyed special tax incentives aimed at the implementation of international trade in a strategic geographical area.

After the Second World War, the area is 'internationalized' by the Peace Treaty of 10 February 1947.[494] The London Memorandum of 1954 establishes the maintenance of the 'Free Port of Trieste' in general accordance with the provisions of the Peace Treaty, while Decree of 19 January 1955, No. 29,[495] and Decree of 21 December 1959, No. 53,[496] contain special rules implementing the international obligation.

The FZ of Venice is first established by Law Decree of 5 January 1948, No. 268,[497] amended by Law of 12 February 1955, No. 41.[498] Later on, Article 5 of Law of 9 January 1991, No. 19,[499] authorizes the transfer of the FZ of Venice in the area of the commercial port of Marghera.

---

492. *See* Section 111 of Act CXXVII of 2007 on Value Added Tax, available at http://www.icnl.org/research/library/files/Hungary/vatact_ENG.pdf.
493. It is wort to note that, before the entry in force of the new provisions of the UCC – with the abolition of Control Type II Free Zones as of 1 May 2016 – there were also two Control Type II FZs in the South of Italy based in Taranto and in Gioia Tauro. Today, such zones are not mentioned anymore in the updated version of the list of existing free zones published by the Commission (last update of 21 August 2019).
494. With reference to the same Peace Treaty (published in United Nations – Treaty Series, 1950, Vol. 49, No. 747), *see* in particular Articles 1-20 of Annex VIII 'Instrument relating to the Free Port of Trieste' and Articles 34 and 35 of Annex VI 'Permanent Statute of the Free Territory of Trieste'. *See also* London Memorandum of 5 October 1954 published in United Nations -Treaty Series, 1956, No. 3297.
495. *Decreto del Commissario Generale del Governo italiano per il territorio di Trieste* of 19 January 1955, No. 29, O.J. of Italy No. 3 of 21 January 1955.
496. *Decreto del Commissario Generale del Governo italiano per il territorio di Trieste* of 21 December 1959, No. 53, O.J. No. 36 of 21 December 1959.
497. O.J. of Italy No. 91 of 17 April 1948.
498. O.J. of Italy No. 51 of 3 March 1955.
499. O.J. of Italy No. 17 of 21 January 1991.

Nowadays, these zones are set under the harmonized EU framework for indirect taxation, as they both consist in a special procedure of storage regulated by the UCC with benefits limited to customs duties, VAT, and excise duties.

The deferral of customs duties is provided pursuant to Article 237 UCC; accordingly, customs duties are not charged on non-Union goods placed in these zones until the same goods are moved out of the zones and imported into the EU or released for consumption.

For what regards VAT and excise duty, the same deferral is established respectively by the Italian VAT Act[500] and by Law Decree of 26 October 1995, No. 504,[501] which represent implementing provisions of the Recast VAT Directive and the Excise Duty Directive.

[2] Urban Tax-Free Zones

The Italian ZFUs are minimal areas of municipal territories where tax relief programmes on direct taxation are set for the creation of small and microenterprises.[502] The main objective is the promotion of the economic and social development of urban areas characterized by a high level of unemployment.

As in the case of France, the Commission has authorized, under the provisions of the TFEU, the creation of the Italian ZFUs, considering them as a form of aid to facilitate the development of certain economic activities or of certain economic areas pursuant to the exception to the State aid prohibition provided by Article 107(3)(c) TFEU.[503]

On these premises, the first ZFU has been established in 2012 in the municipality of the city of L'Aquila after the earthquake of April 2009 and includes the areas affected by the natural disaster with a set of territorial tax advantages in favour of small and microenterprises for supporting the development of the local economy.[504]

More ZFUs have been established in the same year within the macro areas covered by the regional policies of the EU (Campania, Calabria, Sicily, and Puglia) and within the island of Sardinia in the municipalities of the province of Carbonia – Iglesias.[505]

500. *See* Article 67 *Decreto del Presidente della Repubblica* of 26 October 1972, No. 633.
501. O.J. of Italy No. 279 of 29 November 1995.
502. *See* Interministerial Decree 10 April 2013, O.J. of Italy No. 161 of 11 July 2013. For an overview of Italian ZFUs *see* http://www.sviluppoeconomico.gov.it/index.php/it/incentivi/i-mpresa/zone-franche-urbane.
503. The authorization issued by the Commission is provided in the Communication from the Commission of 28 October 2009 (State aid No. 346/2009), COM (2009) No. 8126 final, O.J. 2009, C 299, p. 1.
504. The establishment of the ZFU of L'Aquila is first provided by Article 10(1-*bis*) of Law Decree of 28 April 2009, No. 39 (O.J. of Italy No. 97 of 28 April 2009), converted in Law of 24 June 2009, No. 7 (O.J. of Italy No. 147 of 27 June 2009), while the implementation of the related tax measures is realized through the provisions set by Law Decree of 24 January 2012, No. 1 (O.J. of Italy No. 19 of 24 January 2012), converted in Law of 24 March 2012, No. 27 (O.J. of Italy No. 71 of 24 March 2012). For a comprehensive analysis and evaluation fo the ZFU of L'Aquila *see* F. Miconi, *La Zona Franca Urbana di L'Aquila*, in *supra.*, M. Basilavecchia – L. Del Federico – A. Pace – C. Verrigni, G. Giappichelli (eds), Turin, 2016, pp. 368-383.
505. *See* Law Decree of 18 October 2012, No. 179, O.J. of Italy No. 245 of 19 October 2012.

Later, in 2015, new ZFUs have been established in some areas of the regions of Emilia-Romagna[506] and Lombardia[507] affected by another earthquake occurred in May 2012.

Then, following the recent earthquake of August 2016 in Central Italy, a new group of ZFUs is provided by Law Decree of 24 April 2017, No. 50,[508] with tax benefits in favour of enterprises based in some municipalities of the regions of Lazio, Umbria, Marche, and Abruzzo.

Finally, more initiatives have recently been adopted for the establishment of new ZFUs in the urban areas of Genova,[509] Pescara, Matera, Velletri, Sora, Ventimiglia, Campobasso, Cagliari, Iglesias, Quartu Sant'Elena, and Massa Carrara.[510]

In all the above cases, the tax scheme of the Italian ZFU is defined under the perimeter of the *de minimis rule*[511] and, therefore, the related tax benefits have limited effects compared to the case of French ZFUs.[512]

In particular, enterprises based in the ZFU territory can join a set of tax advantages on direct taxation provided that they fulfil all the conditions described under Article 3 of the Interministerial Decree of 10 April 2013.[513]

For example, they must be micro and small size enterprises pursuant to the provisions of Annex 1 of Regulation (EC) No. 800/2008;[514] they must carry out their

506. *See* Article 12 Law Decree of 19 June 2015, No. 78 (O.J. of Italy No. 140 of 19 June 2015), converted in Law of 6 August 2015, No. 125 (O.J. of Italy No, 188 of 14 August 2015).
507. *See* Article 1(445) Law of 28 December 2015, No. 208 (O.J. of Italy No. 302 of 20 December 2015).
508. O.J. of Italy No. 95 of 24 April 2017.
509. *See* Italian Ministry of Economic Development, *Circolare* No. 73726 of 7 March 2019, available at https://www.mise.gov.it/index.php/it/94-normativa/circolari,-note,-direttive-e-atti-di-indirizzo/2039387-circolare -direttoriale-7-marzo-2019-n-73726-zona-franca-urbana-di-genova.
510. *See Circolare* Italian Ministry of Economic Development No. 172230 of 9 April 2018, available at http://www.sviluppoeconomico.gov.it/index.php/it/incentivi/impresa/zone-franche-urbane/nuove-zone-franche-urbane.
511. Commission Regulation (EU) No. 1407/2013 of 18 December 2013 on the application of Articles 107 and 108 of the Treaty on the Functioning of the European Union to *de minimis* ad, O.J. 2013, L 352, pp. 1-8 (replacing Commission Regulation (EC) No. 1998/2006 of 15 December 2006 on the application of Articles 87 and 88 of the Treaty to *de minimis* aid, O.J. 2006, L 379, pp. 5-10).
512. In this regard, it is important to note that, despite the original authorization issued in 2009 within the exception provided by Article 107(3)(c) TFEU, the Commission has considered the tax measures notified by the Italian government in 2011 for the ZFU of L'Aquila as an amendment to the approved scheme not fulfilling the requirements set by the first authorization. Therefore, in the light of the position held by the Commission and considering the difficulties for obtaining a new authorization – such as, for example, the circumstance that the notified measures have been considered as measures of economic development and not as aid to make good the damage caused by natural disaster or exceptional occurrences – the Italian government has decided to define the ZFU tax scheme within the limits of the *de minimis* rule in order to comply with State aid provisions. For these considerations, *see* F. Miconi, *supra.*, in M. Basilavecchia – L. Del Federico – A. Pace – C. Verrigni, *supra.*, G. Giappichelli (ed.), Turin, 2016, p. 372.
513. Interministerial Decree April 10, 2013, O.J. of Italy No. 161 of 11 July 2013.
514. Commission Regulation (EC) No. 800/2008 of 6 August 2008 declaring certain categories of aid compatible with the internal market in application of Articles 87 and 88 of the Treaty (Block Exemption Regulation), O.J. 2008, L 214, pp. 3-47.

activities within the ZFU pursuant to the provisions of Article 3(5) and (6) of the Interministerial Decree of 10 April 2013;[515] moreover, these enterprises must be in the full and free exercise of their rights, being not subject to a voluntary liquidation or to bankruptcy proceedings.[516]

Legal entities based in the ZFU, both individuals and companies, join a full income tax exemption for the first years of activity, while for the following periods, the exemption is generally limited to a decreasing percentage of their income.

The exemption is granted up to the amount of EUR 100,000 of income derived from the activity carried out in the ZFU, plus an amount of further EUR 5,000 per year for any new employee with a permanent residence within the territory of the zone.[517]

Moreover, in the case that the company carries out a movable activity (e.g., construction company), it can benefit from the income tax exemption as it meets at least one of the following conditions: (a) achieving at least 25% of the volume of business with customers residing in the ZFU; (b) employing at least one full-time employee who performs his job in a stable manner within the perimeter of the ZFU.[518]

Furthermore, within a time limit provided by the law, enterprises based in ZFUs, both individuals and companies, are exempt from the regional tax on productive activities – *Imposta Regionale sulle Attività Produttive* (IRAP) up to the amount of EUR 300,000 for each tax period[519] and from the property tax on real estates located in the ZFU perimeter, provided that the same properties are used for the economic activity.[520]

In the context of the Italian ZFUs, it is also important to remember one recent initiative of the Italian government for the introduction of a tax credit – calculated on the basis of the cost of acquired assets – in favour of enterprises investing in 140 municipalities of the regions of Lazio, Umbria, Marche, and Abruzzo where ZFUs are already operative following the earthquake of August 2016.[521] The Commission, through its authorizing communication, has considered this specific measure as compatible with the internal market pursuant to Article 107(3)(c) of the TFEU, since it pursues a policy objective of common interest, is necessary and proportionate and does not cause undue distortion of competition.[522]

As already seen in the case of ZFUs in France, these zones represent relevant examples of STZs, since their tax advantages are granted according to the same EU law framework described under Chapter 3 and, in particular, according to the exemption to the general State aid prohibition stated by Article 107(3)(c).

515. In particular, according to such provisions, enterprises must have an office within the perimeter of the ZFU.
516. *See* Article 3, Interministerial Decree April 10, 2013, Article 3.
517. *Ibid.*, Article 9.
518. *Ibid.*, Article 3(6).
519. *Ibid.*, Article 11.
520. *Ibid.*, Article 12.
521. On 7 April 2017 the Italian Parliament adopted Law n. 45 (O.J. of Italy No. 84 of 10 April 2017) concerning new urgent measures in favour of the population affected by the earthquakes of 2016 and of 2017. The Law of 7 April 2017 includes Article 18-quarter which represents the legal basis for an aid scheme for new investments in the 140 municipalities of the area surrounding the small towns hit by the earthquakes.
522. Communication from the Commission of 6 April 2018 (State aid No. 48571), COM (2018) No. 1661 final, O.J. 2018, C 180, pp. 1-8.

[3] Special Economic Zones

The Italian government has recently introduced the instrument of 'SEZs' for the establishment of territorial tax incentives aimed at the economic development of the southern and central regions of Campania, Basilicata, Puglia, Calabria, Sicily, Sardinia, Abruzzo, and Molise.

The instrument can be used within the threshold of the maximum aid intensity set by the regional aid map and, therefore, without a formal approval by the Commission according to the exemption from the notification requirement provided under the GBER.[523] In this sense, in fact, Article 5(4) of Decree-Law of 20 June 2017,[524] No. 91, as amended by Law of 3 August 2017, No. 123,[525] provides that the tax incentives of SEZs are granted within the limits set by Article 14 of Regulation (EU) No. 651/2014 where the reference to the maximum aid intensity of the regional aid map is made.

The relevance of the instrument for the scope of this review is evident; tax advantages are here granted according to a general block exemption which represents one of the main characteristic of the EU framework for State aid rules already described in Chapter 3; therefore, Italian SEZs constitute a clear example of regional aid designed within the limits of a general block exemption and, at the same time, an interesting form of expression of the phenomenon of STZs.

The Decree of the President of the Council of Ministers of 25 January 2018, No. 12,[526] defines the modalities for the establishment of SEZs, including their duration (from a minimum of seven years to a maximum of fourteen years),[527] the criteria for identifying and delimiting the SEZ area,[528] the criteria governing company access, and general coordination of development objectives.[529] In particular, the procedure for the establishment of an SEZ includes the submission from the regions to the Italian government of a proposal based on the strategic development.[530]

The tax benefits granted are limited to direct taxation; SEZs in Italy, in fact, include a tax credit for companies initiating their economic activities or investments in such areas. The tax credit corresponds to 20% of investments (limited to a maximum of EUR 50 million) for small undertakings, 15% for average businesses, and 10% for large companies, unless different rates are applied in certain areas.[531]

---

523. *See supra* section §3.02[B][1].
524. O.J. of Italy No. 141 of 20 June 2017.
525. O.J. of Italy No. 188 of 12 August 2017.
526. O.J. of Italy No. 47 of 26 February 2018.
527. *Ibid.*, Article 7.
528. *Ibid.*, Article 3.
529. *Ibid.*, Article 6.
530. *Ibid.* According to this provision, the proposal must include a strategic development plan with data and elements that identify the types of activities intended to be promoted within the area and demonstrate the existence of an economic and functional link with a port area.
531. *See* Article 5(2) of Decree-Law of 20 June 2017, No. 91, as amended by Law of 3 August 2017, No. 123.

The requirements for benefiting from a tax credit are: (i) maintaining the business established in an SEZ for seven years, at least, after the completion of the investment; and (ii) no order of dissolution is allowed.[532]

At the time of writing, on the ground of the above legislation, only two SEZs have been established in Italy in the regions of Campania and Calabria, precisely in the harbour district composed of Naples, Salerno, and Castellammare di Stabia, and in the harbour district of Gioia Tauro.

[4] Livigno

The special tax status of the municipality of Livigno, first introduced by the Austrian Empire in 1840, is based on its disadvantaged geographical condition that affects transports and connections.

This STZ is excluded from the scope of the UCC;[533] accordingly, Article 2 of Italian Law of 1 November 1973, No. 762[534] qualifies Livigno as an area outside the Customs Union line so that customs duties are not applied to goods introduced therein.[535]

Furthermore, Livigno is outside the VAT area;[536] in this sense, in fact, Article 7 of the Decree of the President of the Republic of 26 October 1973, No. 633[537] excludes this territory from the application of VAT.

Livigno is also excluded from the application of excise duties according to Article 5(2) of Directive 2008/118/EC and, thus, the EU common system for excise duties does not apply therein.

On these bases, Livigno represents one more relevant example of STZs essentially based on the exclusion of its territory from the scope of the indirect taxes harmonized at the EU level.

[5] Campione d'Italia

Campione d'Italia is an Italian municipality and enclave surrounded by the Swiss territory and by the Lake of Lugano.

Also Campione d'Italia can be considered as an STZ because of its exclusion from the territorial scope of the harmonized legislation on indirect taxes; this territory, in

532. *Ibid.*, Article 5(3).
533. *See* Article 4 UCC.
534. Law of 1 November 1973, No. 762, O.J. of Italy No. 310 of 1 December 1973.
535. This exemption is also applied to the following goods: liqueurs and spirits, sporting goods, perfumes and beauty products, cameras, radio and television, leather goods, and articles of clothing.
536. *See* Article 4(1) UCC.
537. Decree of the President of the Republic of 26 October 1972, No. 633, O.J. of Italy No. 292 of 11 November 1972.

fact, is not only outside the Customs Union line,[538] but also outside the territorial scope of VAT[539] and the common EU system for excise duty.[540]

Nonetheless, indirect taxes in Campione d'Italia are applied according to Swiss customary law with the imposition of Swiss customs duties, Swiss VAT (8%), and Swiss excise duties.[541]

Otherwise, for what regards direct taxation, the Italian tax regime is regularly applied therein with some minimal exceptions.[542]

[L] Latvia

[1] SEZs in Latvia

SEZs in Latvia have been established in 1997 to promote the international trade, the attraction of investments and the development of production and services, as well as the creation of new jobs.[543]

In 2001 the Latvian Parliament has adopted the Law on 'Tax Application in Free Ports and Special Economic Zones'[544] to unify at national level the regulations applied on direct and indirect taxation. By this instrument, the Latvian legislator simplifies the legal framework of such zones creating a set of norms within a comprehensive legislative text aimed at describing all the elements and conditions of the tax advantages granted therein.

At present, there are five SEZs in Latvia: the Free Port of Riga, the Free Port of Ventspils, the SEZ of Liepaja, the SEZ of Rezekne, and the SEZ of Latgale.

538. *See* Article 4(1) UCC.
539. Article 6(2) of the Council Directive 2006/112/EC of 28 November 2006 on the common system of value added tax, O.J. 2006, L 347, pp. 1-118.
540. Campione d'Italia is excluded from the application of harmonized excise duties according to Article 5(2) of Council Directive 2008/118/EC under which the EU common system for excise duties shall not apply to this territory.
541. From 1 January 2020, the municipality of Campione d'Italia will be included in the EU customs territory and in the EU excise duty area, while continuing to be excluded from the common system of VAT. For the amendments regarding the EU customs territory see Article 1 of Regulation (EU) 2019/474 of the European Parliament and of the Council of 19 March 2019 amending Regulation (EU) No. 952/2013 laying down the Union Customs Code, O.J. 2019, L 83, pp. 38-41; for the amendments regarding the EU excise duty area see Article 2 of Council Directive (EU) 2019/475 of 18 February 2019 amending Directives 2006/112/EC and 2008/118/EC as regards the inclusion of the Italian municipality of Campione d'Italia and the Italian waters of Lake Lugano in the customs territory of the Union and in the territorial application of Directive 2008/118/EC, O.J. 2019, L 83, pp. 42-43.
542. For what concerns direct taxation, individuals that are resident in Campione d'Italia pay taxes on taxable income calculated with a favourable exchange rate. In fact, under Article 188*bis* of the Italian Income Tax Act, (O.J. of Italy No. 302 of 31 December 1986) their income in Swiss currency for a total amount not exceeding CHF 200,000 is converted in EUR – for the purposes of the calculation of their tax debt – on the bases of a 30% flat reduction of the exchange rate.
543. For an economic evaluation of the establishment of STZs in Latvia *see* M.E. Porter, C. Ketels, *Latvia: Economic Strategy after EU Accession*, Harvard Business School Case 707-515, 2007, pp. 1-32, available at http://probni.fpn.bg.ac.rs/wp-content/uploads/Porter-Ketels_Latvia_707515p2.pdf.
544. Law on 'Tax Application in Free Ports and Special Economic Zones' of 27 July 2001, O.J. of Latvia No. 117 (2504) of 10 August 2001.

In order to qualify for tax benefits, companies based in Latvian SEZs must receive permits and sign agreements with the appropriate authorities: the state joint stock company '*Rigas Tirdzniecibas Osta*' (Riga Commercial Port) for the Free Port of Riga, the Ventspils Port Authority for the Ventspils Freeport, the Liepaja SEZ administration, the Rezekne SEZ administration, or the Latgale SEZ administration.[545]

In this context, it is possible to identify a complex set of tax advantages dealing not only with direct taxation, but also with indirect taxation.[546]

For direct taxation, the Commission has authorized the related measures, considering this regime as compatibile with the internal market pursuant to Article 107(3)(a) TFEU.[547]

In details, companies based in Latvian SEZs are entitled to apply a CIT rebate in the amount of 80% of the gross tax due;[548] nevertheless, the same rebate is granted in the limit of a maximum amount compensated to the company corresponding to 35% (45% for medium and 55% for small enterprises) of the accumulated amount of investments in these territories of up to EUR 50 million.[549]

Incentives for large-scale investment projects allow taxpayers to claim tax rebate for initial long-term investment in the following amounts: 35% of a total initial long-term investment up to EUR 50 million and 17.5% of the part of the total initial long-term investment exceeding EUR 50 million up to EUR 100 million.[550]

Companies based in Latvian SEZs are also entitled to apply a RET rebate in the amount of 80% of the tax amount calculated with reference to their immovable properties located in the territory of the zone.[551]

Also in this case, the rebate is granted in the limit of a maximum amount compensated to the company corresponding to 35% (45% for medium and 55% for small enterprises) of the accumulated amount of investments in these territories of up to EUR 50 million.[552]

Furthermore, companies based in Latvian SEZs, which pay dividends, remuneration for management, consultancy services or royalties for intellectual property to a non-resident, withhold income tax from such payments with an 80% rebate of the tax amount calculated.[553]

For what regards indirect taxation, Latvian SEZs are fully harmonized according to the EU rules set for FZs by the UCC; in fact, these zones are mentioned in the updated list of the EU Commission[554] and they have a perimeter fence with entry and exit points under the supervision of customs authorities.

545. *Ibid.*, Section 7(4).
546. *See* Section 8 of Law on Tax Application in Free Ports and Special Economic Zones.
547. Communication from the Commission of 29 October 2014, COM (2014) No. 7812, O.J. 2015, C 44, p. 1.
548. *See* Section 7(1) of Law on Tax Application in Free Ports and Special Economic Zones.
549. *Ibid.*, Section 8(1).
550. *Ibid.*, Section 8(1).
551. *Ibid.*, Section 6(1).
552. *Ibid.*, Section 8(1).
553. *Ibid.*, Section 7(3).
554. *See supra* note 22. It is interesting to note that, even if, as of 2 January 2017, entrepreneurs operating within the newly established Special Economic Zone of Latgale may be eligible for

Therefore, pursuant to Article 237 UCC, customs duties and other indirect taxes are not charged when non-Union goods are introduced in these zones until the same goods are released for circulation or for another customs-approved treatment.

On the ground of the above characteristics, it is clear that SEZs in Latvia are in one important situation to be considered in the context of the present review; the related measures, in fact, are designed in line with the EU law framework for STZs, not only for what regards indirect taxation with the harmonized rules of the UCC, but also with reference to direct taxation under the exemption stated by Article 107(3)(a) TFEU.

[M] Lithuania

[1] FEZs in Lithuania

In Lithuania, the phenomenon of STZs can be identified in the context of the so-called FEZs introduced in 1995 in order to grant a complex set of tax benefits regarding both direct and indirect taxation.[555]

According to the national legislator, a FEZ is defined as '*a territory designated for the purpose of economic-commercial and financial activities within which economic entities are provided with special economic and legal conditions of operation as established by this Law*'.[556]

The aim of the national law is to create favourable conditions in these areas for the establishment of enterprises and the improvement of international trade, production, and export, with the development of foreign investments and the creation of new jobs;[557] in particular, in order to start an activity in a FEZ, a company incorporated according to laws of the Republic of Lithuania must register and get a licence issued by the zone administration company.[558]

Currently there are seven FEZs in Lithuania: Klaipeda FEZ, Akmene FEZ, Siauliai FEZ, Panevezys FEZ, Kaunas FEZ, Marjampole FEZ, and Kedainiai FEZ.[559]

From the point of view of direct taxation, the Commission has authorized a special tax scheme considering it as an aid compatible with the internal market in the light of the exemption provided under Article 107(3)(a) TFEU.[560]

---

certain tax breaks, the same zone is not yet mentioned in the last updated version of the list of existing Free Zones issued by the Commission.

555. Law on the Fundamentals of Free Economic Zones of 28 June 1995, No. I-976, O.J. of Lithuania,1995, No. 59-1462.
556. *Ibid.*, Article 2(1).
557. *Ibid.*, Article 1. For a critical analysis of the establishment of STZs in Lithuania *see* O. Pavuk, T. Narushevich, G. Pilaitis, T. Merkulova, *supra.*, in *The Baltic Course*, 2002, available at http://www.baltic-course.com/archive/eng/winter_2002/03free_zones.htm.
558. *Ibid.*, Article 7 and Article 8(2).
559. US Department of State, Bureau of Economic and Business Affairs, *2017 Investment Climate Statement*, 2017, available at www.state.gov.
560. For what concerns the Kaunas FEZ *see* Communication from the Commission of 1 July 2005, COM (2005) No. 1327 final, O.J. 2005, C 230, p. 1. For FEZs in general *see* Case SA.39365 *Regional State aid in the free economic zones scheme*, notified on 18 August 2014.

In detail, companies based in FEZs whose capital investments in the area are no less than EUR 1 million do not pay any CIT for the first six years. The same companies pay an amount for CIT which is reduced by 50% for the next ten taxable periods.[561]

In any case, the tax benefit above described may be applied only if at least 75% of the company's income during the tax period derives from manufacturing, processing, warehousing activities performed within the zone, from wholesale of goods warehoused within the zone or provision of services related to the activities carried out in the territory of the zone.[562]

Furthermore, dividends earned from investments into an FEZ are exempt from withholding tax,[563] while, according to the Lithuanian Law on Immovable Property Tax,[564] the immovable property of the undertakings based in FEZs is exempt from RET.

As far as indirect taxation is concerned, the Law on the Fundamentals of FEZs provides that '*upon agreement with the Customs Department under the Ministry of Finance, parts of the zone territory may be up in conformity with the requirements for Free Zones defined in Council Regulation (EEC) No 2913/92 of 12 October 1992* [...]';[565] accordingly, these territories should also be considered as FZs within the meaning of the UCC,[566] with a regime of deferral for what regards customs duties and other indirect taxes.[567]

In this regard, there are some national provision which are able to implement the harmonized rules defined at the EU level for the purposes of VAT and excise duty; for example, Article 53 of Law of 5 March 2002, No. IX-751[568] provides that VAT is not charged on the supply of goods placed in a FEZ, while excise duty is not applied in such situations pursuant to Article 13 of Law of 30 October 2001, No. IX-569.[569]

Given the above, it is possible to conclude that, like in the case of Latvia, these zones are relevant for the scope of this review because the set of tax advantages provided is an expression of the same common EU law framework described in Chapter 3, both for what concerns direct and indirect taxation.

561. Article 15(3) of Law on the Fundamentals of Free Economic Zones of 28 June 1995, No. I-976.
562. *Ibid.*, Article 15(3).
563. *Ibid.*, Article 15(4).
564. Article 7(2) of the Law of 7 June 2005, No. X-233, O.J. of Lithuania, 2005, No. 76-2741.
565. Article 2(2) of Law on the Fundamentals of Free Economic Zones of 28 June 1995, No. I-976.
566. *Ibid.*, Article 16. The Union Customs Code has entirely replaced Council Regulation (EEC) No. 2913/92 of 12 October 1992.
567. In this regard, it is worth to note that the last version of the EU list of FZs in operation in the customs territory of the Union (updated as of 21 August 2019) only includes the FEZs of Klaipeda, Kaunas, and Siauliai. At the same time, this same list includes other areas in Lithuania close to Trakai and Vilnius which are not defined as Free Economic Zones under the national law.
568. Law on VAT of 5 March 2002, No. IX-751, O.J. of Lithuania, 2002, No. 35-1271.
569. Law on Excise Duty of 30 October 2001, No. IX-569, O.J. of Lithuania, 2001, No. 98-3482.

[N] Luxembourg

[1] Luxembourg Free Port

In Luxembourg, there is one Free Port established in 2014 as a facility constructed within the Luxembourg airport next to the Air Cargo Terminal.

This area is considered as a FZ under the terms of the UCC and, therefore, it is expressly included in the list of FZs in operation in the customs territory of the Union, as communicated by the Member States to the Commission.[570]

Accordingly, as non-Union goods enter the Luxembourg Free Port, they are automatically set under a special procedure of storage regulated by the UCC with a regime for deferral of customs duties and other charges, such as VAT and excise duty.

Among the relevant national provisions, it is worth to mention the Law of 28 July 2011[571] which enables 'freeport activities' in compliance with EU law, introducing a regime of suspension of VAT and other indirect taxes;[572] according to Article 60*bis* of the Luxembourg VAT Act, in fact, VAT is not charged on the supplies of goods in the territory of the Luxembourg Freeport until the same goods are moved outside the zone or released for consumption.

[O] Malta

[1] Malta Free Port

Malta has a FZ (Malta Freeport) located close to the Marsaxlokk harbour in the southern part of the island.

The tax regime of this STZ entirely complies with the harmonized rules of the UCC and, therefore, the set of benefits there available is limited to indirect taxation, with the deferral of custom duties, VAT and excise duty.

The zone is mentioned in the list of FZs in operation in the EU and has a perimeter fence which is under the control of customs authorities.

In this case, the Malta Freeport Corporation Ltd[573] is the declared authority responsible for the administration of the affairs of the zone by encouraging the establishment of enterprises following the issue of a specific licence.[574]

570. *See supra* note 22.
571. *See* Article 60-*bis*(1) of the VAT Act of 12 February 1979, O.J. of Luxembourg, 1979, Part A, No. 23.
572. Further information are available at http://luxfreeport.lu.
573. *See* Act XXVI of 1989 (Malta Freeports Act), as amended by Legal Notice 103 of 1995 (available at http://www.maltafreeport.com.mt); according to Article 5(1) '*Malta Freeport Corporation Limited, a limited liability company (No. C9353) registered under the Commercial Partnerships Ordinance on the 25th day of January 1988 shall be deemed to be constituted under this Act and shall constitute the Freeport Authority*'.
574. *Ibid.*, Article 6 according to which '*Without prejudice to the generality of the powers conferred upon the Authority by this Act, the Authority may (b) enter into agreements with companies that seek to become licensed to operate in a Freeport*'.

Within national legislation, the Malta Freeports Act, in line with the regime of deferral set by Article 237 UCC, provides that customs duties are not charged on the goods that are intended to be placed into the Freeport.[575]

Furthermore, according to the Maltese VAT Act[576] when goods are, on importation, placed under a customs duty suspension regime (i.e., into the Malta Freeport[577]) – the chargeable event does not take place and VAT becomes chargeable only when goods cease to remain subject to that regime.[578]

Finally, excise duty is not charged pursuant to Article 15(8) of the Customs and Excise Tax Act[579] when non-Union goods are introduced in the Malta Free Port and until the same goods are moved outside the zone and imported in the customs territory of the Union or released for consumption.

[P] Poland

[1] Polish 'Free Customs Duty Areas'

The Polish Law on customs duties of 1989[580] defines a Free Customs Duty Area as a separated and uninhabited part of Poland's customs duty territory, considered as a territory in which Polish, foreign, and international companies are allowed to carry out business activities, excluding retail trading.[581]

The new Polish Customs Code, in force since 1 January 1998, defines these territories in a slightly different manner as zones separated from Poland's customs duty area, in which non-domestic products are regarded to be outside the Poland's customs duty line in the case of charging import duty fees and application of trading policies concerning the importation of goods.[582]

Today, Polish Free Customs Duty Areas are relevant situations in the context of this research since they are entirely regulated according to the harmonized set of rules of the UCC, being a part of the territory of Poland separated from the rest of the State with clearly designated exit and entry points under the control of customs authorities.

Today, seven Free Customs Duty Areas are functioning in Poland: the free area of Mszczonów (the region of Mazowsze), the free area of Gdańsk, the free area of Gliwice, the free area of Szczecin, the free area of Małaszewicze Małe (Terespol), the free area of Świnoujście, and the free area of Warszawa–Okęcie International Airport.[583]

575. *Ibid.*, Article 15(1).
576. *See* Act XXIII of 1998 (VAT Act), available at https://parlament.mt/media/1166/xxiii-of-1998-value-added-tax-act.pdf.
577. *Ibid.*, Fourth Schedule, Article 8(7)(4).
578. *Ibid.*, Fourth Schedule, Article 8(7)(1).
579. Act XII of 1997 (Customs and Excise Tax Act), available at http://www.justiceservices.gov.mt/.
580. Customs Law of 28 December 1989, as amended, O.J. of Poland No. 75/1989.
581. K. Budzowski, *Polish Free Customs Duty Areas, Customs Depots and Special Zones*, in *Zeszyty Naukowe/Polskie Towarzystwo Ekonomiczne*, 2003, No. 1, pp. 49-59.
582. Customs Code Act 1997, O.J. of Poland No. 1997/23/117.
583. *See supra* note 22.

The major objective of these zones is to expand export activities, considering that all these areas have favourable locations in terms of transport and international communication.[584]

The set of tax benefits available is limited to indirect taxation according to the harmonized rules of the UCC, with a regime of deferral for customs duties, VAT, and excise duties.

As far as the national legislation is concerned, the relevant provisions have only an implementing role with respect to the principles and rules stated by the Recast VAT Directive and the Excise Duty Directive; for example, under the Polish VAT Act of 2004,[585] a zero-tax rate applies to the supply of goods into Free Customs Duty Areas intended for export to non-EU countries. At the same time, Article 40(3) of the Polish Excise Duty Act[586] provides that in the case of entry of goods into such zones the application of excise duty is suspended under a suspension arrangement.[587]

[Q] Portugal

[1] Madeira

The Madeira FTZ – also known as 'The International Business Centre of Madeira' – has been established in 1980[588] and is actually composed of an 'Industrial Free Trade Zone', an 'International Shipping Register', an 'International Financial Service Centre' and an 'International Service Centre'.[589]

Today, the legal framework of this territory is characterized by the presence of three different State aid regimes authorized by the Commission under the exemption provided by Article 107(3)(a) TFEU and regulated by Portuguese domestic law.[590] In this regard, in fact, the Commission has considered the tax scheme as compatible with the internal market, as it is targeted to address the specific handicaps of Madeira, as an

584. K. Budzowski, *supra*, in *Zeszyty Naukowe Polskie Towarzystwo Ekonomiczne*, 2003, No. 1, p.51.
585. Article 83(22) of the Polish VAT Act, O.J. of Poland 2004, r. Nr 54, poz. No. 54, Item. 535.535.
586. Excise Duty Act of 6 December 2008, O.J. of Poland 2009, No. 3, Item 11.
587. This provision represents the implementation of the norm set out by Article 7 of Directive 2008/118/EC, under which excise duties become chargeable only at the time of release for consumption or importation, while the Article 4 of the same Directive specifies that '*importation of excise goods means the entry into the territory of the EU of excise goods unless the goods upon their entry into the Union are placed under a customs suspensive procedure or arrangement*' (e.g., Free Zones).
588. Decree Law of 20 October 1980, No. 500, O.J. of Portugal No. 243 of 20 October 1980.
589. S. Vasques, *The Madeira Free Trade Zone: Compliance and Control Issues*, in *European Taxation, IBFD* 2012, p. 149.
590. State Aid Regime No. E19/1994 has been authorized by Commission Decision of 3 November 1995 (SG95 D/1287); State Aid Regimes No. 222/A/2002 and No. 222/B/2002 have been authorized by Communication from the Commission of 11 December 2002, COM (2002) No. 4811 (O.J. 2003, C 134, p. 1), and by Communication from the Commission of 4 February 2003, COM (2003) No. 92; State Aid Regime No. 421/2006 has been authorized by Communication from the Commission of 27 June 2007, COM (2007) No. 3037 final (O.J. 2007, C 240, p. 1). For a comprehensive review of such state aid regimes *see* F. Bras, P. Dewerbe, R. Borges, *The Madeira Free Zone and Its Standpoint Within the European Union*, in *EC Tax Review*, 2004, III, pp. 122-134.

OR, and is proportional, since its conditions do not lead to an overcompensation of the additional costs of the aid beneficiaries; therefore the Commission has considered that the same scheme contributes to the regional development and to the diversification of the economic structure of Madeira, without negative effects on the trade between Member States.[591]

Under the authorized tax scheme, service companies licensed in the Madeira FTZ enjoy many different benefits regarding direct taxation.[592] On these premises, the Madeira FTZ is relevant for this research, considering that the benefits granted are the result of the same EU legal framework described in Chapter 3, with particular reference to State aid rules and their system of exemptions.

In detail, in the Madeira FTZ, according to the Tax Incentives Statute,[593] the income obtained by entities licensed between 1 January 2007 and 31 December 2014 to carry out industrial, commercial, shipping, and other services activities, is subject to taxation, until 31 December 2020, under the following terms: (a) in the years from 2007 to 2009 at a rate of 3%; (b) in the years from 2010 to 2012 at a rate of 4%; (c) in the years from 2013 to 2020 at a rate of 5%.

The entities who wish to enjoy these benefits also have to create one to five jobs in the first six months of their activity and undertake a minimum investment of EUR 75,000 in the acquisition of tangible or intangible fixed assets during the first two years of their activity or to create six or more jobs in the first six months of their activity.[594]

Furthermore, dividends paid to corporate shareholders of companies licensed to operate within the Madeira FTZ, who are resident in EU countries or in countries with which Portugal has an agreement with a tax information exchange clause, benefit from the exemption from withholding tax in Madeira on dividends, royalties, and interests.[595]

In addition, shareholders of companies based in the Madeira FZ are exempt from capital gains tax due on the sale of shares or on any share capital increase,[596] while no

591. *See* Communication from the Commission of 27 June 2007, COM (2007) No. 3037 final (O.J. 2007, C 240, p. 1).
592. The present tax regime is outlined in Article 36 of the Portuguese Tax Incentives Statute approved by Decree Law of 1 July 1989, No. 215, O.J. of Portugal No. 149/1 of 1 July 1989.
593. *See* Article 36 of Statute of Tax Benefits as approved by Decree-Law of 1 July 1989, No. 215, as amended, available at http://www.ibc-madeira.com/images/pdf/en-03-Art_33_34_T-ax_Incent.pdf.
594. *Ibid.*, Article 36(5). Pursuant to this norm, in the case of non-fixed activity (e.g., building trades, street trading, taxis), the enterprise benefits from the tax exemption since it has an effective implementation in the area (e.g., office or workshop) and one of the following conditions is met: (i) it employs at least one full-time employee sedentary who operates in areas assigned to the activity; (ii) it achieves at least 25% of its revenue from customers located in the FTZ territory. In this regard, the European Commission has recently opened an in-depth investigation to examine whether Portugal has applied the Madeira Free Zone regional aid scheme in conformity with the Commission decisions approving it and, in particular, with the requirements that (i) the company profits benefiting from the income tax reductions originated exclusively from activities carried out in Madeira; and (ii) the beneficiary companies actually created and maintained jobs in Madeira (*see* European Commission, Press release of 6 July 2018, available at http://europa.eu/rapid/press-release_IP-18-4384_en.htm.
595. *See* Article 6(b) of Decree Law of 26 June 1986, No. 165, O.J. of Portugal No. 144/1 of 26 June 1986.
596. *Ibid.*, Article 6(c).

property tax is levied from companies based in the Madeira FZ in relation to real estate specifically allocated to the performance of the company's activity.[597]

For what regards indirect taxation, reduced VAT rates are applicable to operations localized in the territory of Madeira, as follows: a standard VAT rate of 22% (instead of 23% applied in mainland Portugal), a reduced VAT rate of 5% (instead of 6% applied in mainland Portugal), and a second reduced VAT rate of 12% (instead of 13% applied in mainland Portugal).[598]

Moreover, in Madeira, oil and energy products are exempt from excise duties when used in the production of electricity or city gas, as well as for entities that develop activities with reference to some categories of products.[599] Then, liqueur and *'crème de'*, which are respectively defined in categories 32 and 33 of Annex II of Regulation (EC) No. 110/2008 and are obtained from regional fruit or plants, are subject to a reduced rate of EUR 296.24 per hectolitre when produced and consumed in the autonomous region of Madeira. A reduced rate of EUR 34.34 per hectolitre applies to 'Madeira Wine' (wine obtained from regional grapes specified in Article 15 of Regulation (EEC) No. 4252/88[600]), when produced and consumed in the autonomous region of Madeira.[601]

Excise duty on tobacco and cigarettes manufactured in Madeira by small producers (with an annual production of less than 500 tonnes) are subject to a reduced rate of up to 50% less than the overall minimum rate when consumed in the autonomous region of Madeira.[602]

Companies established in the FTZ of Madeira are also exempt from property transfer tax due on the acquisition of immovable property for their activities.[603]

Documents, books, papers, contracts, acts, and products included in the stamp tax general table, regarding entities licensed in the Madeira FTZ, are exempt from stamp tax.[604]

In the territory of Madeira, there is also a FZ (*Zona Franca da Madeira*) in the port of Caniçal regulated by the UCC provisions, with entry and exit points under the supervision of customs authorities; thus, goods introduced into this zone are automatically set under a special procedure of storage according to Article 237 UCC, with the deferral of customs duties, VAT, and excise duties.[605]

597. *Ibid.*, Article 7(c).
598. Available at http://exporthelp.europa.eu.
599. *See* Article 89 of Decree of 21 June 2010, No. 73, O.J. of Portugal No. 118/1 of 21 June 2010.
600. Council Regulation (EEC) No. 4252/88 of 21 December 1988 on the preparation and marketing of liqueur wines produced in the Community, O.J. 1998, L 373, pp. 59-65.
601. *See* Article 78 Decree of 21 June 2010, No. 73.
602. *Ibid.*, Article 105.
603. *See* Article 7(a) of Decree Law of 26 June 1986, No. 165.
604. *See* Article 33(11) of the Statute of Tax Benefits as approved by Decree Law of 1 July 1989, No. 215, as amended.
605. This zone is mentioned in the EU Commission list. *See supra* note 22.

[2] Azores

The legal framework of the Azores is characterized by the presence of a regional statute[606] that embodies the system of autonomy envisaged by the constitution of the Portuguese Republic of 1976.

The region exercises its own fiscal power and may adapt the national tax system to the specific characteristics of the zone.[607]

According to the Statute of the Azores, the Legislative Assembly of the region is able to legislate on matters regarding its own powers and to adapt the national tax system,[608] including the power to create and regulate taxes, defining their incidence, rate, liquidation, collection, and tax benefits.[609] Moreover, the Legislative Assembly detains the power to reduce the rates of income tax and VAT in accordance with the current legislation[610] and the power to determine the application, in the Autonomous Region of the Azores, of special reduced rates for CIT.[611] Finally, the fiscal autonomy provides for the power to concede temporary and conditioned tax benefits, related to national and regional taxes, within a contractual regime, applicable to relevant investment projects in the terms of the Finance Law of the Autonomous Regions.[612]

Nevertheless, in the light of a decision of the ECJ,[613] the measures adopted in the past by the Autonomous Region of the Azores under the above institutional framework – consisting, for example, in rate reductions of income tax – have been considered as territorial selective and, therefore, as prohibited State aid. In this regard, in fact, the ECJ has put in evidence the lack of a real financial autonomy of the Azores, considering the presence of budgetary transfers from the central government pursuant to the duties of solidarity provided under the Portuguese Constitution; therefore, according to the same decision, the relevant legal framework for determining the selectivity of the tax measures adopted by the Azores have to be defined with reference to the whole of the Portuguese territory, in the context of which they appear to be selective.

Given the above, the main tax benefits granted in the Azores are now essentially limited to indirect taxation, considering that, at the time of writing, for what regards direct taxation, it is not possible to identify neither a specific authorization issued by the Commission under the exemption of Article 107(3) TFEU, nor any other tax measure covered by a general block exemption for the entities based in the Azores.

606. Law of 12 January 2009, No. 2, on the 'Political and Administrative Statute of the Autonomous Region of the Azores', available at http://www.alra.pt/documentos/estatuto_i-ng.pdf.
607. *Ibid.*, Article 20.
608. *Ibid.*, Article 50(1).
609. *Ibid.*, Article 50(2)(a).
610. *Ibid.*, Article 50(2)(d).
611. *Ibid.*, Article 50(2)(e).
612. *Ibid.*, Article 50(2)(g).
613. Case C-88/03 *Portugal v Commission*, [2006] ECR I-7115.

As far as indirect taxation is concerned, reduced VAT rates are applicable to operations localized in the Azores territory, as follows: a standard VAT rate of 18%, a reduced VAT rate of 4%, and a second reduced VAT rate of 9%.[614]

For what concerns excises, liqueur and *'crème de'*, defined respectively in categories 32 and 33 of Annex II of Regulation (EC) No. 110/2008,[615] obtained from regional fruit or plants, are subject to a rate of EUR 322.32 per hectolitre when produced and consumed in the autonomous region of the Azores.[616]

Cigarettes manufactured in the autonomous region of the Azores by small producers (with an annual production of less than 500 tonnes) are subject to a rate of 36.5% + EUR 15.30 per 1,000 units when consumed in the same territory.[617]

In conclusion, today the relevance of the Azores for this research is essentially limited to a set of tax advantages granted in the field of indirect taxation and, therefore, only under such terms, this territory should be qualified as an STZ with respect to mainland Portugal.

[R] Romania

[1] Romanian FZs

The legal framework of STZs in Romania is mainly represented by Law of 21 July 1992, No. 84,[618] concerning the regime of FZs, by Government Urgency Ordinance of 16 June 1997, No. 31,[619] concerning the regime of foreign investments in Romania, and by Law of 29 June 2001, No. 332,[620] regarding the promotion of foreign investments with significant impact on the economy.

Under the above set of norms, today Romanian FZs only offer advantages on indirect taxation in compliance with the harmonized rules of the UCC, representing one more example of the implementation of STZs according to the EU law framework described in Chapter 3.

Pursuant to Article 1 of Law of 21 July 1992, No. 84, a FZ regime can be set up in maritime and river ports of Romania, along the Danube-Black Sea Channel, along other

614. Article 18(3)(a) of the Portuguese VAT Code. Mainland Portugal standard rate is 23%. An intermediate rate of 13% and a reduced rate of 6% are also applied to some specific products and services in the mainland.
615. Regulation (EC) No. 110/2008 of the European Parliament and of the Council of 15 January on the definition, description, presentation, labelling, and the protection of geographical indications of spirit drinks and repealing Council Regulation (EEC) No. 1576/89, O.J. 2008, L-39, pp. 16-54.
616. *See* Council Decision 376/2014/EU of 12 June 2014 authorizing Portugal to apply a reduced rate of excise duty in the autonomous region of Madeira on locally produced and consumed rum and liqueurs and in the autonomous region of the Azores on locally produced and consumed liqueurs and *eaux-de-vie*, O.J. 2014, L. 182, pp. 1-3.
617. Portugal may apply a reduced rate of up to 50% less than the overall minimum rate to cigarettes consumed in the most remote regions of the Azores and Madeira, made by small-scale manufacturers each of whose annual production does not exceed 500 tonnes.
618. O.J. of Romania, Part I, No. 182 of 30 July 1992.
619. O.J. of Romania, Part I, No. 125 of 19 June 1997.
620. O.J. of Romania, Part I, No. 356 of 3 July 2001.

waterways and in the areas near the border crossing points in order to promote international trade and to attract foreign capital for the introduction of new technologies.

The territorial delimitation of FZs is established by a government decision, following a proposal of the ministries interested and of the local public administration bodies.[621]

Today, six FZs are established in the territory of Romania as confirmed in the updated list of the FZs in operation in the Union[622] (Galati, Curtici - Arad, Sulina, Constantia South and Basarabi, Braila, and Giurgiu).

These zones have entry and exit points controlled by customs authorities[623] and are characterized by the application of a customs suspension regime regulated by the UCC, with the deferral of customs duties and other indirect taxes.

Accordingly, the Romanian Customs Code establishes that customs duties are not charged on non-Union goods introduced in an FZ until the same goods are not realized for free circulation or placed under another procedure.[624]

Other relevant national provisions include Article 144(1) of the Romanian Fiscal Code,[625] according to which operations carried out in a FZ are exempt from VAT[626] except when goods are delivered for use or consumption.[627]

The deferral of excise duty is then provided by Article 14 of Law of 21 July 1992, No. 84,[628] while Article 167 of the Fiscal Code of 2003 specifies that the placement of excisable products in a FZ cannot be considered as import for the purpose of chargeability.[629]

---

621. *See* Article 6 of Law No. 84/1992, O.J. of Romania, Part I, No. 182 of 30 July 1992.
622. *See supra* note 22.
623. *See* Article 3 of Law No. 84/1992, O.J. of Romania, Part I, No. 182 of 30 July 1992.
624. *See* Article 17 of Law No. 84/1992, O.J. of Romania, Part I, No. 182 of 30 July 1992.
625. Law No. 571/2003, O.J. of Romania No. 927 of 23 December 2003.
626. The exempted operations are: (1) the entrance of foreign goods within a Free Zone directly from abroad, for simple storage, without customs formalities; (2) the commercial operation of sale-purchase of a foreign commodity between various operators from a Free Zone or between such operators and other persons from outside a Free Zone; (3) the removal of foreign goods from a Free Zone, outside the country, without customs export declarations, where the goods are in the same state as when they were introduced into the Free Zone; (4) supplies of services that are directly connected with the previously mentioned operations.
627. *See* Article 144(2) of Romanian Fiscal Code.
628. Article 14 of Law No. 84/1992: '*For activities carried out in Free Zones, economic agents shall be exempt from the goods-circulation tax, excise and profits tax throughout the period of activity*'.
629. Article 167 of the Romanian Fiscal Code of 2003: '*The excise is chargeable at the moment of release for consumption or when losses or shortages of excisable products are discovered*'. The national norm fully complies with the scope set out by Article 7 of Directive 2008/118/EC, under which excise duties become chargeable only at the time of release for consumption or importation, considering that according to Article 4 of the same Directive '*importation of excise goods means the entry into the territory of the EU of excise goods unless the goods upon their entry into the Union are placed under a customs suspensive procedure or arrangement*' (e.g., Free Zones).

[S] Slovenia

[1] Free Port of Koper

Today, there is only one FZ operating in Slovenia: the Free Port of Koper located on the Adriatic coastline.

Also in this case, the tax regime of the zone is relevant for this research because it is based on the harmonized rules of the UCC - and, therefore, on the common EU framework of FZs described in Chapter 3 - with a set of benefits limited to indirect taxation and consisting in the deferral of customs duties, VAT, and excise duties.

The zone, which has entry and exit points supervised by the customs authorities,[630] is included in the list of FZs in operation in the customs territory of the Union, as communicated by the Member States to the Commission.[631]

Among the relevant national legislation, Article 57(1) of the Slovenian VAT Act[632] represents an implementation of the rules set by the Recast VAT Directive, providing the exemption from VAT for the supply of goods placed in a FZ (i.e., Free Port of Koper). Furthermore, according to Article 6 of the Slovenian Excise Duty Act,[633] the charge of excise duty is suspended on importation where excise products are placed in a FZ (i.e., Free Port of Koper).

[T] Spain

[1] Spanish FZs

FZs in Spain are located in Vigo, Cadiz, Barcelona, Las Palmas de Gran Canaria, Santa Cruz de Tenerife, Sevilla, and Santander.[634] They are all mentioned in the EU list of FZs[635] and they have a perimeter fence with entry and exit points under the control of customs authorities, thus consisting in a special procedure of storage according to the harmonized rules of the UCC.

The *Zone Franca de Vigo* - managed by a public institution named *Consorcio de la Zona Franca de Vigo* - has been established in 1947 and since then is involved in the promotion of the international trade with third countries.[636]

The *Zone Franca de Cadiz* offers services of warehousing, loading and unloading, handling of goods, classification, stock control, and transport. The zone is managed by

630. *See* in this sense Article 16 of the Economic Zones Act, O.J. of Slovenia of 12 June 1998, No. 45.
631. *See supra* note 22.
632. O.J. of Slovenia No. 117/2006.
633. O.J. of Slovenia No. 97/2010.
634. For the review of the main literature on the topic *see* J. Arteaga Ortiz, X. Martinez Cobas, *Las Zonas Francas en Espana y su utilidad, Delimitacion del concepto y perspectivas de futuro*, in *Boletin Economico de ICE*, 2003, No. 2758, pp. 1-7; J. Arteaga Ortiz, A Conesa Fontes, *Las Zonas Francas en Espana*, in *Boletin Economico de ICE*, 2000, No. 2649, pp. 9-15; F. Trampus, *The Spanish Free Trade Zones as Logistic Platforms for Trade with Latin America*, in *Trasporti - diritto, economia, politica*, 2002, No. 88, pp. 87-105.
635. *See supra* note 22.
636. Available at http://www.zonafrancavigo.com.

the *Cadiz Zona Franca Consortium*, which is an institution of Public Law controlled by the Ministry of Treasury.[637]

The *Zone Franca Aduanera de Barcelona* has been established in 1916 under the original denomination of *Puerto Franco* and it is actually managed by the 'Barcelona Free Zone Consortium'.[638]

The FZ of Las Palmas de Gran Canaria – which belongs to the region of Canary Islands – enjoys the Free Port status since its establishment in 1852 by the *Decreto de Puerto Francos de Canarias* and by the Free Ports Law of 6 May 1900. In addition to the advantages on indirect taxation set by the harmonized EU rules, the FZ of Las Palmas also benefits from a special Fiscal Economic Regime – *Régimen Económico y Fiscal* (REF), which contains a series of favouring measures on direct taxation focused on the establishment of companies in the Canary Islands.[639]

In 2006 the Ministry of Finance authorizes the establishment of one more zone in Santa Cruz de Tenerife, allowing its entire port site area as well as the port of Granadilla, to be used as a FZ. The zone is administrated by the Consortium of Santa Cruz de Tenerife FTZ.[640] Also in this case, companies located therein may benefit from further advantages on direct taxation provided by the REF.[641]

Finally, in 2016, two more FZs have been established in Santander and in Sevilla following the creation of a consortium with administrative functions.[642]

Apart from the general deferral of custom duties provided under Article 237 UCC, Article 23 of the Spanish VAT Law[643] states that the entry of goods into an FZ is exempt from VAT; also in this case, the national norm clearly implements the provision set out by Article 156 of Directive 2006/112/EC according to which Member States are able to exempt, among the others, the supply of goods that are intended to be placed in a FZ.

Furthermore, when non-Union goods are imported into a Spanish FZ from outside EU territory, excise duties are suspended until the goods are moved out of the zone and imported into the EU (where they become 'Union goods') or consumed within the zone; in this regard, in fact, Article 4(19) and (26) of the Spanish '*Ley de Impuestos Especiales*'[644] specifies that the entry of goods into a suspension customs arrangement cannot be considered as importation and, consequently, such operations are not charged for the purposes of excise duties.[645]

637. Available at http://www.zonafrancacadiz.com.
638. Available at http://www.elconsorci.net/.
639. *See infra* section §4.02[T][2].
640. Available at http://www.puertosdetenerife.org/memorias/memoria2010/7/7-port-activity-en.html.
641. *See infra* section §4.02[T][2].
642. *See* Order HAP/1412 of 29 August 2016 which authorizes the establishment of the '*Consorcio de la Zona Franca de Santander*', O.J. of Spain No. 210 of 31 August 2016, pp. 62091-62100; Order HAP/1358 of 25 July 2014 which authorizes the establishment of the '*Consorcio de la Zona Franca de Sevilla*', O.J. of Spain No. 182 of 28 July 2014, pp. 59873-59881.
643. Law of 28 December 1992, No. 37, O.J. of Spain No. 312 of 29 December 1992.
644. Law of 20 December 1992, No. 38, O.J. of Spain No. 312 of 29 December 1992.
645. That is the implementation of the scope set out by Article 7 of the Directive 2008/118/EC, under which excise duties become chargeable only at the time of release for consumption or importation, while Article 4 of the same Directive specifies that '*importation of excise goods*

[2] Canary Islands

In the Canary Islands it is possible to identify a complex set of tax advantages with respect to the standard tax regime applied in the rest of Spain.

For what regards direct taxation, the Commission has authorized the Economic and Fiscal Regime of the Canaries Islands (REF),[646] stating that the same aid fulfils the criteria to be considered compatible with the internal market pursuant to Article 107(3)(a) TFEU.[647]

In this sense, the benefits there granted are shaped on the basis of the guidelines on regional aid and according to the regional aid maps for the period 2014-2020,[648] taking into account the situation of the Canary Islands as an OR of the EU.

The main rules on taxation are contained in Law of 6 July 1994, No. 19,[649] for the amendment of the Economic and Fiscal Regime of the Canary Islands, and in Law of 7 June 1991, No. 20,[650] for the amendment of the tax aspects of the same regime.

One of the main characteristics of this tax scheme is that the most relevant benefits are conditioned to the realization of an investment in the Canary Islands; in fact, the Reserve for Investments in the Canary Islands – *Reserva para Inversiones en Canarias* (RIC) – one of the tax advantages granted in the context of the REF – is a tax benefit to promote investments, which can be applied to corporate entities subject to CIT with an establishment in the Canary Islands, as well as to individuals entrepreneurs that determine their net income by the method of direct appreciation, provided that the income derives from economic activities located in the area.

The RIC can also be applied to individuals and entities not resident in Spain that operate in the Canary Islands through a permanent establishment in order to obtain a reduction in the income taxable base.

In detail, for what concerns companies, up to 90% of the annual undistributed profits can be allocated to a special investment reserve and will not be taxed, provided that the same profits are invested within a four-year period (including the period during which the profits are obtained) in qualifying assets in the Canary Islands or in certain public debt securities or shares in other companies operating in the Canary Islands that invest in qualifying assets.[651]

For individual entrepreneurs the tax benefit consists in a PIT tax credit, based on the net income deriving from business exploitation assigned to the RIC, provided that it derives from activities located therein.

---

means the entry into the territory of the EU of excise goods unless the goods upon their entry into the Union are placed under a customs suspensive procedure or arrangement' (e.g., Free Zones).

646. For a review of the REF regime, *see* Confederacion Regional de Empresarios de las Islas Canarias, *Actualizacion del Regimen Economico y Fiscal de Canaria para el period 2014-2020, Documento de bases*, 2013, available at www.ccelpa.org.
647. Communication from the Commission of 20 December 2006 (State aid No. 377/2006), COM (2006) No. 6635, O.J. 2007, C 30, p. 4.
648. Communication from the Commission – Guidelines on regional State aid for 2014-2020, O.J. 2013, C 209, pp. 1-45.
649. Law of 6 July 1994, No. 19, O.J. of Spain No. 161 of 7 July 1994.
650. Law of 7 June 1991, No. 20, O.J. of Spain No. 137 of 8 June 1991.
651. *Ibid.*, Article 27(2).

The tax credit is determined applying the average tax rate to the annual allocation of the reserve, with the limit of 80% of the tax payable amount.[652]

In the Canary Islands, State aid cannot exceed the 40% of the investment that is financed by the same aid (percentage that increases to 50% for medium-sized companies and 60% for small companies); these limits are applied considering not only the savings in the tax payable due to RIC, but any other aid (e.g., subsidies).

Taxpayers subject to CIT or PIT have the right to apply a rebate of 50% of the payable gross tax that proportionally corresponds to the net income obtained from the sale of goods manufactured in the Canary Islands in the agricultural, livestock, industry, and fishing sectors.[653]

The Special Register for Ships and Shipping Companies – *Registro Especial de Buques y Empresas Navieras* (REB) is a further tax incentive provided under the REF; according to this tax benefit, shipping companies benefit from a CIT rebate of 90% of the gross tax due, which corresponds to the apportion of the taxable base deriving from services rendered – by their ships registered in the Special Register – between the Canary Islands and between the Canary Islands and the rest of the Spanish territory.[654] Contracts and other legal acts executed over ships registered in this Special Register, which are subject to the transfer tax and stamp duty tax, are exempt from taxation.[655]

Other benefits are granted under the Canary Islands Special Zone – *Zona Especial Canaria* (ZEC) which consists in a low taxation plan created within the framework of the Canary Islands Economic and Fiscal Regime (REF) with the intention of encouraging the economic and social development of the Canary Islands and the diversification of their productive structure.[656]

Some requirements must be fulfilled in order to qualify for the application of the ZEC regime.

First, the recipient must be a newly constituted entity with its domicile and effective office in the ZEC territory. At least one of its directors must be resident in the territory of the Canary Islands.[657] The new company must make an investment in the territory of the Canary Islands of at least EUR 100,000 in fixed assets related to the activity within the first two years subsequent to the authorization by the *Consorcio de la Zona Especial Canaria*.[658]

652. *Ibid.*, Article 27(9).
653. *Ibid.*, Article 26(1).
654. *Ibid.*, Article 76.
655. *Ibid.*, Article 74.
656. According to the Commission, the ZEC regime (State aid No. 376/2006) fulfils the criteria to be considered compatible with the internal market pursuant to Article 107(3)(a) of the TFEU. *See* Communication from the Commission of 20 December 2006, COM (2008) No. 6632, O.J. 2007, C 30, p. 4.
657. Article 40 of Law of 6 July 1994, No. 19.
658. *Ibid.*, Article 41. The limit of investments in fixed assets is at least EUR 50,000 in the following islands: La Palma, La Gomera, El Hierro, Fuerteventura, and Lanzarote.

Additionally, the new entity must create at least five jobs within six months from the date it receives the authorization to establish itself as a ZEC Entity, and maintain an average of at least five jobs during the time it is registered as a ZEC Entity.[659]

According to the limit of EU law on accumulation of financial support and under certain conditions, ZEC tax advantages are compatible with other REF tax incentives such as the Reserve for Investments.[660]

The companies in the ZEC territory are subject to CIT at a reduced rate of 4%,[661] while the standard tax rate of CIT in Spain is currently 25%.

The applicable tax rate is levied on the taxable amount arising from operations effectively carried out within the ZEC territory.[662]

Even though the Canary Islands are outside the VAT EU area, a similar local indirect tax, known as the IGIC (*Impuesto General Indirecto de Canarias*), is applied at several different rates on imports.[663] The standard rate is 7%; there are also reduced rates for first necessity products or those which are not manufactured in the Canary Islands (0% and 3%). Nevertheless, under the ZEC, entities are also exempt from IGIC when selling goods and delivering services to other entities based in the ZEC, as well as when importing goods.[664]

Then, the Canary Islands are excluded from the territorial scope of Directive 2008/118/EC on excise duty;[665] therefore, instead of the common EU system for excise duty, the Canary Islands apply a tax authorized under Article 349 TFEU, the so-called *Arbitrio sobre las Importaciones y Entregas de Mercancías* (AIEM). This tax is levied not only on goods originating from the territory of the Canary Islands, but also on importations of goods into the Canary Islands.[666]

ZEC companies are also exempt from transfer tax (*Impuesto sobre Transmisiones Patrimoniales* – ITP) and stamp duty in certain operations such as, for instance, the purchase of goods for the development of the activity.[667]

In conclusion, the Canary Islands, with their complex set of tax benefits, are an important example of an STZ; in this case, in fact, the aspects which are more relevant for the scope of this review involve not only the presence of an authorized State aid regime under the exemption of Article 107(3)(a) TFEU, but also the exclusion of this zone from the territorial scope of the EU legislation for VAT and excise duty.

659. The requirement is at least three jobs in La Palma, La Gomera, El Hierro, Fuerteventura and Lanzarote.
660. *See* Article 42(2) Law of 6 July 1994, No. 19.
661. *Ibid.*, Article 44.
662. *Ibid.*, Article 44(1).
663. *See* Article 2 of Law of 6 July 1994, No. 19.
664. *See* Article 46 Law of 6 July 1994, No. 19.
665. Article 5(2) of Council Directive 2008/118/EC of 16 December 2008 concerning the general arrangements for excise duty and repealing Directive 92/12/EEC.
666. For further details *see* Law of 26 June 2014, No. 4, O.J. of Spain No. 168 of 11 July 2015 pp. 54383-54399.
667. *Ibid.*, Article 45.

[3] Basque Country and Navarra

The Economic Agreement between the Autonomous Community Government of the Basque Country and Spain[668] recognizes the power of the institutions of the provinces of the Basque Country (Álava, Guipúzcoa, and Vizcaya) to regulate taxes. In general, these provinces, being STZs, have full or shared regulatory authority in the area of direct taxation, but far more limited authority in the indirect taxation area.

The institutions of the provinces of the Basque Country also have the power to levy, manage, assess, inspect, review, and collect taxes, except with respect to custom duties and excises. All taxes levied under the Basque system are managed and collected by the Foral Treasuries as stipulated in the Economic Agreement.

As already seen for Azores, this territory is a relevant example of STZ since it involves an assessment of the related tax measures in the perspective of territorial selectivity under State aid rules; also in this case, in fact, the ECJ has analysed the conditions of institutional, procedural, and financial autonomy in order to identify the Basque Country – and not the entire territory of Spain – as the reference framework of the judgement of selectivity.[669]

As far as direct taxation is concerned, the Basque Country has its own PIT and CIT systems; otherwise, indirect taxes are almost completely harmonized at the EU level and the powers of the local authority are limited to specific aspects of managing such taxes.

There are certain provisions in the Economic Agreement regarding CIT that make this region of Spain more attractive for companies; in the Basque Country, for example, a reduced rate of 20% is levied on small companies[670] and on micro companies.[671]

For small companies, other benefits concern the free depreciation for new tangible fixed assets (except buildings) and a general bad debt provision of up to 1% of credit sales and services.

In the case of micro companies, further tax benefits are identified in a general bad debt provision of up to 1% of receivables, a total depreciation/amortization charge of up to 25% of the net tax value or free depreciation for new tangible fixed assets (except

668. *Ley 12/2002 de 23 de mayo 2002, por la que se aprueba el Concierto Económico con la Comunidad Autónoma del País Vasco*, O.J. of Spain No. 124 of 24 May 2002.

669. Joined cases C-428/06 to C-434/06 *Unión General de Trabajadores de La Rioja (UGT-Rioja) and Others v Juntas Generales del Territorio Histórico de Vizcaya and Others*, [2008] I-06747.

670. *See* Article 13 *Norma Foral 2/2014 de 17 de enero, sobre el Impuesto de Sociedades del Territorio Histórico de Gipuzkoa*, O.J. of Spain No. 13 of 22 January 2014, according to which a small company is considered to be a company that meets the following requirements in the year prior to the application of the special tax regime: (i) it carries on a business activity; (ii) its net turnover or assets is under EUR 10 million; (iii) its average number of staff is under 50; (iv) an interest of 25% or more in the company is not held, directly or indirectly, by a company that does not meet the above requirements.

671. *See* Article *13 Norma Foral 2/2014, de 17 de enero, sobre el Impuesto de Sociedades del Territorio Histórico de Gipuzkoa*, O.J. of Spain No. 13 of 22 January 2014, according to which a micro company is considered to be a company that meets the following requirements in the year prior to the application of the special tax regime: (i) it carries on a business activity; (ii) its net turnover or assets is under EUR 2 million; (iii) its average number of staff is under 10; (iv) an interest of 25% or more in the company is not held, directly or indirectly, by a company that does not meet the above requirements.

buildings), and a general tax relief of 10% of prior positive taxable income given as a 'tax compensation' for the difficulties faced by companies of this size.[672]

For holding companies, including, among others, real estate companies, the tax rates are set on a range between 20% and 25%,[673] while other benefits regard the fact that an amount equal to 20% of gross income generated from leases of housing and their financial expenses may be considered tax deductible, as well as an amount equal to 30% of gross income generated from leases of other real estate and their financial expenses.[674]

Beside the Basque Country, also Navarra is an STZ with respect to the CIT rate applied in comparison with the standard tax regime of the rest of Spain. In this case, in fact, the CIT rate is between 19% and 23% for small companies and micro companies[675] and, thus, lower than the average rate for Spain (25%); furthermore, 45% of the amounts accountable for a special investment reserve can here be reduced from the tax base.[676] Other benefits include freedom of depreciation for elements of tangible fixed assets whose unit value does not exceed EUR 1,800 and for elements related, exclusively and permanently, to research and development.[677]

In summary, the tax regime of Navarra, unless not directly investigated by the Commission and the ECJ, clearly represents one more relevant example of STZ; also in this case, in fact, the conditions of institutional, procedural, and financial autonomy qualify this territory as an infra-State body and, therefore, as the only reference framework to be considered for the assessment of selectivity.

---

672. Information available at http://taxsummaries.pwc.com/ID/Spain-Corporate-Other-issues.

673. *See* Article 55 *Norma Foral 2/2014 de 17 de enero, sobre el Impuesto de Sociedades del Territorio Histórico de Gipuzkoa*, O.J. of Spain No. 13 of 22 January 2014. According to Article 14 of the same law, the requirements to be taxed under these rates are as follows:

 (a) the company's shareholders representing at least 75% of its capital are persons, holding companies, or other companies associated with such persons or companies. This requirement should be met throughout the tax period;
 (b) for at least ninety days of the tax period, over half of the company's assets are made up of securities or are not used to carry on business activities. Leased real estate is not considered to be used to carry on a business activity when the company does not have at least five employees on average in a year who work exclusively for the company on a full-time basis;
 (c) companies where at least 80% of their income is generated from assignments of use of real estate that is not considered to be a real estate leasing business activity or is generated from transfers of own capital to third parties or from provisions of services to associated parties and that do not have sufficient personal and material resources may also be taxed under this tax regime.

674. Information available at http://taxsummaries.pwc.com/ID/Spain-Corporate-Other-issues.

675. Article 51 *Ley Foral 26/2016 de 28 de diciembre, del Impuesto sobre Sociedades*, O.J. of Spain No. 55, of 6 March 2017.

676. *Ibid.*, Article 44.

677. *Ibid.*, Article 18.

[4] Ceuta and Melilla

Ceuta and Melilla are Spanish territories located in continental North Africa. These zones belong to Spain since the formation of the modern Spanish State and, therefore, they are also a part of the EU and the Schengen Area.

Pursuant to Article 144(b) of the Spanish Constitution, the cities of Ceuta and Melilla both have Statutes of Autonomy, respectively approved by Organic Law of 13 March 1995, No. 1,[678] and by Organic Law of 13 March 1995, No. 2.[679]

However, on the ground of the same Statutes of Autonomy, these territories do not own any power concerning taxation and, thus, fiscal matters remain an exclusive competence of the central government.

On these bases, Ceuta and Melilla can be identified as STZs with respect to the standard tax regime applied in Spain, considering the presence of a set of tax benefits both on direct and indirect taxation.

In this regard, it is worth to note that the tax scheme on direct taxation for Ceuta and Melilla as provided by the national law[680] – unless not previously investigated by the Commission – clearly represents an exception to the general State aid prohibition within the terms defined under Article 107(3)(a);[681] therefore, both these territories have to be considered as relevant situations for the purposes of the present research.

In detail, the set of tax incentives is characterized by a deduction from CIT and PIT applied in the amount of 50% of the income obtained in Ceuta and Melilla;[682] income generated in trading activities is deemed to be obtained in Ceuta or Melilla, as long as these activities are organized, controlled, managed, and invoiced from these territories through a fixed place of business located therein.[683]

Activities other than trading (e.g., manufacturing or services) can also enjoy the tax relief, although in this case the activity must be performed in these territories. Spanish legislation also provides for specific rules to allocate to Ceuta and Melilla the profits of fishing, shipping, and air transport. These criteria are based on the place of effective management of the company, the place where the contracts are closed and the place where the boats and aircraft are registered.[684]

Then, for what regards indirect taxation, further aspects confirm the possibility to qualify Ceuta and Melilla as STZs; both these territories, in fact, are excluded from the application of VAT[685] and, thus, they are not part of the EU VAT area. They levy an

678. Organic Law No. 1 of 13 March 1995 on the Statute of Autonomy of Ceuta, O.J. of Spain No. 62 of 14 March 1995.
679. Organic Law No. 2 of 13 March 1995, No. 1, on the Statute of Autonomy of Melilla, O.J. of Spain No. 62 of 14 March 1995.
680. *See* Article 69 of Royal Decree of 5 March 2004, No. 3, O.J. of Spain No. 60 of 10 March 2004, pp. 10670-10721.
681. In this sense *see* M. Moron Perez, *El Regimen Fiscal de las Ciudades Autonomas de Ceuta y Melilla: Presente y Futuro, Cronica Triburaria*, in *Crónica tributaria*, 2006, 121, pp. 88 et seq.
682. *See* Article 69 of Royal Decree of 5 March 2004, No. 3.
683. Article 33(2) of Royal Decree of 5 March 2004, No. 4, as amended by Law of 29 October 2013, No. 16, O.J. of Spain No. 260 of 30 October 2013, pp. 87528-87568.
684. *Ibid.*, Article 33(5).
685. *See* Article 3 of Law of 28 December 1992, No. 37, O.J. of Spain No. 312 of 29 December 1992. *See also* Article 6 of Council Directive 2006/112/EC.

indirect tax on production, services, and imports called IPSI (*Impuesto sobre la Producción, los Servicios y la Importación*), but with lower tax rates (from 0.5% to 10%)[686] and with a supplementary levy on tobacco and fuels.[687]

At the same time, customs duties are not applied to goods introduced in Ceuta and Melilla, considering that these territories are outside the line of the Customs Union pursuant to Article 4 UCC.

As Ceuta and Melilla are both excluded from the EU excise area,[688] only a special tax on certain forms of transportation (*Impuesto Especial sobre Determinados Medios de Transporte*)[689] and a special electricity tax (*Impuesto Especial sobre la Electricidad*)[690] are applicable.

[U] United Kingdom

[1] Gibraltar

Gibraltar is a British overseas territory located near the southernmost tip of the Iberian peninsula, sharing its border with Spain to the north. It is part of the EU, having joined the European Economic Community (EEC) under the UK in 1973.

According to Article 355(3) TFEU, the EC Treaty is applied to '*the European territories for whose external relations a Member State is responsible*', a provision which in practice only applies to Gibraltar.

As a separate jurisdiction to the UK, Gibraltar's government and parliament are responsible for the transposition of EU law into local law.

The constitutional status of Gibraltar is unique; although Gibraltar is not a separate Member State,[691] it is a distinct jurisdiction with its own parliament enacting legislation in all areas of local concern, while UK retains responsibility in limited aspects such as foreign affairs and defence.[692]

However, Gibraltar has to be considered an STZ for the purposes of the present research; its tax system, in fact, deviates from the standard regime applied in the mainland UK which remains the Member State responsible for its external relations.

686. *See* Law of 25 March 1991, No. 8, O.J. of Spain No. 73 of 26 March 1991.
687. *Ibid.*, Article 18*bis*.
688. Article 5(2) Council Directive 2008/118/EC of 16 December 2008 concerning the general arrangements for excise duty and repealing Directive 92/12/EEC.
689. Law of 28 December 1992, No. 38, O.J. of Spain No. 312 of 29 December 1992, pp. 44305-44331.
690. *Ibid.*, Article 3.
691. In this sense, *see* Case C-591/15 *The Gibraltar Betting and Gaming Association Limited v Commissioners for Her Majesty's Revenue and Customs and Her Majesty's Treasury*, [2017] ECR I-00000, where the ECJ states that '*Article 355(3) TFEU, in conjunction with Article 56 TFEU, is to be interpreted as meaning that the provision of services by operators established in Gibraltar to persons established in the United Kingdom constitutes, as a matter of EU law, a situation confined in all respects within a single Member State*' (paragraph 56).
692. House of Commons, Foreign Affairs Committee, *Gibraltar: Time to Get Off the Fence, Second Report of Session 2014-15*, House of Commons, London, 2014.

At the same time, Gibraltar is an infra-State body which enjoys enough institutional, procedural, and financial autonomy with respect to the mainland UK; consequently, as stated by the ECJ,[693] the reference framework for the assessment of the selectivity of the tax measures under State aid rules must be identified in Gibraltar a not in the mainland UK.

As far as CIT is concerned, a tax rate of 10% is applied in Gibraltar,[694] but there is a surcharge of an additional 10% on utilities companies and on any company which has a dominant market position.[695]

Gibraltar adopts a territorial source principle of taxation under which income not accrued in or derived from Gibraltar is not taxed in Gibraltar.

Thus, companies are liable to CIT in Gibraltar on specified sources of income that are accrued in, derived from, or received in Gibraltar.

Furthermore, dividend income of a Gibraltar company from foreign investments or from another Gibraltar company is exempt from tax in Gibraltar.

Interests received or receivable from inter-company loans are taxable in Gibraltar if the company receiving the interests is registered in Gibraltar at the following tax rates: 10% for inter-company interests above GBP 100,000; 0% for inter-company interests less than GBP 100,000 unless the income falls within the scope of trading income (e.g., banks, building societies).[696]

Among the other main tax benefits, it is important to note that there is no withholding tax on dividends, interests or royalties paid by a Gibraltar company to a foreign shareholder (company or individual) or to another Gibraltar company.[697]

There is no capital gains tax in Gibraltar, which means that there is no tax or charge payable in respect of gains made by companies in relation to the disposal of capital assets.

According to this principle, the Gibraltar Income Tax Act specifies that capital gains and capital losses shall be excluded in ascertaining the amount of profits or gains.[698]

Further tax advantages derive from the exclusion of Gibraltar from the territorial scope of indirect taxes harmonized at the EU level.

In this regard, in fact, Gibraltar is outside the perimeter of the Customs Union,[699] with a special regime on customs according to which customs duties are levied on goods imported into Gibraltar, mostly at rates from 6% to 12%, while, as of 1 July 2010, import duty on pedal cycles, electric cars, solar panelling, and related equipment is

693. Joined Cases T-211/04 to T-215/04 *Commission and Spain v Government of Gibraltar and United Kingdom*, [2008] II-03745. For the review of the case *see supra* section §3.02[A][5].
694. The standard CIT rate in the United Kingdom is 19%.
695. Legal Notice No. 187 of 2010, O.J. of Gibraltar, II, No. 3827 of 23 December 2010.
696. Income Tax Act, Schedule 5, Article 6(1), available at http://www.gibraltarlaws.gov.gi/-articles/2010-21o.pdf.
697. *Ibid.*, Schedule 5, Article 6(1).
698. *Ibid.*, Schedule 3, Article 1(1).
699. *See* Article 29 of the Treaty of Accession of Denmark, Ireland, and the United Kingdom (1972), O.J. 1972, L 73, pp. 1-204.

reduced to 0%.[700] Furthermore, Gibraltar is outside the EU VAT area[701] and EU excise area[702] and, thus, it is a VAT free jurisdiction with local excises levied mainly on spirits, wines, tobacco, and mineral oil.

§4.03 FINAL REMARKS

The factual experience of the EU outlines a complex framework characterized by the presence of various situations which correspond to the phenomenon of STZs.

As seen in this chapter, it is possible to identify many initiatives aimed at the introduction of a specific set of tax advantages for the entities based in a limited territory at the sub-State level. At the same time, apart from the adoption of a specific tax policy, also the exclusion of some territories from the territorial scope of EU legislation is a relevant situation for the purposes of the present study.

From the structural point of view, the tax advantages cover all the main typologies of taxes, both for what regards direct and indirect taxation, and are granted through different instruments, including exemptions, deductions, rebates, tax credit, etc. Also the objectives pursued can be different; while in some cases, the scope of such initiatives is the development of a specific economic policy, in other cases, the objectives of a social character are the main driver of an STZ, with the inclusion of the same initiative in the context of a social policy.

Given the above, besides the literature and the EU law sources reviewed in the previous chapters, the description of the various STZs in the Member States is one more useful starting point for the analysis of the research questions.

In this direction, all the reviewed sources can now be used as the basis for the next phase of the research where the approach will be focused on a conceptual analysis aimed at the identification of new findings and original results.

700. Imports and Exports Act, 1986 (Act. No. 1986-21), available at http://www.gibraltarlaw-s.gov.gi/articles/1986-21o.pdf.
701. *See* Article 28 of Treaty of Accession of Denmark, Ireland, and the United Kingdom (1972), O.J. 1972, L 73, pp. 1-204.
702. *Ibid.*

CHAPTER 5
Developing a General Legal Theory of STZs

§5.01 INTRODUCTION

The sources reviewed in the previous chapters gives evidence of various situations where tax incentives are reserved to a limited area of a Member State.

As already seen, in fact, STZs are a common phenomenon within the EU framework, representing not only an instrument of tax policy for the public authorities, but also a strategic factor for the allocation choices of the economic operators.

However, the legal bases on which STZs are established are often different, as well as the objectives pursued in the context of such initiatives. Some zones are essentially structured on the ground of the customs legislation or other sources of indirect taxation which are already harmonized at the EU level; in other cases, as far as direct taxation is concerned, national or local legislation fulfils the main role in the definition of the tax regime applied in an STZ, although with important limits due to the fundamental principles and freedoms of the TFEU. At the same time, there are situations where the tax advantages provided within an STZ are clearly aimed to the achievement of objectives of economic policy, with growth-focused measures specifically targeted to improve the margin of profit of enterprises; nonetheless, beside such measures, there are also other examples where STZs are used as an instrument of social cohesion policy for the improvement of the living conditions of disadvantaged groups of individuals.

In this context, the literature on the topic does not offer the possibility to explain the multiform sides of the phenomenon, especially in the area of European tax law, where the aspects of STZs are not properly investigated from a systematic perspective; the previous studies, in fact, as already seen in Chapter 2, are generally limited in their scope and mainly based on an economic approach to the topic.[703]

---

703. For these considerations *see supra* section §2.07.

On these premises, the aim of this chapter is to fill this gap of knowledge with the definition of a general legal theory for all these different experiences of STZs, approaching the issues which involve the following research question:

Research question No. 1

In the context of European tax law, is it possible to develop a general legal theory of STZs able to explain the different experiences of territorial tax incentives in the Member States?

The general legal theory is here developed through the conceptual analysis of the material reviewed in the previous chapters; in this sense, the literature on the topic, the EU law framework for direct and indirect taxation, and the factual experience of the Member States, represent the fields of analysis for the identification of a common reading-key and a set of basic coordinates.

As it will be shown in the next sections, this process valorizes all the different issues related to the phenomenon, with the development of a general legal theory focused on the concept of STZs and on its territorial, structural, and functional dimension.

At the end of this process, the analysis of the findings will include the provision of a comprehensive definition of STZs able to encompass all the different situations identified at the EU level, both for what regards the areas characterized by tax benefits on direct taxation and the other areas with tax benefits limited to indirect taxation.

As the last step, the general legal theory will be completed with the identification of the implementing models adopted in the EU framework; for this scope, the catalogue of STZs described in Chapter 4 will be used as the starting point for the recognition of the common features of each model, with a specific focus on the perspective emerging from the concept of STZs and from its territorial, structural, and functional dimensions.

§5.02 THE CONCEPT

The analysis of the experience of the various Member States outlines a set of essential elements representing the basics of the concept of STZs.

In the light of the legal dimension and the EU law framework respectively explored in Chapter 2 and in Chapter 3, the characteristics of each area can be compared and deeply screened under a three-dimensional approach; in all the cases, in fact, an STZ presents basic features for what regards the territorial limits, the typologies of tax benefits and the methods used for granting them, and, finally, also for what concerns the specific objective pursued by the public authority responsible for the same measures.

Given the above, the next sections will be dedicated to the explanation of the results of the research process, giving evidence of the various aspects which influence the design of a zone.

The resulting concept includes a territorial dimension, mainly related to the necessary presence of a well-defined geographical border, a structural dimension, focusing on the typologies of the tax benefits provided, and, finally, a functional dimension that considers the objectives of tax policy carried out through the establishment of STZs.

The outcome of the research involves a new approach to STZs in the context of European tax law, with the identification of a general concept able to explain the various experiences of the Member States.

In this direction, the research overcomes the limits of the previous studies,[704] opening a new perspective where the territorial, the structural, and the functional dimensions of STZs become the essential reading-key for a better understanding of the phenomenon.

[A] The Territorial Dimension

The territorial dimension is the first issue to be analysed in the process aimed to formulate the definition of the concept of STZs.

In particular, the results of this research put in evidence three different profiles to be considered under the same territorial dimension, namely the geographical delimitation, the reference framework, and the territorial connecting factor which is adopted in the context of each zone.

[1] The Geographical Delimitation

The existence of a geographical border represents the most basic feature of STZs which is immediately recognizable in the factual experience.

The analysis of the literature on the topic confirms the importance and the necessity of a clear delimination of each zone; the scholars, in fact, often focus on this aspect in their attempts to provide a comprehensive definition of the same phenomenon.

In this sense, the 'STZ', regardless of the specific denominations used in each national context, is sometimes defined as a '*preferential tax regime that is ring-fenced*',[705] '*a well-defined geographical area*',[706] or '*as a geographically or administratively limited area*';[707] other scholars, which stress the point of view of customs, define STZs '*as areas with specific definition in or near a port, which are considered external to the customs territory*',[708] '*an area of a port separated from the national customs*

704. For these considerations *see supra* section §2.07.
705. R.S. Avi-Yonah, M. Vallespinos, *Special Tax Zones and the WTO*, University of Michigan Public Law Research Paper No. 545, 2017, available at https://ssrn.com/abstract=2928644.
706. P. Lorot, T. Scwob, *Les Zones franches dans le monde*, in *La Documentation francaise*, 1987, pp. 11 et seq.; A.T. Romero, *ILO's World Labour Report of 1996*, International Labour Organization (ILO), 1996; UNCTAD, *Export Processing Zones: Role of Foreign Direct Investment and Development Impact*, UNCTAD Secretariat, Geneva, 1993, p. 5.
707. M. Ingrosso, O. Nocerino, F. Roccatagliata, C. Sacchetto, *supra.*, Chamber of Commerce of Naples, Naples, 1998, pp. 9 et seq.; A. Basile, D. Germidis, *Investing in Free Export Processing Zones*, OECD Development Centre Studies, Paris, 1984, p. 20.
708. A.L. Lomax, *supra.*, School of Business Administration, University of Oregon, Eugene (Oregon), 1947, p. 5.

territory through a barrier',[709] or as '*a defined area, closed and controlled under the supervision of a special office of federal official'*.[710]

In the context of EU law, the geographical delimitation of STZs emerges from State aid rules considering that the exemptions provided under Article 107(3)(a) and (c) TFEU are set with regard to aid, in order to promote the economic development of 'certain areas'. Then, the same profile is also valorized by the UCC where a FZ is defined as a part of the customs territory of the Union limited from the rest of it,[711] having a perimeter fence supervised by customs authorities.[712]

Furthermore, the recent Guidance of the Code of Conduct Group[713] defines these zones as a 'special geographic area', stressing again the aspect of the geographical delimitation.

Beside the EU law sources, also national legislation offers some opportunities to set a focus on the profile of the geographical delimitation; for example, in the case of Bulgaria, an STZ is defined as '*a delimited part of the territory*',[714] while in Italy such zones are considered as '*a geographically delimited and clearly identified area*'.[715]

Given the above, the geographical delimitation always constitutes a necessary element of STZs; nonetheless, it is also important to distinguish the various ways through which the same geographical delimitation is concretely defined.

In this direction, the analysis and the comparison of the factual experience of the Member States offer important results able to give evidence of the various options available; in fact, beside the construction of an artificial fence requiring the human intervention, there are also situations where the border of an STZ is identified with a natural barrier. Consequently, while in the first case the delimitation of the zone is assured by the presence of a perimeter fence such as a wall, a net, or other artificial constructions,[716] in the second case the natural landscape represents a geographic limit used to precisely identify the area.[717]

A third option consists in the conventional delimitation of the zone through the use of an ideal line on the map, without any artificial or natural barrier set to identify the geographical border of the zone.[718]

Finally, it is also possible to find some hybrid situations where one part of the geographical border is delimited by the natural landscape (e.g., sea or lake) and the

---

709. R.S. Mac Elwee, *supra.*, 1926, p. 381. *See also* R.S. Thoman, *Free Ports and Foreign-Trade Zones*, Cornell Maritime Press, Cambridge, 1956.
710. *See* A. Isaacs, *supra.*, Richard D. Irwin Inc., Chicago (Illinois), 1948, pp. 753 et seq.
711. Article 237 UCC.
712. Article 243(3) UCC.
713. Guidance of the Code of Conduct Group (Business Taxation) on tax privileges related to special economic zones of 19 June 2017, Council of the European Union, Bruxelles, document No. 10487/17.
714. Article 3 of Decree of 14 July 1987, No. 2242, O.J. of Bulgaria No. 55 of 17 July 1987.
715. Article 4(2) Law Decree of 20 June 2017, No. 91, O.J. of Italy No. 141 of 20 June 2017.
716. For example Free Zones under the Union Customs Code where the presence of a perimeter fence is always required.
717. For example Canary Islands, Madeira, Azores where the ocean represents the natural barrier of the STZ.
718. For example Urban Tax-Free Zones in France and in Italy.

other one is delimited by an artificial barrier, such as a perimeter fence,[719] or even conventionally through an ideal line drawn on the map.[720]

[2] The Reference Framework

The territorial dimension also involves some considerations about the reference framework which is relevant for the assessment of the tax incentives; the identification of an STZ, in fact, is always the outcome of a process of critical comparison between the tax benefits there provided and the standard regime applied in the reference framework.

The analysis of the EU experience confirms that the standard tax regime of each Member State represents the fundamental parameter for the identification of the exceptional regime applied in an STZ; in other words, each Member State becomes the sole reference framework for the recognition of the favouring effects produced by the tax regime applied in an STZ.

The same conclusions are also valid for the sub-State bodies with sufficient autonomy, such as the Basque Country, Navarra, Saint-Martin, and Gibraltar; in all the situations, in fact, the reference framework for the concept of STZs corresponds to the territory of the hosting Member State and not to the territory of the infra-State body as stated by the ECJ in the Azores case.[721] This is because the decision of the ECJ in the Azores case, with reference to the conditions of institutional, procedural, and financial autonomy, assumes its relevance in a different context, namely for the purposes of the selectivity test under State aid rules. Differently, for what regards the concept of STZs here developed, the reference framework remains the national territory of the Member State which is responsible for the external relation of the infra-State body,[722] in accordance to the approach used in Chapter 4 for the identification of the various examples of STZs.

In other terms, situations like those of Gibraltar, the Basque Country, Navarra or Saint-Martin, all fulfilling the conditions of institutional, procedural, and financial autonomy according to the position of the ECJ, have to be considered as STZs for the purposes of this study, since their reference framework can always be identified in the territory of the Member State which is responsible for their external relations (i.e., UK, Spain, and France).

On these premises, as far as the reference framework becomes an essential profile of the territorial dimension, it finally can be concluded that STZs can only cover a minor part of the national territory according to a basic scheme with an exceptional tax regime, on one part, and a standard tax regime, on the other; in all the situations reviewed under Chapter 4, in fact, the territory of each STZ is always defined as a minor part of the Member State where a specific set of territorial tax advantages deviates, totally or in part, from the standard system of taxation applied in the rest of the State.

719. For example Campione d'Italia, Mount Athos, Gibraltar, Ceuta, Melilla and French Guyana.
720. For example Saint-Martin.
721. Case C-88/03 *Portugal v Commission*, [2006] ECR I-7115.
722. *See* Article 355(3) TFEU.

In this regard, it is also important to note that the territorial dimension of an STZ only involves cases of asymmetrical autonomy where a minor part of a State claims a special tax treatment that is not applied elsewhere in the same State. Differently, in the case of symmetrical autonomy, namely the situation where a State is equally divided in regions or other infra-State bodies with their own taxing powers, it is not possible to identify any kind of STZs, since in such situations there is not a reference framework with a standard tax regime to be used as a term of comparison.

In summary, the assessment of the tax regime of an STZ has always to be carried out with a focus set on the standard tax regime applied in the Member State concerned; in this sense, the national territory becomes the reference framework for this process of critical comparison.

It is thus possible to conclude that the reference framework represents one more qualifying aspect to be considered in the context of the territorial dimension; this aspect always involves an assessment in terms of comparison between the exceptional tax regime applied in an STZ and the standard tax regime applied in the rest of the hosting Member State.

[3] The Territorial Connecting Factor

Lastly, the territorial dimension involves one more profile concerning the legal criteria used to consider an economic activity as based within the perimeter of an STZ and, thus, as covered by the tax incentives granted therein.

In this regard, the discussion generally deals with the territorial connecting factor adopted by the legislator, namely the rules through which an economic activity carried out by an individual or a company may be linked to the territory of an STZ and benefit from the related tax incentives.[723]

Within the Member States, it is possible to identify a multitude of different criteria on the ground of the various forms of taxation and the corresponding level of harmonization.

For what regards indirect taxation, the UCC identifies the territorial connecting factor for the purposes of custom duties considering the placement of goods; in this sense, Article 237 UCC defines the FZs as a special procedure of storage under which Union or non-Union goods may be placed without being subject to customs duties and other indirect charges.

Then, it is important to consider the territorial connecting factor identified for VAT and excise duty, as this assumes a specific relevance for distinguishing the economic activities which benefit from the exclusion from the territorial scope of the Recast VAT Directive and the Excise Duty Directive.

In the case of VAT, the territorial connecting factor is defined with reference to the place where the goods are located at the time when the supply takes place[724] or the place where the goods are located at the time when dispatch or transport of the goods

723. A. Dagnino, *supra.*, CEDAM, 2008, p. 37.
724. *See* Council Directive 2006/112/EC of 28 November 2006 on the common system of value added tax, O.J. 2006, L 347, pp. 1-118, Article 31.

to the customer begins,[725] or, for supply of services, with reference to the place where the supplier has established his business or has a fixed establishment from which the service is supplied, or, in the absence of such a place of business or fixed establishment, the place where he has his permanent address or usually resides.[726] Differently, for the general arrangements on excise duty, the EU legislation provides that excise duty becomes chargeable at the time, and in the Member State, of release for consumption.[727]

The criteria used sensibly change as far as direct taxation is concerned; in the case of income tax, in fact, Member States are in principle free to determine their own criteria through national legislation, considering the absence of harmonized rules at the EU level.

For example, Madeira, the Canary Islands, and the ZFU in France and in Italy are all characterized by a territorial connecting factor associated to the presence of an economic activity in the area with the fulfilment of some specific requirements, such as the number of employees hired,[728] the volume of business with customers residing in the zone,[729] or the minimum amount of investment in fixed assets.[730] In other cases, the criteria used refer to a 'fixed place of business' from where the economic activity is organized, controlled, managed, and invoiced (e.g., Ceuta and Melilla).[731]

---

725. *Ibid.*, Article 32.
726. *Ibid.*, Article 43.
727. Council Directive 2008/118/EC of 16 December 2008 concerning the general arrangements for excise duty and repealing Directive 92/12/EEC, Article 7 according to which 'release for consumption' means any of the following: (a) the departure of excise goods, including irregular departure, from a duty suspension arrangement; (b) the holding of excise goods outside a duty suspension arrangement where excise duty has not been levied pursuant to the applicable provisions of community law and national legislation; (c) the production of excise goods, including irregular production, outside a duty suspension arrangement; (d) the importation of excise goods, including irregular importation, unless the excise goods are placed, immediately upon importation, under a duty suspension arrangement.
728. In Madeira the entities who wish to enjoy the tax benefits have to create one to five jobs in the first six months of activity (*see supra* section §4.02[Q][1]). In the Canary Islands Special Zone (ZEC), the new entities must create at least five jobs within six months from the date they receive the authorization to establish in the zone and maintain an average of at least five jobs during the time there are registered as a ZEC entity (*see supra* section §4.02[T][2]). In the case of the enterprises established in the French Urban Tax-Free Zones the number of employees living in the zone territory with a permanent contract or with a contract of at least twelve months must be equal to at least half of the total employees; furthermore, the number of employees hired after the fulfilment of the same conditions of contract and residence must be at least half of the employees hired during the same period (*see supra* section §4.02[G][2]). In the Italian Urban Tax-Free Zones, enterprises which benefit from the income tax exemption must employ at least one full-time employee who performs his job in a stable manner within the perimeter of the ZFU (*see supra* section §4.02[K][2]).
729. In the Italian Urban Tax-Free Zones, enterprise must achieve at least 25% of the volume of business with customers residing in the ZFU (*see supra* section §4.02[K][2]).
730. In Madeira the entities who wish to enjoy the tax benefits also have to undertake a minimum investment of EUR 75,000 in the acquisition of tangible or intangible fixed assets during the first two years of activity (*see supra* section §4.02[Q][1]). In the Canary Islands the new companies based in the ZEC must make an investment in the territory of at least EUR 100,000 in fixed assets related to the activity within the first two years subsequent to the authorization by the administrative authority (*see supra* section §4.02[T][2]).
731. *See supra* section §4.02[T][4].

In any case, regardless of some minimal differences in the national legislation, the experience of the Member States, as outlined in the above examples, confirms the possibility to associate the territorial connecting factor for direct taxation to the concept of 'permanent establishment' which is defined, under Article 5 of the OECD Model Tax Convention, as 'a fixed place of business, through which the business of an enterprise is wholly or partly carried on'.[732]

This conclusion finds clear evidence in the situations of Gibraltar and the Basque Country where the national legislation in force explicitly extends the tax benefits granted within such zones to the 'permanent establishment of a non-resident company'.[733]

In this regard, it is important to observe that the general use at the national level of the permanent establishment concept as a territorial connecting factor for STZs is not the result of a random process; the use of such a criterion, in fact, represents the effect of the negative integration of EU law, with particular reference to the limits set by the freedom of establishment to the legislative initiatives of the Member States. Member States, in fact, are generally free to determine their own legislation in the areas of exclusive competence – such as direction taxation – but are obliged, at the same time, to exercise their power in compliance with the basic principles of EU law, including the freedom of establishment.

In this sense, a territorial connecting factor defined by the national legislator with exclusive reference to the residence of an individual or a company – and not also with reference to its permanent establishment – would determine a differentiated tax treatment between the residents and non-residents of an STZ, with the production of a discriminatory effect and the infringement of the freedom of establishment.[734]

According to the ECJ, in fact, the evaluation of a tax measure applied in an STZ, including its territorial connecting factor, has to be carried out in the light of the principle of tax non-discrimination; from this perspective, a national rule with a discriminatory content, with a differential treatment of residents and non-residents, may constitute a restriction on the freedom of establishment where there is no objective difference in the situation which would justify different treatment between various categories of taxpayers.[735]

In other words, as expressly stated in a case concerning the previous tax regime applied in the Basque Country,[736] a permanent establishment of a non-resident

---

732. OECD, *Model Tax Convention on Income and on Capital: Condensed Version 2017*, OECD Publishing, 2017, Paris, available at https://doi.org/10.1787/mtc_cond-2017-en.For a comprehensive review of 'permanent establishments' *see* E. Reimer, N. Urban, S. Schmid, *A Domestic Taxation, Bilateral Tax Treaty, and OECD Perspective*, Kluwer Law International, Alphen aan den Rijn, 2011.

733. *See supra* section §4.02[T][3] (for the case of the Basque Country) and section §4.02[U][1] (for the case of Gibraltar).

734. *See* Case C-169/08 *Presidente del Consiglio dei Ministri v Regione Sardegna*, [2009] I-10821.

735. Case C-169/08 *Presidente del Consiglio dei Ministri v Regione Sardegna*, [2009] I-10821, paragraph 37.

736. Opinion of Advocate General Saggio delivered on 1 July 1999. Joined cases C-400/97, C-401/97 and C-402/97 *Administración General del Estado v Juntas Generales de Guipúzcoa and Diputación Foral de Guipúzcoa, Juntas Generales d'Alava and Diputación Foral d'Alava and Juntas Generales de Vizcaya*, [2000] ECR I-01073.

company cannot be excluded from the tax benefits provided in the same zone solely on the ground of the lack of the condition of residence.[737]

In conclusion, from the analysis of the EU framework and the experiences of the Member States it is clear that the territorial connecting factor assumes different forms in the case of indirect taxation, on one part, and in the case of direct taxation, on the other. While in the first situation, the criteria used correspond to the place where the goods are located at the time of the relevant operation - except for the supply of services under VAT rules where the place of business or fixed establishment is considered - differently, in the case of direct taxation, Member States generally define the territorial connecting factor in accordance with the limits set by the ECJ in order to avoid an infringement of the freedom of establishment; in this sense, in fact, the permanent establishment, even with the specific characteristics of each national context, represents today the parameter in accordance with EU law which is normally used to set a link between a business entity and the tax benefits available within an STZ.

[B] The Structural Dimension

The structural dimension of STZs is probably the most decisive factor from the economic operator's point of view, since the strategic choice of establishing a business within a zone is usually linked to the exploitation of the related tax benefits. In this sense, the focus turns to the specific provisions able to introduce exceptions to the standard rules applied in the hosting State with the final aim of reducing the tax burden.

Given the above, it is now necessary to switch to a more technical approach and to deepen the analysis of the structural aspects of STZs by the review of the different types of tax benefits usually introduced therein.

Preliminary, it must be noted that, in such cases, the standard rules of the tax system of the hosting Member State - namely the reference framework - are not applied in the area, in whole or in part; in this sense, the tax benefits introduced in STZs are based on a negative conception characterized by the total or partial denial of the standard tax rules applied in the reference framework.[738]

The denial of the standard tax rules is set in various forms in the experiences of the Member States and can lead to different outcomes that are described here below under the conceptual categories of the 'exclusion regimes', on one part, and 'subtractive regimes', on the other.[739]

737. *Ibid.*, paragraph 25.
738. P. Boria, *Il sistema tributario*, Wolters Kluwer Italia, Milan, 2008, p. 1035.
739. *Ibid.*, p. 1039.

[1] Exclusion Regimes

The 'exclusion regimes' are the result of an intervention through which the legislator limits the effects of the standard rules relevant under the discipline of one or more taxes, with the consequent refusal of such rules within the territory of the zone.

The term 'exclusion', in fact, can be used to identify those areas that are entirely outside the perimeter in which the standard tax rules produce their effects.

In these cases, it is not possible to identify the presence of a subtractive scheme with positive rules for counterbalancing the effects of the exclusion and, thus, the structural dimension merely corresponds to the negative result of the limitation of the area of application of one or more taxes.

In other words, a situation of 'exclusion' is characterized by the mere outlining of the external perimeter of the national territory where tax rules produce their effects; at the same time, the national legislator does not provide any special regime for the STZ whose territory remains outside the geographical limits of application of the same rules.[740]

On these bases, the exclusion regimes clearly differ from the concept of exemption where - as it will be explained in the next section - there is a subtractive regime provided by the legislator with exceptions to the standard rules of taxation generally applied in the rest of the hosting State.

Following the analysis of the material reviewed in the previous chapters, typical examples of tax benefits belonging to the category of the 'exclusion regimes' may be identified with the zones that are entirely set outside the Union Customs line[741] or the EU VAT area[742] where customs duties and VAT are not applied and where, at the same time, no subtractive regimes have been introduced for the regulation of the same taxes.

[2] Subtractive Regimes

In other cases, STZs are characterized by the presence of a subtractive regime with a positive discipline that differs from the standard one applied throughout the rest of the State. These rules usually affect the elements of the tax structure, such as the tax base or the tax rate, by the modification of the sequence that leads from the general factual element relevant under the tax rule to the determination of the final amount due by the taxpayer.[743]

740. For a comparison between exclusions and exemptions, *see* S. La Rosa, *Esclusioni tributarie*, *Enc. Giur.*, XIII, Rome, 1989; N. D'Amati, *Agevolazioni ed esenzioni tributarie*, in *Noviss. Dig. It.*, Appendix, I, Turin, 1980, pp. 153 et seq.; V. Uckmar, *Principi comuni di diritto costituzionale tributario*, CEDAM, Padova, 1999, pp. 71 et seq.

741. For example Livigno (Italy), Ceuta and Melilla (Spain), Gibraltar (United Kingdom), Mayotte and French Guyana (France).

742. For example Mount Athos (Greece), Livigno (Italy), Ceuta and Melilla (Spain), Gibraltar (United Kingdom).

743. P. Boria, *supra.*, Wolters Kluwer Italia, Milan, 2008, p. 1039.

All these situations are considered as exceptions to the standard rules of taxation, given the fact that, otherwise, the activities carried out in the zone would be subject to the standard tax discipline applied in the reference framework.

Therefore, there is always a relationship and a comparison between the basic situation (the standard tax treatment applied in the reference framework) and the subtractive discipline and, consequently, the result of this comparison highlights a negative difference suitable to generate a benefit to the taxpayer.

The subtractive discipline consists of a rule of positive law according to which the standard norm does not produce its effects, definitely or temporarily, with reference to one or more elements of the tax structure.[744]

Under these subtractive regimes it is possible to work out a classification according to the way through which the tax structure is affected, considering that tax benefits, both as they are temporary or perpetual, may intervene on the premises of the tax, on the tax base, on the tax rate, or on the procedures of assessment or those of collection.[745]

On these bases, it is possible to analyse the factual experience of the EU, with reference to the tax benefits classification proposed by Sandford,[746] later used by Cedefop,[747] which distinguishes five categories of incentives:

(1) tax exemptions: the income produced by entities based in STZs is exempted from taxation and, thus, it is not considered as taxable income. Among such tax incentives, it is possible to identify situations of full[748] or partial exemption[749] in which the subtractive discipline is aimed to exclude the income produced, totally or in part, from the application of taxation;
(2) tax allowances:[750] the deduction from the gross income (gross tax base) of an amount usually corresponding to the expenses occurred for some specific needs previously identified by the legislator. The result of the deduction determines the net taxable income;
(3) tax credits:[751] the deduction from the gross tax due of an amount (tax credit) usually corresponding to a percentage of the total expenses made by the

744. *Ibid.*, p. 1037.
745. F. Fichera, *Le agevolazioni fiscali*, CEDAM, Padova, 1992, p. 67.
746. C. Sanford, *Why Tax Systems Differ: A Comparative Study of the Political Economy of Taxation*, Fiscal Publications, Bath, 2000.
747. CEDEFOP, *Using Tax Incentive to Promote Education and Training*, European Centre for the Development of Vocational Training (ed.), CEDEFOP panorama series, Luxembourg, 2009, p. 21.
748. For example CIT and PIT exemption for *Zone Franche Urbaine* (ZFU) in France; IRAP and RET exemption for *Zone Franche Urbane* (ZFU) in Italy; CIT and RET exemption for Free Economic Zones in Lithuania; PIT and RET exemption for Madeira in Portugal.
749. For example CIT and PIT exemption for ZFUs in Italy, limited to 60% from the sixth to the tenth year, to 40% from the eleventh to the twelfth year and to 20% from the thirteenth to the fourteenth year; CIT dividends exemption for Canary Islands Economic and Fiscal Regime (REF) up to 90% of annual undistributed profits.
750. For example PIT reduction for Overseas departments (DOM) in France; PIT and CIT deduction for Ceuta and Melilla in Spain.
751. For example PIT tax credit for Overseas departments (DOM) in France; PIT tax credit for Canary Islands Economic and Fiscal Regime (REF), CIT tax credit for Special Economic Zones in Italy.

taxpayer for some specific needs previously identified by the legislator. The result of the deduction determines the net tax due;

(4) tax relief:[752] the application of a lower tax rate to the net taxable income;

(5) tax deferrals: the delay in the payment of taxes with the consequent suspension of any obligation set by the tax rule. Such provisions simply postpone the withdrawal, without changing the amount of the tax. The most classic example is the FZ regulated by the UCC where the tax benefit consists of a mere suspension of the taxation, given the fact that the same goods introduced into the FZ may be subjected to the levy once they exit the zone or are released for consumption.

Furthermore, apart from the above classification proposed by Sandford, the analysis of STZs in the EU context, as already carried out in Chapter 4, offers the opportunity to recognize other situations belonging to the category of subtractive regimes as follows:

(6) tax rebate:[753] a reduction in the amount of tax to be paid, generally expressed in the form of a percentage;

(7) tax replacement regime:[754] in this case the subtractive discipline does not represent a mere modification of one or more elements of the existing tax structure applied in the rest of the State, but it contains a replacement regime with regulations able to introduce a totally different tax structure, even through the introduction of a new tax.

[C] The Functional Dimension

Beside the structural and the territorial dimension, there is one more perspective to be used for the definition of the concept of STZs which is mainly focused on the reasons according to which territorial tax benefits are granted.

In this direction, the functional dimension involves the analysis of the tax policies and the government functions associated with the establishment of STZs with a teleological approach to the topic where the objectives pursued become the main aspect to be considered.[755]

---

752. For example CIT rate reduction for Saint-Martin in France; CIT, PIT, Excise, and VAT rate reduction for Azores; CIT rate reduction for Madeira; CIT rate reduction for Canary Islands Special Economic Zone (ZEC) in Spain.

753. For example CIT, RET and withholding tax rebate for Special Economic Zones in Latvia; CIT and PIT rebate for the production of corporal goods in the Canary Islands; CIT rebate for the Special Register for Ships and Shipping Companies Regime (REB) in Canary Islands.

754. For example Special import duties and local excise are applied in Gibraltar; in Ceuta and Melilla IPSI is applied instead of VAT; in Canary Islands IGIC and AIEM are applied instead of VAT and excise; in French Overseas departments OM and OMR are applied instead of excise duties, while an alternative VAT system is applied in the same zones; in Saint-Martin *Tax Generale sur le Chiffre d'Affaire* is applied instead of VAT.

755. S. La Rosa, *Le agevolazioni tributarie*, in *Trattato di diritto tributario, diretto da Amatucci A.*, Padova, 1994, I, 1, pp. 401 et seq.

Only a few previous studies have outlined the importance of this perspective; under the theory of tax expenditures,[756] for example, scholars identify a strict link between the favouring tax measures, on one part, and the objectives of tax policy which are pursued by the government, on the other.[757]

In this case, tax benefits are seen as a tool in the hands of governments to grant, indirectly, a form of subsidy which could also be introduced through different rules not belonging to the tax law field (i.e., contributions and other public grants); therefore, the concept of tax expenditures is representative of the active role of the State in the management of public resources through the establishment of tax benefits aimed at pursuing some specific objectives of tax policy.

The conclusion is that the introduction of tax advantages in a limited territory of a Member State always represents the result of a political choice involving the management of public resources and, thus, assuming relevance in the context of the functional dimension.

Given the above, the experience of the Member States confirms the existence of a functional dimension of STZs; all the related tax measures, in fact, are defined on the ground of a specific objective of economic and/or social policy pursued at the national level.

In this sense, the adoption of a functional perspective offers the opportunity to associate each tax measure in an STZ with a specific government function; under this approach it is thus possible to distinguish between economic policies, on one part, including government functions like commerce and economic development, and social policies, on the other, including government functions such as welfare, employment or social services.

On the ground of these ideas, the analysis of the material of the previous chapters finally outlines the possibility of a classification of tax incentives based on the same perspective; in this regard, in fact, the category of economic tax incentives, on one part, and the category of social tax incentives, on the other, represent the systematic approach used in the next sections to explore and to explain the functional dimension of STZs.

[1] Economic Tax Incentives

The analysis of the experience of the Member States gives evidence of many situations where the tax incentives granted in an STZ are univocally aimed at pursuing economic objectives.

756. *See* P.R. Mc Daniel, S.S. Surrey, *International Aspects of Tax Expenditures: A Comparative Study*, Springer Netherlands, Deventer, 1985; SS. Surrey, *Pathways to Tax Reform: The Concept of Tax Expenditures*, Harvard University Press, 1973. The results of these studies have been later used by international organizations. *See*, for instance, OECD Committee on Fiscal Affairs, *Tax Expenditures. A Review of the Issues and Country Practices*, OECD publications, Paris, 1984; V. Halberstadt, *Tax Incentives as an Instrument for Achievement of Governmental Goal, Report from the Netherlands for the 1976 Congress of the International Fiscal Association, Jerusalem (Israel), 13-17 September 1976*, Deventer, 1976.

757. A. Dagnino, *supra*, CEDAM, Padova, 2008, p. 20.

As far as indirect taxation is concerned, the level of harmonization achieved at the EU level clearly influences the same objective pursued in the context of an STZ; the establishment of the internal market, in fact, is the main driver of the process of harmonization and, therefore, the tax incentives on indirect taxation, including those introduced within an STZ, are generally addressed to objectives of an economic character.

For example, in the case of FZs, the deferral of customs duties and other indirect charges, as established under the UCC, is clearly aimed at the improvement of the efficiency in the import/export process and, thus, to the development of the international trade of goods.

The economic objective can also be found in the STZs which are excluded from the territorial scope of the EU legislation on indirect taxation, such as Ceuta and Melilla in Spain[758] or Helgoland and Busingen in Germany.[759] In these situations, the exclusion from the territorial scope of the UCC, the Recast VAT Directive and the Excise Duty Directive is established on the ground of some historical privileges due to the local communities in consideration of the disadvantaged geographical location; the tax benefits, in fact, – which are there granted through the establishment of an 'exclusion regime' – represent a form of compensation of the high transportation costs and are aimed at promoting domestic products and services in the international market.

For what regards direct taxation, there are also many situations where the tax incentives are targeted at the achievement of the same objectives of an economic character.

In this sense, there is the example of SEZs in Italy which have been established to encourage the creation of favourable conditions in economic, financial, and administrative terms, for the development, in some areas of the State, of existing economic activities or for the settlement of new ones.[760]

The same purposes can be identified in the case of SEZs in Latvia[761] and FEZs in Lithuania,[762] or also in the case of the business entities established in Saint-Martin,[763] where the objective is associated to the development of the international trade and the improvement of the attractiveness of such zones for foreign investments.

The Basque Country and Navarra are also characterized by the presence of a set of tax incentives which are addressed to the improvement of the competitiveness of the economic activities based in these territories and to the development of the international trade.[764]

Finally, in the case of Gibraltar it is evident that the tax advantages there granted are aimed at the pursuit of economic objectives; the territorial source principle of taxation and the withholding tax exemption for dividends, interests, and royalties paid

758. *See supra* section §4.02[T][4].
759. *See supra* section §4.02[H][2].
760. *See* Article 4 of Decree-Law of 20 June 2017, No. 91, O.J. of Italy No. 141 of 20 June 2017.
761. *See supra* section §4.02[L][1].
762. *See supra* section §4.02[M][1].
763. *See supra* section §4.02[G][4].
764. *See supra* section §4.02[T][3].

by a Gibraltar company to foreign shareholders give evidence of an objective which is associated with the development of foreign investments in the same territory.[765]

In all the aforementioned situations, it is clear that the government functions which can be associated with the tax advantages granted are exclusively related to economic development and commerce in general, while it is not possible to recognize any social function under the same tax measures.

These conclusions are also confirmed by the analysis of the conditions under which the tax benefits are granted in each STZ; in most of the cases, in fact, the eligibility requirements are related to a certain minimum amount of investments[766] or to the establishment of the economic activity in the STZ for a minimum number of years.[767] Differently, there are no conditions of a social character regarding, for example, the creation of a certain number of new jobs or the hiring of workers belonging to a disadvantaged category.

Given the above, the results of the present research finally outline the fundamentals of a first category of tax incentives which characterize the functional dimension of STZs; in this context, in fact, it is possible to identify the category of 'economic tax incentives' – also defined as 'business related tax incentives' or 'income related tax incentives'[768] – which include all the tax measures addressed to the pursuit of objectives of an economic character.

As already seen, economic tax incentives are widely used across the various Member States as an instrument of economic policy under specific government functions. In such situations, economic tax incentives are used to promote the economic development of certain areas and the international trade between the operators based therein; the aim is often to change the trend of the macroeconomic system and the level of different economic indicators, with the improvement of the results in terms of marginal profits for the undertakings which are active in the area concerned.[769]

In summary, in the light of the experience of the Member States, it is possible to define the category of economic tax incentives in a broad manner through a series of different coordinates. First, it is necessary that tax incentives are aimed at pursuing a specific objective of economic character which is generally related to (i) the competitiveness in respect to the international trade, (ii) the attractiveness of the area for foreign investments, or (iii) the efficiency in the production and distribution chain in the import export/process. Second, it is necessary that the same objective is pursued under the impulse of a government function like economic development or commerce in general. Third, the outcome of the tax incentives programme, from the perspective

765. *See supra* section §4.02[U][1].

766. For example, in the case of Free Economic Zones in Lithuania, companies whose capital investments in the area are no less than EUR 1 million do not pay any CIT for the first six years of activity (*see supra* section §4.02[M][1]).

767. In the case of Special Economic Zones in Italy (*see supra* section §4.02[K][3]) enterprises benefit from a tax credit provided that they maintain the business established in the zone for seven years, at least, after the completion of the investment.

768. E. Traversa, *Tax Incentives and Territoriality Within the European Union: Balancing the Internal Market with the Tax Sovereignty of Member States*, in *World Tax Journal*, 2014, p. 339.

769. *Ibid.*

of the taxpayer, is always linked to the improvement of the economic environment with a focus on the development of trade between economic operators; in this case, in fact, positive effects on employees and resident population in general are only an eventual result which is not directly pursued by the legislator.

[2] Social Tax Incentives

Beside the category of economic tax incentives, it is possible to identify other tax measures in the context of STZs which are instead addressed to objectives of a social character.

In this sense, the aim of the present section is to identify the boundaries of one more category which is relevant under the functional dimension of STZs: the category of 'social tax incentives'.

For this purpose, the research process is based on the analysis of the various resources which have been reviewed under the previous chapters, including the legal dimension of STZs with the relevant literature, the EU law framework, and the experience of the Member States.

The literature on the topic of tax expenditures tries to investigate the concept of social tax incentives in general, without a direct link to the phenomenon of STZs. In particular, according to some scholars, the establishment of social tax incentives is a matter of fact as far as two conditions are fulfilled: first, tax benefits must be addressed to disadvantaged groups of individuals belonging to the low and the middle-income class; second, the same tax benefits must be designed within a specific government function related to social welfare objectives, such as income security, health, employment, training, housing, education, or social services.[770]

The EU law framework offers more opportunities to define the category of social tax incentives and to explore its substantial content. In this direction, in fact, specific notions used at the EU level, such as 'social services of general interest' (SSGIs), 'social advantages' and social enterprises', can be associated with the concept of social tax incentives and, therefore, can contribute to better define what the social character of these incentives really entails.

The Commission, for example, provides a list of services which constitute SSGIs, giving a positive content to the social dimension of such initiatives; in this sense, Article 2(1)(c) of Decision 2012/21/EU makes reference to services related to '*health and long term care, childcare, access to and reintegration into the labour market, social housing and the care and social inclusion of vulnerable groups*'.

In particular, for the purposes of the present research, the concept of 'inclusion of vulnerable groups' assumes a fundamental relevance for the establishment of the boundaries of the category of social tax incentives. In fact, as far as this concept is intended in a flexible and broad way, Member States are allowed to determine what they qualify as 'social' with a wide margin of discretion.

770. *See* C. Howard, *The Hidden Welfare State: Tax Expenditure and Social Policy in the United States*, Princeton University Press, Princeton, 1997, pp. 18 et seq.

Nevertheless, some limits are imposed by EU law in case of a manifest error of assessment in the identification of what constitutes 'inclusion of vulnerable groups';[771] in this sense, certain minimum criteria have to be fulfilled concerning the universal and compulsory character of such measures.[772]

In the context of the *Almunia* Package, this perspective is confirmed by the Commission staff working document[773] where SSGIs cover not only health services and social security schemes, but also other essential services - of a more flexible and broad scope - playing a prevention and social cohesion role with customized assistance to facilitate social inclusion and to safeguard fundamental rights.[774] Therefore, it is clear that the social character of SSGIs, as defined under the above resources, can be associated to the social character of the tax benefits granted in an STZ, giving a positive content to the category of social tax incentives.

Within the EU law framework, also the notion of social advantages is contiguous to the category of social tax incentives, including all the advantages which, whether or not linked to a contract of employment, are granted to national workers mainly because of their objective status or by virtue of their residence on the national territory.[775]

Nevertheless, this definition is very broad and general[776] and, thus, it is not able to support the research path aimed at the identification of the conceptual limits of the category of social tax incentives.

On the contrary, the notion of social enterprises[777] is a more useful instrument; in particular, social enterprises assume relevance when the perspective of analysis is shifted on the recipient of the social tax incentives and, thus, on the specific rules according to which such entities operate in respect to vulnerable groups of individuals. In this sense, in fact, the boundaries of the category of social tax incentives can be better defined as long as the focus is set on the governance criteria, economic criteria,

771. Case T-289/03 *BUPA and others v Commission*, [2008] ECR II-00081, paragraph 166; Case T-17/02 *Fred Olsen, SA v Commission*, [2005] ECR II-02031, paragraph 216. In this sense, *see also* A. Koukiadaki, *EU Governance and Social Services of General Interest: When Even the UK Is Concerned*, in, *EU Law, Governance and Social Policy European Integration Online Papers*, J.C. Barbier (ed.) 2012, Special Mini-Issue 1, Vol. 16, Article 5 available at http://eiop.or.at/eiop/texte/2012-005a.htm.
772. *Ibid.*, paragraphs 188-190.
773. *See supra* section §3.02[D][5].
774. In particular, according to the Commission staff working document, in the first place such services '*offer assistance to persons faced by personal challenges or crises (such as debt, unemployment, drug addiction or family breakdown). Secondly, they include activities to ensure that the people concerned are able to completely reintegrate into society (rehabilitation, language training for immigrants) and, in particular, return to the labour market (occupational training and reintegration). These services complement and support the role of families in caring for the youngest and oldest members of society in particular. Thirdly, these services include activities to integrate people with long-term health or disability problems. Fourthly, they also include social housing, which provides housing for disadvantaged citizens or socially less advantaged groups*'.
775. *See supra* section §3.03[B][4].
776. A. Czekay-Dancewicz, *Access to Social Benefits and Advantages for EU Migrant Workers, Members of Their Families and Other Categories of Migrating EU Citizens*, 2013, p. 1, available at http://ec.europa.eu/social/BlobServlet?d ocId = 11714&langId = en.
777. *See supra* section §3.03[B][5].

and social criteria which characterize social enterprises;[778] in this direction, social enterprises and social tax incentives seem to be part of the same framework which is related to the management of a government function within the welfare domain. In particular, social enterprises become a sort of vehicle to grant social tax incentives and, at the same time, a selective filter between public finance and the citizens.

After the literature and the EU law framework, the analysis must finally be oriented to the factual experience of the Member States.

In this regard, ZFU in France and in Italy represent important examples of areas with social tax incentives established on the ground of the same principles. Within these areas, the development of economic activities is directly addressed to social cohesion and to the creation of employment for local residents within the welfare domain in general and the related government functions; in particular, under such tax regimes, the minimum number of resident employees to be hired by the recipient undertakings is a condition able to confirm the pursuit of an objective of social policy.

Also Madeira and the Canary Islands are equally characterized by a set of tax incentives with a clear social objective and conditioned on the creation of a certain number of new jobs for local residents; also in this case, the scope is the creation of employment and, therefore, the welfare domain is again the government function interested by the related tax measures.

Given the above, it is now necessary to summarize the results of this process of analysis, identifying the characteristics able to distinguish the category of social tax incentives from the category of economic tax incentives.

In this direction, the scope of the tax measure, the filtering role of enterprises, and the conditions under which the incentives are granted, finally represent three aspects to be considered in order to identify the presence of social tax incentives under the functional dimension of STZs.

---

778. *See* Article 2 of Regulation (EU) No. 1296/2013 according to which a 'social enterprise' is an undertaking, regardless of its legal form, which: (a) in accordance with its Articles of Association, Statutes or with any other legal document, has as its primary objective the achievement of measurable, positive social impacts rather than generating profit for its owners, members, and shareholders, and which: (i) provides services or goods able to generate a social return and/or (ii) employs a method of production of goods or services that embodies its social objective; (b) uses its profits first and foremost to achieve its primary objective and has predefined procedures and rules covering any distribution of profits to shareholders and owners which ensure that such distribution does not undermine the primary objective; and (c) is managed in an entrepreneurial, accountable, and transparent way, in particular by involving workers, customers, and stakeholders affected by its business activities. *See also See* Communication from the Commission to the European Parliament, the Council, the European Economic and Social Committee and the Committee of Regions, *Social business initiative creating a favourable climate for social enterprises, key stakeholders in the social economy and innovation*, COM(2011) No. 0682 final, paragraph 1. According to this Communication, a social enterprise is 'an operator in the social economy whose main objective is to have a social impact rather than make a profit for their owners or shareholders. It operates by providing goods and services for the market in an entrepreneurial and innovative fashion and uses its profits primarily to achieve social objectives. It is managed in an open and responsible manner and, in particular, involves employees, consumers, and stakeholders affected by its commercial activities'.

The scope, as the first aspect to be considered, is always connected to the exercise of a specific government function within the social welfare domain, such as employment, housing or social services in general; here, the primacy of the social objective over capital and profits is the qualifying feature, being able to highlight the government function and the context of social policy where the same tax measures are adopted. Within the welfare domain and the related government functions, the social inclusion of vulnerable groups – or, more simply, the 'social cohesion' – becomes a flexible and broad objective allowing Member State to valorize the peculiarities and the specific needs of each national context.

Then, the autonomy of the concept of social tax incentives is also based on the role of enterprises within the same framework where such incentives are granted. In this sense, in fact, it is important to observe that enterprises, as the direct recipient of the favouring tax treatment, assume a filtering role between public finance and groups of individuals who require more protection; they become a sort of a vehicle through which social tax incentives are finally brought to vulnerable groups of people usually identified with the new employees hired according to the conditions set under the tax scheme of an STZ. Under this mechanism, enterprises become a selective tool for the identification of vulnerable groups of individuals according to a set of conditions provided by the law and regarding the eligibility for the same tax incentives.

Finally, the last aspect to be considered is related to the specific conditions under which tax incentives are granted within STZs. From the functional perspective, in fact, a certain number of conditions are necessary to address the tax measure to the effective achievement of an objective of a social character. Social tax incentives, in fact, as far as they are granted to entities carrying out an economic activity, have to be carefully designed in order to influence the behaviour of enterprises towards vulnerable groups of people, with an effect consisting in the creation of new jobs, for example. Differently, without these conditions, the category of social tax incentives would be inconsistent since the enterprises would be free to join the tax benefits and, at the same time, to pursue different objectives of an economic character related to the improvement of marginal profits.

Therefore, enterprises, in order to qualify for the tax benefits, must comply with conditions concerning the creation of employment for residents or the reinvestment of the profits in projects or other activities related with social cohesion in general. Through the fulfilment of such conditions, social tax incentives are finally targeted to vulnerable groups of people, despite the fact that the same tax incentives are formally granted in favour of enterprises, allowing the reduction of their tax burden.

Given the above, in the light of the material analysed under the present research, it is possible to conclude that social tax incentives are an autonomous category which, beside economic tax incentives, characterizes the functional dimension of STZs. The scope of the related tax measure, the role of enterprises, and the conditions for eligibility give a positive content to the same conceptual category, with a series of requirements and qualifying features able to define the conceptual boundaries and to valorize the systematic perspective.

[D] The Definition

The term 'STZs' is used in this study to identify a comprehensive concept able to encompass all the geographic areas characterized by the presence of tax benefits according to the territorial, structural, and functional dimensions analysed in the previous sections.

In this context, in fact, the other denominations used in literature and in legislation (e.g., FZs, SEZs, Tax Free Zones, etc.) are not able to clearly set the borders and the essential elements of the phenomenon in a comprehensive way, especially for what regards the legal aspects.[779]

This lexical choice is thus supported by the idea of a macro-category able to include the different experiences of territorial tax benefits within the EU; in this regard, in fact, the present phenomenon does not only correspond to the situation of a tax-free zone where taxation is not applied,[780] but also to other situations with a more favourable regime of taxation compared to the standard regime applied in the rest of the State.[781]

On these premises, the approach to the research question formulated in the introduction of the present chapter, as far as it is aimed at the development of a general legal theory of STZs, should also include a comprehensive definition on the ground of the territorial, structural, and functional dimensions explored in the previous sections.

For this scope, it is thus necessary to summarize in a few words the key features of the concept of STZs, highlighting its basic elements as resulting from the research process.

First, under the territorial dimension, it is important to remember that the geographical delimitation of an STZ always involves the presence of a natural, artificial or conventional border; in this sense, the territory within which the tax incentives are available is a well-defined geographical area and, at the same time, a minor part of the reference framework represented by the hosting Member State. Entities and goods which can benefit from the favouring tax regimes are those considered as based within the STZ according to a territorial connecting factor provided by law.

Second, from the structural point of view, these areas are characterized by a special tax treatment which deviates, in total or in part, from the standard tax regime applied in the rest of the Member State; thus, the tax benefits introduced in STZs are based on a negative conception characterized by the total or partial denial of the standard tax rules applied in the reference framework. As seen, the deviation from the standard tax rules can be set through the establishment of 'exclusion regimes' or 'subtractive regimes'. In the former case, the legislator limits the effects of the standard rules relevant under the discipline of one or more taxes, with the consequent refusal of such rules within the territory of the zone. In the latter case, STZs are characterized by

779. For these considerations *see supra* section §1.08.
780. For example the Free Zones established under the EU customs legislation where no custom duties and other charges are applied.
781. For example the Canary Islands Economic and Fiscal Regime (REF) characterized by the presence of a lower taxation.

a positive discipline that differs from the standard one applied throughout the rest of the State; in this situation, the positive discipline introduced in the STZ affects the elements of the tax structure, such as the tax base or the tax rate, by the modification of the sequence that leads from the general factual element relevant under the tax rule to the determination of the final amount due by the taxpayer.

Third, for what regards the functional dimension, it is evident that the tax measures of an STZ are defined on the ground of a specific objective of economic or social policy pursued at the national level; in other words, each tax measure is associated to a specific government function, with a fundamental distinction between economic policies, on one part, including government functions like commerce and economic development, and social policies, on the other, including government functions such as welfare, employment or social services.

On the ground of this summary of the main characteristics of the phenomenon, it is finally possible to outline a comprehensive definition within the general legal theory of STZs. In this sense, STZs can be defined as 'areas delimited by a natural, artificial or conventional border where entities and goods, selected through a territorial connecting factor provided by the law, can benefit from a favouring tax treatment which deviates, under an exclusion regime or a subtractive regime, from the standard tax treatment applied in the rest of the hosting State on the ground of objectives of an economic or social character defined within a specific government function'.

The proposed definition, essentially based on the identification of a territorial, a structural and a functional dimension, represents one more result of the research process, offering theoretical support for the comprehension of the phenomenon from the perspective of European tax law.

§5.03 THE IMPLEMENTING MODELS

The analysis of the experience of the Member States also offers the opportunity to recognize different implementing models which are the direct expression of the concept of STZs developed according to the territorial, the structural, and the functional dimensions.

In this direction, the examples of STZs reviewed in Chapter 4 are sometimes characterized by a set of common features, especially for what regards the legal background under which they are established.

Accordingly, the research puts in evidence the presence of three implementing models respectively based on the UCC (FZs), on State aid rules (State Aid Zones), and on the territorial scope of the indirect taxes harmonized at EU level (Extraterritorial Zones).

[A] The 'FZ' Model

The first model of STZs identified under the present research corresponds to the areas defined as 'FZs' within the UCC.

In this case, the tax benefits granted are exclusively relevant in the context of indirect taxation, with a specific deferral regime provided for customs duties, VAT, and excise duties, while no advantages can generally be identified for what concerns direct taxation.

As seen in Chapter 4, this implementing model is widely used in the experience of the Member States, considering that the list of FZs in operation in the Union, as communicated by the Member States to the Commission,[782] includes areas which are part of the national territory of Bulgaria, Croatia, Czech Republic, Denmark, Estonia, Finland, France, Germany, Greece, Hungary, Italy, Latvia, Lithuania, Luxembourg, Malta, Poland, Portugal, Romania, Slovenia, and Spain.

The recognition of the basic features of the 'FZ' model is the direct result of the analysis of the EU legal framework; its main legal source, in fact, is represented by the UCC which includes a comprehensive regime for the application of custom duties.

In general, according to Article 210 UCC, FZs are identified as a special procedure of storage under which Union or non-Union goods may be placed. More precisely, a FZ, as defined by Article 237 UCC, is a part of the customs territory of the Union limited from the rest of it, in which non-EU goods introduced therein are considered, both for customs duties and for trade policy measures, as not situated in the territory of the Union, provided that they are not released for free circulation or placed under another customs procedure or used or consumed under conditions other than those provided by customs regulations.

The Articles 243 and 244 UCC recognize the possibility for Member States to designate parts of the customs territory of the Union as FZs; in particular, for what regards the territorial dimension, Member States determine the area covered and the entry and exit points, considering that FZs are always ring-fenced and subjected to customs supervision.

From the structural point of view, the tax benefits of the FZ generally consist in the suspension of the levy of customs duties thanks to a deferral regime for goods introduced into the area.

In this regard, in fact, Article 237(a) UCC provides that under a storage procedure – such as the FZ – non-Union goods may be stored in the customs territory of the Union without being subject to import duties until they are not assigned to the final exportation to non-EU countries or released for free circulation in the Union.

The FZ model is also characterized by the presence of further tax advantages granted by Directive 2006/112/EC and by Directive 2008/118/EC regarding, respectively, VAT and excise duty.

In the case of VAT, Member States are allowed to exempt from VAT the supply of goods and services carried out in a FZ; according to Article 156 of Directive 2006/112/EC, in fact, Member States are able to exempt, among others, the supply of goods that are intended to be placed in a FZ, while the following Article 159 specifies that the same Member States may also exempt the supply of services related to the

782. Communication from the Commission of 23 February 2002 publishing the list of free zones in existence and in operation in the Community, O.J. 2002, C 50, pp. 16-18 (last update 21 August 2019).

supply of goods referred to in Article 156. In this regard, it is important to note that the tax incentives here provided only refer to the supplies of goods and services made between entities based within the FZ territory. Differently, the supply between a non-EU operator and an operator based in a FZ is regulated by Article 237 UCC according to which under a FZ, '*non-Union goods may be stored in the customs territory of the Union without being subject to other charges as provided for under other relevant provisions in force*'.

The VAT exemption provided according to the above discipline is merely temporary and, thus, it consists in a form of tax deferral with the suspension of taxation; the same goods brought into the FZ regime, in fact, are subjected to VAT once they exit the zone to enter the Union territory or are released for consumption.

In other words, any time goods are introduced into a FZ, the chargeable event of VAT - as in the case of customs duties - is delayed until such goods remain placed within the perimeter of the FZ.

These conclusions are also confirmed by Article 202 of Directive 2006/112/EC according to which '*VAT shall be payable by any person who causes goods to cease to be covered by the arrangements or situations listed in Articles 156* [referring to Free Zones], *157, 160 and 161*'.

For what regards excise duty, the deferral is equally granted through the delay of the chargeable event which corresponds, in this case, to the importation of the goods into the territory of the EU. The chargeable event, in fact, is excluded any time the goods are placed under the FZ regime, assuming that a FZ is a customs suspensive procedure and not a form of importation or release for consumption.

Finally, from the functional point of view, it is worth to note that the tax benefits granted within the model of the FZ - represented by the suspension of custom duties, VAT and excise duty - are the result of the economic policy carried out by the hosting State, within a government function corresponding to the development of the international trade. No other objectives can be recognized under the establishment of FZs and, thus, the management of social policy and welfare remains an external issue not directly linked to the provision of such tax incentives.

[B] The 'State Aid Zone' Model

Within the EU law framework also State aid rules assume a fundamental role for the discipline of STZs, especially as far as the topic of regional aid and the issue of territorial selectivity are concerned.

By the analysis of the experience of the Member States, in fact, it is possible to identify many examples of STZs where the special tax treatment - compared to the standard one applied in the reference framework - is defined on the ground of the discipline of State aid as set by Article 107 TFEU.

In this regard, the resulting 'State Aid Zone' model can be implemented in two different forms: as an exemption to the general State aid prohibition according to the situations of regional aid described under paragraph 3, letters (a) and (c) of Article 107 TFEU, on one part, or as an infra-State body with sufficient institutional, procedural, and financial autonomy with tax measures considered as not selective according to ECJ case law, on the other part.

[1] Regional Aid

In the first case, the tax measures adopted in an STZ are in principle prohibited State aid, falling within the conditions set out by Article 107 TFEU; in particular, the tax advantages are considered territorial selective with reference to the territory of the Member State, in the sense that they favour only certain undertakings or certain products.

Nonetheless, in such situations, the tax advantages may be structured as an exemption to the general State aid prohibition in the terms defined under Article 107(3) TFEU and on the ground of a discretional assessment by the Commission under which tax benefits may be declared acceptable if certain conditions are met.

In this sense, in fact, paragraphs (a) and (c) of Article 107(3) TFEU identify two different categories of regional aid that may be authorized by the Commission.

First, Article 107(3)(a) TFEU provides that aid may be granted to promote the economic development of areas where the standard of living is abnormally low or where there is serious underemployment and of the 'ORs' referred to in Article 349 TFEU, in view of their structural, economic, and social situation. This exemption concerns only those regions where the economic situation is extremely unfavourable in relation to the entire territory of the EU, so that the assessment of these factors must be made with reference to the EU level, and not with reference to the national average in the Member State concerned.[783]

Second, Article 107(3)(c) TFEU allows for the approval of aid to facilitate the development of certain economic activities or of certain economic areas; this second exception is wider in scope than that available under Article 107(3)(a) TFEU since it permits the development of certain areas without being restricted by the economic conditions necessary for the application of the first exception, allowing regional aid intended to favour the economic development of areas which are disadvantaged in relation to the national average.[784]

In both cases, the Commission has the responsibility, under a system of prior authorizations, to ensure that every Member State only conceives and designs aid measures useful to help companies in producing goods and services that would not otherwise be provided in the internal market, avoiding measures that distort competition.[785]

Nevertheless, it is worth remembering that, following the introduction of the GBER, STZs may also be established within the threshold of the maximum aid intensity set by the regional aid map without a formal prior approval by the Commission as long as some conditions are fulfilled.[786]

783. *See supra* section §3.02[A][2].
784. *See supra* section §3.02[A][3].
785. For the role of the Commission *see supra* section §3.02[A][4].
786. *See supra* section §3.02[B][1].

Today, the 'State Aid Zone' model is often implemented in the Member States through the introduction of regional aid; in fact, there are various examples of zones characterized by a set of territorial tax advantaged established on the ground of the exemptions provided by Article 107(3) TFEU, such as in the case of Madeira in Portugal, ZFU in France and in Italy and SEZs in Italy.

The common features of these zones are mainly recognizable under the structural dimension since in all the cases the tax advantages are granted with the establishment of a subtractive regime, namely a positive special discipline able to modify elements of the tax structure already defined at the national level, such as the tax base or the tax rate. On the contrary, for what regards the functional dimension, such zones are not always addressed towards the same aim, since they may pursue both objectives of a social character (i.e., ZFU in France and in Italy) or of an economic character (i.e., Madeira in Portugal and SEZs in Italy).

[2] The 'Infra-State Body'

The State Aid Zone model may also be implemented through the establishment of an infra-State body where the tax incentives are not considered territorial selective as long as some requirements are fulfilled.

According to ECJ case law, this possibility is associated to the situations in which an infra-State body, such as a region or a municipality, enjoys sufficient institutional, procedural, and economic autonomy to be able to determine its own tax system, defining the political and economic environment in which undertakings operate.[787]

Under this approach, the autonomy of the infra-State body excludes in principle the territorial selectivity for the scope of State aid rules, regardless of any further evaluation of the disadvantaged economic conditions of the same territory.

In particular, the infra-State body must enjoy a legal and factual status which makes it sufficiently autonomous in relation to the central government of a Member State, with the result that, by the measures it adopts, it is that body and not the central government which plays a fundamental role in the definition of the political and economic environment. In such a case, it is the area in which the infra-State body exercises its powers, and not the State as a whole, that constitutes the reference framework for the assessment of whether a measure adopted by such a body favours certain undertakings with respect to others in a comparable legal and factual situation.[788]

In more details, three conditions must be fulfilled in order to obtain the requirement of autonomy under which tax benefits introduced within an infra-State body may not be considered as selective for the scope of State aid rules.

First, by a constitutional point of view, the regional authority needs to have a separate political and administrative status from the national government (institutional autonomy).

787. Case C-88/03 *Portugal v Commission*, [2006] ECR I-7115.
788. *Ibid.*

Second, the measure must be adopted with no central government authorized to directly affect the decision (procedural autonomy).

Third, the financial consequences of the beneficial treatment given to undertakings in the region must not be offset by aid or subsidies from other regions or from the central government (economic and financial autonomy).[789]

In conclusion, according to the above elements, it is always necessary to verify if the region plays a key role in the definition of a political and economic environment not constrained by decisions taken by the general economic policy of the Member State; in other words, the regional authority must assume the responsibility for the political and financial consequences of the tax measures implemented.

On these premises, the model of STZs at issue represents an evident result of the phenomenon of asymmetrical fiscal federalism, being clear that the infra-State body is set in a context where the political priority is the devolution of powers from the central State to a specific regional or local authority.[790]

Therefore, it is clear that the main common feature of the State Aid Zone implemented through an infra-State body is related to its territorial dimension and, in particular, to the identification of the reference framework for the purposes of the selectivity test under State aid rules.[791]

From the structural point of view, the tax benefits granted are generally introduced in the form of a subtractive regime exclusively defined by the regional authority with reference to the standard regime adopted in the rest of the hosting State (e.g., Basque Country and Navarra). In some cases, the tax benefits are directly implemented by the local authority in the context of an autonomous tax system with the definition of an alternative legal framework under which the tax due is determined (e.g., Gibraltar).

Finally, the functional dimension of the infra-State bodies recognized in the EU experience is generally characterized by the pursuit of objectives of an economic character, since the examples of Basque Country, Navarra, and Gibraltar are all addressed in that sense; nonetheless, it is not possible to exclude in principle future

789. *Ibid.*

790. In this regard, it is important to note that the model of STZ here identified – the infra-State body – only refers to cases of asymmetrical autonomy where a single region (or a minor number of regions) of a State claims a special tax treatment that is not applied elsewhere in the same State. Otherwise, in the case of symmetrical autonomy, namely the situation where a State is equally divided in regions or other infra-State bodies with their own taxing powers, it is not possible to identify any kind of STZs, considering that the territorial dimension always requires that the zone with the special tax treatment represents a minor part of the political territory of the hosting State (*see supra* section §5.02[A][2]). For some interesting considerations about the different approach of the Commission to asymmetrical and symmetrical autonomy *see* R. Luja, *Do State Aid Rules Still Allow European Union Member States to Claim Fiscal Sovereignty?*, in *EC Tax Review*, 2016, No. 5-6, pp. 318-319.

791. It is important to remember that the reference framework for the purposes of the selectivity test is different from the reference framework which is used to confirm the existence of an STZ; in the latter case, in fact, the reference framework always corresponds to the territory of the Member State which is responsible for the external relations of the infra-State body, regardless of any further investigation on the fulfilment of the conditions of institutional, procedural, and financial autonomy.

initiatives for the establishment of infra-State bodies addressed to objectives belonging to the social and welfare domain.

[C] The 'Extraterritorial Zone' Model

The third and last implementing model identified in the experience of the Member States includes the so-called Extraterritorial Zones where the tax incentives are merely the result of the exclusion of the area from the territorial scope of one or more taxes.

In such situations, the effects of the standard rules are limited to the rest of the hosting State, with the consequent exclusion of the application of the same rules within the territory of the zone.

Extraterritorial Zones are entirely outside the perimeter in which standard tax rules produce their effects and, therefore, the favouring treatment is the negative result of the limitation of the territorial scope of the tax norm.

On these bases, this model of STZs is founded on the definition of the geographical limits within which tax rules produce their effects, with the exclusion of a specific area of the national territory from the scope of application of one or more taxes.

In all these situations, it is not possible to identify the introduction of a subtractive regime with a set of positive norms reserved to the area, considering that the favouring treatment is the mere result of the non-application of the standard tax rules implemented in the rest of the hosting State.

Therefore, it is evident that the common feature of this model is defined under the structural dimension, considering that the special tax treatment is here provided through the establishment of 'exclusion regimes' for one or more taxes.[792]

Then, from the functional point of view, these zones usually represent an instrument for the development of economic policy; they are established on the ground of some historical privileges due to the local community based in the zone, as the result of compromises between national and local authorities signed at the time of the foundation of the State; these historical privileges are generally justified on the base of economic reasons related to the disadvantaged geographical position of the zone, especially when located far away from the main national financial centres.

Therefore, the model of the Extraterritorial Zone is generally associated with objectives of an economic character and it is aimed at improving the volume of the international trade and at offsetting the gap related to the distance from the main financial centres of the Member State; such zones, in fact, are generally located in disadvantages areas such as mountain areas (Livigno, Mount Athos), remote islands

---

792. For the territories excluded from the scope of customs duties *see* Article 4 of Regulation (EU) No. 952/2013 of the European Parliament and of the Council of 9 October 2013 laying down the Union Customs Code, O.J. 2013, L. 269, pp. 1-101; for the territories excluded from the scope of VAT *see* Article 6 of Council Directive 2006/112/EC of 28 November 2006 on the common system of value added tax, O.J. 2006, L 347, pp. 1-118; for the territories excluded from the scope of excise duty see Article 5(2) of Council Directive 2008/118/EC of 16 December 2008 concerning the general arrangements for excise duty and repealing Directive 92/12/EEC, O.J. 2009, L 9, pp. 12-30.

(Aland Island and Helgoland) or enclaves in the political territories of other States (Busingen, Campione d'Italia, Ceuta, and Melilla).

[D] Hybrid Situations

In the EU context, the models of STZs described in the present chapter do not exclude the presence of hybrid situations where different features are combined together giving birth to original solutions.

In general, there are examples in which both the elements of the State Aid Zone and of the Extraterritorial Zone characterize the complex set of tax advantages granted to a limited area of land (e.g., Canary Islands, Ceuta and Melilla, French Overseas Departments, and Saint-Martin).

In other cases, the 'FZ' model is combined with the 'State Aid Zone' model, with a mix of different tax benefits dealing not only with indirect taxation, but also with direct taxation (e.g., FEZs in Lithuania and SEZs in Latvia).

Given the above, the implementing models identified in this research should always be considered as flexible instruments, both for what regards the analysis of the factual experience and the development of future initiatives for the establishment of new zones.

In this sense, STZs may always be designed as a combination of the implementing models above described in order to adapt the set of tax advantages to the features of each national legal system and to the specific objectives pursued by the governments of the respective states.

§5.04 SUMMARY OF THE RESULTS

At the end of this chapter, it is necessary to summarize the results achieved with reference to the analysis of the research question formulated in the beginning.

The research process has been carried out focusing on three main aspects: the concept of STZs with its territorial, structural and functional dimension, the definition of STZs in terms of a comprehensive macro-category, and, finally, the implementing models of STZs identified in the experience of the Member States.

The same results can now be valorized as essential parts of a general legal theory of STZs in order to allow a better understanding of the phenomenon within European tax law.

Starting from the concept of STZ, the first fundamental element to be considered is the territorial dimension and, in particular, the geographical border, the reference framework and the territorial connecting factor. In this regard, in fact, an STZ is always a well-defined area delimited by a natural, artificial or conventional border; then, the favouring tax treatment granted in the same area has to be measured and assessed in comparison with the standard tax treatment applied in the reference framework corresponding to the territory of the hosting Member State; furthermore, the entities and the goods which can benefit from the favouring tax treatment have to be selected according to a territorial connecting factor provided by law which may be identified in the place where the goods are stored (e.g., in the case of FZs) or with the permanent establishment (e.g., in the case of the State Aid Zone).

The second element which characterizes the concept of STZs corresponds to the structural dimension and generally refers to the presence of a regime of exception compared to the standard rules on taxation applied in the rest of the hosting State. In this sense, all the examples of STZs are characterized by the identification of a tax regime which, in whole or in part, deviates from the one normally applied in the hosting State. In detail, the tax treatment provided in an STZ may be purely and simply the negative result of a mere exclusion of the standard rules on taxation (i.e., exclusion regimes), or it may correspond to a subtractive scheme when the legislator introduces therein a set of special rules in place of the standard regime applied in the rest of the State (e.g., subtractive regimes with exemptions, exclusions, deferrals, etc.)

The third element of the concept of STZ deals with the functional dimension and it is linked to the objectives pursued by the government of a state through the establishment of STZs; the favouring tax regime of an STZ, in fact, is always designed in the context of a specific government function, with the introduction of a set of tax benefits addressed to objectives of an economic or social character. In this regard, STZs may be established with the introduction of economic tax incentives, on one part, as long as the objectives pursued are of an economic character, or with the introduction of social tax incentives, on the other, any time the objectives are set within the social and welfare domain.

Beside the concept of STZs, the general legal theory includes a comprehensive definition which has been outlined on the ground of the territorial, structural, and functional dimensions through the summary of the respective key features. In this direction, STZs have been defined as 'areas delimited by a natural, artificial or conventional border where entities and goods, selected through a territorial connecting factor provided by the law, can benefit from a favouring tax treatment which deviates, under an exclusion regime or a subtractive regime, from the standard tax treatment applied in the rest of the hosting State on the ground of objectives of an economic or social character defined within a specific government function'. This definition is able to encompass under its umbrella all the different experiences of STZs in the Member States and, at the same time, it is set in accordance with the legal dimension and the EU law framework as resulting from the material reviewed in Chapter 2 and Chapter 3.

The last step of the research process has involved the identification of the implementing models of STZs within the EU.

In particular, three different models assume an autonomous relevance in this context; first, the 'FZ' model which is set on the ground of the provisions of the UCC where FZs are defined as a customs special procedure of storage according to which the charge of customs duties and other indirect charges is suspended under a regime of deferral; second, the 'State Aid Zone' model which is developed, on one part, on the ground of State aid rules in the form of regional aid and as an exemption to the general State aid prohibition, or, on the other, in the form of an infra-State body with sufficient autonomy, where the tax advantages granted are not considered as territorial selective; third, the 'Extraterritorial Zone' model where the tax incentives are merely the result of the exclusion of the area from the territorial scope of one or more taxes.

§5.05 FINAL REMARKS

In the light of the above outcomes, the concept of STZs, the definition, and the implementing models represent the fundamentals of the general legal theory of STZs as resulting from the research process.

In this context, the same general legal theory, which is the point of arrival of the present chapter, is able to explain under a common reading-key not only the EU law framework on the topic, but also the factual experience of the Member States, improving the systematic perspective within the field of European tax law.

In the end, the results of the present research offer enough support for a positive answer to the research question formulated at the beginning of this chapter, as it will be better outlined in the conclusions of this book.

CHAPTER 6
Towards a New Model for Social Cohesion Policies

§6.01 INTRODUCTION

The experience of the Member States is currently characterized by the presence of three different implementing models of STZs whose territorial, structural, and functional dimensions assume various configurations, according to a common set of basic features identified in the previous chapter.

The first model, which corresponds to the FZ regulated by the UCC, is addressed to undertakings active in the import-export process with economic tax incentives granted exclusively on indirect taxation through the deferral of customs duties, VAT, and excise duties.

The second model, namely the State Aid Zone, covers both economic and social tax incentives on direct taxation defined on the ground of State aid rules according to the following two solutions: through the exemptions provided for regional aid under paragraphs (a) and (c) of Article 107(3) TFEU, on one part, or through the establishment of an infra-State body with sufficient institutional, procedural, and financial autonomy, on the other.

The third and last model includes economic tax incentives granted in the geographical areas which are outside the territorial scope of the indirect taxes already harmonized at the EU level, namely customs duties, VAT and excise duty; the so-called Extraterritorial Zones, in fact, may be established out of the Customs Union line, or, in other cases, outside the EU VAT area or the EU excise duty area, with the definition of tax-free territories pursuant to some historical privileges.

On these premises, the research must now be addressed to verify the space left for future initiatives of the Member States aimed at the establishment of new STZs in accordance with EU law, even beyond the legal background of the implementing models already identified in the previous chapter. In other words, it is necessary to verify whether or not the three implementing models recognized in the factual experience cover all the possibilities for the establishment of territorial tax incentives according to the EU law framework.

In this regard, it is interesting to note that none of the models recognized in the factual experience is specifically targeted at the development of social cohesion policies based on social tax incentives; even the examples of ZFU in France and in Italy, in fact, have been developed under a model – the State Aid Zone – which is neutral from the point of view of the functional dimension, considering that the related zones may pursue both objectives of a social or of an economic nature.

This lack of an implementing model of STZs specifically based on social tax incentives sounds as a missed opportunity for the autonomous initiatives of the Member States aimed at developing social cohesion policies for their most disadvantaged areas. In this sense, it is thus necessary to measure the space left for such initiatives and to find the coordinates of a new model of STZs to be implemented beside the FZ, the State Aid Zone, and the Extraterritorial Zone.

Therefore, on the ground of the above considerations, it is finally possible to outline the following research question:

> Research question No. 2
>
> *Is it possible to identify a new implementing model of STZs within the EU law framework addressed to the development of social cohesion policies for the most disadvantaged areas of the Union?*

The declared objective becomes relevant in the current stage of European integration as long as the situation of the disadvantaged areas of the Union is considered in the context of social cohesion policies.

The main priority, in fact, is to preserve the integrity and cohesion of the Union, through an approach to EU law able to support not only the growth of the internal market, but also the harmonious development of welfare and social cohesion in each Member State.

On the ground of the research question, the following sections will first outline the design of the new model in ideal terms within its territorial, structural, and functional dimensions, defining the related profiles and its denomination in coherence with the idea resulting from the research question, namely the creation of an instrument for the development of social cohesion policies for the most disadvantaged areas of the Union.

Then, the research will approach the analysis of the EU law framework testing the design of the new model under each of the relevant variables. In this regard, State aid rules, the fundamental freedoms and harmful tax competition will represent the fundamental variables to be considered.

At the end of this process, the eventual space left for the autonomous initiatives of the Member States will be measured; accordingly, the research will finally outline the results of the analysis in order to verify whether and how the design of the new model can be implemented in accordance with the EU law framework.

§6.02 DESIGN OF THE MODEL

The methodology used for the development of the new model starts from a choice involving the characteristics of the territorial, the structural, and the functional dimensions in coherence with the scope of the research question. The initial idea, in fact, is that STZs may also be used for the management of social cohesion policies under a specific government function at the Member States' level; accordingly, the design of the new model has to be structured in line with that idea, putting in evidence a set of characteristics addressed to the pursuit of the related objectives of a social nature.

For the moment, the characteristics of the new model - such as the typologies of tax incentives provided, or the conditions established for the undertakings to be eligible for the same advantages - are exclusively set on the ground of the factual experience in order to address the tax measures in the context of social cohesion policies.

This means that, in this first stage of the research, the selection of the options available is carried out regardless of the limits of compatibility of the EU law framework, leaving to the second stage of the research any assessment of the resulting design with reference to the variables of EU law.

[A] The Territorial Dimension

[1] Geographical Delimitation

In the design of the new model, the territorial dimension first leads to some considerations about the geographical borders of the area where tax incentives are granted; as seen, in fact, the geographical delimitation under the general legal theory of STZs may be defined through a natural barrier, through an artificial fence or simply through a conventional line on the map.

Among the various options available, the use of a conventional line seems to be the most flexible solution for the targeted areas of the new model. By this way, the border of an STZ can be clearly defined also in the situations where the natural landscape does not offer any physical element for the same scope (e.g., a lake or a river) or in the situations where the presence of artificial or natural cutoffs would undermine the continuity and the accessibility of the zone. Such barriers, in fact, are often able to physically isolate the zone from the surrounding locations with negative effects on the development of the economic activities based therein.[793]

For example, in the case of urban areas, the geographical delimitation through a conventional line is the only feasible solution to preserve the existing transport connections with the territories outside the zone; ZFUs in France and in Italy, in fact, are characterized by a geographical delimitation of the areas which is achieved through the definition of an ideal line on the map without any further intervention aimed at the

793. For these considerations *see* A. Briant, L. Miren, S. Benoit, *Can Tax Breaks Beat Geography? Lessons from the French Enterprise Zone Experience*, in *American Economic Journal: Economic Policy*, 2015, No. 7(2), pp. 88-124.

construction of a perimeter fence or to the use of different physical elements forming part of the natural landscape. Starting from these experiences, the new model of STZs should replicate the same approach to the territorial dimension, confirming the choice adopted in the mentioned case of ZFU in consideration of the broader possibilities offered.

In summary, the use of a conventional line for the geographical limitation of the zone should be considered as the first fixed value of the territorial dimension of the new model; by this way, in fact, it is possible to guarantee a flexible design for the implementation of the new model not only in the case of the remote areas, but also in the case of urban areas where continuity and accessibility are fundamental parameters for the attractiveness of the zone.

[2] Reference Framework

The next profile to be considered in the context of the territorial dimension is the reference framework; the design of the new model, in fact, requires the identification of a standard tax regime to be compared with the special tax treatment applied in the zone in order to detect the favouring effect reserved to the entities based therein. In this regard, it is possible to conclude that, in the new model, the reference framework does not assume any specific form; in fact, as in all the other implementing models of STZs, the reference framework basically corresponds to the territory of the Member State which is responsible for the external relations of the zone according to the fundamentals of the general legal theory developed in the previous chapter.[794] This is because the objectives of the social character, which represent the main driver of the new model, do not require for this specific profile any deviation from the standard features identified under the general legal theory.

[3] Territorial Connecting Factor

The last profile of the territorial dimension is the so-called territorial connecting factor which has been defined as the set of rules through which an economic activity carried out by an individual or a company may be linked to the territory of an STZ and benefit from the related tax incentives.

In this case, the definition of the related criteria involves multiple aspects essentially focused on the distinction between indirect taxation and direct taxation. As far as the tax benefits are related to indirect taxation, the territorial connecting factor is generally defined according to secondary law and the harmonized EU rules on customs duties, VAT, and excise duties. Differently, in the case of direct taxation, the definition of the territorial connecting factor is influenced by the limits set by primary law and, in particular, by the freedom of establishment as interpreted by the ECJ. The main point,

794. As seen in Chapter 5 (section §5.02[A][2]), this perspective is based on Article 355(3) TFEU according to which the Treaty is applied to '*the European territories for whose external relations a Member State is responsible*'.

in fact, is that, as far as direct taxation is concerned, the adoption of a specific territorial connecting factor might determine a discriminatory treatment between residents and non-residents with the possible infringement of the freedom of establishment.

Within this context, the design of the new model should include a territorial connecting factor able to ensure the pursuit of the objectives of a social character; in this sense, the effective presence of the economic operator within the zone becomes a serious issue to be considered, as well as the definition of a territorial connecting factor able to guarantee the establishment of a fruitful relationship between the economic operator and the local community.

For these purposes, it seems possible to confirm that the criterion of the permanent establishment is sufficient to ensure the objective, since it sets a link between the place of business and a specific geographic point, as well as a certain degree of permanence within the area concerned.

However, the adoption of a territorial connecting factor linked to the permanent establishment of a non-resident entity should always be carefully considered; as it will be explained under the functional dimension, in such cases, in fact, it is always necessary to provide a set of specific conditions in order to ensure that the same permanent establishment carries out a substantial economic activity, assuming an effective role in the support of the vulnerable groups of individuals resident of the zone.

In conclusion, the territorial dimension of the new model assumes some qualifying features which are essentially based on the geographical delimitation of the area; in this case, in fact, the border of the zone should be defined through the use of a conventional line on the map, instead than through a natural barrier or an artificial fence. Differently, for what concerns the profiles of the reference framework and the territorial connecting factor, the design of the new model does not deviate from the standard characteristics identified within the general legal theory of STZs.

[B] The Structural Dimension

[1] Tax Allowances and Tax Credits

For what regards the structural dimension, the design of the new model requires to focus on the specific provisions able to introduce exceptions to the standard rules applied in the hosting State with the final aim of reducing the tax burden.

As seen under the general legal theory of STZs, the denial of the standard tax rules may be set in various forms and can lead to different outcomes corresponding to the categories of the 'exclusion regimes', on one part, and 'subtractive regimes', on the other.

The exclusion regimes are the result of an intervention through which the legislator limits the effects of the standard rules relevant under the discipline of one or more taxes; consequently, the areas with the favouring tax treatment are entirely outside the perimeter in which the standard tax rules produce their effects.

In the subtractive regimes, STZs are instead characterized by the presence of a positive discipline that differs from the standard one applied throughout the rest of the

State. These rules usually affect the elements of the tax structure, such as the tax base or the tax rate, by the modification of the sequence that leads from the general factual element relevant under the tax rule to the determination of the final amount due by the taxpayer.

Given the above, the structural dimension in the design of the new model involves the identification of the best options available to address the tax incentives towards the objectives of a social character according to the scope of the research question.

For this purpose, the exclusion regimes do not seem a proper solution since, in such cases, the favouring tax treatment is merely the negative result of the limitation of the areas of application of one or more taxes; this means that, under the exclusion regimes, it is not possible to identify an active role of the legislator in the definition of a set of positive rules to pursue the objectives of a social cohesion policy.

In other words, the establishment of exclusion regimes results as a neutral situation where the government is not the main character in the regulation and in the measurement of the value of the tax expenditures. Exclusion regimes, in fact, are essentially founded on the alternative between taxation or no taxation and, therefore, they do not offer the possibility of a broader set of options in order to better address the tax incentives to the expected results.

On the contrary, in the case of subtractive regimes, the legislator introduces a positive discipline under which the standard tax norm does not produce its effects with reference to specific elements of the tax structure, such as the tax base or the tax rate. Consequently, under the subtractive regimes, there are many different alternatives in the regulation and in the measurement of the value of the tax expenditures, considering the possibilities offered by incentives like tax exemptions, tax allowances, tax credits, tax reliefs, tax deferrals, tax rebates, or tax replacement regimes.

For these reasons, it is clear that the design of the new model should exclusively include tax incentives belonging to the category of the subtractive regimes, since only in such cases, it is possible to safeguard the active role of the governments and to shape the structural dimension with a specific focus on the aims pursued by the related tax measures.

In particular, within the various options available under the category of the subtractive regimes, tax allowances and tax credits seem to be the most interesting types of tax incentives for the purposes of this model. In both cases, in fact, it is possible to clearly measure the value of the tax expenditures by reference to the nature and the value of the expenses which can be deducted from the gross income (tax allowances) or from the gross tax due (tax credits).

On the contrary, in the case of tax exemptions, tax reliefs, and tax rebates, it is more difficult to precisely define the cap of the value of tax expenditures, considering that such types of tax incentives are not generally associated to the amount of the expenses effectively incurred by the economic operator.

Also tax deferrals and tax replacement regimes cannot be considered an interesting option under the design of the new model. Tax deferrals, in fact, determine a mere delay in the payment of taxes and, therefore, cannot be concretely addressed to grant a definitive advantage in favour of vulnerable groups of individuals. Then, tax replacement regimes, as far as they introduce a new tax and not a mere modification of one or more elements of the tax applied in the rest of the State, limit the possibilities of a clear comparison between the special tax treatment applied in the zone and the standard tax treatment applied in the reference framework.

Therefore, the structural dimension of the new model should be characterized by the establishment of a set of tax incentives in the form of tax allowances or tax credits, being these the best options available to ensure the measurement of the value of the tax expenditures in coherence with the objectives of a social character pursued.

In this sense, in fact, only tax allowances and tax credits, different from what happens for other types of tax incentives, ensure that the government continues to keep the control of the effects of the STZ programme, with a better monitoring and a continuous comparison between the value of tax expenditures and the effects over the local community.

[2] The Focus on Direct Taxation

Finally, the structural dimension of the new model involves a choice between the typologies of taxes which are established by the incentive programme adopted under the STZ regime. This choice is essentially associated to the distinction between indirect taxes and direct taxes and to the different outcomes that the related tax incentives may produce with reference to the objectives of a social character pursued through the new model.

In this regard, it is not possible to put indirect taxes and direct taxes on the same level, considering that indirect taxation is always characterized by the shift of the tax burden from the economic operator to the final consumer through a mechanism of reimbursement. In other words, indirect taxes are generally neutral for the economic operator since the related tax burden is shifted over the final consumer.

Therefore, it is evident that an incentive programme based on direct taxation could better pursue the objectives of a social character, since direct taxes cannot be shifted to the final consumer and, thus, they have a stronger influence on the allocation choices of enterprises.

In this regard, in fact, the objective of the new model is the improvement of the employment rate through the introduction of tax measures able to lower the tax burden of business entities as long as new workers are hired. On these premises, it is clear that the incentive programme can produce the expected results only where the tax measures are concretely able to favour the position of the economic operator, such as in the case of an incentive programme based on business direct taxation.[795] In conclusion, the design of the new model should be characterized, for what regards its structural dimension, by the establishment of an incentive programme based on direct taxation, with the introduction of a set of tax incentives in the form of tax allowances or tax credits associated to the amount of expenses occurred by the economic operator

795. Differently, an incentive programme based on indirect taxation (e.g., with the use of lower VAT-rates) would only improve the financial situation of final consumers without any concrete effect on the job market.

for specific purposes defined under the functional dimension (e.g., expenses for new employees hired).

Accordingly, the structural dimension can here assume a form in coherence with the social objectives pursued, addressing the design of the new model within the scope of the research question.

[C] The Functional Dimension

The functional dimension covers the most qualifying aspects of the design of the new model, focusing on the objectives pursued by the related tax measures.

The approach is driven by the scope of the research question formulated at the beginning of the chapter; the new model, in fact, must be aimed towards the development of social cohesion policies for the most disadvantaged areas of the Union and, accordingly, the tax incentives granted must univocally be addressed to objectives of a social character.

In this direction, the category of social tax incentives must characterize the design of the new model with respect to the various profiles identified under the general legal theory, such as those related to the scope of the tax measure or the conditions under which the incentives are granted.

Given the above, it is now necessary to define the design of the new model under its functional dimension outlining the corresponding values for the various profiles involved.

[1] The Scope of the Tax Measures

The first profile is related to the scope of the tax measures; in this regard, according to the research question, the new model should support a specific government function under the social cohesion policy domain with a focus on the employment factor and, in particular, on the social inclusion and work integration of low-income individuals which reside in disadvantaged areas. Therefore, as far as work integration is concerned, the main priority becomes the adoption of a series of actions addressed to the creation of new jobs for low-income individuals; the expected result, in fact, is the improvement of the living conditions of people residing in disadvantaged areas affected by a high unemployment rate; thus, the functional dimension involves the development of social cohesion policies aimed at reducing the differences between low-income areas and high-income areas of Member States.

[2] Eligible Undertakings

The second profile which is able to influence the design of the new model and its functional dimension is associated with the position of the recipient of the tax advantages; in this regard, in fact, it always necessary that the subjective characteristics of the economic operator are compatible, coherent, and suitable with respect to the objectives pursued under the functional dimension.

In this context, the recipient undertakings assume a filtering role in the selection of the individuals which are the ultimate target of the tax measures (i.e., employees and small and medium-sized enterprises); this basically means that each recipient undertaking, in consideration of its crucial role within the tax incentive mechanism, must ensure sufficient financial and economic strength and reliability. In this sense, in fact, the success of an STZ programme strictly depends on the effective fulfilment by the recipient undertakings of the obligations set by the various conditions under which tax incentives are granted, such as the hiring of a minimum number of new employees or a minimum volume of purchases from the local suppliers. The eventual non-fulfilment of the same obligations would seriously undermine the results of the entire incentive programme, with the failure of the substantial scope set under the establishment of an STZ.

For these reasons, the financial capacity of the recipient undertakings becomes an essential element to be considered. In this regard, serious doubts arise about the financial and economic capacity of small and medium enterprises (SME) to manage such a responsibility since they usually do not have sufficient strength and solidity to comply with the strict conditions which are now set under the design of this new model.

On the ground of these considerations, the design of the new model should limit the granting of social tax incentives to large enterprises which can provide enough guarantees about their economical and financial strength and solidity. Large enterprises, in fact, generally have the economical and financial capacity to follow long-term programmes and, thus, to ensure the fulfilment of their obligations and the compliance with the set of conditions provided for the granting of the tax incentives available in the zone.[796]

Beside large enterprises, it should also be considered the option of extending the tax benefits to social enterprises. In this case, in fact, regardless of the size of the economic operator, the legislation already offers enough guarantees to properly ensure the achievement of objectives of a social character. This is because the various requirements established under EU law to be qualified as a social enterprise already address the behaviour of such entities to the effective fulfilment of the same obligations, concerning, for example, the hiring of a minimum number of new employees resident of the area. In particular, the social criteria for the qualification as a social enterprise are able to counterbalance any issue related to the economic and financial strength of the economic operator; for example, it is important to mention the existence of an explicit social purpose defined in the articles of the association, such as to benefit the local community or a disadvantaged group of people, or the pursuit of social goals rather than making profits. In other words, any risk of non-fulfilment associated to

796. A proportional approach to the issue should be based on the assumption that the tax benefits must be limited to enterprises having sufficient financial resources in order to fulfil the social obligations concerned. In this case, having regard to the meaning of Article 2(1) of Annex I to Commission Regulation (EU) No. 651/2014 of 17 June 2014, the notion of large enterprises seems to be appropriate for such a purpose, considering that it covers all the enterprises whose balance sheet total exceeds EUR 43 million or whose total annual turnover exceeds EUR 50 million regardless of the number of employees (*see infra* section §7.05[A][1]).

insolvency can be counterbalanced by the subjective qualifications of social enterprises, considering that they have to respond to a series of specific requirements defined under EU law which already ensure the effective pursuit of their statutory social goals.

For the above reasons, it seems thus possible to include social enterprises among the recipient undertakings in the context of the new model, regardless of any consideration on their financial and economic size.

Differently, for what regards the other SME, which are not qualified as social enterprises, the doubts concerning their financial and economic strengths, associated with the consequent risk of non-fulfilment and insolvency, do not allow to confer them a filtering role which is crucial for the success of a tax incentive programme.

[3] Obligations of the Recipient Undertakings

The third and last profile, concerning the conditions under which the incentives are granted, assumes a fundamental relevance for the design of the new model. In order to ensure the effective pursuit of the same objectives of a social character, in fact, it is necessary to define a set of specific conditions to be fulfilled by the recipient undertakings which should involve the hiring of new employees, on one part, and the purchases made from local suppliers, on the other.

In this sense, the enterprise, in order to qualify for the benefits available under the STZ regime, should first hire a minimum number of new employees in the first year of its activity; under this condition, in fact, it seems possible to ensure that the tax expenditures are concretely addressed to the creation of employment, establishing a link between the tax incentives, the economic operators, and the employees. In particular, the focus should be set on the residence of the employees, introducing one more condition according to which the new workers hired have to maintain their residence in the area for a certain minimum period of time; by this way, in fact, it is possible to avoid the situation of a temporary residence registered by the employee only for tax purposes, ensuring that the tax advantages are granted only to the economic operators which effectively respond to the substantial scope of the tax measure. Then, it is necessary to establish a minimum duration of the employment contract; by this condition, in fact, it seems possible to avoid a situation where the abuse of short-term contracts could undermine the objectives set under the establishment of such zones. In this direction, the creation of stable employment should be supported through long-term relationships between the economic operators and the new employees in order to ensure the effective improvement of the living conditions of the residents of the zone on a long-term basis. The functional dimension of the new model should also focus on the qualification of the new employees hired by the economic operators based in the zone; particular attention should be paid to the definition of a balanced solution where high-qualified employees and low-qualified employees could benefit from the same opportunities of the STZ regime. In this regard, one more condition should regard the hiring of a minimum number of high-qualified employees, thus extending the effects of social tax incentives to a broader audience of individuals which reside in the disadvantaged areas of the Member States.

Furthermore, in order to qualify for the same tax benefits, the recipient undertakings should guarantee a minimum volume of purchases from the suppliers based within the zone. The idea, in fact, is to limit the social tax incentives only to those undertakings which are able to guarantee a minimum annual volume of purchases of goods or services from the suppliers which are based in the zone, thus maximizing the positive effects of such tax measures with the creation of a virtuous circle in the productive and distributive chain. In this regard, the suppliers considered under the same condition should be limited to the small and medium-sized enterprises based in the zone;[797] this category of suppliers, in fact, is the most affected by the issues of the disadvantaged areas, especially in the case of self-employed economic activities requiring more protection.

In summary, the functional dimension in the design of the new model is essentially defined around the scope of the research question. The declared objective, in fact, is the development of social cohesion policies for the most disadvantaged areas of the Union; therefore, the profiles above described are all set in a coherent way in order to address the tax measures towards the same aim pursued in the context of the new model.

[D] The Denomination

As seen in the previous sections, the design of the new model includes a series of qualifying elements which are mainly focused on the functional dimension and on the category of social tax incentives.

In particular, a profile which clearly emerges from this design is related to the possible implementation of the new model in the context of the social cohesion policies targeted at low-income individuals which reside in the disadvantaged areas of the Union.

On these premises, the new model will be defined from now onwards as 'Social Cohesion Zone' in order to stress its functional dimension and its possible implementation for the development of new social cohesion policies within the EU framework.

The choice of such a denomination is justified under many profiles. First of all, the wording 'social' refers to the aim pursued by the related tax measures, involving the social inclusion of vulnerable group of individuals which reside in disadvantaged areas of the EU with high unemployment rates. Then, the wording 'cohesion' refers to the possibility of implementing the same model in the context of the cohesion policy to solve the issues related to the disparities between high-income and low-income areas of the Union. In this sense, the cohesion policy is generally set to address such regional disparities and to bring structural changes to the most disadvantaged areas.

797. The category of micro, small and medium-sized enterprises ('SMEs') is made up of enterprises which employ fewer than 250 persons and which have an annual turnover not exceeding EUR 50 million, and/or an annual balance sheet total not exceeding EUR 43 million (*see* Commission Regulation (EU) No. 651/2014 of 17 June 2014, Annex 1, Article 2(1)).

Therefore, social policy and cohesion policy are addressed in the same direction and assume a unified dimension in the new model of the Social Cohesion Zone; in this sense, in fact, it seems possible to identify a common area of influence where the objectives of social policy, such as, the improvement of the employment rate, interact with the classic objectives of cohesion policy (e.g., reduction of regional disparities).

§6.03 ANALYSIS OF THE VARIABLES IN THE EU LAW FRAMEWORK

In the previous sections, the design of the Social Cohesion Zone has been defined according to scope of the research question regardless of any assessment with reference to its compatibility with the EU law framework.

In other words, the first stage of the research process has merely been focus on the identification of a model which could be suitable for the aim pursued, namely the development of social cohesion policies addressed to the disadvantaged areas of the Member States. This has been done in ideal terms without a concrete assessment of the multitude of implications and limits deriving from the application of EU law.

Therefore, at this point, the design of the new model needs to be tested with respect to the variables of the EU law framework following the coordinates described in Chapter 3, with regard to State aid rules, the fundamental freedoms, and harmful tax competition.

The research process, in fact, has now to be oriented towards the following step: to verify whether and how the design of the Social Cohesion Zone, as defined under the above sections, can be compatible with EU law and, therefore, can be used as a new implementing model in the Member States.

Accordingly, the next sections are dedicated to follow this research path, exploring the possibilities offered by the EU law framework and the related limits, with the aim to find an answer to the research question formulated at the beginning of this chapter.

[A] State Aid Rules

State aid rules are the first variable to be considered for testing the design of the Social Cohesion Zone within the EU law framework.

For this purpose, it is necessary to clarify that the territorial dimension, as outlined in the design of the new model, does not assume any relevance in this part of the research process; this is because the geographical delimitation through a conventional line – instead of through an artificial or a natural barrier – is a neutral factor with respect to the discipline of State aid and, as a consequence, the analysis does not require any investigation about the different profiles of the territorial dimension.

On the contrary, as far as the structural dimension is concerned, State aid rules become a serious issue; in this sense, a measure on direct taxation for the Social Cohesion Zone, such as a subtractive regime with tax credits or tax allowances, may be considered territorial selective as long as the tax advantages are exclusively granted to the enterprises based in the zone, with potential negative effects on the internal market and on the trade between Member States.[798]

In such a situation, the functional dimension of the new model gives evidence of a specific characteristic which is relevant for the analysis with respect to State aid rules: as seen, in fact, the use of social tax incentives under a subtractive regime assumes a fundamental role in the design of the Social Cohesion Zone.

On these premises, social tax incentives become the main focus of the analysis for State aid rules, opening the possibility of an alternative path for the implementation of the Social Cohesion Zone within the EU law framework.

Therefore, it is now necessary to test the functioning of the new model within State aid rules, assuming, as the starting point of the analysis, the presence of a set of social tax incentives granted in the form of a subtractive regime and specifically addressed to the economic operators based in the limited territory of the Social Cohesion Zone.

Such kind of tax measures, being exclusively reserved to the economic operators which are based within the geographical limits of the Social Cohesion Zone, are generally considered as territorial selective, falling under the general prohibition set by Article 107(1) TFEU; nonetheless, the same measures may be declared compatible with the internal market when they are set according to the exemptions for regional aid provided under paragraphs (a) and (c) of Article 107(3) TFEU

In this regard, it should be observed that the possibilities offered by Article 107(3) have already been exploited in the context of the State Aid Zone model, which has been identified and described in Chapter 5; the situations defined under paragraphs (a) and (c) are the legal background for many examples of STZs established in the Member States, such as in the case of Urban Tax Free Zones in France and in Italy or Madeira in Portugal.

Therefore, the research must be moved out of the exemptions provided under Article 107(3) TFEU, setting a focus on a different area of analysis able to offer more original solutions.

On the ground of this basic framework, it is thus necessary to explore the other possibilities left by the *Altmark* criteria and by Article 106(2) TFEU (with specific reference to the Commission Decision 2012/21/EU), approaching the following research sub-question:

> Research sub-question No. 2.1
>
> *Can a tax measure of a social character addressed to a limited area of a Member State be considered compatible with the internal market and be exempt from the notification obligation under State aid rules?*

In this direction, the presence of social tax incentives offers the opportunity to begin a new research path outside the exemptions for regional aid set by Article 107(3) TFEU. The objective, in fact, is to verify the space left by State aid rules for the

798. *See, inter alia,* Joined cases C-400/97, C-401/97 and C-402/97 *Administración General del Estado v Juntas Generales de Guipúzcoa and Diputación Foral de Guipúzcoa, Juntas Generales d'Alava and Diputación Foral d'Alava and Juntas Generales de Vizcaya,* [2000] ECR I-01073.

implementation of the Social Cohesion Zone, assuming a different perspective of analysis focused on the discipline of Social Services of General Interest (SSGIs).

[1] Social Tax Incentives and SSGIs

The discipline of SSGIs opens a new room of study in coherence with the objectives of a social character pursued under the design of the Social Cohesion Zone. The new model, in fact, has to be tested with respect to State aid rules, focusing on the relationship between its functional dimension and the concept of SSGIs.

In this direction, it seems possible to establish a strict connection between the concept of SSGIs and the concept of social tax incentives, addressing the research process related to State aid rules towards the core of the functional dimension.

Both concepts, in fact, become overlapping when the beneficiaries of the social tax incentives are also the same providers of SSGIs; in other words, in such situations, social tax incentives are granted to the entities which are directly involved in the provision of SSGIs. On the background of these concepts there is the domain of social cohesion policies within which the design of the new model has been shaped according to the research question formulated at the beginning of the present chapter.

SSGIs include a broad set of services which are addressed to disadvantaged groups of individuals; the pursued objective is to improve the living conditions by providing accessible services and, in particular, by achieving high levels of employment, human health protection and social cohesion in general. In particular, these services play a prevention and social cohesion role with customized assistance to facilitate social inclusion and safeguard fundamental rights.

In this regard, it is important to remember that SSGIs, as well as Services of General Economic Interest (SGEIs), are a subset of the macro-category of Services of General Interest (SGIs), which covers all those services that public authorities classify as being of general interest and, therefore, are subject to specific public service obligations.

In particular, as already seen under Chapter 3, measures constituting SSGIs are generally subject to the same rules applicable to SGEIs; according to the Commission, in fact, 'almost all services offered in the social field can be considered economic activities'.[799] In other words, the fact that the aim pursued by the provision of such services is not economic but rather social does not preclude that the activity carried out is economic in nature, especially when the same activity is carried out by an economic operator involved in the provision of goods or services on the market.

For these reasons, in the next sections, the references made to the discipline of SGEIs must also be deemed valid for SSGIs, considering that the recipient undertakings within the Social Cohesion Zone Model are always economic operators active in the market.

799. *See* Communication from the Commission of 26 April 2006, *Implementing the Community Lisbon programme: Social services of general interest in the European Union*, COM (2006) No. 177 final, paragraph 2.1.

[2] *Outcomes under the Altmark Criteria*

According to the above premises, the analysis of State aid rules must start from the criteria identified in the *Altmark* case to consider a measure of compensation for a public service as falling outside the notion of State aid set by Article 107(1) TFEU. In first approximation, in fact, the social tax incentives provided under the new model could represent a form of compensation for the economic operator involved in the provision of a public service related to the objectives of a social character which are pursued in the context of the Social Cohesion Zone.

In this regard, the ECJ identifies four cumulative criteria to be fulfilled in order for such a measure to be considered out of the scope of State aid rules and, therefore, exempt from the notification requirement provided by Article 108(3) TFEU.

First, the beneficiary must have a clearly defined public service obligation to discharge according to the definition of an SGEI set by Article 106(2) TFEU.

Second, the parameters on which compensation is calculated must be established in advance in an objective and transparent manner to avoid overcompensation which may confer economic advantage to the recipient.

Third, the compensation cannot exceed what is necessary to cover all costs incurred in the discharge of the public service in question, taking into account the relevant receipts and a reasonable profit for the undertaking.

Fourth, the undertaking must be selected pursuant to a public procurement procedure or, in alternative, the compensation to the beneficiary must not exceed that of a typical well-run undertaking which meets all the necessary public service requirements.

Given the above, it is now necessary to test the design of the Social Cohesion Zone with reference to each of the above criteria; the objective, in fact, is to verify whether or not the related tax measures, which consist in the introduction of social tax incentives, can fall outside the scope of application of State aid rules and, thus, not be subject to the notification requirement set by Article 108 TFEU.

First criterion (clearly defined public service obligation to discharge)

The first *Altmark* criterion involves the nature and the scope of the activity carried out by the beneficiary of the tax measure, establishing a clearly defined public obligation to discharge.

In this regard, the concept of public service obligation corresponds to the concept of an SSGI as referred to in Article 106(2) TFEU; nevertheless, it is not possible to identify a clear and precise regulatory definition of the concept of an SSGI within the EU law framework.[800]

800. M. Klasse, *The Impact of Altmark: The European Commission Case Law Responses*, in *Financing Services of General Economic Interest*, E. Szyszczak, J.W. van de Gronden (eds), TMC Asser Press, The Hague, 2013, p. 39.

Consequently, it follows from the case law that Member States have a wide discretion to define what they regard as SSGIs and to determine the nature and scope of an SSGI mission within the meaning of the Treaty.[801]

The same flexible approach is confirmed in the Communication within the *Almunia* package where the Commission clarifies that Member States have a wide margin of discretion in defining a service as an SSGI and in granting compensation to the service provider, since the Commission's competence in this respect is essentially limited to manifest errors.[802]

One more aspect of the first *Altmark* criterion is related to the entrustment act which is associated to the SSGI mission; in this sense, in fact, the Commission always requires an official act having binding legal force under national law able to establish an obligation over the operator to provide the services in question.[803]

Moving from these premises on the first *Altmark* criterion, the analysis must now clarify whether or not the beneficiary of social tax incentives can assume a clearly defined public service obligation to discharge in the context of the Social Cohesion Zone, namely whether or not the beneficiary is carrying out an SSGI in the same terms defined under EU law.

As already seen, the design of the Social Cohesion Zone provides evidence of a series of strict conditions to be fulfilled by the beneficiary to ensure the pursuit of the objectives of a social character. For example, the hiring of a minimum number of new employees resident in the zone, as well as the purchase of a minimum volume of goods and/or services from local suppliers are both obligations assumed in the general interest; the creation of new jobs in disadvantaged areas, in fact, represents an initiative for social cohesion and, in particular, for work integration of low-income individuals, with an important outcome with respect to the general interest.

From these considerations, it seems possible to configure the activities of the recipient undertakings of social tax incentives as SSGIs as long as they are based on the fulfilment of a set of conditions in the public interest, instead of in the interest of the same economic operator.

In this perspective, the granting of social tax incentives becomes a form of compensation in favour of the economic operator for the obligations related to the minimum number of new employees to be hired or the minimum volume of purchases to be made from local suppliers.

Therefore, the entrustment act is the document which summarizes the same perspective, establishing the granting of social tax incentives, on one part, and the obligations assumed in the general interest, on the other.

---

801. Case T-289/03 *British United Provident Association Ltd (BUPA), BUPA Insurance Ltd and BUPA Ireland Ltd v Commission of the European Communities*, [2005] ECR II-741, paragraph 167.
802. *See* Case T-17/02 *Fred Olsen v Commission*, [2005] ECR II-2031, paragraph 216.
803. Commission staff working document, *Guide to the application of the European Union rules on state aid, public procurement and the internal market to services of general economic interest, and in particular to social services of general interest*, Brussels, 2013, SWD(2013) 53 final/2, p. 21; *see also* M. Klasse, *supra.*, in E. Szyzyczak, J.W. van de Gronden, *Financing Services of General Economic Interest*, TMC Asser Press, The Hague, 2013, p. 41.

Further arguments can support the configuration as SSGIs of the work integration activities carried out by the recipient of the tax measures in the Social Cohesion Zone.

First of all, it should be noted that, when the obligation defined in the entrustment act is referred to the hiring of a minimum number of new employees resident in the area, the activity of the enterprise, involving a real work integration service, cannot be considered as carried out for the mere purpose of making profits; in such cases, in fact, the activity of the enterprises is aimed at the fulfilment of the obligations assumed in the same entrustment act and, therefore, the same activity finally results as carried out according to a social objective in the general interest of the society.

Second, once the entrustment act is signed and the obligation is assumed, the statutory goals of the undertaking - even when related to the scope of making profits - remain on the background, while the sole aspect to be considered becomes the object of the obligation assumed by the enterprise within the same entrustment act; therefore, any time the object of that obligation is of a clear social nature, the activities carried out should be considered as a genuine SSGI for the purposes of the first *Altmark* criterion.

According to these considerations, the first *Altmark* criterion does not involve any specific requirement for what regards the legal form and the size of the economic operator which is the beneficiary of the social tax incentives; in this sense, the Social Cohesion Zone may offer its incentives both to large enterprises and social enterprises, as long as the same recipient undertakings provide work integration services under a specific obligation assumed towards the public authority, thus confirming the same approach used at the beginning of this chapter for the definition of the design of the new model. In this sense, the only requirement is that in both cases the recipient undertakings are involved in a work integration service - as their main activity or even as an additional activity - and fulfil the obligations defined under the Social Cohesion Zone Model, regarding the minimum number of new resident employees and the minimum volume of purchases from the local suppliers.

However, it is worth noting that the social character of the obligations assumed in the entrustment act could be further valorized as far as social enterprises become the beneficiary of the social tax incentives.

In this case, in fact, not only the object of the obligations in the entrustment act, but also the statutory goals defined in the articles of association are able to provide evidence of the existence of a genuine SSGI within the Social Cohesion Zone. Social enterprises, in fact, according to Article 2(1) of Regulation (EU) No. 1296/2013, have as primary objective the achievement of social goals and are characterized by the prevalence of the social goals over profits and by specific social criteria enshrined in the existence of an explicit social purpose.

These considerations offer the opportunity to recognize social enterprises as the most defendable solution for the selection of the provider of SSGIs. In this case, in fact, the existence of a 'genuine and correctly defined' SSGI can also be supported by the statutory goals of social enterprises with respect to the activities effectively carried out; thus, it seems clear that, under this framework, the services provided by social enterprises perfectly fulfil the first *Altmark* criterion, considering that not only the object of the obligation assumed in the entrustment act, but also the statutory goals are specifically addressed to aims of a social character which are pursued in the public interest.

In summary, the analysis of the first *Altmark* criterion with respect to the design of the new model gives evidence of the possibility of identifying a public service obligation and, therefore, a genuine SSGI, any time the content of the obligations assumed by the economic operator is defined through an entrustment act with the identification of a set of clear conditions to be fulfilled related to objectives of a social character. Within this framework, large enterprises and social enterprises can both be identified, in principle, as the beneficiaries of the social tax incentives granted in the Social Cohesion Zone as long as the object of the obligation assumed is the only parameter to be considered to identify the existence of genuine SSGIs. Nevertheless, it is important to note that the adoption of a narrow approach focused on the statutory goals of the economic operator would produce more limitations, considering that in such a case, only social enterprises would be selected as legal entities eligible for the social tax incentives.

In any case, it is worth pointing out that, since Member States have a wide margin of discretion in defining a service as an SSGI, not only the EU framework, but also the national legislation should allow the identification of a genuine SSGI as long as the obligations assumed by the economic operator are related to objectives of a social character in the terms above described.

The logical consequence is that, regardless of the aspects of compatibility with EU law, the identification of a genuine SSGI also requires a national legal order with provisions suitable for such a purpose; in other words, the introduction of national norms able to include such kind of work integration services under the concept of SSGI becomes a fundamental issue for the practical implementation of the new model in the light of the first *Altmark* criterion.

Second criterion (objective parameters)

The second *Altmark* criterion requires that the parameters for calculating the compensation are established in advance and in an objective and transparent manner.

This excludes the possibility of changing *ex post* the parameters of the calculation of the compensation. In this regard, it should be noted that the requirement refers to the *ex ante* establishment of the parameters and does not necessarily encompass the establishment of the amount of compensation.[804] In the decisions of the Commission, the criterion is found to be satisfied, for example, in cases concerning public service compensation for regional passenger transport in which the compensation is calculated on the basis of a price per kilometre and the total number of kilometres provided for in the contract.[805] Similarly, a compensation based on the number of users meets the second requirement.[806] In other cases, the Commission accepts that a multi-annual

804. M. Klasse, *supra.*, in E. Szyzyczak, J.W. van de Gronden, *Financing Services of General Economic Interest*, TMC Asser Press, The Hague, 2013, p. 42.
805. Commission Decision of 26 November 2008 (State aid C 16/2007 *Postbus AG*) O.J. 2009, L 306, p. 26, paragraphs 72 et seq.
806. Communication from the Commission of 16 May 2006 (State aid No. 604/2005 *Busverkehr Landkreis Wittenberg*) O.J. 2006, C 207, pp. 2, et. seq.

budget planning fulfils the second requirement where this budget is based on data and hypotheses which are reasonable and sufficiently detailed.[807]

On these bases, in the case of the Social Cohesion Zone, the parameters for calculating the compensation should be referred to the number of new employees hired and the monetary value of the purchases made from local suppliers. For this purpose, the content of the entrustment act must be valorized in order to ensure the fulfilment of the second *Altmark* criterion, with a detailed description of each of the parameters used to calculate the maximum amount of the compensation.

In summary, the parameters defined *ex ante* in the entrustment act must ensure the possibility of a precise calculation *ex post* of the total value of the compensation granted to the economic operators, with the indication of the exact value of the tax expenditure with reference to each operator in the year of activity.

Third criterion: avoiding overcompensation (necessity)

Under the third *Altmark* criterion it is necessary to establish whether the compensation (i.e., the value of social tax incentives) does not exceed the costs related to the public service mission. This involves an *ex post* assessment of the costs effectively borne and a comparison with the tax expenditure value of the compensation measures for the public services carried out by the beneficiaries.

The Commission practice is generally based on Article 6 of the Decision which provides some guidance on how this criterion may be concretely fulfilled.

In particular, the amount of compensation must not exceed what is necessary to cover the net cost incurred in discharging the public service obligations, including a reasonable profit.[808] In this regard, the costs to be taken into consideration shall include all the costs incurred in operating the SGI.

Thus, within the new model, it will be necessary to calculate the difference between the entire revenue earned from the SSGI and all the costs incurred in operating the same SSGI.

In this regard, when the beneficiary of the social tax incentives is a large enterprise carrying out activities falling both inside and outside the scope of the SSGI, the internal accounts shall separately show the costs and receipts associated with the SSGI and those of other services, as well as the parameters for allocating costs and revenues. No compensation shall be granted in respect of these costs.[809]

This point assumes a specific relevance in the context of the Social Cohesion Zone Model as long as large enterprises are included among the recipient undertakings; here, in fact, it is necessary to consider only the costs related to the SSGI, namely those referred to the gross wages paid for the new employees hired or those deriving from the

807. Commission Decision of 24 February 2010 (State aid C 41/08 *DSB*) O.J. 2011, L 7, pp. 1 et seq., paragraph 281.

808. M. Klasse, *supra.*, in E. Szyzyczak, J.W. van de Gronden, *Financing Services of General Economic Interest*, TMC Asser Press, The Hague, 2013, p. 43.

809. *See* Commission Decision 2012/21/EU of 20 December 2011 on the application of Article 106(2) of the Treaty on the Functioning of the European Union to State aid in the form of public service compensation granted to certain undertakings entrusted with the operation of services of general economic interest, O.J. 2012, L 7, pp. 3-10, Article 5(9).

purchases made from the local suppliers of the area. All the other costs, as long as they are related to activities falling outside the SSGI will not be taken into consideration. Nevertheless, in such cases, the costs linked to investments, notably concerning infrastructures (e.g., offices for the new employees and other instrumental goods), may be taken into account when necessary for the operation of the SSGI.[810]

Within the third Altmark criterion, the ECJ also clarifies that for any compensation to fall outside Article 107(1) TFEU the compensation may not only cover the costs of the public service but also a reasonable profit.

In this regard, the Commission in its case law applies not only sales-based (such as EBITDA[811]) profitability indicators, but also capital-based (such as ROCE[812]) indicators. For instance, in the French broadband infrastructure case *Pyrénées-Atlantiques* the Commission comes to the conclusion that a ROCE of approximately 11% is reasonable for the sector.[813] Then, in *Southern Moravia Bus Companies*, the Commission considers a margin of close to 8% as reasonable for the passenger transport in question,[814] while in a case of public passenger transport service compensation (*Anhalt-Bitterfeld*), the Commission considers that the proposed margin cap of 5% (turnover margin) over the costs of providing the service allows for a reasonable margin.[815] Furthermore, in *Danske Statsbaner (DSB)*, the Commission accepts that the reasonable profit varies between 6% and 12% (return on equity), with an annual cap set at 10% over three years, to take account of the efficiency gains and/or the improvement in the quality of the rail passenger services to be provided by the company DSB.[816]

On these bases, in order to fulfil the third *Altmark* criterion, the reasonable profits for the recipient undertakings of the Social Cohesion Zone should be set with reference to one of the above indicators, giving precedence to the most practical solution.

810. *Ibid.*, Article 5(3)(d).
811. A company's earnings before interest, taxes, depreciation, and amortization (EBITDA) is an accounting measure calculated using company net earnings, before interest expenses, taxes, depreciation, and amortization are subtracted, as a proxy for a company current operating profitability.
812. Return on capital employed (ROCE) is a financial ratio that measures a company profitability and the efficiency with which its capital is employed. ROCE is calculated as: ROCE = Earnings Before Interest and Tax (EBIT) / Capital Employed.
813. Communication from the Commission of 16 November 2004 (State aid No. 381/2004 *Broadband Infrastructure Project Pyrénées-Atlantiques*) COM (2004) No. 4343 final, paragraph 82; Communication from the Commission of 16 November 2004 (State Aid No. 381/2004 *Broadband Infrastructure Project Pyrénées-Atlantiques*) COM (2004) No. 4343 final, O.J. 2005, C 162..
814. Commission Decision of 26 November 2008 (State aid C 3/08 *Southern Moravia Bus Companies*) O.J. 2009, L 97, p. 14, paragraph 71.
815. Communication from the Commission of 15 September 2009 (State aid No. 206/2009 *Financing of the public transport services in district of Anhalt-Bitterfeld*) COM (2009) No. 6777 final, paragraph 46; Communication from the Commission of 15 September 2009 (State aid No 206/2009 *Financing of the public transport services in district of Anhalt-Bitterfeld*) COM (2009) No. 6777 final, O.J. 2009, C 255.
816. Commission Decision of 24 February 2010 (State aid C 41/08 *DSB*) O.J. 2011, L 7, pp. 1 et seq., paragraph 359.

Fourth criterion: competitive tendering or efficient undertaking comparator

Under the fourth *Altmark* criterion the undertaking must be selected pursuant to a public procurement procedure or, in alternative, the compensation to the beneficiary must not exceed that of a typical well-run undertaking which meets all the necessary public service requirements.

In particular, for what regards the public procurement procedure, the fourth *Altmark* criterion requires to verify whether the procedure has resulted in genuinely competitive tendering, and, in particular, whether the SSGI is assigned to the undertaking requesting the lowest level of compensation. Under the relevant case law, 'qualitative' tenders, where the undertaking is selected on the basis of the most advantageous bid and not on the basis of the lowest level of compensation, are generally considered as not able to avoid the risk of overcompensation. In the same direction, the Commission recommends the adoption of an open, transparent and non-discriminatory public procurement procedure with award criteria based on the lowest level of compensation, while the 'most economically advantageous tender' is deemed sufficient only where '*the award criteria are closely related to the subject-matter* [...] *and allow for the most economically advantageous offer to match the value of the market*'.[817]

Where the undertaking is not chosen pursuant to a public procurement procedure, the fourth *Altmark* criterion requires that the level of compensation is determined on the basis of an analysis of the costs that a typical well-run undertaking would have incurred in the same situation. This is an alternative test based on the efficiency of the provider of the service and on the least cost for the community. The benchmark is the would-be price referred to the situation of the same public service assigned by way of a competitive tender.[818]

However, the application of the alternative test involves a high degree of legal uncertainty with unpredictability of the results because of a lack of comparable undertakings to be used as benchmarks.[819]

Given the above, it is possible to conclude that, within the design of the new model, the economic operator which benefits from the social tax incentives, should always be selected through an open, transparent, and non-discriminatory public procurement procedure. Otherwise, the alternative test, which is based on the costs of a well-run business, does not offer sufficient guarantees for its practical implementation considering the lack of objective parameters.

Furthermore, the public procurement procedure adopted for the selection of the beneficiaries in the Social Cohesion Zone should always involve awarding criteria

817. Communication from the Commission of 11 January 2012 on the application of the European Union State aid rules to compensation granted for the provision of services of general economic interest, O.J. 2012, C 8, pp. 4-14, paragraph 67.
818. Commission Decision of 26 November 2008 (State aid C 3/08 *Southern Moravia Bus Companies*) O.J. 2009, L 97, p. 14, paragraph 83.
819. *See* Opinion by the State Aid Group of EAGCP, Services of general economic interest, 29 June 2006, p. 7, available at http://ec.europa.eu/competition/state_aid/legislation/sgei.pdf.

based on the lowest level of compensation in order to avoid the risk of overcompensation in conformity with the views of the ECJ and the Commission.[820]

At the end of the analysis of the *Altmark* criteria, it is necessary to summarize the main outcomes and, in particular, to verify whether the design of the Social Cohesion Zone, as outlined at the beginning of this chapter, can be adapted within the EU law framework as far as the variable of State aid rules is considered.

The research process has been addressed to investigate the possibility of tax measures – in the form of social tax incentives – which could fall outside the scope of application of State aid rules and, thus, not be subject to the notification requirement set by Article 108 TFEU.

For this purpose, the results of the analysis outline the possibility of a Social Cohesion Zone with a set of social tax incentives defined out of the scope of the State aid discipline – and, therefore, not constituting State aid under the notion of Article 107(1) TFEU – as long as some specific requirements are fulfilled on the ground of the *Altmark* criteria.

First of all, the economic operators which benefit from the social tax incentives granted in the zone must be selected through an open, transparent, and non-discriminatory public procurement procedure, with awarding criteria based on the lowest level of compensation. In particular, the call for tenders should anticipate the content of the obligations and the conditions which will be included in the entrustment act and, at the same time, it should specify a set of eligibility requirements for the applications of the economic operators.

In this context, the entrustment act, which represents the conclusion of the public procurement procedure, assumes a critical role for the admissibility of the tax measures under the *Altmark* criteria. This document, in fact, should precisely define the duration and the content of the obligations assumed by the recipient undertakings involved in a work integration service, both in the case of social enterprises (where the work integration service is the main statutory activity) and in the case of large enterprises (where work integration is a mere additional service beside the other main statutory goals). The same document should also include a description of the compensation mechanism (with the use of tax exemptions and tax credits) and, in particular, the parameters for calculating, controlling, and reviewing the compensation, including the indicator used to establish the reasonable profit.

In conclusion, the outcome of the analysis of the *Altmark* criteria gives evidence of a Social Cohesion Zone Model which can be designed in a form compatible with the internal market from the perspective of State aid rules; in particular, it has been demonstrated that, as long as the use of the public procurement procedure and the entrustment act are set according to the requirements above described, the tax measures granted in the Social Cohesion Zone can be considered as not constituting State aid under the notion of Article 107(1) and, therefore, be exempt from the notification requirement.

820. For practical solutions regarding the implementation of the public procurement procedure and the selection of economic operators in the context of social tax incentives *see infra* section §7.05[B][2].

[3] Outcomes under Article 106(2) TFEU

The second part of the analysis of State aid rules must be focused on those situations where the recipient undertaking is unable to comply with all the *Altmark* criteria.

This could happen, for example, when the beneficiary is selected without an open, transparent, and non-discriminatory public procurement procedure, or when the parameters for calculating the compensation are not established in advance.

In such cases, the tax measures granted within the Social Cohesion Zone will be considered as State aid according to the notion of Article 107(1) TFEU; nevertheless, when a tax measure addressed to an SSGI fails to comply with the *Altmark* criteria, it is still possible to find a space left within Article 106(2) TFEU in order to consider such a measure as a State aid compatible with the internal market.

Being this the case, the general consequence is that the tax measures have to be previously notified pursuant to Article 108(3) TFEU with an assessment from the Commission based on the conditions of compatibility set by Article 106(2).

Nevertheless, even in this context, the Commission Decision 2012/21/EU, which is part of the *Almunia* package, still offers some possibilities for the introduction of tax measures exempt from the notification obligation, giving evidence of one more field of investigation for the purposes of the research question. The Decision, in fact, provides a sort of block exemption according to which State aid in the form of public service compensation meeting a series of specific conditions are automatically compatible with the internal market and exempt from the prior notification obligation provided for in Article 108(3) TFEU.

Therefore, also in this case, the conditions set by the same Decision assume a fundamental relevance in order to verify the space left for the autonomous initiatives of the Member States for the implementation of the Social Cohesion Zone Model within the EU law framework.

By the analysis of this instrument, it first entails that the tax measures adopted in the context of the Social Cohesion Zone can effectively be covered by the scope of the Decision; the reference to the 'social inclusion of vulnerable groups', in fact, underlines the possibility for Member States to include various social services within a flexible concept, with the consequent exemption from the notification requirement when the related tax measures are addressed to objectives of social policies.[821] Accordingly, as far as the design of the Social Cohesion Zone is concerned, it seems possible to include under the concept of 'social inclusion of vulnerable groups' all the objectives of a social character associated with the work integration of the low-income individuals resident in the area. This means that the social tax incentives provided in the new model can be qualified as a form of public service compensation in favour of the economic operators which are involved in the provision of work integration services in favour of vulnerable groups of individuals. By this way, the tax measures adopted in the Social Cohesion Zone, even though considered as State aid pursuant to Article 107(1)TFEU, may in

821. *See* Commission Decision 2012/21/EU of 20 December 2011, Article 2(1)(c).

principle become block exempted from the notification requirement according to the provisions of the Decision.

The Decision also provides that the exemption is subject to the existence of an entrustment act through which the beneficiary is specifically entrusted by the public authority. In particular, the entrustment act must include the content and the duration of the public service obligation (maximum ten years), the undertaking and the territory concerned, the nature of any exclusive or special rights assigned to the undertaking by the granting authority, a description of the compensation mechanism, the parameters for calculating, controlling, and reviewing the compensation, and a specific reference to the same Decision. In more details, the duration of the period of entrustment must be justified by reference to objective criteria, such as the need to amortize non-transferable fixed assets; in principle, the duration of the period of entrustment must not exceed the period required for the depreciation of the most significant assets required to provide the SSGI.[822]

Further conditions provided by the Decision concern the control of overcompensation. Also in this case, in fact, the amount of compensation must not exceed what is necessary to cover the net cost incurred in discharging the public service obligations, including a reasonable profit. The net cost is calculated as the difference between the costs incurred in operating the SSGI and the revenues; In particular, where the undertaking also carries out activities falling outside the scope of the SSGI, only the costs related to the SSGI will be taken into consideration, while the cost linked with investments may be taken into account only when necessary for the operation of the SSGI.[823]

The Decision also contains some further guidance for what regards the concept of 'reasonable profit'; in this sense, reasonable profit means the rate of return on capital that would be required by a typical undertaking considering whether or not to provide the SSGI for the whole period of entrustment, taking into account the level of risk.[824] Where, by reasons of specific circumstances, it is not appropriate to use the rate of return on capital, Member States may rely on profit level indicators other than the rate of return on capital to determine what the reasonable profit should be, such as the average return on equity, ROCE, return on assets or return on sales.[825] Furthermore, where an undertaking carries out activities falling both inside and outside the scope of the SSGI, according to the Decision the internal accounts must show separately the costs and receipts associated with the SSGI and those of other services, as well as the parameters for allocating costs and revenues.[826]

822. Communication from the Commission on the application of the European Union State aid rules to compensation granted for the provision of services of general economic interest, O.J. 2012, C 8, pp. 4-14, paragraph 17.
823. *Ibid.*, paragraph 31.
824. In more details, the Decision provides that a rate of return on capital that does not exceed the relevant swap rate plus a premium of 100 basis points shall be regarded as reasonable in any event.
825. Communication from the Commission on the application of the European Union State aid rules to compensation granted for the provision of services of general economic interest, O.J. 2012, C 8, pp. 4-14, paragraph 34.
826. Commission Decision 2012/21/EU of 20 December 2011, Article 5(9).

Finally, it is important to observe that in the recitals of the Decision it is expressly provided that the exemption at issue has to be applied without prejudice to the Union provisions in the field of public procurement.[827] This basically means that, regardless of the fourth *Altmark* criterion, the obligation to follow a public procurement procedure has become, in the eyes of the Commission, a standard requirement for contracts related to SSGIs.

In definitive, if the tax measures provided within the Social Cohesion Zone fulfil the conditions laid down in the Decision, then the measures are considered to be compatible with the internal market and exempt from the notification requirement set by Article 108(3) TFEU.

Otherwise, where the Decision is not applicable, the tax measures can still in principle be evaluated under Article 106(2) TFEU according to the criteria specifically defined in the Framework included in the *Almunia* package. Nevertheless, this being the case, the tax measures will need the approval of the Commission after notification pursuant to Article 108(3) of the TFEU and, therefore, it will not be possible to identify a space left for the autonomous initiatives of the Member States.

Therefore, the evaluation of the tax measures of the Social Cohesion Zone under the criteria defined in the Framework must be excluded from the scope of the present analysis since it would involve a perspective not in line with the object of the research question (which is related to the possibility of tax measures not only compatible with the internal market, but also exempt from the notification requirement).

At the same time, the perspective of the SGEI *de minimis* regulation cannot be considered; the *de minimis* rule, in fact, which provides that an aid below EUR 500,000 on a three-year period does not have the characteristic of distorting competition, is not sufficient from the point of view of the expenditure value since it essentially reproduces a mechanism which is already used in the context of the current regional aid policy. Therefore, the analysis of any eventual perspective offered by the SGEI *de minimis* regulation would finally re-propose the dimension of the State Aid Zone model, excluding the possibility of original results from the development of the research question.

In summary, on the ground of the above considerations, the analysis of the scope and the conditions of the Commission Decision is finally able to define one more space left for the Social Cohesion Zone under the perspective of Article 106(2) TFEU in addition to the outcomes resulting from the analysis of the *Altmark* criteria.

In this regard, it is necessary to verify whether the same space is wider than that provided under the *Altmark* criteria through a comparison of the different outcomes with reference to the design of the new model.

For what regards the first *Altmark* criterion, it seems that the scope of the Decision, which refers to the social inclusion of vulnerable groups of people, essentially re-proposes the same substance of the principles defined under *Altmark*. In both cases, in fact, it is necessary that the SSGI is clearly defined and, at the same time, Member States join a wide margin of discretion in defining what they considered as an SSGI.

827. *Ibid.*, recital 29.

The second and the third *Altmark* criteria find the same evidence in the outcomes from the analysis of the Decision. In this sense, Articles 4 and 5 of the Decision, respectively dedicated to 'entrustment' and 'compensation', contain references to the same principles developed under *Altmark*; for example, the entrustment act under the Decision must include the parameters for calculating the compensation, in line with the substance of the second *Altmark* criterion. Furthermore, also Article 5 of the Decision refers to the prohibition of overcompensation and to the concept of reasonable profits in a way which is analogous to the third *Altmark* criterion.

On the contrary, important differences emerge as far as the fourth *Altmark* criterion is considered. In this case, in fact, the Decision does not specifically provide any condition related to the use of a public procurement procedure for awarding contracts.

On the ground of this outcome, it is possible to conclude that the space left to Member States for the implementation of the Social Cohesion Zone is wider in the case of the Commission Decision than in the case of *Altmark*; in the former case, in fact, it seems possible to grant the tax incentives within the Social Cohesion Zone without a prior selection of the beneficiaries though a public procurement procedure.

Nevertheless, the practical effects of such conclusion should be mitigated by a basic consideration.

As stated in the same recital of the Decision,[828] in fact, the exemption at issue has to be applied without prejudice to the Union provisions in the field of public procurement. This basically means that Member States have to comply with public procurement EU rules, regardless of the scope of State aid rules. As a consequence, it is hard to believe that, from the practical point of view, the implementation of the Social Cohesion Zone under the Decision could lead to more flexible outcomes than under the *Altmark* criteria, since in both cases, the compliance with public procurement EU rules seems to be a fundamental aspect to be considered.

This conclusion is coherent with the position of the case law considering that in several cases it is possible to note a certain similarity between the conditions for the application of Article 106(2) TFEU and the aspects of the *Altmark* criteria.[829]

[B] Fundamental Freedoms

The fundamental freedoms are the second variable to be considered for the analysis of the design of the Social Cohesion Zone within the EU law framework.

As already seen, the fundamental freedoms play a relevant role in this field, considering that the introduction of tax incentives for a limited area of a Member State generally determines a differentiated tax treatment between resident and non-resident entities.

---

828. *Ibid.*
829. *See, inter alia*, Case T-289/03 *BUPA and others v Commission* [2008] ECR II-00081, paragraphs 160, 162 and 224.

The design of the new model is characterized by the presence of tax measures of a social character addressed to recipient undertakings which are considered as based in the territory of the zone according to the criterion of the permanent establishment.[830]

Nonetheless, the same undertakings must comply with a set of conditions concerning the hiring of a minimum number of resident employees or the purchasing of a minimum volume of services and goods from the local suppliers.

On these premises, the variable of the fundamental freedoms involves two different levels of analysis related to the free movement of persons: first, the position of the undertakings which are the direct recipient of tax advantages granted through the package of social tax incentives (with respect to the freedom of establishment); second, the employees and the suppliers resident in the zone which indirectly benefit from the tax measures adopted in the context of the Social Cohesion Zone, enjoying the positive effects generated by the fulfilment of the obligations assumed by the recipient undertakings (with respect to the free movement of workers and the freedom of establishment).

On these premises, it is now necessary to test the Social Cohesion Zone under the same variable, approaching the following research sub-question:

> Research sub-question No. 2.2
>
> *Can a tax measure of a social character addressed to a limited area of a Member State, including conditions also based on the residence of the actors involved, be considered compatible with the free movement of persons?*

Therefore, the next sections will be dedicated to the analysis of the issues related to the above research sub-question, exploring first the position of the recipient undertakings and then the position of the employees and suppliers resident in the area which represent the ultimate target of the tax policy carried out under the Social Cohesion Zone.

[1] The Situation of the Recipient Undertakings

In the design of the Social Cohesion Zone, the territorial dimension has been shaped assuming the permanent establishment as the connecting factor for considering an undertaking as based within the perimeter of the zone.

Accordingly, the social tax incentives defined under the new model may be granted not only to resident undertakings but also to permanent establishment of non-resident undertakings, expanding the set of recipients which are eligible for the same tax measures.

830. For what regards the territorial dimension of the new model, the permanent establishment is here assumed as a minimum requirement to ensure a sufficient link between the place of business and a specific geographic point, as well as a certain degree of permanence within the area concerned (*see supra* section §6.02[A][3]). This means that, under the same territorial dimension, a business can also operate in the zone through more structured forms of organization, such as a subsidiary company. In all these cases, in fact, there will be a sufficient link between the place of business and the territory of the zone.

The analysis of the EU law framework confirms this possibility as a comfortable solution to exclude the presence of a discriminatory treatment or a restriction for what concerns the freedom of establishment.

In such cases, in fact, the terms of comparison are between a non-resident company with a permanent establishment in the STZ territory, on one part, and a resident company based in the same STZ, on the other; here, it is evident that the permanent establishment of the non-resident company is generally in a comparable situation with the resident company and, thus, both situations have to be treated in the same manner.[831]

Consequently, the identification of the permanent establishment as the territorial connecting factor is an element which ensures the freedom of establishment in the context of the Social Cohesion Zone, at least for what regards the situation of the recipient undertakings based within the perimeter of the zone.

These conclusions are in line with the settled case law reviewed in the context of Chapter 3; it has been already stated, in fact, that the attribution of tax incentives only to undertakings having their registered office in the territory of the Social Cohesion Zone and not to non-resident companies with a permanent establishment in the same territory may determine a discrimination against the non-resident company with the consequent infringement of the freedom of establishment.[832] In particular, in the case *Avoir Fiscal* the ECJ comes to the conclusion that the permanent establishment of a non-resident company and a resident company are in comparable situations as the national tax law does not distinguish between resident companies and permanent establishment of non-resident companies for the purpose of tax liability. Both entities, in fact, are subject to CIT and, consequently, they are on the same footing under national law for the purposes of direct taxation. The different treatment of the two comparable situations, therefore, constitutes discrimination; therefore, the permanent establishment of a non-resident company has to be treated in the same manner as resident companies.

On the ground of these considerations, it is possible to conclude that the situation of the non-resident undertakings in the new model does not involve any issue related to the freedom of establishment and the principle of tax non-discrimination. This is because, as long as the territorial connecting factor is defined with reference to the permanent establishment, any concern about a differentiated tax treatment does not emerge; in other words, the extension of the set of recipients, with the inclusion of the permanent establishment of non-resident entities, is able to set aside any discussion about the discrimination or the restriction of the freedom of establishment.

Therefore, from the point of view of the recipient undertakings, the Social Cohesion Zone Model can pass the test of compatibility within the variable of the freedom of establishment without any further investigation.

---

831. K. Dziurdz, C. Marchgraber, *Non-Discrimination in European and Tax Treaty Law*, Series on International Tax Law, M. Lang (ed.), Wien, 2015, p. 52.

832. Case C-270/83 *Commission of the European Communities v French Republic (Avoir fiscale)*, [1986] ECR 273; Joined cases C-400/97, C-401/97 and C-402/97 *Administración General del Estado v Juntas Generales de Guipúzcoa and Diputación Foral de Guipúzcoa, Juntas Generales d'Alava and Diputación Foral d'Alava and Juntas Generales de Vizcaya*, [2000] ECR I-01073.

[2] The Situation of the Employees

The tax measures provided under the Social Cohesion Zone Model are characterized by a series of conditions to be fulfilled by the recipient undertaking which regard, among the others, the hiring of a minimum number of new employees resident in the area.

In the resulting framework the recipient undertakings are the beneficiaries of the tax incentives with a favouring effect consisting in the reduction of their tax burden, while the new hired employees become the real ultimate target of the initiatives assumed by the Member State within the domain of social cohesion policy.

In such a situation, some concerns may arise with reference to the free movement of workers and the issues related to the discrimination or the restriction against the individuals which do not have their residence in the same area.

Within the design of the new model, in fact, the terms of comparison may be set between the situation of the employees resident of the zone and the employees non-resident of the same zone; furthermore, for what regards the second situation, it is also possible to make one more distinction between the workers which are resident of the hosting Member State and the workers which are non-resident with respect to the hosting Member State.

As long as these situations are considered as comparable, the tax incentives provided under the Social Cohesion Zone Model could be seen as a discriminatory measure with respect to the position of the workers not resident in the same area.

Before any further analysis based on the judgement of discrimination, it should first be noted that the design of the new model offers some important arguments to refuse, in principle, the above doubts.

First of all, the discriminatory content of a tax measure is usually measured with regard to the position of the recipient of the tax advantages, namely the undertaking which benefits from the reduction of the tax burden. In this case, as far as the perspective is shifted to the employees, the tax measures at issue do not determine any favourable effect with reference to their tax liability. In such situations, in fact, the factual evidence is only characterized by an indirect effect which is not of a fiscal nature as it merely consists in the increase of the employment offers available in the job market of the area.

Therefore, it seems not possible to expand the scope of the judgement of discrimination on the indirect effects of the tax measures, especially when the indirect effects do not include a reduction of the tax liability of the same employees.

Then, the second argument is that the employees resident in the Social Cohesion Zone are not in a comparable situation with respect to all the other employees which reside outside the territory of the zone. In this regard, in fact, it is important to remember that the crucial element for the decision of establishing a Social Cohesion Zone in a limited area of the Member State is always related to the disadvantaged conditions of a specific territory with respect to the national average or the EU average. In this sense, in fact, the social tax incentives provided under the Social Cohesion Zone regime are specifically tailored to improve the living conditions of low-income individuals in the light of the disadvantaged geographical position of the territory in which they reside. Consequently, it is clear that the employees who reside in more competi tive territories of the Member States cannot claim to be within a comparable situation with respect to the employees based in the Social Cohesion Zone.

On the ground of these considerations, it should be hard to suppose an infringement of the free movement of workers following the adoption of the tax measures provided within the Social Cohesion Zone Model; the situation of the new employees hired by the recipient undertaking, in fact, seems to be set outside the perimeter of any judgement of discrimination which should be limited to the direct effects of the related tax measures and the consequent reduction of the tax burden.

However, the scope of the present analysis is also intended to consider the case where the ECJ would challenge these conclusions, assuming a more invasive approach with the extension of the scope of the judgement of discrimination to the situations of the employees which indirectly benefit from the tax measures at issue.

Being this the case, it is now necessary to analyse the situation of the new employees hired by the recipient undertakings following the steps of the judgement of discrimination.

Comparability test

The first aspect to be considered under the judgement of discrimination is related to the comparability of the two situations.

In this case, the terms of the comparison are set between the situation of the workers who have their residence in the zone and the other workers who have their residence out of the perimeter of the same zone.

On these premises, the analysis should be carried out according to the overall comparison approach which has been consolidated since the Schumacker case.[833] In this sense, the comparability between residents and non-residents exists only when there is an equivalence between residents and non-residents with respect to the overall ability to pay; in other words, the relevant factor for comparability is identified in the evaluation of the general situation of the taxpayer, with specific reference to the Member State where the overall income (or, at least, the most part of the income) is produced. Therefore, in the Social Cohesion Zone Model, the comparability will be detected only as long as the non-resident produces at least the most part of his/her income within the perimeter of the STZ.[834]

As a consequence, the comparability between the situations of the resident and non-resident of the Social Cohesion Zone will be generally excluded, considering the usual presence of important elements of differentiation for what regards the place where the income is produced; however, such general rule may be subject to relevant deviations, with the consequent formulation of a judgement of non-discrimination, if it is possible to identify an equivalence between residents and non-residents with reference to the overall ability to pay and the area where their income is produced.

833. Case C-279/93 *Finanzamt Köln-Altstadt v Roland Schumacker*, [1995] ECR I-225.
834. *Ibid.*, paragraph 38.

This could happen, for example, in the case of the workers which have their residence in the areas immediately outside the external perimeter of the zone[835] and, at the same time, which produce the most part of their income in the Social Cohesion Zone, since they are hired by undertakings or permanent establishment of undertakings based within the perimeter of the same zone.

Being that the case, it is necessary to proceed with the next steps of the judgement of discrimination in order to verify the eventual infringement of the free movement of workers.

Discrimination test

The second step of the judgement of discrimination involves the verification of the existence of a national rule with a discriminatory content, with a differential treatment of the two comparable situations.

For the purposes of the discriminatory test, it is first necessary to make a distinction; the focus, in fact, can be set on the differentiated treatment between the resident employees of the Social Cohesion Zone and the other workers who are resident of the same hosting Member State or on the differentiated treatment between the same resident employees of the zone and the workers which have their residence in another Member State.

This distinction is important since Article 45 TFEU does not apply to a 'wholly internal' situation, such as in the case of the workers who are non-resident with respect to the Social Cohesion Zone but, at the same time, have their residence in another area of the same hosting Member State.[836]

In such cases, in fact, it is possible to identify a situation of 'reverse discrimination', where national workers cannot claim in their own Member States the rights which can instead be claimed by the workers who reside in another Member State. As expressly stated in *Saunders*, a resident of a Member State cannot rely on Article 45 TFEU in his or her own Member State to challenge a restriction on the free movement of persons, since there is no factor connecting the situation with Union law.[837] In other words, the residents of a Member State who have never exercised the right to the free movement of persons within the Union, have no rights to be invoked under Union law;[838] this is because a worker can rely on Article 45 TFEU against his or her own state only where that worker has been employed in another Member State.[839]

On the ground of the above considerations, it is finally clear that it is not possible to identify any discriminatory measure as long as the terms of comparison are between the resident employees of the Social Cohesion Zone and the other workers who are

835. In such a case it would be necessary to define a reasonable distance from the perimeter of the zone in order to consider the situation of the non-resident workers as relevant for the purposes of the comparability test.
836. P. Craig, G. De Búrca, *EU Law: Text, Cases, and Materials*, 6th Edition, Oxford University Press, New York, 2015, pp. 762-763.
837. Case C-178/78 *R v Sanders*, [1979] ECR 1129.
838. Joined Cases C-35/83 and C-36/83 *Morson and Jhanjan v Netherlands*, [1982] ECR 3723.
839. Case C-18/95 *FC Terhoeve v Inspecteur van de Belastingdienst Particulieren/Ondernemingen Buitenland*, [1999] ECR I-345.

resident of the same hosting Member State. In such cases, in fact, the absence of a cross-border factor determines, under the views of the ECJ, the impossibility of invoking the free movement of persons against the hosting Member State.

Otherwise, a discriminatory treatment relevant under the judgement of discrimination may exist when the comparison is between the same resident employees of the zone and the workers who have their residence in another Member State.

For example, such a situation may occur in case of a Social Cohesion Zone located close to the border of a Member State; in such case, in fact, the workers who have their residence in the other Member State, in the areas immediately outside the external perimeter of the zone, could be affected by a discriminatory treatment as long as they produce the most part of their income in the Social Cohesion Zone.

Justification test

Within the limits of relevance set by the comparability test and the discrimination test, it is now necessary to verify the tax measures of the Social Cohesion Zone under the third step of the judgement of discrimination; in this case, the aim is the identification of possible objective grounds for justifying a discriminatory rule based on the residence of the workers.

Within the EU framework, the free movement of workers may be subject to limitations on grounds of public policy, public security or public health as provided by Article 45 TFEU; in particular, as regards the public policy exception, the ECJ states that Member States retain a certain margin of discretion since 'the particular circumstances justifying recourse to the concept of public policy may vary from one country to another and from one period to another'.[840]

In addition to the grounds explicitly mentioned in the TFEU, the ECJ, since the *Cassis de Dijon judgment*, states that the infringement of the fundamental freedoms may also be justified by general grounds of public interest.[841]

However, the case law of the ECJ does not provide a comprehensive definition of public interest, limiting its decisions to the description of a series of examples of situations that are relevant under such notion.

The lack of a systematic approach is mainly justified by the need of flexibility which usually characterizes the measures of social policy adopted at the national level, while no uniform code of values can be imposed by EU law;[842] for example, in the case of the UK, the Joint Committee on Privacy and Injunctions assumes the same approach stating that '*the decision of where the public interest lies in a particular case is a matter of judgment, and is best taken by the courts in privacy cases*'.[843] In other words, the

840. Case C-41/74, *Yvonne van Duyn v Home Office*, [1974] ECR 01337.
841. Case C-120/78 *Rewe-Zentral AG v Bundesmonopolverwaltung für Branntwein*, [1979] ECR 00649.
842. Case C-268/99 *Aldona Malgorzata Jany and Others v Staatssecretaris van Justitie*, [2001] ECR I-08615.
843. House of Lords – Joint Committee on Privacy and Injunctions, *Paper No. 273*, House of Commons Paper No. 1443, Session 2010-12, 2012, p. 19.

general opinion is that a non-exhaustive list of public interest matters is more appropriate and useful than a strict definition of public interest.[844]

Therefore, the ECJ always leaves open the list of public interests, on the ground of the fact that the choice of public interests which a Member State wishes to promote by granting tax incentives is a matter of its own discretion.[845]

In particular, as far as the scope of the public interests is concerned, the ECJ puts in evidence that both the EU and the Member States are required to respect fundamental rights, considering that 'the protection of those rights is a legitimate interest which, in principle, justifies a restriction of the obligations imposed by EU law, even under a fundamental freedom guaranteed by the Treaty'.[846] In the light of these general grounds of public interest, the ECJ sometimes accepts the cohesion of the tax system as justification,[847] as well as the territoriality argument,[848] the effectiveness of fiscal supervision[849] or the need to safeguard the balanced allocation of taxing rights.[850] Nonetheless, such cases, which belong to the tax law field, do not offer any support to valorize the social element which characterizes the new model of STZs here developed.

However, the ECJ also explores other situations where the concept of social protection is better addressed for the purposes of the present analysis. According to the ECJ, in fact, overriding reasons relating to the public interest capable of justifying a restriction on the free movement of persons include the protection of workers,[851] the fight against undeclared work, as well as the protection of the financial balance of social security systems.[852]

On these bases, it is possible to conclude that the tax measures provided under the Social Cohesion Zone should be allowed under a public interest justification, as long as they are univocally addressed to the work integration and the social inclusion of low-income groups of individuals in the disadvantaged areas of the Member States within the domain of a social policy initiative.[853]

844. For example, the Australian Press Council defines public interest as '*involving a matter capable of affecting the people at large so they might be legitimately interested in, or concerned about, what is going on, or what may happen to them or to others*' (*See* Australian Press Council, *General Statement of Principles*, 2011, available at http://www.presscouncil.org.au/uploads/52321/ufiles/APC_General_Statement_of_Principles.pdf).

845. *See* E. Traversa, *supra.*, in *World Tax Journal*, 2014, p. 339. *See also* G. Bizioli, *Impact of the Freedom of Establishment on Tax Law*, in *EC Tax Review*, 1998, No. 4, pp. 239-247, where the author stresses the relativity of concepts such as public policy or public security (often used by the ECJ to refer to the general concept of public interest) '*because they change in time, national usage, and geographic location*'.

846. Case C-112/00 *Eugen Schmidberger, Internationale Transporte und Planzüge v Republik Österreich*, [2003] ECR I-05659.

847. Case C-204/90 *Bachmann*, [1992] ECR I-249.

848. Case C-250/95 *Futura Participations*, [1997] ECR I-2471.

849. *Ibid.*

850. Case C-446/03 *Marks & Spencer*, [2005] ECR I-10837.

851. Case C-515/08 *Dos Santos Palhota and Others*, [2010] ECR I-09133, paragraph 47. *See also* Case C-445/03 *Commission v Luxembourg* [2004] ECR I-10191, paragraph 29.

852. *See* Case C–346/06 *Dirk Rüffert v Land Niedersachsen*, [2008] ECR I-01989, paragraph 42.

853. *Ibid.*

In this direction, the individual rights defined on the ground of the fundamental freedoms can be counterbalanced by social considerations and public interests, within a broader conception of the internal market, including social protection.[854]

Within the Social Cohesion Zone Model, the specific conditions to be fulfilled by the recipient undertakings give evidence of a public interest which can be defined according to principles already stated by the ECJ in the relevant case law. In this regard, in fact, the hiring of a minimum number of new employees is an obligation evidently assumed in the public interest, being addressed to the protection of the employment in the most disadvantaged areas of the Member States.

Proportionality test

The last step of the analysis regarding the situation of the employees involves the application of the principle of proportionality.

When a ground of justification exists, in fact, it is always necessary to verify the proportionality of the same measure with respect to the objective pursued. According to the ECJ, tax incentives always must be proportionate to the legitimate objective of the national provisions on the ground of the public interest defined by the State at its own discretion.[855]

The ECJ has to interpret the principle of proportionality in the light of the Member State's values, considering also public policy justifications which determine a margin of discretion within the limits imposed by the Treaty.

In the proportionality test there are usually three stages concerning the suitability, the necessity, and the proportionality *stricto sensu* of a tax measure.[856]

The suitability of the tax measure deals with the relationship between the means and the end: the question asked is whether the chosen measure is suitable or appropriate to achieve the given aim proposed. In this regard, the assessment of suitability is strongly related to the facts and circumstances of the case and, therefore, the same assessment is usually left to the relevant national authorities or, in preliminary proceedings, to the national courts.[857]

In the second stage the measure's proportionality is assessed under the profile of its necessity; here, the Court assesses whether the chosen measure is necessary to achieve the proposed goal. In many cases, the ECJ interprets the 'necessity' strictly in a variety of different ways according to the different areas of law and according to the substance of the conflicting interests at stake. In particular, the 'least restrictive

---

854. *See* P. Craig, *The Evolution of the Single Market*, in *The law of the Single European Market – Unpacking the Premises*, C. Barnard, J. Scott (eds), Hart Publishing, Oxford and Portland, 2002, p. 32.

855. *See*, *inter alia*, Case C-406/04 *Gérald De Cuyper v Office National de l'emploi*, [2006] I-06947, paragraph 40; Case C-192/05 *K. Tas-Hagen and R. A. Tas v Raadskamer WUBO van de Pensioen- en Uitkeringsraad*, [2006] I-10451, paragraph 33; Case C-499/06 *Halina Nerkowska v Zakład Ubezpieczeń Społecznych Oddział w Koszalinie*, [2008] ECR I-03993.

856. T.I. Harbo, *The Function of the Proportionality Principle in EU Law*, in *European Law Journal*, 2010, Vol. 16, No. 2, p. 165.

857. *See* in this regard Case C-145/88 *Torfaen Borough Council v B&Q plc*, [1989] ECR I-3815; Case C-169/91 *Stoke-on-Trent CC v B&Q plc*, [1992] ECR I-6457.

alternative' usually represents the basic concept around which such interpretation is carried out;[858] the Court sets strict requirements for necessity in the sense that the measure must be 'indispensable for attaining the objective pursued if the situation is such that the free movement of persons is greatly restricted'.[859] In this sense, the focus of the necessity test is 'the examination of whether there are less restrictive alternatives available to achieve the objective pursued'.[860]

Finally, the test of proportionality involves the so-called proportionality *stricto sensu*, meaning that a measure is disproportionate if it imposes an excessive burden on the individual;[861] in this regard, the Court usually determines the interests served by the contested measure or decision, checking if the balance of all the interests is opportunely defined.

On these methodological premises, the design of the new model has to be tested pursuant to the principle of proportionality.

For what regards the first stage – i.e., the suitability of the tax measures – it should be noted that the social tax incentives are granted to the recipient undertakings provided that a specific set of conditions are fulfilled; therefore, in order to verify the suitability of the tax measure it is necessary to verify whether or not the effective fulfilment of these conditions determines the establishment of a fruitful relationship between the means and the ends.

In this case, the hiring of a minimum number of employees has been identified as the proper mean to pursue the objective of the Social Cohesion Zone; by the obligation assumed by the recipient undertaking, in fact, it is possible to improve the number of jobs available in the disadvantaged area, supporting the development of the employment factor. Thus, it seems that the proportionality of the tax measures is ensured under the criterion of suitability, considering that the condition of the minimum number of new employees hired is univocally aimed to the effective pursuit of the social goals of the Social Cohesion Zone.

Then, as far as the necessity of the tax measure is concerned (second stage of the proportionality test), the question is whether the social tax incentives granted to the recipient undertakings are necessary to achieve the improvement of the living conditions of the residents of the Social Cohesion Zone.

---

858. *See, ex multis*, Case C-312/89 and C-332/89 *Union départementale des syndicats CGT de l'Aisne v SIDEF Conforama, Société Arts et Meubles and Société Jima*, [1991] *ECR* I-00997, (Opinion of the Advocate General Van Gerven) paragraph 14. *See also* T.I. Harbo, *supra.*, in *European Law Journal*, 2010, Vol. 16, No. 2, p. 172.

859. D. Weber, *Tax Avoidance and the EC Treaty Freedoms: A Study of the Limitations under European Law to the Prevention of Tax Avoidance*, in *Eucotax Series on European Taxation 11*, Kluwer law international, The Hague, 2005, p. 209. *See* Case C-101/94 *Commission of the European Communities v Italian Republic*, [1996] ECR I-02691.

860. *Ibid.* It is also worth to remember that, in some cases, the requirement of 'necessity' has been interpreted in a weaker form by the ECJ, using as a parameter the 'manifestly inappropriateness' of a tax measure (*see* Case C-331/88 *The Queen v Minister of Agriculture, Fisheries and Food and Secretary of State for Health, ex parte: Fedesa and Others*, [1990] ECR I-04023).

861. R. Alexy, *A Theory of Constitutional Rights*, Oxford University Press, Oxford, 2002, p. 66.

In this case, the parameter of 'fiscal residue'[862] – which will be better discussed with some examples in next chapter[863] – can be used to confirm the necessity of the Social Cohesion Zone, even when the 'least restrictive alternative' becomes the concept adopted the carry out the same assessment.

The fiscal residue, in fact, is able to identify the ratio between the tax burden set in a region and the value of the public services available in the same region; thus, it can be used as a parameter to manage the allocation of tax expenditures among different areas of a Member State and to carry out an evaluation on the necessity of the Social Cohesion Zone.[864]

More precisely, the introduction of social tax incentives under the new model will become necessary as far as the parameter of the fiscal residue gives evidence of a negative ratio between the tax burden on undertakings based in the area (excessively high) and the value of the public services received by the same undertakings (excessively low). Accordingly, the Social Cohesion Zone may become the least restrictive alternative, especially when the previous policies adopted for the area have not achieved the expected results with reference to the localization choices of the undertakings and the improvement of the employment factor.

The last stage of the analysis deals with the proportionality *stricto sensu*. In this regard, the proportionality of the tax incentives granted in the Social Cohesion Zone can be easily confirmed, assuming that it is not possible to identify an excessive burden on the workers which do not reside in the zone; in this sense, in fact, for the non-resident workers the standard tax treatment provided at the level of the hosting Member State will be ensured. Furthermore, in the disadvantaged territory of the Social Cohesion Zone the employment factor remains the prevailing interest to be defended in the context of a social cohesion policy, in contrast with the position of the residents of high-income areas of the same Member State.

In summary, on the ground of the above analysis, it is possible to conclude that the proportionality test can be positively carried out with reference to the tax measures adopted under the Social Cohesion Zone Model; the specific conditions to be fulfilled by the recipient undertakings represent the fundamental element to be considered for achieving a positive outcome under the same test. In any case, it will also be necessary to pay specific attention to the selection of the eligible areas according to the parameter of the fiscal residue to ensure the necessity of the tax measures.

[3] The Situation of the Suppliers

Among the conditions to be fulfilled by the recipient undertaking, the design of the Social Cohesion Zone also includes the purchase of a minimum annual volume of

862. For an explanation of the concept of fiscal residue *see* B. Moro, *Incentivi fiscali e politiche di sviluppo economico regionale in Europa*, in *Moneta e Credito*, 2001, Vol. 52, pp. 343-388.
863. *See infra* section §7.04.
864. *Ibid.*, p. 383; P. Musgrave, *Interjurisdictional Coordination of Taxes on Capital Income*, in *Tax Coordination in the EC*, S. Cnossen (ed.) Kluwer Law International, Deventer, 1987, pp. 218-235.

goods and/or services from local suppliers (i.e., small and medium-sized enterprises registered in the zone).

Also in this case, the suppliers are the real ultimate target of the social cohesion policy; the objective of the Social Cohesion Zone, in fact, is essentially focused on the improvement of the living conditions not only of the resident employees, but also of the other categories requiring more protection, including, for example, the owners of the self-employed activities based in the same territory.

In such a situation, it is necessary to verify whether the freedom of establishment set by Article 49 TFEU may be invoked by the non-residents in order to access to economic activities under the same conditions defined for the SMEs registered in the territory of the Social Cohesion Zone.

In this regard, it seems possible to consider the same doubts already developed for the free movement of workers.

Also in this case, in fact, it is evident that there are no tax measures able to directly affect the tax liability of the suppliers with a reduction of the related tax burden; as a consequence, it seems not possible to identify a tax measure of a discriminatory content with reference to the position of the suppliers. This is because the set of social tax incentives is exclusively granted to the recipient undertakings and not directly to the local suppliers.

On these premises, it is hard to conceive an expansion of the scope of the judgement of discrimination on the suppliers, considering that the tax incentives of the Social Cohesion Zone do not involve any form of reduction of their tax liability. Consequently, it seems that not only the situations of the employees but also the situations of the suppliers are outside the perimeter of the judgement of discrimination regarding the tax measures adopted in the new model.

With these serious concerns in mind, as far as the perspective is however focused on the steps of the judgement of discrimination, the terms of the comparison should be set on the situation of the economic activities carried out by SMEs registered in the zone, on one part, and the economic activities carried out by SMEs with no registered office in the same territory, on the other. Being this the case, it would be difficult to suppose the comparability of such situations considering that SMEs with a registered office out of the zone are usually characterized by better results in terms of economic and financial indicators.

Furthermore, even when the two situations would be comparable,[865] a discriminatory treatment for the purposes of freedom of establishment cannot be identified with reference to the situation of the SMEs having a registered office in another area of the hosting Member State. In such a situation, in fact, Article 49 cannot be invoked as long as it not possible to identify a cross-border element. By this way, it is evident that a violation of the freedom of establishment under the Social Cohesion Zone Model

865. For example, that is the case of an individual entrepreneur residing in a Member State in proximity of the external limit of a Social Cohesion Zone which is part of another Member State, provided that the same entrepreneur earns the (almost) entire income in the territory of the Social Cohesion Zone.

might be identified only in a limited number of cases where the terms of comparison involve an SME with its registered office in another Member State.

In that case, as already seen for the employees, any eventual discrimination could be set under the public interest exception according to the possibilities offered by the recent case law of the ECJ,[866] especially as far as the protection of the employment factor is considered as a general ground of public interest; in particular, this is evident in the case of the owners of self-employed activities which usually meet the same difficulties of the employees, considering the low level of their income in the disadvantaged areas of the Union.

Finally, the situation of the suppliers should however involve the application of the principle of proportionality under the last step of the judgement of discrimination.

In this regard, the suitability of the tax measures can easily be confirmed; through the obligations assumed by the recipient undertaking, in fact, it is possible to ensure an increase of the volume of purchases from the local suppliers and, therefore, an improvement of the financial and economic situation of SMEs based in the same zone. The result is the increase of the annual revenue in consideration of the higher volume of the orders, with subsequent positive effects on the living conditions of the owners of these activities. Furthermore, the necessity and the proportionality *stricto sensu* of the tax measures can be ensured by the application of the parameter of the fiscal residue according to the same approach already described for the situation of the employees.

[C] The Code of Conduct for Business Taxation

The Code of Conduct for business taxation is the third and last variable to be considered for the analysis of the new model.

This document is a legally non-binding political commitment between Member States and it embodies a soft law process strategy designed to circumvent the Member States' propensity to disagree about taxation.[867]

The scope of the Code of Conduct is to contrast the harmful tax measures which affect or may affect in a significant way the location of business activities in the EU territory and which provide for a significantly lower level of taxation than the standard one applied in the Member State concerned.

In this direction, social tax incentives have to be scrutinized under the criteria of the Code of Conduct in order to verify the eventual presence of harmful tax measures within the Social Cohesion Zone Model.

Given the above, it is necessary to test the Social Cohesion Zone for the purposes of the Code of Conduct, approaching the following research sub-question:

Research sub-question No. 2.3

866. Case C-515/08 *Dos Santos Palhota and Others*, [2010] ECR I-09133, paragraph 47. *See*, also Case C–346/06 *Dirk Rüffert v Land Niedersachsen*, [2008] ECR I-01989, paragraph 42.

867. W.W. Bratton, J. A. Mc Cahery, *Tax Coordination and Tax Competition in the European Union: Evaluating the Code of Conduct on Business Taxation*, in *Internal Market Law Review*, 2001, No. 3, pp. 677-718.

Can a tax measure of a social character addressed to a limited area of a Member State be considered acceptable under the criteria of the Code of Conduct for business taxation?

On these bases, the next sections will approach the analysis of the above research sub-question, with a review of the design of the Social Cohesion Zone under the criteria of the Code of Conduct for business taxation, including the circumstances described in the recent guidance on tax privileges related to STZs.[868]

[1] The Code of Conduct Criteria

The provisions of the Code of Conduct essentially focus on the position of the foreign investor and on the tax measures able to influence the capital allocation choices in consideration of a preferential lower tax charge. On these premises, the practical implementation of the Code of Conduct should not usually involve situations where national governments implement a tax measure - such as those provided under the Social Cohesion Zone - with the exclusive aim of developing a social policy.

Nonetheless, this starting assumption must be verified with reference to each single criterion provided under the Code of Conduct for the identification of a harmful tax measure.

The first criterion (availability of the tax advantage only for non-residents, or for transactions with non-residents) has clearly to be excluded from the scope of the Social Cohesion Zone Model. It is evident, in fact, that the social tax incentives are here addressed in the opposite sense, limiting the related advantages to the recipient undertakings which are resident, or at least, established in the territory of the zone.

The second criterion is the ring-fencing, namely the protection of the domestic market so that the measure does not erode the domestic tax base of the State concerned. In this regard, the tax measures adopted under the Social Cohesion Zone Model are characterized by the reduction of the tax burden of all the eligible undertakings with a permanent establishment in the area regardless of their nationality; accordingly, the subsequent erosion of the tax base may indifferently affect the domestic tax base or non-domestic tax base, considering the absence of specific conditions related to the nationality of the eligible undertakings.

The third criterion refers to the lack of substance and real economic activity. In the Social Cohesion Zone Model, the substance is ensured by the fulfilment of the conditions of the hiring of a minimum number of new resident employees and a minimum volume of purchases from the local suppliers; as far as the recipient undertaking complies with these obligations, there will be a real economic activity carried out in the zone.

The fourth criterion, which concerns the lack of the arm's-length dealing, might involve the transactions between the recipient undertaking, as the customer, on one

868. Guidance of the Code of Conduct Group (Business Taxation) on tax privileges related to special economic zones of 19 June 2017, Council of the European Union, Brussels, document No. 10487/17.

part, and SMEs having the registered office in the zone, as suppliers, on the other. In this regard, the tax measures granted under the Social Cohesion Zone Model could be evaluated as harmful in the case of a prior relationship existing between the customer and the suppliers with a possible collusion between the same parties of the business relationship. For this reason, the design of the new model must be shaped ensuring that both the recipient undertakings and the local suppliers are acting in their own interest and that neither party is being pressured by the other party to go ahead with the transaction. These conditions can be ensured paying attention to the content of the entrustment act between the public authority and the recipient undertaking providing that it contains a specific clause in order to exclude from the calculation of the minimum volume of purchases the orders made between parties with a prior different relationship (e.g., an employee which starts a self-employed activity establishing a trade with his previous employer).

The fifth and last criterion is focused on non-transparency with particular reference to unpublished advance rulings and negotiability of the tax burden. With this in mind, the design of the Social Cohesion Zone must be conceived as the result of a legal background completely defined under national law, excluding the setting of differentiated conditions following a ruling made for a specific case; in other terms, the content of the entrustment act, with particular reference to the size of the tax incentives granted and the object of the obligations assumed by the recipient undertaking, must merely implement the provisions set by the national law in a transparent manner. Differently, in fact, the entrustment act would offer a space for the negotiability of the tax burden, giving evidence of the harmful character of the related tax measure.

On the ground of this analysis, it finally results that the Code of Conduct for business taxation is a relevant variable under the Social Cohesion Zone Model as far as the position of the recipient undertaking is concerned.

As seen, in fact, while the first, the second, and the third criteria do not determine any specific correction to the design of the model as resulting from the previous stages of the analysis, on the contrary, the fourth and the fifth criteria suggest to pay attention to some aspects in the implementation of the Social Cohesion Zone Model in the Member States. In this sense, in fact, the exclusion from the eligible costs of the purchases made between non-independent parties, as well as the transparency and non-negotiability with reference to the tax benefits and the obligation assumed in the entrustment act, become more essential qualifying features of the model resulting from the present analysis.

[2] *The Guidance on Tax Privileges Related to SEZs*

For the purpose of the Code of Conduct and the implementation of the related criteria, the analysis must also include the content of the recent guidance of tax privileges related to SEZs.[869]

This document issued by the Code of Conduct Group (business taxation) better defines a series of circumstances under which the tax measures adopted in a SEZ – this is the term here adopted – will be scrutinized by the Code of Conduct Group.

These circumstances essentially reproduce the five criteria analysed in the previous section, with some further specifications which can be useful for the assessment of the related tax measures.

Among the same circumstances, it is interesting to note that the guidance specifically sets the focus on the tax privileges available also for highly mobile activities, considering this factor as an indicator of possible harmful tax measures.

With reference to the movable activities, in fact, a question emerges about the possibility of including, between the eligible undertakings for the tax incentives granted in the Social Cohesion Zone, the economic operators active in the banking and insurance industry or in the information technology sector. In this regard, it is important to defend such a possibility, considering the strategic role of highly mobile activities in the improvement of the employment factor as demonstrated in many successful experiences throughout the world (e.g., companies of the IT sector based in the Silicon Valley in California).

On these premises, the conclusion must be assumed in consideration of the practical role of this guidance; the circumstances there described, in fact, merely suggest the existence of a harmful tax measure, while the final scrutiny always has to be carried out with exclusive reference to the five criteria defined under the Code of Conduct. This basically means that a tax measure, even when it is also available for highly mobile activities, must be assessed under the third criterion of the Code of Conduct which refers to the lack of substance, intended as a broader concept related to the existence of a real economic activity. Therefore, on these bases, the final outcome will be positive as long as the undertakings carrying out a highly mobile activity assume the obligation of hiring a minimum number of employees in the zone and of purchasing a minimum volume of goods and services from local suppliers; through the fulfilment of these conditions, in fact, the substance of a real economic activity will however be ensured even in case of highly mobile activities, excluding the harmful character of the related tax measure.

Finally, it should be mentioned that, under the guidance, one more circumstance deals with the lack of regular tax audits aimed at verifying that the profits accruing in the zone are associated to the activities allocated therein.

869. Guidance of the Code of Conduct Group (Business Taxation) on tax privileges related to special economic zones of 19 June 2017, Council of the European Union, Bruxelles, document No. 10487/17.

This point suggests to include in the Social Cohesion Zone Model the provision of a periodical monitoring and control from the public authority on the effective connection between the profits and the activities from which the same profits are supposed to be generated. In this sense, it will be for the national legislator to define the terms and the conditions of the supervision activity.

§6.04 SUMMARY OF THE RESULTS

On the ground of the analysis of the EU law framework, it is finally possible to summarize the results of the research process carried out in the present chapter.

The starting idea has been identified in an instrument to be used at the Member States level for the development of social cohesion policies for the most disadvantaged areas of the Union in coherence with the scope of the research question.

The first stage of the research process has thus been focused on the identification of a design which could be suitable for the aim pursued, in ideal terms, without the assessment of the variables resulting from the application of EU law.

Accordingly, the initial version of the new model has been structured in accordance with the same idea, assuming a set of characteristics under the territorial, the structural, and the functional dimensions all addressed to the same objective of a social nature.

The second stage of the research process has instead been addressed to test the same model with respect to the variables of the EU law framework following the coordinates described in Chapter 3, with regard to State aid rules, the fundamental freedoms, and harmful tax competition.

At the end of this process of analysis, it is necessary to proceed with a summary of the corresponding results.

The first variable of State aid rules has given evidence of a double track which can be followed in order to shape the tax advantages of the Social Cohesion Zone Model in a form compatible with the internal market and exempt from the notification obligation of State aid.

The first track is the most ambitious and is aimed at setting the social tax incentives out of the scope of the State aid discipline, as not constituting State aid under the notion of Article 107(1) TFEU. For this purpose, the tax measures must comply with the *Altmark* criteria and, therefore, must first be designed as a compensation for the recipient undertakings involved in the provision of an SSGI.

In in this regard, the possibility has been considered of including large enterprises among the beneficiaries of the related tax measures. By the analysis of the substance of SSGIs, it seems that a solution in positive or negative sense should be linked to the parameter used for the identification of a genuine SSGI; the idea, in fact, is that, when the parameter is the object of the obligation assumed from the undertaking, large enterprises might be included among the possible recipients of the advantages, considering the social character of the conditions to be fulfilled under the Social Cohesion Zone Model (e.g., minimum number of employees to be hired); otherwise, as far as the parameter is instead focused on the statutory goals of the undertaking, then only social enterprises seem to provide an SSGI eligible for the tax incentives of the Social Cohesion Zone. Nevertheless, through the analysis of the EU law framework, it has not been possible to identify any common reference or limit for this parameter (except for the case of a manifest error), considering that Member States continue to enjoy a wide margin of discretion in deciding what to consider as an SSGI. On these premises, there is then a space left for Member States in order to include not only social enterprises, but also large enterprises among the eligible undertakings within the Social Cohesion Zone Model.

In any case, the economic operators which benefit from the social tax incentives granted in the zone must be selected through an open, transparent, and non-discriminatory public procurement procedure, with awarding criteria based on the lowest level of compensation; the call for tenders must define the content of the obligations and the conditions under which the tax benefits will be granted, as well as the eligibility requirements for the economic operators. Furthermore, the entrustment act, which represents the conclusion of the public procurement procedure, must precisely define the duration and the content of the social obligations for the economic operators, concerning the minimum number of resident employees to be hired and the minimum annual volume of purchases from local suppliers. The same document must also include a description of the compensation mechanism and, in particular, the parameters for calculating, controlling, and reviewing the compensation, including the indicators used to establish the reasonable profit.

The second track is instead based on the exemption defined under Article 106(2) TFEU, assuming that the tax measures at issue fails to comply with the *Altmark* criteria and, therefore, must be considered as State aid under the notion of Article 107(1) TFEU.

In this case, the analysis defines, at least at first sight, a wider space left to Member States for the implementation of the Social Cohesion Zone, in consideration of the block exemption provided by the Commission Decision in order to consider a tax measure as a State aid compatible with the internal market and exempt from the notification obligation. This is because the prior selection of the beneficiaries through a public procurement procedure is not expressly mentioned by the Decision among the requirements for enjoying this exemption.

Nevertheless, it has been underlined that, beyond the formal absence of this requirement, Member States always have to comply with public procurement EU rules, regardless of the scope of State aid rules; therefore, even within this second track, the compliance with public procurement EU rules cannot be excluded from the horizon of the Social Cohesion Zone Model.

The second variable of the fundamental freedoms assumes different outcomes as far as the perspectives of the recipient undertakings, the employees and the suppliers are separately considered.

For what regards the recipient undertaking, any issue related to the possible infringement of the freedom of establishment can be set apart as long as the territorial connecting factor of the new model is defined allowing the eligibility of the tax incentives also for the permanent establishment of a non-resident undertaking.

The same results have been substantially achieved for the situations of the employees and the suppliers, even through a more complex process of analysis also involving the various steps of the judgement of discrimination.

In these cases, it has first been observed that the tax measures at issue do not determine any favourable effect with reference to the tax liability of the employees and the suppliers. In such situations, in fact, the factual evidence is only characterized by an indirect effect which is not of a fiscal nature as it merely consists in the increase of the job offers and of the purchasing orders in the area concerned. The conclusion is thus in the sense that it seems not possible to expand the scope of the judgement of discrimination to the indirect effects of the tax measures.

However, regardless of these first conclusions, the absence of discrimination or a restriction with reference to the free movement of workers or the freedom of establishment has also been confirmed following the analysis of each step of the judgement of discrimination. In particular, it has not been possible to identify any discriminatory measure as long as the terms of comparison are between the resident employees of the Social Cohesion Zone and the other workers which are resident of the same hosting Member State; in such cases, in fact, the absence of a cross-border dimension determines, according to the views of the ECJ, the impossibility of invoking against the hosting Member State the right of free movement under EU law. In any case, the residual situations which could be negatively evaluated under the comparability test and the discrimination test may finally be resolved under the justification test and the proportionality test; this is because the tax measures provided under the Social Cohesion Zone Model may be allowed under a public interest justification, as long as they are univocally addressed to the protection of the employment factor in the disadvantaged areas of the Member States. Moreover, as seen, the analysis of the specific conditions to be fulfilled by the recipient undertakings offers the opportunity to confirm the proportionality of the related tax measures on the ground of the parameter of the fiscal residue.

The third and last variable of the EU law framework deals with the Code of Conduct for business taxation.

In this regard, the fourth and the fifth criteria for considering a tax measure as harmful suggest to exclude from the eligible costs the purchases made between non-independent parties, as well as to ensure the transparency and non-negotiability through the introduction of specific provisions. Moreover, as far as highly mobile activities are concerned, it is possible to confirm the real economic substance of the activity carried out by the recipient undertaking in consideration of the object of the obligations defined in the entrustment act, namely the minimum number of new employees to be hired and the minimum volume of purchases from local suppliers. Finally, the analysis of the recent guidance issued by the Code of Conduct Group suggests to provide monitoring activities from the public authorities addressed to verify the effective connection between the activities carried out within the Social Cohesion Zone and the profits generated.

§6.05 SYNTHESIS OF THE MODEL

The outcomes of the present research are able to support a positive answer to the research question formulated at the beginning of this chapter.

The results illustrated in the previous section, in fact, offer the opportunity to outline a synthesis of the new model of the Social Cohesion Zone according to its territorial, structural, and functional dimensions.

[A] Territorial Dimension

For what regards the territorial dimension, the analysis of the EU law framework which is relevant for direct taxation does not involve any requirement or condition for the profile of the geographical delimitation. The ring-fencing of STZs, in fact, becomes a requirement only in the case of the FZs of the UCC which exclusively cover the different field of indirect taxation.

Therefore, it is possible to confirm the value set within the initial design of the Social Cohesion Zone corresponding to a conventional limitation of the area through a line on the map; by this way, in fact, it is possible to guarantee a flexible solution which is also suitable for ensuring the continuity and the accessibility of urban areas.

One more profile which has been considered in the context of the territorial dimension is the reference framework. In the new model, as well as in all the other implementing models described in Chapter 5, the reference framework basically corresponds to the territory of the Member State which is responsible for the external relations of the zone as stated by Article 355 TFEU.

Beside the geographical delimitation and the reference framework, also the territorial connecting factor has been considered in the context of the territorial dimension. For this purpose, the analysis of the variable of the free movement of persons has given evidence of the compatibility of the original solution outlined in the initial design. As seen, in fact, as far as the tax incentives are extended to the permanent establishment of a non-resident undertaking, the infringement of the freedom of establishment must be excluded.

[B] Structural Dimension

The initial design of the new model has been characterized by a structural dimension focused on the use of tax incentives limited to direct taxation.

In this regard, it is important to note that the Social Cohesion Zone, as resulting from the analysis of the EU law framework, may cover all the typologies of direct taxes since under this profile the variables of EU law do not set any limitation. The main point is that direct taxes are not harmonized at the EU level, except for what regards some marginal aspects of cross-border situations; therefore, the structural dimension of the new model, for what concerns the types of direct taxes involved, can be freely developed through the autonomous initiative of the Member States which retain an exclusive competence in the field of direct taxation.

Under the initial design, the same tax incentives have been structured in the form of a subtractive regime and, in particular, through the introduction of tax allowances and tax credits. This is a choice of opportunity since, in both situations, it is possible to clearly set the value of the tax expenditures by reference to the number of new employees hired and the amount of the eligible costs incurred for purchases from local suppliers. In any case, from the analysis of the EU law framework no limitation against the same choice has been identified; in fact, the definition of such aspect of the structural dimension remains a matter of exclusive competence of the Member States which are in principle free of determining the most suitable solution for the objectives pursued.

Nevertheless, the results of the analysis carried out in the present chapter have identified some further requirements to be fulfilled under the structural dimension in order to adapt the design of the Social Cohesion Zone Model to the current EU law framework.

First, the undertakings which benefit from the social tax incentives available in the zone must be selected through an open, transparent, and non-discriminatory public procurement procedure, with awarding criteria based on the lowest level of compensation (i.e., the value of the tax expenditure). In particular, it is necessary to pay attention to the content of the call for tenders which must define the obligations and the conditions under which the tax benefits will be granted, as well as the eligibility requirements for the economic operators.

Second, the entrustment act, which represents the conclusion of the public procurement procedure, must precisely define the duration and the content of the obligations for the economic operators. The same document must also include a description of the compensation mechanism (i.e., tax credits and tax allowances) and, in particular, the parameters for calculating, controlling, and reviewing the compensation, including the indicators used to establish the reasonable profit. In this sense, the parameter for compensation will be set making reference, for example, to a certain fixed amount of tax credit or tax allowance for each new employee or to a tax credit or a tax allowance corresponding to a percentage of the costs incurred for the purchases made from local suppliers.

All these requirements, which emerge from the analysis of the *Altmark* criteria, must then be provided within the structural dimension of the Social Cohesion Zone Model in order to ensure its compatibility with EU law, considering also the relevant rules on public procurement.

The structural dimension of the new model is finally completed by provisions addressed to exclude from the eligible costs the purchases made between non-independent parties and to ensure monitoring activities from the public authorities, as well as to guarantee the transparency and the non-negotiability of the related tax measures.

[C] Functional Dimension

The starting idea of the Social Cohesion Zone has been focused on the development of social cohesion policies aimed at reducing the differences in the living conditions between low-income areas and high-income areas of Member States.

For this purpose, the main target has been set on the employment factor and, consequently, on the low-income individuals who reside in the most disadvantaged areas.

Accordingly, the tax measures of the Social Cohesion Zone Model have been designed, from the functional point of view, as social tax incentives in the terms defined under the general legal theory of STZs.

Following the analysis of the first *Altmark* criterion, social tax incentives in the new model must be designed as a compensation for the recipient undertakings involved in the provision of an SSGI in order to be set out of the scope of State aid rules. Therefore, it is crucial to clearly define the objects of the obligations assumed by the undertakings through the signature of the entrustment act, establishing a solid link between means and ends in order to give evidence of the social character of the tax measure. By this way, in fact, the economic activity carried out by the economic operator will be deemed to be a genuine SSGI, as long as the obligations are specifically targeted to the public interest (i.e., involving government functions related to employment under the welfare domain, such as in the case of work integration services) and not to the mere pursuit of making profits.

These aspects must be valorized in the context of the entrustment act with clear written evidence of the public interest justification which is referred to the protection of the employment factor in the disadvantaged areas of the Member States. Moreover, public authorities will provide evidence of the reasons under the selection of a specific area of the Member State as a Social Cohesion Zone; in this regard, a reference will be made to the parameter of the fiscal residue in order to allow a comprehensive assessment of the related tax measures also for what regards their proportionality.

Furthermore, in order to ensure the effective pursuit of the same objectives, a set of specific conditions has been outlined to be fulfilled by the economic operators which intend to benefit from the tax incentives granted in the area.

The first subset of these conditions refers to the minimum number of new employees to be hired by the recipient undertaking in the first year of activity, as well as the residence of the same employees, the minimum duration of the employment contract and the qualification of the new employees in order to guarantee the hiring of a balanced number of units of high-qualified employees and low-qualified employees.

The second subset of conditions concerns the minimum volume of purchases to be made by the recipient undertaking from the local suppliers, namely SMEs having their registered office in the territory of the Social Cohesion Zone.

Beside this set of conditions, the functional dimension of the new model has been characterized by the provision of some specific eligibility requirements for the recipient undertakings which intend to benefit from the tax incentives available in the zone. In this regard, in fact, one more choice of opportunity is in the sense of limiting the tax incentives to entities, such as social enterprises and large enterprises, which can provide enough guarantees for what concerns their statutory social goals or their economical and financial strength.

§6.06 FINAL REMARKS

The outcomes of the analysis carried out in the present chapter give evidence of a new implementing model, the Social Cohesion Zone, which can be set within the general legal theory of STZs and beside the other existing models recognized in the factual experience (i.e., FZ, State Aid Zone, and Extraterritorial Zone).

The set of characteristics described under the territorial, the structural and the functional dimension confirms the possibility of a positive answer to the second research question, offering support for the conclusions of the book which will be presented in Chapter 8.

CHAPTER 7

Implementation Aspects of the Social Cohesion Zone

§7.01 INTRODUCTION

After the analysis of the results with reference to each research question, it is now necessary to discuss the main outcomes and the possible implementations.

In the previous chapters, the possibility has been demonstrated of a general legal theory of STZs able to explain under a common reading-key not only the EU law framework on the topic, but also the factual experience of the Member States. This result has been achieved setting a focus on three main aspects: the concept of STZs with its territorial, structural, and functional dimensions, the definition of STZs as a comprehensive macro-category and, finally the implementing models of STZs identified on the basis of the experience of the Member States.

On the ground of this systematic perspective, the possibility has been demonstrated of a new model of STZs within the EU law framework to be implemented beside the FZ, the State Aid Zone, and the Extraterritorial Zone. The Social Cohesion Zone, in fact, exploits the space left for the Member States within the negative limits of EU law, addressing its tax measures to the development of social cohesion policies for the most disadvantaged areas of the Union.

Starting from these findings, the following sections will first proceed with a comparison between the new model of the Social Cohesion Zone and the other implementing models identified under the general legal theory of STZs; the objective is to find a motivation for the Social Cohesion Zone, highlighting the opportunity aspects for giving precedence to this instrument for the development of social cohesion policies.

Then, the idea of the Social Cohesion Zone will be discussed as an innovative instrument for the Commission in the context of the EU cohesion policy outlining a possible solution for its governance; in this sense, in fact, the assumption according to which Member States are free to take autonomous initiatives for the establishment of the Social Cohesion Zone does not exclude the EU competence in the adoption of supporting, coordinating or complementary actions.

Furthermore, the discussion will cover the issues related to protectionism with particular reference to the parameter used to verify the proportionality of the tax measures. In this regard, the fiscal residue will be proposed as the parameter to measure the legitimacy of the Social Cohesion Zone in order to avoid the establishment of protectionist measures with restrictive effects on the internal market and the consequent infringement of the free movement of persons.

At the end of this chapter, a practical example of a package of tax incentives for the establishment of Social Cohesion Zones will be outlined, with the description of a set of qualifying features developed on the ground of the results of the research.

§7.02 COMPARISON OF THE MODELS UNDER THE GENERAL LEGAL THEORY OF STZs

The new model of the Social Cohesion Zone has been developed as an instrument for social cohesion policies; the related tax measures, in fact, being configured as social tax incentives, are univocally addressed to improve the living conditions of the individuals which reside in the most disadvantaged areas of the EU.

The improvement of the employment factor in these areas is the ultimate target of the tax incentives granted to the recipient undertakings; in this regard, the starting assumption is the necessity of reducing the disparities between low-income and high-income areas of the Union through a series of public initiatives concretely aimed at changing the conditions of the employment market in the disadvantaged areas.

Given the above, the overview of the EU law framework confirms that the other existing models of STZs do not offer sufficient support for the development of such kind of policies.

In the case of FZs, the tax benefits belong to the category of economic tax incentives; such zones, in fact, represent an instrument focused on the import/export process where it is usually not possible to identify any important effect on the employment factor for the individuals resident in the area.

Extraterritorial Zones are always established on the ground of specific historical privileges and, therefore, also in this case, the corresponding model of STZs cannot be used as a general instrument for the management of social cohesion policies; in particular, the model is not easily replicable in absence of historical privileges and, in any case, it would require important amendments to the EU law with a different definition of the boundaries of the Customs Union or of the VAT and the excise duty common area.

Differently, as far as State Aid Zones are concerned, some possibilities for social cohesion policies can emerge from the exemptions for regional aid set by paragraphs (a) and (c) of Article 107(3) TFEU. In the both situations, in fact, tax incentives may be used for favouring the development of certain economic areas where the standard of living is abnormally low with respect to the national average or with reference to the EU level.

Nonetheless, the analysis of the experience of the Member States points out the presence of important limits for the introduction of social tax incentives under the State Aid Zone model. The system of prior authorizations and the criteria for the assessment carried out by the Commission determine a situation where the initiatives of the Member States often limit their objectives, especially for what regards the size of the tax expenditures and the consequent effectiveness of the related measures.

Despite the recent openings of the Commission and a more relaxed control on regional aid in the context of the State aid modernization process, it is a matter of fact that today the conditions and tests for the evaluation of the compatibility of a tax measure under such exemptions remain very strict. For instance, the guidelines on regional State aid set a maximum aid intensity[870] and requires that the measures are limited to the minimum necessary in order to avoid any potential distortion on competition and trade.[871] Therefore, it is evident that the approach of the Commission for the purposes of State aid rules is still consistently based on the defence of the internal market.

As a consequence, Member States can only assume minor initiatives for the development of social cohesion policies. In this regard, in fact, according to the GBER, investment aid is compatible with the internal market and exempt from the notification obligation as long as they are in compliance with the map for regional aid approved by the Commission, considering a maximum aid intensity defined as a percentage of the eligible costs.[872] Furthermore, under the *de minimis* regulation, the measures become exempt from the notification requirement when they are in compliance with specific conditions, such as those concerning the total amount of the aid not exceeding EUR 200,000[873] (for each enterprise over a period of three years), the method of calculation and the method of control.

In definitive, the quantitative limits set by EU law for regional aid, both for what concerns the maximum aid intensity and the notification threshold, represent an important obstacle for the development of social cohesion policies at the national level. For example, the recent experience of ZFU in Italy gives evidence of the insufficiency of regional aid designed under the exemptions of Article 107(3) TFEU;[874] the same quantitative limits, in fact, undermine the attractiveness of the related tax measures, especially for the allocation choices of large enterprises, while the effects are generally limited to SME which do not have enough financial strength to support a real improvement of the employment factor in the area.

Therefore, the result is that today Member States are not able to assume relevant initiatives for their disadvantaged regions, considering the limits set in terms of

870. *See* Communication from the Commission – Guidelines on regional State aid for 2014-2020, O.J. 2013, C 209, paragraph 3.6.
871. *Ibid.*, paragraph 3.7.
872. *See* Article 14(12), Commission Regulation (EU) No. 651/2014 of 17 June 2014 declaring certain categories of aid compatible with the internal market in application of Article 107 and 107 of the Treaty, O.J. 2014, L 187, pp. 1-78.
873. Commission Regulation (EU) No. 1407/2013 of 18 December 2013 on the application of Articles 107 and 108 of the Treaty on the Functioning of the European Union to *de minimis* ad, O.J. 2013, L 352, pp. 1-8.
874. *See supra* note 512.

maximum aid intensity, the notification threshold, and all the other strict conditions laid down in the guidelines on regional State aid.

Also when the State Aid Zone is implemented through an 'infra-State body' there are evident difficulties in the development of social cohesion policies through the adoption of this instrument.

The infra-State body, in fact, needs to be set in accordance with a specific constitutional framework at the national level, with the fulfilment of the requirements of the institutional, procedural, and financial autonomy; in this regard, the experience of the Member States does not give evidence of many examples able to comply with such requirements, with the practical impossibility of implementing the same model of STZs in absence of important amendments to the constitutional environment of the hosting State; therefore, the option of the intra-State body cannot represent a concrete track in the EU for the improvement of the living conditions of the most disadvantaged areas.[875]

On these premises, it is possible to conclude that there is enough motivation and need for the Social Cohesion Zone Model as developed in the present study.

In this case, in fact, the measures consisting of social tax incentives may offer the opportunity of more incisive initiatives, being not subject to the limit of the maximum aid intensity and to the notification thresholds provided for regional State aid. In the situation of the Social Cohesion Zone, the maximum value of the tax expenditures may cover the total amount of the eligible costs and not a mere percentage (in terms of maximum aid intensity) as it happens for the regional aid covered by the GBER.[876] Moreover, the value of tax expenditures in the Social Cohesion Zone may also cover a reasonable profit, thus improving the attractiveness of the related tax measures for the economic operators which are interested in investing in the zone. Within these new parameters, the value of the tax expenditures will thus be determined in a way able to cover the entire or, at least, the most part of the investments made by the recipient undertakings, plus a percentage for the reasonable profit, without being subject to the maximum aid intensity limits or to the notification thresholds established by the GBER.

At the same time, from a different perspective, it is worth to observe that the fulfilment of the *Altmark* criteria will exclude any potential distortive effect on the internal market and the trade between Member States, supporting the establishment of the new model in a more relaxed framework focused on the social character of the tax measures without the strict limits for regional aid.

On these conceptual bases, the Social Cohesion Zone Model can fulfil an important gap in the EU law framework, allowing the use of a more effective instrument for the development of social cohesion policies, with a set of tax measures able to support more incisive actions.

---

875. For instance, it is not possible to implement the model of the infra-State body in Italy, considering that the constitutional framework is there not able to fulfil the requirements set by the ECJ, especially because of the transfers of funds existing between the central government and local institutions.
876. *See supra* section §3.02[B][1].

By this way, the Social Cohesion Zone can become a new instrument able to overcome the quantitative limits of the State Aid Zone model, opening a space for future initiatives addressed to influence the allocation choices of large enterprises and to improve the employment factor in the most disadvantaged areas of the Union.

§7.03 THE SOCIAL COHESION ZONE: AN OPPORTUNITY FOR EU COHESION POLICY?

The new model of the Social Cohesion Zone is based on a fundamental assumption: Member States are in principle free to assume autonomous initiatives for the establishment of social tax incentives for a limited area of their territory as long as a set of specific conditions is fulfilled, including, for example, the compliance with all the four *Altmark* criteria.

Nevertheless, the present research is not intended to support the idea of a weak EU where the Member States are the exclusive players in the definition of their own social cohesion policies; in this sense, it is necessary to guarantee a coordination between the Member States, defining the essential features of a multilevel framework where the objectives are set according to a vision of territorial cohesion developed at the EU level.

Therefore, on the ground of the above thoughts, the Social Cohesion Zone can represent a serious opportunity also for the EU Cohesion Policy managed by the Commission, offering an innovative instrument for the introduction of territorial tax incentives of a social character.

On these premises, the discussion will here be focused on the possibility to reconcile the tax sovereignty of the Member States with a supporting and coordinating role of the EU institutions, thus ensuring the achievement of the same goals in the most effective form.

[A] General Aspects

In general, the EU cohesion policy is set to address regional disparities and to bring structural changes to the economies of European regions. The idea of the EU cohesion policy starts along with the Treaty of Rome in 1957[877] and is intended to enhance socio-economic cohesion among regions of the Member States by supporting the development of the poorest areas of the Union.

Today, the EU cohesion policy is organized under the guidance of three different policy threads following different aims and involving different European actors: (i) the cohesion policy in a strict sense, under the responsibility of the EU Directorate-General for Regional Affairs, (ii) the Europe 2020 Strategy consisting of strategic agendas under

877. In this sense, according to Article 2 of the EEC Treaty one of the objectives of the EU is to achieve '*a harmonious, balanced and sustainable development of economic activities*' throughout the Union.

the joint responsibility of the EU Council and EU Commission, and (iii) the EU State aid control under the responsibility of the EU Directorate-General Competition.[878]

The first thread – namely EU cohesion policy in a strict sense – has its legal basis in Article 174 TFEU and is thus committed to the goals of promoting a harmonious development, strengthening economic, social, and territorial cohesion, and reducing disparities between regions under the principles of multi-annual programming, coordination and additionality; its main instruments are the Structural Funds[879] and a number of EU initiatives.[880] The Structural Funds provide a mechanism for redistributing an element of the EU budget and are all allocated on a territorial basis, except the Objective 3 that regards the whole territory of the Union.[881]

Differently, the Europe 2020 Strategy focuses on strategic agendas for definite periods, drawing up a vision of the European future and setting out a framework for joint and coordinated reforms and investments within the EU as a whole and its Member States. The current Europe 2020 Strategy, officially constituted by the Conclusion of the European Council in 2010 for the period 2010-2020,[882] is thus supposed to be a growth strategy for the Union; its three priorities – smart, sustainable, and inclusive growth – are substantiated by five targets on employment, research and development, environment, education, and social inclusion.

Finally, State Aid Control, as the third policy thread, concerns the control of State aid by the EU Directorate-General Competition aimed at safeguarding undistorted competition between economic operators in the EU.

Thus, the framework above described is characterized by the fundamental role of the Commission which is responsible for the management of a set of different actions all aimed at the objective of social cohesion within the Union.

In this context, the results of the present study suggest to move towards the development of one more thread in the context of the EU cohesion policy with a new line of intervention based on the implementation of the Social Cohesion Zone. The Social Cohesion Zone, in fact, can be a valuable instrument for the improvement of a series of economic indicators, such as the employment factor, which are all already set among the main objectives of the EU cohesion policy of the Commission; in this sense, in fact, social tax incentives introduced in the Social Cohesion Zone are always functional to the achievement of objectives of territorial cohesion, thus favouring the convergence between underdeveloped and developed regions of the Union.

Therefore, beside the cohesion policy in a strict sense, the Europe 2020 strategy and the State aid control policy, the Social Cohesion Zone can become the fourth line

878. For more details about the past and present organization of the EU cohesion policy, *see* C. Krieger-Boden, *EU Cohesion Policy, Past and Present: Sustaining a Prospering and Fair European Union?*, Kiel Institute for the World Economy, Kiel Working Paper, No. 2037, 2016.
879. Today, among the most important Structural Funds, there are the European Regional Development Fund (ERDF), the European Social Fund (ESF), the European Agricultural Guidance and Guarantee Fund (EAGGF), and the Financial Instrument for Fisheries (FIFG).
880. The main EU initiatives in the field are named as follows: Interreg, Urban, Equal, and Leader.
881. *See* G. Stahl, D. Lluna, *A Cohesion Policy for the Future*, in *Intereconomics*, 2003, Vol. 38, No. 6, pp. 295-305.
882. Conclusions of the European Council of 25/26 March 2010, EUCO 7/10, available at http://register.consilium.europa.eu/doc/srv?l=EN&f=ST%207%202010%20INIT.

of action within the general EU cohesion policy, offering a new tool to the Commission for the implementation of better targeted initiatives.

[B] Legal Background

The idea of including the new model within the EU cohesion policy can be supported by the valorization of some fundamental values of the Treaties. The principles of solidarity and equality, for example, are strictly related to the development of the EU cohesion policy, as they are both able to counterbalance other policies which are exclusively aimed to the defence of the internal market.

In detail, Article 2 TEU identifies solidarity and equality as bases of the European society and founding values common to the Member States; even though these principles are very general, they represent the fundamentals over which the EU cohesion policy has to be developed, leaving the doors open to the implementation of all those instruments - such as the Social Cohesion Zone - whose final aim is the reduction of the social disparities between high-income and low-income regions.

Then, Article 3(3) TEU offers one more supporting argument since it univocally identifies the promotion of social and territorial cohesion and solidarity as specific objectives of the Union.

Moreover, other reasons for the implementation of the Social Cohesion Zone in the context of the EU cohesion policy can also be recognized in the TFEU; according to Article 174 TFEU, in fact, *'the Union shall aim at reducing disparities between the levels of development of the various regions and the backwardness of the least favoured regions. Among the regions concerned, particular attention shall be paid to rural areas, areas affected by industrial transition, and regions which suffer from severe and permanent natural or demographic handicaps such as the northernmost regions with very low population density and islands, cross-border and mountain regions'.*

On these bases, the idea of implementing the Social Cohesion Zone within the EU cohesion policy is coherent with the resulting framework, finding its legal supporting arguments in a comprehensive set of norms belonging to EU primary law.

Furthermore, it is important to observe that the same values of solidarity and social cohesion are strongly considered also in the constitutional tradition of Member States, with the aim of refusing any unilateral approach based on the mere defence of the internal market.[883] The constitutional orders of Member States, in fact, already contain a set of fundamental principles which operate as 'checks and balances' for the defence of the values of solidarity and social cohesion; according to the ECJ, in fact, such principles can allow important derogations from EU law when a public interest to be pursued is recognized.[884]

883. In this sense, *see* F. GALLO, *Le ragioni del fisco. Etica e giustizia nella tassatione*, 2nd Edition, Il Mulino, Bologna, 2011, pp. 134 et seq.; G. MOSCHETTI, *Diniego di detrazione per consapevolezza nel contrasto alle frodi Iva, alla luce dei principi di certezza del diritto e proporzionalità*, CEDAM, Padova, 2013, p. 174.

884. *See, inter alia*, Case C-386/04 *Centro di Musicologia Walter Stauffer*, [2006] ECR I-8203, paragraph 39; Case C-406/04 *Gérald De Cuyper v Office National de l'emploi*, [2006] ECR I6947,

On the ground of these ideas, it is possible to conclude that the implementation of the Social Cohesion Zone within the EU cohesion policy finds its supporting arguments not only in a set of norms belonging to EU primary law, but also in the constitutional tradition common to Member States; in this regard, the position recently held by the ECJ around the concept of public interest[885] opens a new space for the valorization of the principles of solidarity and cohesion, pointing out the urgent need of new instruments for the development of a social cohesion policy in line with the common constitutional tradition of the Member States.

[C] The EU Governance of the Social Cohesion Zone

As far as the Social Cohesion Zone becomes a new line of action within the EU cohesion policy, it is then necessary to identify the level of government at which the various aspects must be defined, finding out the best way to set up a favourable legal environment for the implementation of the new model.

In this direction, the discussion has to focus on the governance of the Social Cohesion Zone, identifying a valuable solution where the EU and Member States can share their different role, with a set of coordinated actions aimed at maximizing the results and at improving the social cohesion between different areas of the Union.

As already seen, the Social Cohesion Zone is a measure defined in the context of a social cohesion policy, namely an area where Member States are always reluctant to confer their competence to the Union;[886] in particular, at the present stage of the integration process, the field of social and cohesion policy is still primarily within the domain of the Member States according to the principle of subsidiarity, even if forming part of the shared competences.[887]

The widespread idea, in fact, is that such policies are implemented more effectively at the national level than at the European level and, thus, the role of EU institutions is limited to the support and the coordination of the activities of the same Member States.

Moreover, when the perspective changes from the functional to the structural dimension, it is worth to note that the model of the Social Cohesion Zone exclusively involves the area of direct taxation, namely an area where Member States conserve their prerogatives and their autonomous tax systems.

On these bases, as far as the new model is concerned, it is not feasible to reserve an active role for the EU Institutions in the hard-law making process, since both social

paragraph 40; Case C-192/05 *K. Tas-Hagen and R. A. Tas v Raadskamer WUBO van de Pensioen- en Uitkeringsraad*, [2006] I-10451, paragraph 33; Case C-499/06 *Halina Nerkowska v Zakład Ubezpieczeń Społecznych Oddział w Koszalinie*, [2008] ECR I-03993.

885. Case C–287/10 *Tankreederei I SA v Directeur de l'administration des contributions directes*, [2010] ECR I-14233, paragraph 27; Case C-192/05 *K. Tas-Hagen and R. A. Tas v Raadskamer WUBO van de Pensioen- en Uitkeringsraad*) [2006] I-10451, paragraph 33 and 35.

886. W. Streeck, *Neo-Voluntarism: A New European Social Policy Regime?*, in *European Law Journal*, 1995, No. 1, pp. 31-59.

887. *See* Article 4(2)(b) TFEU.

policy and direct taxation are areas of competence of the Member States pursuant to the principle of subsidiarity.

Nonetheless, the inclusion of the Social Cohesion Zone within the EU cohesion policy presupposes a coordination and a supervision at the EU level, with the definition of strategic objectives and general principles; in other words, the objective of social cohesion between different areas of the EU necessarily requires a coordination at the EU level.[888]

On the ground of the above ideas, the system of governance should be defined according to the principle of subsidiarity with a dialogue between regulatory norms (Member States level) and general principles (EU level). In this sense, while, on one part, the statutory planning of the Social Cohesion Zone is reserved for the national governments, EU institutions, on the other, should be responsible for different tasks, such as the formulation of general policies and overall territorial strategies.[889]

This objective may be achieved through the adoption of the so-called Open Method of Coordination (hereinafter OMC), thus ensuring a role for the EU institutions in supporting the establishment of the Social Cohesion Zone in the most disadvantaged areas of the EU.

The OMC is a form of EU governance based on a soft law approach; the objective deals with the reinforcement of the pillar of European integration through a set of new measures able to complement - rather than substitute - the Member States' action in areas with a limited scope for EU law.[890] The legitimacy of the OMC within the EU framework is based on the provision of Article 2(5) TFEU; beside the first and the second categories of exclusive and shared competence, in fact, the OMC falls within a third category, namely of 'supporting, coordination, and supplementing' competence.[891] The OMC involves various mechanisms of coordination, such as guidelines, quantitative and qualitative indicators and benchmarks, and national and regional targets, backed by periodic evaluations and peer reviews, all finalized to provide a concrete help to Member States in learning from one another and consequently improve their domestic policies.[892]

In the case of the Social Cohesion Zone, a model of governance based on OMC does not preclude the possibility for each Member State to adapt that general framework to the features of its economy and society, with the full exercise of its legislative competence in the regulation of the detailed tax measures to be implemented in the context of the Social Cohesion Zone.

---

888. J. Rivolin, A. Faludi, *The Hidden Face of European Spatial Planning: Innovations in Governance*, in *European Planning Studies*, 2005, Vol. 13, No. 2, pp. 195-215.
889. U.J. Rivolin, *Cohesion and Subsidiarity Towards Good Territorial Governance in Europe*, in *Town Planning Review*, 2005, Vol. 76, No. 1.
890. For a brief analysis of the main features of the Open Method of Coordination *see* European Parliament, Member's Research Service, *The Open Method of Coordination*, European Parliament Publications, 2014.
891. K. Amstrong, *The Open Method of Coordination - Obstinate or Obsolete?*, University of Cambridge Faculty of Law, Research Paper No. 45/2016, available at https://papers.ssrn.com/sol3/papers.cfm?abstract_id=2839840.
892. *See* C. De La Porte, *Good Governance via the OMC? The Cases of Employment and Social Inclusion*, in *European Journal of Legal Studies*, 2007, Vol. 1, No. 1.

In particular, the OMC should include a series of coordinated actions at the EU level with the adoption of instruments of soft law focused on the definition of the concept of Social Cohesion Zone, on the criteria for the selection of the eligible areas, and on the monitoring of the various examples of Social Cohesion Zones established across the EU, with the introduction of a set of mechanisms of evaluation and peer review at the EU level.

Within such lines of intervention, the set of general principles defined at the EU level may be translated at the national level into the development of initiatives aimed at the establishment of the Social Cohesion Zone according to the principle of subsidiarity; at that point, as far as the role of the national government is concerned, EU institutions must remain excluded by the definition of statutory regulations, such as those concerning the type of tax benefits to be granted (e.g., deduction, tax credit) or the specific direct tax involved.

In conclusion, the resulting model of governance of the Social Cohesion Zone includes a 'politics of strategies', where the development of ideas takes place at the EU level, and a 'politics of reaction', where the national governments decode the guidelines according to national differences, implement policies in line with the principle of subsidiarity, and provide feedback.[893] In these terms, EU institutions can assume a fundamental role of impulse, with the definition of a favourable environment for the implementation of the Social Cohesion Zone within the EU cohesion policy.

§7.04 THE SOCIAL COHESION ZONE AND THE FISCAL RESIDUE

The tax measures adopted in the Social Cohesion Zone for the recipient undertakings produce an indirect effect in favour of resident employees and resident suppliers, consisting in the improvement of the opportunities on the local market.

In this regard, as seen in the previous chapter, when the situations of a resident and of a non-resident are comparable, the tax measures of the Social Cohesion Zone may determine a discriminatory or a restrictive tax treatment of the non-residents. In such a case, in order to avoid the adoption of protectionist measures, it is then necessary to verify whether an overriding reason of public interest exists and, finally, whether the same tax measure does not go beyond what it is necessary to attain the objective pursued.

For these purposes, the proportionality test is usually carried out under three different stages concerning the suitability, the necessity, and the proportionality *stricto sensu* of a tax measure.[894]

The first stage, which is based on the suitability, does not require particular attention in the case of the Social Cohesion Zone, considering that the obligations assumed by the recipient undertakings are clearly addressed to the achievement of

893. *See* in this sense G. Pagoulatos, M. Stasinopoulou, D.A. Sotiropoulos, *Governance in EU Social and Employment Policy: A Survey*, Athens University of Economics and Business, available at http://www.eliamep.gr/wp-content/uploads/2009/01/r-cwowe1.pdf.

894. T.I. Harbo, *The Function of the Proportionality Principle in EU Law*, in *European Law Journal*, 2010, Vol. 16, No. 2, p. 165.

objectives of a social character, especially for what regards the minimum number of new employees to be hired in the first year of activity.

More complicated are the issues related to the second and third stages where the measure's proportionality is respectively assessed under the profile of its necessity and its 'proportionality *stricto sensu*'. In both cases, in fact, it seems that the judgements of the ECJ are characterized by a wide discretionality; in particular, as far as the necessity is concerned, the review of the national measure by the ECJ is generally based on the 'least restrictive alternative', a concept which leads to uncertainty as regards the norm to be applied.[895]

For these purposes, it is now necessary to discuss a possible option to limit such a discretionality, introducing the concept of 'fiscal residue' and allowing an assessment based on a more objective parameter.

The so-called fiscal residue is generally referred to as the 'net benefits from tax-expenditure programme, i.e., the benefits from expenditure minus disutility from tax payment';[896] in this sense, the fiscal residue is a parameter able to identify the ratio between the tax burden set in a region and the value of the public services available in the same region.[897] The same concept is strictly related to the allocation of tax expenditures among different areas of a State even through a differentiated tax treatment on a regional basis.

The parameter of the fiscal residue finds a theoretical support in the concept of fair tax competition which is essentially linked to the proportion existing between the total tax burden in an area and the value of the public services available in the same area.

Accordingly, Member States should modulate the extent of the tax burden at the territorial level on the ground of the public services locally available in order to achieve a neutral value of the fiscal residue and the horizontal fiscal balance across the different areas of the national territory. By this way, 'high tax-high spend' zones could perfectly coexist along with 'low tax–low spend' zones,[898] without any negative effect on the internal market.

The neutralization of the fiscal residue leads to the rationalization of public expenditures, moving resources towards objectives related to the improvement of the living and social conditions in the most disadvantaged areas. As far as it is possible to set differentiated tax rates among different areas, residents are able to get access to public services at a fair price on the ground of the proportional relation existing between the tax burden and the value of the public services available.

---

895. D. Weber, *Tax Avoidance and the EC Treaty Freedoms: A Study of the Limitations under European Law to the Prevention of Tax Avoidance*, in *Eucotax Series on European Taxation 11*, The Hague, Kluwer law international, 2005, p. 210.
896. J. M. Buchanan, *Federalism and Fiscal Equity*, in *American* Economic *Review*, 1950, Vol. 40, No. 4, pp. 583-599.
897. *See* B. Moro, *Incentivi fiscali e politiche di sviluppo economico regionale in Europa*, in *Moneta e Credito*, 2001, Vol. 52, pp. 343-388.
898. A. Steichen, *Tax Competition in Europe or the Taming of Leviathan*, in Vv.Aa., *Tax Competition in Europe*, IBFD – International Bureau of Fiscal Documentation, Amsterdam, 2003, p. 49.

The concept of fiscal residue can also be valorized on the ground of the principle of tax equity. Tax equity is generally associated with the fundamental right of every taxpayer to claim tax justice with the proper destination of public resources.[899] This principle, in fact, is generally intended as equity among taxpayers (taxpayer equity), assuming that taxpayers who are in the same economic position should be treated in the same way for tax purposes; in other words, the equity of a tax system concerns whether the tax burden is distributed fairly among the population and, therefore, the principle of tax equity implies that all the productive members of society should contribute to the public finance and should pay their fair share through taxation.[900] In particular, the content of the principle of tax equity can be defined according to the benefit principle.[901] In this sense, the benefit principle is based on the equitable measure of economic distribution and on the rule according to which the entire tax burden should be distributed in the same proportion as it occurs in the case of benefits granted by the State.[902] Therefore, a differentiated allocation of tax expenditures finds its justification in the lower value of the public services available in the area and in the mentioned rule according to which the tax burden has to be set in proportion to the benefits granted by the State.

Given the above, the parameter of fiscal residue may represent the instrument to be used for the assessment of the proportionality of a tax measure.

In this case, in fact, the tax measures at issue will be considered as the 'least restrictive alternative' – and, therefore, as necessary to achieve the improvement of the living conditions of the residents of the Social Cohesion Zone – as long as they are addressed to the neutralization of the fiscal residue and to the achievement of the horizontal fiscal balance between the various areas of a Member State. In this sense, in fact, when the Social Cohesion Zone covers a territory characterized by a low value of the public services available compared to the tax burden applied to the residents of the same area, then the fiscal residue will assume a negative value and, consequently, the related tax measures will be the 'least restrictive alternative' until the negative value of the fiscal residue is neutralized. The necessity, in fact, will be identified in the lack of an alternative to the legislative choice, given the absence of other equally effective means to achieve the neutralization of the fiscal residue; in this regard, in fact, it is important to observe that the only alternative track for the neutralization of the fiscal residue, which is the improvement of the value of the public services available in the area (e.g., construction of new roads or new hospitals), is not usually a feasible solution considering the strict limits of State resources as generally defined by the public budget.

---

899. P. Musgrave, *Harmonization of Direct Business Taxes: A Case Study*, in C.S. Shoup, *Fiscal Harmonization in Internal Markets*, Vol. II, Columbia University Press, New York, 1967, pp. 211-32; *Ibid.*, *US. Taxation of Foreign Investment and Income: Issues and Arguments*, Harvard Law School, Cambridge, 1969.

900. G.L. Salis, *A Brief Introduction to the Principle of Tax Equity*, 2007, available at http://aafm.us/article1967.html?id=214, 2007.

901. J. Rice Steven, *Introduction to Taxation: A Decision-Making Approach*, Dame Publishing, Dublin, 1996, pp. 15-17.

902. D.G. Duff, *Benefit Taxes and User Fees in Theory and Practice*, in *The University of Toronto Law Journal*, 2004, No. 54, pp. 435-446.

The parameter of fiscal residue may also assume a role in the third stage of the proportionality test which is focused on the 'proportionality *stricto sensu*'. In this case, in fact, the balance between the different interests involved, namely those of the residents of the zone, on one part, and of the non-residents of the zone, on the other, will be achieved through a process of neutralization of the fiscal residue; in other words, until the value of the fiscal residue is negative, the interests of the residents of the Social Cohesion Zone will be considered prevalent with respect to the interests of the non-residents.

In summary, the proportionality of the tax measures introduced in the Social Cohesion Zone should be founded on an assessment based on the parameter of the fiscal residue, considering not only the relevance of the tax burden in the area, but also the value of the public services there available. By this way, it seems possible to definitely overcome the discretionary element of the ECJ in the proportionality test, with an evaluation of the necessity and the proportionality *stricto sensu* of a measure carried out on the ground of an objective parameter.

At the same time, the parameter of the fiscal residue will ensure the implementation of the Social Cohesion Zone in the proper areas, without any detrimental effect on the surrounding territories of the same Member State; in this sense, in fact, as long as the fiscal residue is defined according to the EU average, the horizontal fiscal balance resulting from its application will be able to guarantee a fair taxation to all the citizens irrespective of the territory of residence.

On these bases, it is evident that a differentiated allocation of tax expenditures within a Member State – with the establishment of the Social Cohesion Zone – finds its justification in a negative value of the fiscal residue of the same area; accordingly, the proportionality of the related tax measures will be ensured until the same parameter of the fiscal residue is completely neutralized. In principle, this mechanism should imply that, where the value of the public services available in the area would eventually increase, the same tax incentives will be lowered in order to keep a neutral value for the parameter of the fiscal residue.

In conclusion, as far as the Social Cohesion Zone is based on the neutralization of the fiscal residue, the overriding reasons relating to the public interest will be considered as proportional, overcoming any issue of protectionism in the context of the present discussion.

§7.05 THE SOCIAL COHESION ZONE: THE PRACTICAL IMPLEMENTATION

The last part of the discussion must now be addressed to the outline of the substantial and procedural aspects in the practical implementation of the Social Cohesion Zone Model in the EU context, as resulting from the analysis of the findings and from the issues approached in the present chapter.

[A] Substantial Aspects

The substantial aspects of the implementation process include relevant provisions concerning the eligibility conditions of the recipient undertakings, the content and the mechanism of the tax incentives, and the obligations to be assumed by the same recipient undertakings.

[1] Eligibility Conditions

The eligibility conditions deal with the situation of the recipient undertakings which intend to qualify for the favouring tax measures.

A first group of eligibility conditions must focus on the legal status of the recipient undertaking. In this regard, the eligible undertaking must be identified in an enterprise, namely a legal entity engaged in an economic activity, irrespective of its legal form, possessing the right to conduct business on its own and, thus, to enter into contracts, own property, and incur liabilities. In line with the results achieved by the analysis of the EU law framework. eligibility must be extended to the permanent establishment of a non-resident enterprise which is defined under Article 5 of the OECD Model Tax Convention, as 'a fixed place of business, through which the business of an enterprise is wholly or partly carried on'.

A second group of eligibility conditions must instead focus on the size and on the statutory goals of the recipient undertakings, with the outline of two alternative situations both eligible for the tax incentives, namely those of large enterprises, on one part, and social enterprises, on the other.

In the first situation the eligibility is reserved to large enterprises having certain size requirements (irrespective of their statutory goals) in order to ensure sufficient financial and economic strength for the fulfilment of the obligations assumed in the context of the Social Cohesion Zone regime. In this case, large enterprises must be identified as enterprises other than micro, small or medium enterprises within the meaning of Annex I to the Commission Regulation (EU) No. 651/2014 of 17 June 2014 declaring certain categories of aid compatible with the internal market in application of Articles 107 and 108 TFEU. On these bases, the eligibility conditions will require that the enterprise, based on the data of the last approved accounting period, meets one of the following criteria: (a) it employs 250 or more employees; (b) it employs fewer than 250 employees but the enterprise's balance sheet total exceeds EUR 43 million or the total annual turnover exceeds EUR 50 million.[903]

Otherwise, in the second situation, the eligibility is reserved to social enterprises having statutory goals of a social character, irrespective of any size requirement, according to the definition set out by Article 2(1) of Regulation (EU) No. 1296/2013. In this case, in fact, social enterprises are eligible for the tax incentives not in consideration of their size, but in consideration of their statutory goals which are univocally addressed to the pursuit of a social objective.

903. *See* Commission Regulation (EU) No. 651/2014 of 17 June 2014, Annex 1, Article 2(1).

In other words, while in the case of large enterprises the reasons for the eligibility must be identified in their economic and financial strengths - which are able to ensure the fulfilment of the obligations assumed under the Social Cohesion Zone regime - differently, in the case of social enterprises, the justification for the same eligibility must be found in the clarity of the statutory goals which generally ensure the prevalence of social objectives over profits, regardless of any size requirement.

[2] Tax Incentive Mechanism

The tax incentives must exclusively be granted in the area of direct taxation with measures specifically addressed to income tax. As seen, in fact, the process of harmonization of indirect taxes, such as customs duties, VAT, and excise duties does not allow autonomous initiatives of the Member States and, therefore, the tax measures related to indirect taxes have to be excluded from the horizon of the Social Cohesion Zone.

In this case, the tax incentives on income tax have to be granted in the form of tax allowances or tax credits considering that, in both cases, the choice of such subtractive regimes allows to calculate in advance the value of the tax expenditures starting from the amount of the eligible items. Therefore, the identification of the eligible items becomes a fundamental aspect of the tax incentives mechanism, since it determines a connection between the tax advantages granted and the specific expenses supported by objectives of a social policy (i.e., wages for new employees and costs for purchase orders sent to local suppliers).

In a first variable, the tax incentives have to be set in form of tax allowances allowing the deduction from the gross income (gross tax base) of a monetary value related to the following eligible items: (i) the number of new employees hired, (ii) the volume of the purchase orders of goods and services sent to local suppliers, and (iii) a reasonable profit.

On these bases, the amount of the deductible items will be calculated as follows:

(i) a fixed amount for each new employee hired in the tax year;
(ii) a variable amount corresponding to the costs incurred in the tax year for purchase orders of goods and services sent to local suppliers;
(iii) a variable amount corresponding to the reasonable profit defined on the ground of an objective parameter (e.g., ROCE).

In a second variable the tax incentives have to be granted in form of tax credits with the deduction from the gross tax due of a monetary value (tax credit) related to the same items, namely: (i) the number of new employees hired, (ii) the volume of the purchase orders of goods or services sent to local suppliers, and (iii) a reasonable profit.

On these bases, the amount of the tax credit will be calculated as follows:

(i) a fixed amount for each new employee hired in the tax year;
(ii) a variable amount corresponding to a percentage of the costs incurred in the tax year for purchase orders of goods and services sent to local suppliers;

(iii) a variable amount corresponding to a percentage of the reasonable profit defined on the ground of an objective parameter (e.g., ROCE).

The tax incentive mechanism here described represents one of the main substantial aspects and offers a concrete idea of the incisiveness of the Social Cohesion Zone compared to the other implementing models of STZs recognized in the experience of the Member States. In this case, in fact, it is evident that the amount of the deductible items and of the tax credits may be determined without any external limit; while in the case of the State Aid Zone, for instance, the value of the tax expenditures finds a cap in the fixed threshold under the *de minimis* regulation or in the maximum aid intensity provided by the regional aid map under the GBER, in the case of the Social Cohesion Zone the same cap is established only by internal limits which are exclusively associated with the investments made by the recipient undertaking, without any maximum aid intensity or fixed threshold.

[3] Obligations of the Recipient Undertakings

The tax regime of the Social Cohesion Zone includes a series of obligations to be fulfilled by the recipient undertaking.

The first obligation concerns the minimum number of employees to be hired in the first year of activity.

In particular, the new employees must be resident of the zone since a minimum period of time before the beginning of the employment contract and must maintain their residence in the area concerned for the entire period of the labour contract; by this way, in fact, it is possible to avoid abusive practices, such as in the case of a temporary residence registered only for tax purposes, ensuring that the tax advantages are granted only to the economic operators which effectively respond to the substantial scope of the tax measure. Furthermore, the new employees must be hired with a long-term contract or other contractual forms able to guarantee a certain stability to the employment relation; this is necessary to avoid the abuse of short-term contracts which could undermine the objectives set under the establishment of such zones. Finally, the hiring mechanism must ensure the numerical balance between high-qualified employees and low-qualified employees, thus extending the effects of social tax incentives to a broader audience of individuals which reside in the disadvantaged areas of the Member States. In this sense, the obligation assumed by the recipient undertaking will also involve the hiring of a minimum percentage of high-qualified workers in respect to the total number of employees hired in the same tax period.[904]

The second obligation is focused on the minimum volume of the purchase orders of goods and services to be sent to the small and medium-sized enterprises based in the

904. The possibility of limiting the obligation to the hiring of new employees belonging to the low-income and the middle-income class should also be considered. For example, the obligation could be fulfilled by the hiring of new employees with a salary under a certain threshold; by this way, the tax measures would be better addressed to their scope, consisting in the improvement of the employment factor, especially with reference to the most disadvantaged individuals who reside in the zone.

zone.[905] The idea, in fact, is to limit the social tax incentives only to those undertakings which are able to guarantee a minimum annual volume of purchases of goods or services from local suppliers, thus maximizing the positive effects of such tax measures with the creation of a virtuous circle in the productive and distributive chain.

By the provision of these obligations, the social character of the tax measures granted in favour of the eligible undertakings will be ensured, establishing a strong link between means and ends; consequently, it will be possible to qualify the economic activity of the recipient undertakings as a work integration service carried out in the general interest and, therefore, as a genuine SSGI where the social goals prevail over the profit.

[B] Procedural Aspects

In this implementation process, the establishment of a Social Cohesion Zone involves some important procedural aspects.

In particular, it is possible to identify three different chronological stages which characterize the relationship between public authorities and recipient undertakings within the implementation process of a Social Cohesion Zone.

[1] Selection of the Eligible Areas

The first stage of the implementation process is focused on the selection of the eligible areas for the establishment of a Social Cohesion Zone.

In this regard, the parameter of the fiscal residue assumes a fundamental role, being able to identify the ratio between the tax burden set in a region and the value of the public services available in the same region.

By this way, the outcome of the process of selection is the identification of the areas where the parameter of the fiscal residue assumes a negative value with respect to the EU average ratio, considering the presence of a high tax burden and, at the same time, a low-quality level of the public services available in these areas.

Therefore, the eligible areas will be the areas with a negative value of the parameter of the fiscal residue; in such cases, in fact, the establishment of a Social Cohesion Zone is a necessary instrument of social cohesion policy to be used to neutralize the parameter of the fiscal residue (from a negative value to a neutral value)

The process of detection of the parameter of the fiscal residue in respect to the EU average and the corresponding identification of the eligible areas in the Member States should lead to the definition of a mapping at the EU level. In this sense, there is a space for a significant role of the EU institutions, through the adoption of the OMC for supporting the establishment of the Social Cohesion Zone according to objective criteria. In particular, among the various actions, the OMC should first provide an

905. The category of micro, small, and medium-sized enterprises ('SMEs') is made up of enterprises which employ fewer than 250 persons and which have an annual turnover not exceeding EUR 50 million, and/or an annual balance sheet total not exceeding EUR 43 million (*see* Commission Regulation (EU) No. 651/2014 of 17 June 2014, Annex 1, Article 2(1)).

instrument to define the criteria for the identification of the value of the public services in an area for the purposes of the fiscal residue, making reference to a set of factors, such as the presence of transport connections, hospitals, schools, etc. with the measurement of their respective quality level according to a series of ranking parameters. Moreover, the same OMC should involve the detection of the EU average of the fiscal residue, the mapping process of the eligible areas where the values are negative with respect to the same average, and the periodical update of the database in order to eventually amend the maps defined at the EU level with the inclusion of new eligible areas or the exclusion of the old eligible areas.

Through this process, it is possible to ensure the coordination role of the EU institutions, improving the performance and the coherence of the initiatives assumed at the Member States' level; in this regard, in fact, the use of an objective criterion for the selection of the eligible areas, such as the fiscal residue, represents a guarantee for the proportionality of the tax measures assumed in the context of a Social Cohesion Zone.

[2] Public Procurement Procedure

Following the selection of the eligible areas with a mapping at the EU level, the second stage of the implementation process deals with the public procurement procedures for the selection of the eligible undertakings.

In any case, in fact, the economic operators which benefit from the social tax incentives of the Social Cohesion Zone must be selected through an open, transparent, and non-discriminatory public procurement procedure, with awarding criteria based on the lowest level of compensation.

The first step of the public procurement procedure involves the publishing of the call for tenders whose content must include, among others, the eligibility conditions, the tax benefit mechanism with the indication of the cap for deductible items and tax credits, and the object of the obligations which will be assumed by the awarded undertakings. Furthermore, the same call for tenders should include detailed information about the awarding criteria making reference to the lowest level of compensation intended as a percentage of the total amount of the investment; in this sense, the participants should set their offers presenting a business plan about the work integration service to be provided, with the indication of their best discount, in terms of a percentage, on the total amount of the eligible items, including a reasonable profit.

The second step deals with the entrustment act to be signed between the public authority and the awarded undertakings; the document will essentially reproduce the content of the clauses of the call for tenders, with a specific focus on the description of the compensation mechanism and, in particular, on the parameters for calculating, controlling, and reviewing the compensation, including the indicators used to establish the reasonable profit.

[3] Monitoring

The last procedural aspect to be considered is related to the control *ex post* of the activities carried out by the recipient undertakings and of the results obtained with reference to the employment factor.

Also in this case, the EU institutions can assume a fundamental role of coordination and support through the OMC; EU institutions, in fact, may define a set of mechanisms of evaluation and peer review, best practices, and benchmarks for the monitoring of the various examples of Social Cohesion Zones established across the EU.

By this way, it is possible to improve the quantity and the quality of the statistical data available with a process of continuous update, allowing the Member States to better set and achieve their short, medium, and long-term goals.

§7.06 FINAL REMARKS

The outcomes of the discussion highlight the possibility of a practical implementation of the results achieved at the end of the present research.

The model of the Social Cohesion Zone can finally be presented as a concrete instrument which exploits the space left for Member States in areas of competence still not harmonized at the EU level; moreover, the tax incentives granted on direct taxation are defined in a form compatible with EU primary law, including the critical variables of State aid rules and free movement of persons.

Therefore, the Social Cohesion Zone Model becomes one more implementing model beside the FZ, the Extraterritorial Zone, and the State Aid Zone, assuming its qualifying features within the general legal theory of STZs.

On these premises, the use of the Social Cohesion Zone Model in the context of the EU cohesion policy has been discussed, focusing on the possible reconciliation between the role of the EU institutions, on one part, and the Member States, on the other. For this purpose, the opportunity of an action of support and coordination from the EU institutions has emerged, through instruments of soft law able to define objective parameters, strategies, and best practices.

Furthermore, the discussion has led to the introduction of the fiscal residue as an essential parameter for the selection of the eligible areas; in this sense, in fact, as long as the neutralization of the fiscal residue becomes the target of such initiatives, it is still possible to ensure the proportionality of the tax measures of the Social Cohesion Zone, overcoming any issue related to the infringement of the free movement of persons.

In conclusion, the resulting framework assumes a concrete dimension with the definition of a practical instrument for social cohesion policies addressed to the most disadvantaged areas of the Union.

CHAPTER 8

Conclusions and Recommendations

§8.01 SUMMARY OF THE RESEARCH PROCESS

The aim of this study has been addressed to the definition of a general legal theory of STZs within European tax law and to the identification of a new implementing model for the development of social cohesion policies for the most disadvantaged areas of the Union.

In this direction, the objective has first been focused on the development of a theoretical concept able to work as a reading-key of the factual experience of the Member States, allowing a deeper understanding of the phenomenon in the context of legal studies; the starting point, in fact, is the disorganic approach of the previous works and the lack of a systematic perspective from the point of view of tax law.

At the same time, further motivation has been found starting from the presumption that the existing models of STZs are not able to face the economic issues of the disadvantaged areas of the Union. On these bases, the consequent assumption is the need of creating a new instrument of policy action to tackle the issues of the low-income areas of the Union, with particular reference to the high rate of unemployment; in this sense, the focus has been set on the need to contrast, through new suitable tax measures, the continuous growth of population in the most developed areas of the EU, on one part, and the corresponding depopulation of the underdeveloped areas characterized by lack of employment, on the other.

On these premises, it is necessary to start this conclusion chapter with a brief overview of the contents of the book, summarizing the results achieved with reference to each research question.

The first stage of the study, which covers the content of Chapter 2, has involved the review of the literature on the topic with the outline of the corresponding legal dimension of STZs, especially for what concerns the different views of the scholars about the concepts, the definitions and the denominations used in the various national and international contexts.

The content of Chapter 3 has been focused on the EU law framework with the review of the instruments of hard law and soft law which influence the phenomenon of STZs. In this case, the different perspective from the field of indirect taxation and direct taxation has emerged together with the different role which primary law and secondary law may assume in the same fields; furthermore, the review has underlined for direct taxation the crucial role of the Commission for interpreting the relevant provisions of State aid rules.

Chapter 4 has been dedicated to the review of the factual experience of the Member States with the description of the situations which correspond to the phenomenon of STZs.

The first result of the research process has been outlined in Chapter 5 and consists in the development of a general legal theory of STZs on the ground of three main pillars: the concept of STZs with its territorial, structural, and functional dimensions, the definition of STZs in terms of a comprehensive macro-category, and, finally, the implementing models of STZs as resulting from the experience of the Member States.

In particular, for what regards the concept of STZs, the relevance of the functional dimension has been underlined, with the opening of a new room for the analysis of the phenomenon under a different perspective; in this regard, in fact, the functional dimension highlights the objectives pursued by the government through the establishment of STZs and the distinction between measures constituting economic tax incentives, on one part, and measures constituting social tax incentives, on the other.

The general legal theory has then been enriched by the inclusion of a comprehensive definition of STZs able to summarize the key features and by the identification of a series of implementing models as resulting from the factual experience.

The second result of the research, which is outlined in Chapter 6, deals with the development of a new model of STZs corresponding and addressed as the Social Cohesion Zone Model.

The new model is here developed starting from the presumption that the existing models of STZs are not able to tackle the economic hardships of the most disadvantaged areas of the Union, with the consequent assumption that an additional model for STZs is needed.

In this case, the analysis of the variables of EU law has given evidence of the possibility of shaping the tax measures of the Social Cohesion Zone Model in a form compatible with the internal market and exempt from the notification obligation under State aid rules.

For this purpose, a design has been considered characterized by the introduction of social tax incentives in compliance with the *Altmark* criteria or, as an alternative, with the criteria of Article 106(2) TFEU as defined by the Commission Decision under the *Almunia* package. In this regard, attention has been paid to configure the tax incentives as a compensation in favour of the recipient undertakings for the provision of a SSGI, focusing the attention on the social character of the obligations assumed by the same undertakings. In particular, the analysis has put in evidence the possibility of a broad interpretation of the concept of SSGIs allowing the inclusion of large enterprises among the eligible undertakings as long as they assume the obligation of providing work integration services even if outside of their general statutory goals;

otherwise, a narrow interpretation of the same concept would limit the eligible undertakings to the category of social enterprises where the obligation of providing work integration services is already assumed in coherence with the statutory goals. In any case, the use of a public procurement procedure for the selection of the recipient undertakings, as well as the signature of an entrustment act of a specific content, have been resulted as fundamental aspects for ensuring the compliance of the Social Cohesion Zone with the EU law framework.

Furthermore, when the variable of the free movement of persons is considered, the results of the study have put the opportunity in evidence to extend the tax incentives available in the Social Cohesion Zone Model to the permanent establishments of non-resident undertakings. At the same time, as far as the position of the resident employees and the local suppliers are concerned, the analysis of the ECJ case law has offered many arguments to exclude the infringement of the free movement of persons; in this sense, in fact, even when a tax measure would result in a discriminatory or restrictive treatment with reference to the situation of the non-resident, the tax measures provided under the Social Cohesion Zone Model may be allowed under a public interest justification, as long as they are univocally addressed to the protection of the employment factor in the disadvantaged areas of the Member States, while the proportionality of the same tax measures would be ensured through the application of the parameter of the fiscal residue.

Also in the case of the Code of Conduct Group for business taxation, the Social Cohesion Zone Model has not presented any negative outlook as long as certain requirements are fulfilled; in this sense, in fact, it is sufficient to exclude among the eligible costs the purchases made between non-independent parties and, at the same time, to ensure the transparency and non-negotiability through the introduction of specific provisions.

Finally, in Chapter 7, the discussion of the findings has offered more support for the use of the Social Cohesion Zone Model in the context of the EU cohesion policy, suggesting an action of coordination from the EU institutions through instruments of soft law able to define objectives parameters, strategies, and best practices. In this regard, the parameter of the fiscal residue has been proposed as the proper instrument for the selection of the eligible areas in order to progressively achieve the horizontal fiscal balance across the Union and, at the same time, in order to ensure the proportionality of the related tax measures.

§8.02 ANSWERS TO THE RESEARCH QUESTIONS AND CONCLUSIONS

After the summary of the main findings, it is finally possible to answer the research questions formulated at the beginning of this book, with the enunciation of the conclusion statements in the light of the results achieved.

[A] The General Legal Theory of STZs

In the introductory chapter the first research question has been outlined in the following terms:

Research question No. 1

In the context of European tax law, is it possible to develop a general legal theory of STZs able to explain the different experiences of territorial tax incentives in the Member States?

At the end of the research process, the results achieved confirm the possibility of a positive answer to the first research question.

Through the analysis of the relevant sources, in fact, it is possible to define a general legal theory of STZs based on three fundamental pillars: the concept of STZs, the definition, and the implementing models.

This theory is a general theory in the sense that it offers a common reading-key for a comprehensive understanding of the phenomenon within the EU law framework and within the experience of the Member States; in this sense, the territorial, the structural, and the functional dimensions are able to highlight the common characteristics of each example of STZs recognized in the Member States.

This general theory is also a legal theory as it is specifically developed within the field of European tax law. In fact, the selection of the relevant material over which the theory has been worked out is focused on legal sources of the EU law framework, including primary law and secondary law, with specific references to the instruments related to the phenomenon of taxation, both for what regards indirect taxes and direct taxes.

The general theory is also a comprehensive theory, being able to encompass under its umbrella all the different experiences of STZs in the Member States. In this sense, in fact, STZs have been defined in a broad sense as 'areas delimited by a natural, artificial or conventional border where entities and goods, selected through a territorial connecting factor provided by the law, can benefit from a favouring tax treatment which deviates, under an exclusion regime or a subtractive regime, from the standard tax treatment applied in the rest of the hosting State on the ground of objectives of an economic or social character defined within a specific government function'. Furthermore, the general theory includes the identification of three different models which are able to explain the different situations of territorial tax incentives in the EU context, namely the FZ, the State Aid Zone, and the Extraterritorial Zone.

In conclusion, it is possible to answer in a positive sense to the first research question, considering the results achieved and the general legal theory here developed in the context of European tax law.

By this way, the resulting theory can fill the gap of knowledge recognized at the beginning of the present study in consideration of the lack of a systematic perspective of the topic, especially as far as the field of tax law is concerned. In this sense, in fact, the reviewed literature gives evidence of a disorganic approach to the phenomenon which is essentially based on the specific characteristics of the national context in which each single research is carried out, with different denominations, definitions, and classifications.

Therefore, the new theory is an original result of the research process as it definitely overcomes all the issues involved and sensibly changes the systematic perspective, offering new categories for a deeper understanding of the phenomenon; the new reading-key, in fact, which is based on the territorial, the structural, and the functional dimensions, is finally able to highlight the substantial aspects of STZs opening a new room of study within the field of European tax law. In particular, one of the main findings is that under the functional dimension, the distinction between the category of economic tax incentives and the category of social tax incentives seriously influences the way in which the variables of the EU legal framework work. Only in case of social tax incentives, in fact, it is possible to support the introduction of an incentive programme on the ground of the discipline provided for SSGIs, including the Altmark criteria and Article 106(2) TFEU.

In conclusion, the general theory which has been developed under the present study is an original result, considering that the literature review does not provide any evidence of similar systematic efforts as far as the area of European tax law is concerned.

[B] The New Model of the Social Cohesion Zone

The second research question, which involves the development of a new model of STZs for social cohesion policies, has been outlined as follows:

> Research question No. 2
>
> *Is it possible to identify a new implementing model of STZs within the EU law framework addressed to the development of social cohesion policies for the most disadvantaged areas of the Union?*

The new model has been developed starting from the presumption that the existing STZs are not able to face the economic issues of the most disadvantages areas of the Union, with the consequent assumption that a new model of STZs is needed at the current stage of European integration.

At the end of the research process, the results of the analysis under the variables of EU law provide sufficient support for a positive answer to the research question.

In this sense, it is possible to conclude that, as far as direct taxation is concerned, there is a space left for Member States to assume autonomous initiatives for the development of social cohesion policies within the strict limits set by EU law.

Nonetheless, the resulting model of the Social Cohesion Zone requires to pay a special attention to the definition of the related tax regime in consideration of the outer limits of EU law; in this sense, in fact, State aid rules, the free movement of persons and harmful tax competition set some important boundaries to the design of the new model which result in a series of strict requirements and conditions to be fulfilled in order to establish a Social Cohesion Zone Model compatible with EU law.

For example, the tax measures must comply with the *Altmark* criteria - or, as an alternative, with the conditions set by the Commission Decision of the *Almunia* package - and, therefore, must first be configured as a compensation for the recipient undertakings involved in the provision of an SSGI; the eligible undertakings must be limited to social enterprises and large enterprises (in the latter case as long as a broad interpretation of the concept of SSGI is adopted), while the related measures must exclusively include tax incentives of a genuine social character (i.e., social tax incentives). Furthermore, the use of a public procurement procedure and the signature of the entrustment act assume a fundamental role in the process of selection of the recipient undertakings, with the consequent need for Member States to adapt their internal rules to the framework resulting from the variables of EU law. Then, among the various conditions to be fulfilled, also the territorial connecting factor influences the design of the new model with the need of a choice including, within the eligible undertakings, the permanent establishments of non-resident undertakings.

In the context of the new model, the research puts in evidence the fact that the obligations assumed by the recipient undertakings, with reference to the hiring of a minimum number of resident employees, may be positively assessed under a general public interest justification, thus excluding any form of illegitimate discrimination or restriction with respect to the free movement of persons.

Nevertheless, the same measures must also be proportional to the objectives pursued in the sense that they do not go beyond what is necessary to achieve the same objectives. For what regards this specific profile, the research brings new insights to the discussion setting a focus on the concept of fiscal residue. As seen, in fact, the fiscal residue can be used as a parameter to measure the proportionality of a tax measure as far as it identifies the ratio between the tax burden in a certain area and the corresponding value of the public services there available; in other words, the same parameter determines the possibility to identify the areas with a negative ratio where the establishment of a Social Cohesion Zone is a necessary measure to achieve the objectives set in the context of a social cohesion policy. This is a new perspective that can be used to approach the issue of proportionality under the judgment of discrimination, addressing the tax measures for a certain area to the neutralization of the fiscal residue and to the consequent achievement of a horizontal fiscal balance across the various regions of the Union; in this context, in fact, the fiscal residue becomes an objective parameter to be used for considering the tax measures as proportional, thus overcoming the broad discretionality which generally characterizes the proportionality test in the case law of the ECJ.

Therefore, the findings which result from the development of this second research question allow some important considerations with respect to the starting background and the ideas generally spread in the EU law framework.

First, the results of the research give evidence of the possibility of overcoming the negative outlook traditionally assumed by the tax measures reserved to a limited area of the national territory; in this sense, the issue of the territorial selectivity of the tax measures and the concerns related to possible negative effects on the internal market may finally be set apart as far as the design of the Social Cohesion Zone is shaped on the ground of the *Altmark* criteria or of the Commission Decision of the *Almunia* package. The valorization of the functional perspective of the Social Cohesion Zone, in fact, offers the opportunity of assuming a different track for the development of the related tax measures, even out of the scope of State aid rules. The new track here developed is then an original finding of the present research, being based on the idea of designing the tax measures reserved for a limited area of a Member State in the form of compensation measures addressed to a SSGI (i.e., a work integration service carried out by the eligible undertakings).

Second, at the current stage of EU law, it is a matter of fact that the assessment of the discriminatory or restrictive character of a tax measure, including those introduced within the Social Cohesion Zone, is still left to the broad discretionality of the ECJ; the proportionality test, in fact, generally involves the use of a parameter based on the 'least restrictive measure', with consequent difficulties in predicting the decision of the ECJ, especially when there is a lack of objective terms of comparison. In this regard, one more original outcome which derives from the discussion of the same findings is the possibility of a new approach to the proportionality test based on the parameter of the fiscal residue; in this sense, in fact, the innovative perspective is addressed to the selection of the eligible areas according to an objective parameter, the fiscal residue, which is associated to the idea of an horizontal fiscal balance to be achieved between the various areas of the Union. In other words, the idea of neutralizing the fiscal residue in a certain area can provide support for configuring the establishment of the Social Cohesion Zone as the least restrictive measure in order to achieve the same objective in a proportional manner.

Thanks to these new findings, it is then possible to conclude that the Social Cohesion Zone, as the innovative result of the research process, is a new implementing model of STZs in compliance with the EU law framework which can be used for the development of social cohesion policies for the most disadvantaged areas of the Union, provided that certain specific conditions are fulfilled. Therefore, the research fills one more gap in the existing EU framework, providing a new instrument for social cohesion policies and a new model of STZs beside the FZ, the State Aid Zone, and the Extraterritorial Zone.

§8.03 RECOMMENDATIONS FOR FUTURE EU INITIATIVES

At the current stage of development of the EU law framework the Social Cohesion Zone Model is a hidden instrument, considering the lack of explicit references both in the context of hard law and soft law.

The present research discloses the fundamentals of the new model through an intense process of analysis where the variables of EU law are deeply scrutinized in order to find the space left for the autonomous initiatives of the Member States.

On these premises, the recommendations resulting from this study are addressed to the adoption of a soft law tool able to give evidence of the Social Cohesion Zone within the area of European tax law, presenting it as a visible instrument in the context of the EU cohesion policy; for this purpose, a new communication from the Commission could represent an interesting option for releasing the potential of the Social Cohesion Zone in all its qualifying features.

Different orders of reasons are set on the ground of this choice.

First, as long as the answers to the research questions are positive, it is not necessary to intervene through hard law tools since it has been demonstrated that the current EU law framework already offers some space for the initiatives of the Member States in the area of direct taxation.

Second, a soft law tool is able to improve the EU framework from the point of view of legal certainty, allowing Member States to take actions in a legal environment with well-defined limits; in this regard, there is a need to definitely overcome the case-by-case approach of the Commission and the broad discretionality in interpreting the interactions between social tax incentives and the main EU law variables, such as in the case of State aid rules, free movement of persons, or harmful tax competition.

Third, a soft law tool seems to be the appropriate solution from the perspective of the EU cohesion policy in order to guarantee a continuous progress in the development of social cohesion in the most disadvantaged areas of the Union; in this sense, in fact, a communication including guidelines, best practices, and benchmarks can offer a support to the actions of the Member States while, at the same time, they remain free to exercise their legislative competence in the field of direct taxation.

In more detail, the communication from the Commission should present the Social Cohesion Zone Model as an instrument defined on the track of the *Altmark* criteria, clarifying in which terms the concept of social tax incentives can be associated with the concept of social services of a general interest.

For this purpose, there is a need of a clear statement about the role of work integration services within the first Altmark criterion and, in particular, about the possibility of identifying a genuine SSGI any time an enterprise assumes the obligation of providing such kind of services, irrespective of the statutory goals; only by this way, in fact, it is possible to extend the package of social tax incentives to large enterprises, as long as they are entrusted with a public service obligation consisting in a work integration service in favour of resident employees and local suppliers.

Then, the content of the communication should also involve more aspects concerning the parameters and the calculation mechanism for the maximum amount of the compensation, the content of the entrustment act and the public procurement procedure to be used for the selection of the recipient undertakings.

Furthermore, the communication should deal with the criteria for the selection of the eligible areas. In this regard, it is first necessary to illustrate the factors which determine the fiscal residue, with the identification of the mechanism for calculating the tax burden and the value of the public services in the area concerned; this part of the communication should include a set of rules for the detection of the EU average value of the fiscal residue, for the mapping of the territory of the Member States and for the periodical update of the same maps. Then, the range of negative values under which Social Cohesion Zones may be established for a certain period of time should also be defined; in this direction, in fact, the communication should establish a methodology for the classification of the eligible areas starting from the detection of a negative value for the parameter of the fiscal residue, with a distinction in categories according to a specific range of the corresponding value.

Finally, it is recommended that the same communication includes monitoring instruments, with the definition of a set of mechanisms of evaluation and peer review at the EU level, as well as mutual learning processes between the Member States for achieving short, medium, and long-term goals.

§8.04 AREAS FOR FUTURE RESEARCH

Despite the originality of the results achieved, there are also some important limitations embodied in this work which are able to highlight the corresponding areas for future research.

The first limit regards the resources reviewed and analysed under the research process; as far as legislation is concerned, in fact, the phenomenon of STZs has been explored with exclusive reference to European tax law, on one part, and to the national tax legislation of the Member States, on the other.

As a consequence, there are no references to other important variables such as international tax treaties, WTO commercial policies or the Base Erosion and Profit Shifting (BEPS) actions of the OECD, which remain out of the field of investigation of the present study. This concretely means that the results achieved should require to also be tested with respect to such external resources in order to assume a validity in the field of international tax law.

The second limit is external to the field of legal studies and regards the econometric evaluation of the effects of the related tax measures.

Questions related to the efficiency or the effectiveness of STZs, including the new model of the Social Cohesion Zone, remain open, as they are linked to the definition of valuable instruments of econometric evaluation. In particular, the value of the tax expenditures, the duration of the programme, the instruments and parameters used to evaluate the performance are all aspects that would require further studies in the context of economics; in this sense, the establishment of a dialogue between the field of legal studies and the field of economics would improve the results not only from the point of view of the legitimacy under the EU law framework, but also from the point of view of the efficiency and effectiveness of a tax incentive programme at the territorial level.

Therefore, the conclusion is that many crucial aspects for the success or a failure of a programme based on the Social Cohesion Zone Model are outside the field of legal studies, being related to the field of economic studies aimed to the definition of a set of parameters and methods for monitoring the results achieved.

On the ground of the above considerations, it is finally possible to identify the areas for future research which are related to the scope of the present study. International tax law, including tax treaties, WTO commercial policies, and the BEPS actions of the OECD, is the first area where the results of this research should be carefully tested to verify whether or not the general legal theory of STZs and the Social Cohesion Zone Model may be confirmed as scientific categories of international value.

Then, the field of economics is the second area for future research where the Social Cohesion Zone Model should require to be deeply assessed from the point of view of its efficiency and effectiveness.

§8.05 FINAL CONCLUSIONS

At the end of this study, the phenomenon of STZs assumes an autonomous value in the context of European tax law thanks to a new outlook based on a set of original findings.

The research process has given evidence of a general legal theory able to explain the different variables of STZs from the perspective of tax law studies, through the valorization of the territorial, the structural, and the functional dimensions.

This first point of arrival fills an important gap of knowledge in the field; the theory here developed, in fact, offers new insights for a better understanding of the phenomenon focusing on a comprehensive concept able to encompass all the various experiences of STZs within the EU.

The corresponding effect is that the various examples of STZs across the EU now find, for the first time, a theoretical framework within the field of tax law studies, with a more consistent legal approach to the topic.

Nonetheless, the ideas resulting from the present research are not merely based on systematic considerations related to the development of a general legal theory; the further step here made, in fact, is wider in perspective and covers relevant issues in the context of social cohesion policy.

In this sense, it has been demonstrated that there is still a space left for Member States for autonomous initiatives through the Social Cohesion Zone Model as long as the tax measures exclusively deal with direct taxation and fulfil a specific set of requirements.

The results achieved are associated to the most important challenges of the future of the Union, especially for what regards the issues of the most disadvantaged territories which are affected by serious delays and unemployment.

In the last years, social and economic disparities have dramatically increased in most Member States, on the ground of the economic crisis started in 2008 and the emerging scepticism against the process of European integration.

As a response to these negative feedbacks, the results of this study promote a renewed image of the Union offering support to the adoption of a new instrument for the development of social cohesion policies addressed to the low-income areas; the Social Cohesion Zone Model, in fact, opens a new perspective where the values of solidarity and social cohesion finally become the main engine for the neutralization of the fiscal residue and the achievement of the horizontal fiscal balance between the different territories of the Union.

In this new context, the Social Cohesion Zone Model becomes a strategic instrument for the future of the process of European integration and for tackling of issues related to the overpopulation and the underpopulation which respectively affect high-income and low-income areas of the EU. In this regard, in fact, the significant movement of European citizens from low-income to high-income areas of the Union and the continuous growth of the population in the most developed regions of the EU is leading to many issues in consideration of the limited resources of the public services there available.

On the ground of these considerations, the general legal theory of STZs, together with the new model of the Social Cohesion Zone, represents an original contribution to the knowledge in the field of European tax law in the light of the future challenges of the Union.

In this context, the final message of the present study is addressed to the implementation of the Social Cohesion Zone Model for supporting the track towards the realization of a Social Europe. In this sense, EU institutions should definitely change their route towards a more comprehensive idea of Europe aimed not only at the defence of the principles of the internal market, but also to the valorization of the constitutional traditions common to the various Member States, including the value of social cohesion at the territorial level.

Bibliography

ADONNINO P., *Non-discrimination Rules in International Taxation, General Report*, in *Cahiers de droit fiscal international*, IFA, Periodicals Service Company, Vol. 78b, Deventer, 1993, pp. 26 et seq.

AKINCI G., CRITTLE J., *Special Economic Zone: Performance, Lessons Learned, and Implication for Zone Development (English)*. Foreign Investment Advisory Service (FIAS) occasional paper. Washington, DC: World Bank, 2008, available at http://documents.worldbank.org/curated/en/343901468330977533/Special-economi c-zone-performance-lessons-learned-and-implication-for-zone-develop ment.

ALEXY R., *A Theory of Constitutional Rights*, Oxford University Press, Oxford, 2002.

AVI-YONAH R.S., VALLESPINOS M., *Special Tax Zones and the WTO*, University of Michigan, Research Paper No. 545, 2017, available at https://ssrn.com/abstract =2928644.

ARMSTRONG K., *The Open Method of Coordination – Obstinate or Obsolete?* University of Cambridge Faculty of Law, Research Paper No. 45, 2016, available at https:// papers.ssrn.com/sol3/papers.cfm?abstract_id=2839840.

ARTEAGA ORTIZ J., MARTINEZ COBAS X., *Las Zonas Francas en Espana y su utilidad, Delimitacion del concepto y perspectivas de futuro*, in *Boletin Economico de ICE*, 2003, No. 2758, pp. 1-7.

ARTEAGA ORTIZ J., CONESA FONTES A., *Las Zonas Francas en Espana*, in *Boletin Economico de ICE*, 2000, No. 2649.

AUSTRALIAN PRESS COUNCIL, *General Statement of Principles*, 2011, available at http:// www.presscouncil.org.au/uploads/52321/ufiles/APC_General_Stat-ement_of_ Principles.pdf.

BACON K., *Differential Taxes, State Aids and the Lunn Poly Case*, in *European Competition Law Review*, 1999, p. 384.

BACON K., *European Union Law of State Aid*, 3rd Edition, Oxford University Press, Oxford, 2017.

BARRETT J., VEAL J., *Social Enterprise: Some Tax Policy Considerations*, in *Journal of the Australasian Tax Teachers Association*, 2013.

Basile A., Germidis D., *Investing in Free Export Processing Zones*, OECD Development Centre, Paris, 1984.

Basinger S.J., Hallerberg M., *Remodeling the Competition for Capital: How Domestic Politics Erase the Race to Bottom*, in *American Political Science Review*, 2004, Vol. 98, No. 2, pp. 261-276.

Bizioli G., *Impact of the Freedom of Establishment on Tax Law*, in *EC Tax Review*, 1998, No. 4, pp. 239-247.

Bizioli G., *L'autonomia finanziaria e tributaria regionale*, Giappichelli, G. (ed.), Turin, 2012.

Bolin R.L., *The Global Network of Export Processing Zones*, in *Journal of the Flagstaff Institute*, 1998, Vol. 22, p. 15.

Borghi S., *Il ruolo delle zone franche industriali nel dialogo nord-sud: il sud-est asiatico*, in *Economia e Politica industriale*, 1985, No. 47, pp. 267 et seq.

Boria P., *Il sistema tributario*, Wolters Kluwer Italia, Milan, 2008.

Boria P., *Diritto tributario europeo*, Giuffrè A. (ed.), Milan, 2010.

Boria P., *Taxation in European Union*, 2nd Edition, Springer International Publishing, Cham, 2017.

Borozan D., *Free zone – the Source of Socio-Economic Benefit*, in *Interdisciplinary Management Research Journal*, Osijek, 2007, Vol. 3, pp. 75-91.

Bras F., Dewerbe P., Borges R., *The Madeira Free Zone and Its Standpoint Within the European Union*, in *EC Tax Review*, 2004, Vol. III, pp. 122-134.

Bratton W.W., Mc Cahery J. A., *Tax Coordination and Tax Competition in the European Union: Evaluating the Code of Conduct on Business Taxation*, in *Internal Market Law Review*, 2001, No. 3, pp. 677-718.

Brautigam D., Fjeldstad O., Moore M., *Taxation and State-Building in Developing Countries: Capacity and Consent*, Cambridge University Press, Cambridge, 2008.

Briant A., Miren L., Benoit S., *Can Tax Breaks Beat Geography? Lessons from the French Enterprise Zone Experience*, in *American Economic Journal: Economic Policy*, 2015, No. 7(2), pp. 88-124.

Bucicco C., *Il fondamento giuridico delle zone franche urbane e l'equivoco con le zone franche di diritto doganale*, in *Diritto e Pratica Tributaria*, 2008, I, pp. 105 et seq.

Bucicco C., *Compatibilità europea degli interventi a sostegno delle aree colpite da calamità naturali*, in M. Basilavecchia – L. Del Federico – A. Pace – C. Verrigni, *Interventi finanziari e tributari per le aree colpite da calamità, tra norme interne e principi europei*, Giappichelli, G. (ed.), Turin, 2016, pp. 147-196.

Budzowski K., *Polish Free Customs Duty Areas, Customs Depots and Special Zones*, in *Zeszyty Naukowe/Polskie Towarzystwo Ekonomiczne*, 2003, No. 1, pp. 49-59.

Carinci A., *Autonomia impositiva degli enti sub-statali e divieto di aiuti di Stato*, in *Rassegna Tributaria*, 2006, No. 5, pp. 1783 et seq.

Carpenter G., Keller Lauritzen J.R., *Promoting Social Enterprise Financing* (Discussion paper), Danish Technological Institute, Centre for Policy and Business Analysis, Taastrup (Denmark), 2016.

Casson L., *The Grain Trade of the Hellenistic World*, in Casson, L. (ed.) *Ancient Trade and Society*, Wayne State University Press, Detroit, 1984, p. 76.

CEDEFOP, *Using Tax Incentive to Promote Education and Training*, European Centre for the Development of Vocational Training (ed.), CEDEFOP panorama series, Luxembourg, 2009.

CHANG W.N., RADULESCU D.M., *Types of Tax Concessions for Attracting Foreign Direct Investment in Free Economic Zones*, in *CESifo Working Paper Series*, 2004, No. 1175, available at https://papers.ssrn.com/sol3/papers.cfm?abstra- ct_id = 534 707.

CHAPMAN O., *Les zones franches dans le monde et aux Etats-Unis*, in *Problemes Economiques*, 1986, p. 28.

CHAISSE J., HU J., *International Economic Law and the Challenges of the Free Zones*, Kluwer Law International, 2019.

COLLIE D., *State Aid in the European Union: The Prohibition of Subsidies in an Integrated Market*, in *International Journal of Industrial Organization*, 2000, pp. 867-884.

CONFEDERACION REGIONAL DE EMPRESARIOS DE LAS ISLAS CANARIAS, *Actualizacion del Regimen Economico y Fiscal de Canaria para el period 2014-2020, Documento de bases*, 2013, available at www.ccelpa.org.

CRAIG P., *The Evolution of the Single Market*, in BARNARD C., SCOTT J. (eds), *The Law of the Single European Market - Unpacking the Premises*, Hart Publishing, Oxford and Portland, 2002.

CRAIG P., DE BÚRCA G., *EU Law: Text, Cases, and Materials*, 6th Edition, Oxford University Press, New York, 2015.

CZEKAY-DANCEWICZ A., *Access to Social Benefits and Advantages for EU Migrant Workers, Members of Their Families and Other Categories of Migrating EU Citizens*, 2013, p. 1, available at http://ec.europa.eu/social/BlobServlet?d ocId = 11714&langId = en.

D'AMATI N., *Agevolazioni ed esenzioni tributarie*, in *Noviss. Dig. It.*, Appendix, I, Turin, 1980, pp. 153 et seq.

DAGNINO A., *Agevolazioni fiscali e potestà normativa*, CEDAM, Padova, 2008.

DALLA COSTA G.F., NARDO S., MENINI M., *Le zone franche nella globalizzazione. Definizioni, tipologie, percorsi di sviluppo*, CLEUP SC, Padova, 2006, pp. 57 et seq.

DE JONG W., *Establishing Free Zones for Regional Development*, Library of the European Parliament, 2013, available at http://www.europarl.europa.eu/Reg-Data/bibliotheque/briefing/2013/130481/LDM_BRI(2013)130481REVEN.pdf.

DE LA PORTE C., *Good Governance via the OMC? The Cases of Employment and Social Inclusion*, in *European Journal of Legal Studies*, 2007, Vol. 1, No. 1.

DE LIGT L., *Fairs and Markets in the Roman Empire. Economic and Social Aspects of Periodic Trade in a Pre-industrial Society*, J.C. Gieben, Amsterdam, 1993.

DEFOURNY J., NYSSENS M., *Social Enterprise in Europe: Recent Trends and Developments*, in *Social Enterprise Journal*, 2008, pp. 5 et seq.

DEL FEDERICO L., *Introduzione allo studio della finanza pubblica per le aree colpite da calamità*, in M. BASILAVECCHIA - L. DEL FEDERICO - A. PACE - C. VERRIGNI, *Interventi finanziari e tributari per le aree colpite da calamità, tra norme interne e principi europei*, GIAPPICHELLI, G. (ed.), Turin, 2016, pp. 1-23.

DIAMOND W., DIAMOND D., *Tax-Free Trade Zones of the World*, M. Bender, New York, 1990.

DRABBE H., *The Test of Selectivity in State Aid Litigation: The Relevance of Drawing Internal and External Comparison to Identify the Reference Framework*, in RUST, A., MICHEAU, C. (eds), *State Aid and Tax Law*, Wolters Kluwer International, The Hague, 2013, pp. 87 et seq.

DUFF D.G., *Benefit Taxes and User Fees in Theory and Practice*, in *The University of Toronto Law Journal*, 2004, No. 54, pp. 435-446.

DZIURDZ K., MARCHGRABER C., *Non-discrimination in European and Tax Treaty Law*, Series on International Tax Law, LANG, M. (ed.), Wien, 2015.

EUROPEAN COMMISSION, *A map of social enterprises and their eco-systems in Europe. Synthesis Report*, European Commission Publications, 2014.

EUROPEAN COMMISSION – DIRECTORATE-GENERAL FOR INTERNAL MARKET, INDUSTRY, ENTREPRENEURSHIP AND SMEs, *Social enterprises and the social economy going forward. A call for action from the Commission Expert Group on Social Entrepreneurship (GECES)*, 2016, available at http://ec.europa.eu/growth/sectors/social-economy/enterprises/expert-groups.

EUROPEAN COMMISSION – EMPLOYMENT SOCIAL AFFAIRS AND INCLUSION, *The relationship between social security coordination and tax law, Analytical report 2014*, European Commission Publications, 2014.

EUROPEAN PARLIAMENT, MEMBER'S RESEARCH SERVICE, *The Open Method of Coordination*, European Parliament Publications, 2014.

FAROLE T., *Special Economic Zones in Africa: Comparing Performance and Learning from Global Experiences*, The World Bank Ed., Washington DC, 2011.

FICARI V., *Aiuti fiscali regionali, selettività e 'insularità': dalle Azzorre agli enti locali italiani*, in *Diritto e pratica tributaria internazionale*, 2007, pp. 319 et seq.

FICHERA F., *Le agevolazioni fiscali*, CEDAM, Padova, 1992.

FINARDI F., MORONI E., *Stati d'eccezione, Zone e Porti Franchi nell'economia–mondo*, FrancoAngeli, Milan, 2001.

FLORA P., HEIDENHEIMER A., *The Historical Core and Changing Boundaries of the Welfare State*, in FLORA P., HEIDENHEIMER A. (eds), *The Development of Welfare States in Europe and America*, Transaction Bookis, New Brunswick, 1981, pp. 26 et seq.

FONTANA C., *Gli aiuti di Stato di natura fiscale*, GIAPPICHELLI, G. (ed.), Turin, 2012.

FURLOTTI M., *Le zone franche industriali in una prospettiva di cooperazione tra Europa e America Latina*, in *Economia e politica industriale*, 1986, No. 52, p. 237.

GALLO F., *Le ragioni del fisco. Etica e giustizia nella tassazione*, 2nd Edition, Il Mulino, Bologna, 2011.

GEBAUER A., CHANG WOON N., PARSCHE R., *Lessons of the 1999 Abolition of Intra-EU Duty-Free Sales for the New EU Member States*, in *CESifo Economic Studies*, Oxford, 2005, Vol. 51.1., pp. 133-157.

GRAVELLE J.G., *Tax Havens: International Tax Avoidance and Evasion*, Congressional Research Service, 2010, Washington DC.

GREVE B., *The Hidden Welfare State, Tax Expenditure and Social Policy*, in *Scandinavian Journal of Social Welfare*, 1994, p. 206.

HALBERSTADT V., *Tax Incentives as an Instrument for Achievement of Governmental Goal, Report from the Netherlands for the 1976 Congress of the International Fiscal Association, Jerusalem (Israel), 13-17 September 1976*, Deventer, 1976.

HEANEY V., *Investing in Social Enterprise: The Role of Tax Incentives*, Centre for the Study of Financial Innovation (CSFI), London, 2010.

HARBO T.I., *The Function of the Proportionality Principle in EU Law*, in *European Law Journal*, 2010, Vol. 16, No. 2, p. 158.

HOUSE OF COMMONS, FOREIGN AFFAIRS COMMITTEE, *Gibraltar: Time to Get Off the Fence, Second Report of Session 2014-15*, House of Commons, London, 2014.

HOUSE OF LORDS – JOINT COMMITTEE ON PRIVACY AND INJUNCTIONS, *Paper No. 273*, House of Commons Paper No. 1443, Session 2010-12, 2012.

HOWARD C., *The Hidden Welfare State: Tax Expenditure and Social Policy in the United States*, Princeton University Press, Princeton, 1997.

INGROSSO M., NOCERINO O., ROCCATAGLIATA F., SACCHETTO C., *Le Zone Franche*, Chamber of Commerce of Naples, Naples, 1998.

ISAACS A., *International Trade Tariff and Commercial Policies*, Richard D. Irwin Inc., Chicago (Illinois), 1948.

KIRETA I., *Tax Incentive Regimes in Croatia, Macedonia (FYR) and Serbia – Should They Compete?*, in *European Taxation*, 2013, pp. 215 et seq.

KLASSE M., *The Impact of Altmark: The European Commission Case Law Responses*, in SZYZYCZAK E., VAN DE GRONDEN J.W. (eds), *Financing Services of General Economic Interest*, TMC Asser Press, The Hague, 2013.

KRIEGER-BODEN C., *EU Cohesion Policy, Past and Present: Sustaining a Prospering and Fair European Union?*, Kiel Institute for the World Economy, Kiel Working Paper, No. 2037, 2016.

KOCHENOV D., *Introducing EU Law of the Overseas*, in KOCHENOV, D. (ed.), *EU Law of the Overseas, Outermost Regions, Associated Overseas Countries and Territories, Territories Sui Generis*, Wolters Kluwer, The Hague, 2011, pp. 3-69.

KOCHENOV D., *The Application of EU Law in the EU's Overseas Regions, Countries and Territories After the Entry Into Force of the Treaty of Lisbon*, in *Journal of International Law and Practice*, 2012, Vol. 20, pp. 669-743.

KOUKIADAKI A., *EU Governance and Social Services of General Interest: When Even the UK Is Concerned*, in BARBIER, J.C. (ed.), *EU Law, Governance and Social Policy European Integration Online Papers*, 2012, Special Mini-Issue 1, Vol. 16, Article 5, available at http://eiop.or.at/eiop/texte/2012-005a.htm.

LA ROSA S., *Esclusioni tributarie, Enc. Giur.*, XIII, Rome, 1989.

LA ROSA S., *Le agevolazioni tributarie*, in *Trattato di diritto tributario, diretto da Amatucci A.*, Padova, 1994, I, 1, pp. 401 et seq.

LANG M., PISTONE P., SCHUCH J., STARINGER C., *Introduction to European Tax Law: Direct Taxation*, 3rd Edition, Spiramus Press, Wien, 2013.

LAUKKANEN A., *The Development Aspects of Special Tax Zones*, in *Bulletin for International Taxation*, 2016, Vol. 70, No. 3, pp. 152-162.

LAUKKANEN A., PISTONE P., DE GOEDE J., *Special Tax Zones in the Era of International Tax Coordination*, IBFD, 2019.

LLOYD T.H., *England and the German Hanse, 1157-1611: A Study of Their Trade and Commercial Diplomacy*, Cambridge University Press, Cambridge, 1991.

LOMAX A.L., *The Foreign Trade Zone*, School of Business Administration, University of Oregon, Eugene (Oregon), 1947.

LOROT P., SCWOB T., *Les Zones franches dans le monde*, in *La Documentation francaise*, 1987, pp. 11 et seq.

LUJA R., *Revisiting the Balance Between Aid, Selectivity and Selective Aid in Respect of Taxes and Special Levies*, in *European State Aid Law Quarterly*, 2010, No. 1, pp. 161-168.

LUJA R., *The Selectivity Test: The Concept of Sectorial Aid*, in RUST, A., MICHEAU, C. (eds), *State Aid and Tax Law*, Wolters Kluwer International, The Hague, 2013, pp. 107-118.

LUJA R., *Do State Aid Rules Still Allow European Union Member States to Claim Fiscal Sovereignty?*, in *EC Tax Review*, 2016, No. 5-6, pp. 312-324.

MAC ELWEE R. S., *Port Development*, McGraw Hill, 1926, New York.

MARMOR T.R., MARSHAW, J.L. HARVEY P.L., *America's Misunderstood Welfare State*, Basic Books, New York, 1990.

MC DANIEL R., SURREY S.S., *International Aspects of Tax Expenditures: A Comparative Study*, Springer Netherlands, Deventer, 1985.

MC DANIEL W.R., KOSSACK E.W., *The Financial Benefits of users of foreign-trade zones*, in *Columbia Journal of World Business*, 1983, pp. 33 et seq.

MELIS G., *La delega sul federalismo fiscale e la cosiddetta 'fiscalità di vantaggio': profili comunitari*, in *Rassegna Tributaria*, 2009, No. 4, pp. 1003 et seq.

MENG G.W., *Evolutionary Model of Free Economic Zones – Different Generations and Structural Features*, in *Chinese Geographical Science*, 2005, Vol. 15, pp. 103-112.

MICONI F., *La Zona Franca Urbana di L'Aquila*, in M. BASILAVECCHIA – L. DEL FEDERICO – A. PACE – C. VERRIGNI, *Interventi finanziari e tributari per le aree colpite da calamità, tra norme interne e principi europei*, GIAPPICHELLI, G. (ed.), Turin, 2016, pp. 368-383.

MOBERG L., *The Political Economy of Special Economic Zones: Concentrating Economic*, Routledge, 2017.

MORO B., *Incentivi fiscali e politiche di sviluppo economico regionale in Europa*, in *Moneta e Credito*, 2001, Vol. 52, pp. 343-388.

MORON PEREZ M., *El Regimen Fiscal de las Ciudades Autonomas de Ceuta y Melilla: Presente y Futuro, Cronica Triburaria*, in *Crónica tributaria*, 2006, 121, pp. 88 et seq.

MOSCHETTI G., *Diniego di detrazione per consapevolezza nel contrasto alle frodi Iva, alla luce dei principi di certezza del diritto e proporzionalità*, CEDAM, Padova, 2013, p. 174.

MURRAY F., *The European Union and Member State Territories: A New Legal Framework under the EU Treaties*, Springer, The Hague, 2012, pp. 131 et seq.

MUSGRAVE P., *Harmonization of Direct Business Taxes: A Case Study*, in SHOUP, C.S. (ed.), *Fiscal Harmonization in Internal markets*, Vol. II, Columbia University Press, New York, 1967, pp. 211-232.

MUSGRAVE P., *US Taxation of Foreign Investment and Income: Issues and Arguments*, Harvard Law School, Cambridge, 1969.

MUSGRAVE P., *Interjurisdictional Coordination of Taxes on Capital Income*, in CNOSSEN, S. (ed.), *Tax Coordination in the EC*, Kluwer Law International, Deventer, 1987, pp. 218-35.

NICOLAIDES P., *Fiscal State Aid in the EU: The Limits of Tax Autonomy*, in *World Competition*, 2004, p. 365.

NICOLAIDES P., *Developments in Fiscal Aid: New Interpretations and New Problems with the Concept of Selectivity*, in *European State Aid Law Quarterly*, 2007, Vol. I, pp. 43 et seq.

NICOLAIDES P., *Altmark Requires Efficiency; Article 106(2) TFEU Does Not!*, 2017, available at http://www.sipotra.it/wp-content/uploads/2017/03/Altmark-Requires-Efficiency.pdf.

NYSSEN M., *Social Enterprise – At the Crossroads of Market, Public Policies and Civil Society*, Routledge, London and New York, 2006.

OECD, CENTRE FOR ENTREPRENEURSHIP, SMEs, REGIONS AND CITIES, *Social Enterprises*, OECD publications, Paris, 1999.

OECD COMMITTEE ON FISCAL AFFAIRS, *Tax Expenditures. A Review of the Issues and Country Practices*, OECD publications, Paris, 1984.

OWENS J. P., *Tax Expenditures and Direct Expenditures as Instruments of Social Policy*, CNOSSEN, S. (ed.), Comparative Tax Studies, Amsterdam, 1983.

PAGOULATOS G., STASINOPOULOU M., SOTIROPOULOS D.A., *Governance in EU Social and Employment Policy: A Survey*, Athens University of Economics and Business, available at http://www.eliamep.gr/wp-content/uploads/2009/0-1/recwowe1.pdf.

PAMPEL F.C., WILLIAMSON J.B., *Age, Class, Politics, and the Welfare State*, Cambridge, University Press, Cambridge, 1989.

PAVUK O., NARUSHEVICH, T. PILAITIS G., MERKULOVA T., *Free Zones on the Fence*, in *The Baltic Course*, 2002, available at http://www.baltic-course.com/archive/eng/winter_2002/03free_zones.htm.

PORTER E., KETELS C., *Latvia: Economic Strategy after EU Accession*, Harvard Business School Case 707-515, 2007, pp. 1-32, available at http://probni.fpn.- bg.ac.rs/wp -content/uploads/Porter Ketels_Latvia_707515p2.pdf.

RADAELLI C.M., *The Code of Conduct Against Harmful Tax Competition: Open Method of Coordination in Disguise?* in *Public Administration*, 2003, Vol. 81, No. 3, p. 522.

RADVAN M., *System of Financial Law: System of Tax Law: Conference Proceedings. 1*, Masaryk University, Faculty of Law, Brno, 2015.

RAUH N.K., *The Sacred Bonds of Commerce: Religion, Economy, and Trade Society at Hellenistic Roman Delos, 166-87 B.C.*, J.C. Gieben, Amsterdam, 1993.

REGER G., *Regionalism and Change in the Economy of Independent Delos, 314-167 B.C.*, University of California Press, Berkeley, 1994.

REIMER E., URBAN N., SCHMID S., *A Domestic Taxation, Bilateral Tax Treaty, and OECD Perspective*, Kluwer Law International, Alphen aan den Rijn, 2011.

RICE STEVEN J., *Introduction to Taxation: A Decision-Making Approach*, Dame Publishing, Dublin, 1996.

RIVOLIN J., FALUDI A., *The Hidden Face of European Spatial Planning: Innovations in Governance*, in *European Planning Studies*, 2005, Vol. 13, No. 2, pp. 195-215.

RIVOLIN J., *Cohesion and Subsidiarity. Towards Good Territorial Governance in Europe*, in *Town Planning Review*, 2005, Vol. 76, No. 1.

ROMERO A. T., *ILO's World Labour Report of 1996*, International Labour Organization (ILO), 1996.

SANFORD C., *Why Tax Systems Differ: A Comparative Study of the Political Economy of Taxation*, Fiscal Publications, Bath, 2000.

SCHOEN W., *Taxation and State Aid Law in the European Union*, in *Internal Market Law Review*, Kluwer Law International, The Hague, 1999, Vol. 36, No. 5, pp. 911-936.

SCHULZE H.C., *Free Trade Zones at the Beginning of the 21st Century*, in *The Comparative and International Law Journal of Southern Africa*, 2002, Vol. 35.

SHATZ K.W., SPINANGER D., *Zone Franche e prospettive nella Repubblica Federale di Germania*, in *Economia e Banca*, 1986, pp. 250 et seq.

SOARE I., NECHITA D., *Free Zones Development in Romania – Premises, Determining Factors and Perspective*, in *Economics and Applied Informatics*, 2010, No. 1, pp. 117-124.

SPINANGER D., *Objectives and Impact of Economic Activity Zones – Some Evidence from Asia*, in *Weltwirtschaftliches Archiv*, 1984, Vol. 120, No. 1, pp. 64 et seq.

STAHL G., LLUNA D., *A Cohesion Policy for the Future*, in *Intereconomics*, 2003, Vol. 38, No. 6, pp. 295-305.

STARCHILD A., *Tax Havens for International Business*, Macmillan Press, London, 1994, p. 1.

STEICHEN A., *Tax Competition in Europe or the Taming of Leviathan*, in VV.AA., *Tax Competition in Europe*, IBFD – International Bureau of Fiscal Documentation, Amsterdam, 2003, p. 73.

STREECK W., *Neo-Voluntarism: A New European Social Policy Regime?*, in *European Law Journal*, 1995, No. 1, pp. 31-59.

SURREY SS., *Pathways to Tax Reform: The Concept of Tax Expenditures*, Harvard University Press, Cambridge, 1973.

TRAVERSA E., *The Selectivity Test: The Concept of Regional Aid*, in RUST, A., MICHEAU, C. (eds), *State Aid and Tax Law*, Wolters Kluwer International, Alphen aan den Rijn, 2013, pp. 119 et seq.

TRAVERSA E., *Tax Incentives and Territoriality Within the European Union: Balancing the Internal Market with the Tax Sovereignty of Member States*, in *World Tax Journal*, 2014, pp. 337 et seq.

TERRA B. J.M., WATTEL P. J., *European Tax Law*, 6th Edition, Kluwer Law International, Alphen aan den Rijn, 2012.

TITMUSS R., *Essays on the Welfare State*, Yale University Press, New Haven, 1959.

TRAMPUS F., *The Spanish Free Trade Zones as Logistic Platforms for Trade with Latin America*, in *Trasporti – diritto, economia, politica*, 2002, No. 88, pp. 87-105.

THOMAN R.S., *Free Ports and Foreign-Trade Zones*, Cornell Maritime Press, Cambridge, 1956.

UDINA M., CONETTI G., *Zone Franche*, in *Enc. Giuridica Treccani*, Rome, 1994.

UCKMAR V., *Principi comuni di diritto costituzionale tributario*, CEDAM, Padova, 1999.

UNITED NATIONS: CENTRE ON TRANSNATIONAL CORPORATIONS, *The Challenge of Free Economic Zones in Central and Eastern Europe*, United Nations Publications, New York, 1991.

UNITED NATIONS CONFERENCE ON TRADE AND DEVELOPMENT, *Export Processing Zones: Role of Foreign Direct Investment and Development Impact, UNCTAD Secretariat Report*, United Nations Publications, Geneva, 1993.

UNITED NATIONS DEVELOPMENT PROGRAMME, *Legal Framework for Social Economy and Social Enterprises: A Comparative Report*, European Center for Not-for-Profit Law, 2012, available at http://ecnl.org/dindocuments/442_ECNL%20UNDP%20 Social%20Economy%20Report.pdf.

UNITED NATIONS – ECONOMIC AND SOCIAL COMMISSION FOR ASIA AND PACIFIC, *Commercial Development of Regional Ports as Logistic Centres*, United Nations Publications, New York, 2002.

US CONGRESS – JOINT COMMITTEE ON TAXATION, *Estimates of Federal Tax Expenditures for Fiscal Years 1992-1996*, Government Printing Office, Washington D.C., 1991.

US CONGRESS – OFFICE OF MANAGEMENT AND BUDGET (OMB), *Analytical Perspectives, Budget of the United States Government, Fiscal Year 1996*, Government Printing Office, Washington, D.C., 1995.

US DEPARTMENT OF STATE, BUREAU OF ECONOMIC AND BUSINESS AFFAIRS, *2013 Investment Climate Statement – Denmark*, April 2013, Report, available at http://www.state .gov.

US DEPARTMENT OF STATE, BUREAU OF ECONOMIC AND BUSINESS AFFAIRS, *2014 Investment Climate Statement*, June 2014, available at www.state.gov.

US DEPARTMENT OF STATE, BUREAU OF ECONOMIC AND BUSINESS AFFAIRS, *2017 Investment Climate Statement*, 2017, available at www.state.gov.

VASQUES S., *The Madeira Free Trade Zone: Compliance and Control Issues*, in *European Taxation, IBFD* 2012, p. 149.

VIMERCATI G., *Le zone franche industriali nei paesi emergenti. Il sud est asiatico*, FrancoAngeli, Milan 1985.

WALL D., *Export Processing Zones*, in *Journal of World Law*, No. 10, 1976, pp. 478-489.

WARR P., *Export Processing Zones*, in MILNER, C. (ed.) *Export Promotion Strategies; Theory and Evidence from Developing Countries*. New York University Press, New York, 1990.

WEBER D., *Tax Avoidance and the EC Treaty Freedoms: A Study of the Limitations under European Law to the Prevention of Tax Avoidance*, in *Eucotax Series on European Taxation 11*, The Hague, Kluwer law international, 2005.

WISHLADE F.G., *Regional State Aid and Competition Policy in the European Union*, Kluwer Law International, The Hague, 2003.

WOLLMANN H., MARCOU G., The *Provision of Public Services in Europe: Between State, Local Government and Market*, Edward Elgar Publishing, Cheltenham, 2010.

WORLD CUSTOMS ORGANIZATION, *International Convention on the Simplification and Harmonization of Customs Procedures*, Kyoto, 18 May, 1973.

WORLD TRADE ORGANIZATION, *World Trade Report 2006*, pp. 47 et seq., available at https://www.wto.org/english/res_e/booksp_e/anrep_e/wtr06-2b_-e.pdf.

WORTHSTONE, WRAGGE & CO LLP, *The Role of tax Incentives in Encouraging social Investment*, City of London Economic Development, London, 2013.

XIANGMING C., *The Evolution of Free Economic Zones and the Recent Development of Cross-National Growth Zones*, in *International Journal of Urban and Regional Research*, 1995, Vol. 19, No. 4, pp. 593-621.

ZILLER J., *Outermost Regions, Overseas Countries and Territories and Others after the Entry into Force of the Lisbon Treaty*, in KOCHENOV, D. (ed.), *EU Law of the Overseas, Outermost Regions, Associated Overseas Countries and Territories, Territories Sui Generis*, Wolters Kluwer, The Hague, 2011, p. 78.

Table of Cases

Court of Justice of the EU

Case	Name	Reported	Page Numbers
C-30/59	*Steenkolenmijnen v High Authority*	[1961] ECR I	46
C-75/63	*Hoekstra v Bestuur der Bedrijfsvereniging voor detailhandel en Ambachten*	[1964] ECR 987	96
C-173/73	*Italy v Commission*	[1974] ECR 709	62
C-41/74	*Yvonne van Duyn v Home Office*	[1974] ECR 01337	216
C-32/75	*Cristini v SNCF*	[1975] ECR 1085	96
C-148/77	*Hansen v Hauptzollamt Flensburg*	[1978] ECR 01787	216
C-120/78	*Rewe-Zentral AG v Bundesmonopolverwaltung fur Branntwein*	[1979] ECR 649	51, 216
C-178/78	*R v Sanders*	[1979] ECR 1129	215
C-35/83 to C-36/83	*Morson and Jhanjan v Netherlands,*	[1982] ECR 3723	215
C-270/83	*Commission of the European Communities v French Republic (Avoir fiscal)*	[1986] ECR 273	86, 212
C-310/85	*Deufil GmbH & Co. KG v Commission*	[1987] ECR 00901	61, 62
C-248/84	*Federal Republic of Germany v Commission*	[1987] ECR 04013	50

Case	Name	Reported	Page Numbers
C-118/85	*Commission v Italy*	[1987] ECR 2599	45
C-263/86	*Belgian State v René Humbel and Marie-Thérèse Edel,*	[1988] ECR 05365	81
C-237/87	*Volvo AB v Erik Veng (UK) Ltd.*	[1988] ECR 6211	96
C-145/88	*Torfaen Borough Council v B&Q plc*	[1989] ECR I-3815	86, 218
C-331/88	*The Queen v Minister of Agriculture, Fisheries and Food and Secretary of State for Health, ex parte: Fedesa and Others*	[1990] ECR I-04023	219
C-312/89 and C-332/89	*Union départementale des syndicats CGT de l'Aisne v SIDEF Conforama, Société Arts et Meubles and Société Jima*	[1991] *ECR* I-00997	219
C-3/90	*Bernini (MJE) v Netherlands Ministry of Education and Science*	[1992] ECR I-1071	96
C-204/90	*Hanns-Martin Bachmann v Belgian State*	[1992] ECR I-00249	83, 86, 217
C-169/91	*Stoke-on-Trent CC v B&Q plc*	[1992] ECR I-6457	86, 218
C-109/92	*Stephan Max Wirth v Landeshauptstadt Hannover*	[1993] ECR I-06447	81
C-387/92	*Banco de Credito Industrial SA, now Banco Exterior de Espana SA v Ayuntamiento de Valencia*	[1994] ECR I-00877	46
C-278/92 to C-280/92	*Kingdom of Spain v Commission*	[1994] ECR I-04103	62
C-279/93	*Finanzamt Köln-Altstadt v Roland Schumacker*	[1995] ECR I-225	84, 85, 214
C-80/94	*H. E. J. Wielockx* v *Inspecteur der Directe Belastingen*	[1995] ECR I-2493	85
C-101/94	*Commission v Italian Republic*	[1996] ECR I-02691	86, 219
C-107/94	*P. H. Asscher v Staatssecretaris van Financiën*	[1996] ECR I-03089	85
C-237/94	*O'Flynn v Adjudication Officer*	[1996] ECR I-2617	96
C-241/94	*France v Commission*	[1996] ECR I-4551	62
C-250/95	*Futura Participations SA and Singer v Administration des contributions*	[1997] ECR I-02471	85, 217

Case	Name	Reported	Page Numbers
C-169/95	*Spain v Commission*	[1997] ECR I-00135	62
C-118/96	*Jessica Safir v Skattemyndigheten i Dalarnas Län, formerly Skattemyndigheten i Kopparbergs Län*	[1998] ECR I-01897	85
C-264/96	*Imperial Chemical Industries plc (ICI) v Kenneth Hall Colmer*	[1998] ECR I-04695	86
C-85/96	*María Martínez Sala v Freistaat Bayern*	[1998] ECR I–2691	96
C-75/97	*Belgium v Commission*	[1999] ECR I-3671	62
C-251/97	*France v Commission of the European Communities*	[1999] ECR I-6639	73
C-400/97 to C-402/97	*Administración General del Estado v Juntas Generales de Guipúzcoa and Diputación Foral de Guipúzcoa, Juntas Generales d'Alava and Diputación Foral d'Alava and Juntas Generales de Vizcaya*	[2000] ECR I-01073	53, 54, 88, 89, 162, 197, 212
C-310/99	*Italy v Commission*	[2002] ECR I-2289	50
C-172/98	*Commission of the European Communities v Kingdom of Belgium*	[1999] ECR I-03999	80
C-157/99	B.S.M. *Geraets-Smits v Stichting Ziekenfonds VGZ and H.T.M. Peerbooms v Stichting CZ Groep Zorgverzekeringen,*	[2001] ECR I-05473	81
C-268/99	*Aldona Malgorzata Jany and Others v Staatssecretaris van Justitie*	[2001] ECR I-08615	216
C-328/99	*Italian Republic and SIM 2 Multimedia S.p.A. v Commission of the European Communities*	[2003] ECR I-04035	46
C-42/02	*Diana Elisabeth Lindman*	[2003] ECR I-13519	51
C-112/00	*Eugen Schmidberger, Internationale Transporte und Planzüge v Republik Österreich*	[2003] ECR I-05659	217
C-276/02	*Spain c. Commission of the European Communities*	[2004] ECR I-08091	46
C-280/00	*Altmark Trans GmbH and Regierungspräsidium Magdeburg v Nahverkehrsgesellschaft Altmark GmbH, and Oberbundesanwalt beim Bundesverwaltungsgericht*	[2003] ECR I-07747	72, 73

Case	Name	Reported	Page Numbers
C-355/00	*Freskot AE v Elliniko Dimosio*	[2003] ECR I-05264	81
C-445/03	*Commission v Luxembourg*	[2004] ECR I-10191	217
C-446/03	*Marks & Spencer*	[2005] ECR I-10837	217
C-88/03	*Portugal v Commission*	[2006] ECR I-7115	54, 55, 122, 140, 159, 179
C-386/04	*Centro di Musicologia Walter Stauffer*	[2006] ECR I-8203	239
C-406/04	*Gérald De Cuyper v Office National de l'emploi*	[2006] ECR I-06947	218, 239
C-192/05	*K. Tas-Hagen and R. A. Tas v Raadskamer WUBO van de Pensioen- en Uitkeringsraad*	[2006] ECR I-10451	218, 240
C-346/06	*Dirk Rüffert v Land Niedersachsen*	[2008] ECR I-01989	90, 217, 222
C-499/06	*Halina Nerkowska v Zakład Ubezpieczeń Społecznych Oddział w Koszalinie*	[2008] ECR I-03993	218, 240
C-487/06	*British Aggregates Association v Commission*	[2008] ECR I-10515	62
C-527/06	*Renneberg*	[2008] ECR I-7735	87
C-428/06 to C-434/06	*Unión General de Trabajadores de La Rioja (UGT-Rioja) and Others v Juntas Generales del Territorio Histórico de Vizcaya and Others*	[2008] ECR I-06747	57, 58, 148
C-169/08	*Presidente del Consiglio dei Ministri v Regione Sardegna*	[2009] ECR I-10821	60, 61, 84, 87, 88, 162
C-447/08 to C-448/08	*Criminal proceedings against Otto Sjöberg (C-447/08) and Anders Gerdin (C-448/08),*	[2010] ECR I-06921	86, 90
C-515/08	*Dos Santos Palhota and Others*	[2010] ECR I-09133	90, 217, 222
C-287/10	*Tankreederei I SA v Directeur de l'administration des contributions directes*	[2010] ECR I-14233	240
C-106/09	*Commission and Spain v Government of Gibraltar and United Kingdom*	[2011] ECR I-11113	60
C-542/09	*Commission v Kingdom of the Netherlands*	[2012] ECR I-0000	96

Case	Name	Reported	Page Numbers
C-20/15 P and C-21/15 P	*Commission v World Duty Free Group SA, formerly Autogrill España SA, Banco Santander SA, Santusa Holding SL*	[2016] ECR I-0000	48, 60
C-591/15	*The Gibraltar Betting and Gaming Association Limited v Commissioners for Her Majesty's Revenue and Customs and Her Majesty's Treasury*	[2017] ECR I-0000	151
C-571/15	*Wallenborn Transports SA v Hauptzollamt GießenCase*	[2017] ECR I-0000	94

General Court of the EU

Case	Name	Reported	Page Numbers
T-17/02	*Fred Olsen, SA v Commission*	[2005] ECR II-02031	71, 171, 200
T-289/03	*BUPA and others v Commission*	[2008] ECR II-00081	71, 171, 200, 210
T-349/03	*Corsica Ferries France sas c Commission*	[2005] ECR II-2197	51
T-211/04 and T-215/04	*Government of Gibraltar and United Kingdom v Commission*	[2008] ECR II-3745	59, 152
T-81/07	*KG Holding NV c Commission*	[2009] ECR II-2411	45
T-52/12	*Greece v Commission*	[2014] ECR II-0000	45

Table of Legislation and Policy Documents

EU Legislation

Document	Reported	Page Numbers
Act concerning the conditions of accession of the Kingdom of Norway, the Republic of Austria, the Republic of Finland and the Kingdom of Sweden and the adjustments to the treaties on which the European Union is founded	O.J. 1994, C 241, pp. 9–404	117
Commission Decision of 3 November 1995 (SG95 D/1287)	Not published	137
Commission Decision 82/371/EEC of 17 December 1981 relating to a proceeding under Article 85 of the EEC Treaty (IV/29.995 – NAVEWA-ANSEAU)	O.J. 1982, L 167, pp 39-52	71
Commission Decision of 26 November 2008 (State Aid C 16/2007 *Postbus AG*)	O.J. 2009, L 306, p. 26	202
Commission Decision of 26 November 2008 (State aid C 3/08 *Southern Moravia Bus Companies*)	O.J. 2009, L 97, p. 14	204, 205
Commission Decision of 24 February 2010 (State aid C 41/08 *DSB*)	O.J. 2011, L 7, p. 1 et seq.	203, 204
Commission Decision 2012/21/EU of 20 December 2011 on the application of Article 106(2) of the Treaty on the Functioning of the European Union to State aid in the form of public service compensation granted to certain undertakings entrusted with the operation of services of general economic interest	O.J. 2012, L 7, p. 3–10	74, 203

Document	Reported	Page Numbers
Commission Recommendation of 6 May 2003 concerning the definition of micro, small and medium-sized enterprises	O.J. 2003, L 124, pp. 36-41	110
Commission Regulation (EC) No. 800/2008 of 6 August 2008 declaring certain categories of aid compatible with the internal market in application of Articles 87 and 88 of the Treaty (Block Exemption Regulation)	O.J. 2008, L 214, pp. 3–47	127
Commission Regulation (EU) No. 360/2012 of 25 April 2012 on the application of Articles 107 and 108 of the Treaty on the Functioning of the European Union to *de minimis* aid granted to undertakings providing services of general economic interest	O.J. L 114, p. 8–13	77
Commission Regulation (EU) No. 1407/2013 of 18 December 2013 on the application of Articles 107 and 108 of the Treaty on the Functioning of the European Union to *de minimis* aid	O.J. 2013, L 352, pp. 1-8	64, 106, 127, 235
Commission Regulation (EU) No. 651/2014 of 17 June 2014 declaring certain categories of aid compatible with the internal market in application of Article 107 and 108 of the Treaty	O.J. 2014, L 187, pp. 1-78	63, 106, 235
Commission Regulation (EU) No. 1084/2017 of 14 June 2017, amending Commission Regulation (EU) No. 651/2014 of 17 June 2014, as regards aid for port and airport infrastructure, notification thresholds for aid for culture and heritage conservation and for aid for sport and multifunctional recreational infrastructures, and regional operating aid schemes for outermost regions and amending Regulation (EU) No. 702/2014 as regards the calculation of eligible costs	O.J. 2017, L 156, pp. 1-18	63
Council Decision 2012/419/EU of 11 July 2012	O.J. 2012, L 204, p. 131	15
Council Decision 376/2014/EU of 12 June 2014 authorizing Portugal to apply a reduced rate of excise duty in the autonomous region of Madeira on locally produced and consumed rum and liqueurs and in the autonomous region of the Azores on locally produced and consumed liqueurs and *eaux-de-vie*	O.J. 2014, L. 182, pp. 1-3	141

Document	Reported	Page Numbers
Council Directive 69/75/EEC of 4 March 1969 on harmonization of legal action, regulatory and administrative arrangements for the free zones regimes	O.J. 1969, L 58, pp. 11-13	5, 22
Council Directive 2006/112/EC of 28 November 2006 on the common system of value added tax	O.J. 2006, L 347, pp. 1-118	181, 123, 131, 160, 181
Council Directive 2008/118/EC of 16 December 2008 concerning the general arrangements for excise duty and repealing Directive 92/12/EEC	O.J. 2009, L 9, pp. 12-30	94, 123, 181
Council Directive (EU) 2019/475 of 18 February 2019 amending Directives 2006/112/EC and 2008/118/EC as regards the inclusion of the Italian municipality of Campione d'Italia and the Italian waters of Lake Lugano in the customs territory of the Union and in the territorial application of Directive 2008/118/EC	O.J. 2019, L 83, pp. 42–43	131
Council Regulation (EEC) No. 2504/88 of 25 July 1988 on free zones and free warehouses	O.J. 1988, L 225, pp. 8-13	6
Council Regulation (EEC) No. 4252/88 of 21 December 1988 on the preparation and marketing of liqueur wines produced in the Community	O.J. 1988, L 373, pp. 59-65	139
Council Regulation (EEC) No. 2913/92 of 12 October 1992 establishing the Community Customs Code	O.J. 1992, L 302, pp. 1-50	6, 91
Council Regulation (EEC) No. 2454/93 of 2 July 1993 laying down provisions for the implementation of Council Regulation (EEC) No. 2913/92 establishing the Community Customs Code	O.J. 1993, L 253, pp. 1-766	92
Council Regulation (EC) No. 994/98 of 7 May 1998 on the application of Articles 92 and 93 of the Treaty establishing the European Community to certain categories of horizontal State aid	O.J. 1998, L 142, pp. 1–4	63, 64
Council Regulation (EC) No. 2700/2000 of 16 November 2000 amending Council Regulation (EEC) No. 2913/92 establishing the Community Customs Code	O.J. 2000, L 311, pp. 17-20	91
Council Regulation (EC) No. 450/2008 of 23 April 2008 laying down the Community Customs Code (Modernized Customs Code)	O.J. 2008, L 145, pp. 1–64	7, 92

Document	Reported	Page Numbers
Council Regulation (EU) No. 1588/2015 of 13 July 2015 on the application of Articles 107 and 108 of the Treaty on the Functioning of the European Union to certain categories of horizontal State aid	O.J. 2015, L 248, pp. 1-8	63, 64
Regulation (EC) No. 110/2008 of the European Parliament and of the Council of 15 January on the definition, description, presentation, labelling and the protection of geographical indications of spirit drinks and repealing Council Regulation (EEC) No. 1576/89	O.J. 2008, L 39, pp. 16-54	141
Regulation (EC) No. 450/2008 of the European Parliament and of the Council of 23 April 2008 laying down the Community Customs Code	O.J. 2008, L 145, pp. 1-64	7, 92
Regulation (EU) No. 492/2011 of the European Parliament and of the Council of 5 April 2011 on freedom of movement for workers within the Union	O.J. 2011, L 141, p. 1-12	95
Regulation (EU) No. 952/2013 of the European Parliament and of the Council of 9 October 2013 laying down the Union Customs Code	O.J. 2013, L. 269, pp. 1-101	7, 29, 91, 181
Regulation (EU) No. 1296/2013 of the European Parliament and of the Council of 11 December 2013 on a European Union Programme for Employment and Social Innovation ('EaSI') and amending Decision No 283/2010/EU establishing a European Progress Microfinance Facility for employment and social inclusion	O.J. 2013, L 347, pp. 238–252	97
Regulation (EU) 2019/474 of the European Parliament and of the Council of 19 March 2019 amending Regulation (EU) No 952/2013 laying down the Union Customs Code	O.J. 2019, L 83, pp. 38–41	131
Treaty of Accession of Denmark, Ireland, and the United Kingdom (1972)	O.J. 1972, L 73, pp. 1-204	152, 153
Treaty concerning the accession of the Republic of Croatia to the European Union	O.J. 2012, L 112, pp. 10-20	15
Treaty on European Union (consolidated version)	O.J. 2012, C 236, pp. 13-390	15
Treaty on the Functioning of the European Union	O.J. 2012, C 326, pp. 47-390	7

EU Policy Documents

Document	Reported	Page Numbers
Commission notice on the notion of State aid as referred to in Article 107(1) TFEU	O.J. 2016, C 262, pp. 1-50	45, 46, 47, 49
Commission staff working document, Guide to the application of the European Union rules on state aid, public procurement and the internal market to services of general economic interest, and in particular to social services of general interest, SWD (2013) 53 final/2	available at *http://ec.europa.eu/competition/state_aid/overview/new_guide_eu_rules_procurement_en.pdf*	70, 79, 81, 89, 90, 200
Communication from the Commission – Guidelines on national regional aid	O.J. 1998, C 74, pp. 9-18	65
Communication from the Commission of 19 January 2001, *Services of general interest in Europe*	O.J. 2001, C 17	71
Communication from the Commission of 23 February 2002 publishing the list of free zones in existence and in operation in the Community	O.J. 2002, C 50, pp. 16-18	6, 176
Communication from the Commission of 11 December 2002, COM (2002) No. 4811	O.J. 2003, C 134, p. 1	137
Communication from the Commission of 16 November 2004 (State Aid No. 381/2004 *Broadband Infrastructure Project Pyrénées-Atlantiques*) COM (2004) No. 4343 final	O.J. 2005, C 162	204
Communication from the Commission of 1 July 2005, COM (2005) No. 1327 final	O.J. 2005, C 230, p. 1	133
Communication from the Commission – Guidelines on national regional aid for 2007-2013	O.J. 2006, C 54, pp. 13-44	65
Communication from the Commission of 26 April 2006, *Implementing the Community Lisbon programme: Social services of general interest in the European Union*, COM (2006) No. 177 final	Not published	70, 80, 81, 198
Communication from the Commission of 16 May 2006 (State Aid No. 604/2005 *Busverkehr Landkreis Wittenberg*)	O.J. 2006, C 207, p. 2, et. seq.	203
Communication from the Commission of 22 June 2006 (State aid No. 70/A/2006), COM (2006) No. 2329 final	O.J. 2006, C 242, pp. 18	119
Communication from the Commission of 20 December 2006 (State aid No. 377/2006), COM (2006) No. 6635	O.J. 2007, C 30, p. 4	145, 146

Document	Reported	Page Numbers
Communication from the Commission of 27 June 2007, COM (2007) No. 3037 final	O.J. 2007, C 240, p. 1	137, 138
Communication from the Commission of 23 October 2007 (State aid No. 21502), COM (2007) No. 5115	O.J. 2008, C 14, p. 10	120
Communication from the Commission of 3 June 2009 (State aid No. 326/08 *Réduction des taux d'imposition à Saint-Martin*), COM (2009) No. 4026 final	O.J. 2009, C 264, p. 3	122
Communication from the Commission of 15 September 2009 (State aid No 206/2009 *Financing of the public transport services in district of Anhalt-Bitterfeld*) COM (2009) No. 6777 final	O.J. 2009, C 255	204
Communication from the Commission of 28 October 2009 (State aid No. 346/2009), COM (2009) No. 8126 final	O.J. 2009, C 299, p. 1	126
Communication from the Commission of 29 September 2010 (State aid No. 325/08 *Aide fiscale à l'investissement à Saint-Martin*), COM (2010) No. 6471 final	O.J. 2011, C 181, p. 31	122
Communication from the Commission – Guidelines on regional State aid for 2014-2020	O.J. 2013, C 209, pp. 1-45	50, 66, 106, 145
Communication from the Commission of 29 October 2014, COM (2014) No. 7812	O.J. 2015, C 44, p. 1	132
Communication from the Commission of 4 February 2003, COM (2003) No. 92	Not published	137
Communication from the Commission of 25 October 2011, COM (2011) No. 682	Not published	172
Communication from the Commission of 11 January 2012 on the application of the European Union State aid rules to compensation granted for the provision of services of general economic interest	O.J. 2012, C 8, pp. 4-14	75, 205
Communication from the Commission of 10 December 2014 (State aid No. 38566), COM (2014) No. 9316 final	O.J. 2015, C 44, pp. 1-12	121
Communication from the Commission, *European Union framework for State aid in the form of public service compensation*	O.J. 2012, C 8, p. 15–22	78
Communication from the Commission of 6 April 2018 (State aid No. 48571), COM (2018) No. 1661 final	O.J. 2018, C 180, pp. 1-8	69, 128

Document	Reported	Page Numbers
Communication from the Commission of 19 July 2018 (State aid No. 50370), COM (2018) No. 4545 final	O.J. 2018, C 317, pp. 1-10	120–121
Communication from the Commission of 15 May 2019 (State aid No. 50299), COM (2019) No. 3592 final	O.J. 2019, C 221, pp. 1-5	120
Conclusions of the ECOFIN Council Meeting on 1 December 1997 concerning taxation policy - Resolution of the Council and the Representatives of the Governments of the Member States, meeting within the Council of 1 December 1997 on conduct for business taxation	O.J. 1998, C 2, pp. 1-6	8, 100
Conclusions of the European Council of 25/26 March 2010, EUCO 7/10	Not published	238
Guidance of the Code of Conduct Group (Business Taxation) on tax privileges related to special economic zones (document No. 10487/17 of 19 June 2017)	Not published	104, 105, 158, 223, 225
Opinion by the State Aid Group of EAGCP, Services of general economic interest, 29 June 2006, p. 7	available at *http://ec.europa.eu/competition/state_aid/legislation/sgei.pdf*	205
Parliamentary question E-3120/07 of 21 June 2007	O.J. 2008, C 45, pp. 1–226	21
Report from the Code of Conduct Group (Business Taxation) to ECOFIN Council of 23 November 1999, SN(1999) 4901, Annex A	Not published	102
Report from the Code of Conduct Group (Business Taxation) to the ECOFIN Council of 25 May 2010, Council of the European Union, document No. 10033/10.	Not published	104

International Legislation

Document	Reported	Page Numbers
London Memorandum of 5 October 1954 (signed in London)	United Nations - Treaty Series, 1956, No. 3297	125
Peace Treaty of 10 February 1947 (signed in Paris)	United Nations - Treaty Series, 1950, Vol. 49, No. 747	125

Bulgarian Legislation

Document	Reported	Page Numbers
VAT Act	O.J. of Bulgaria No. 63 of 4 August 2006	112
Customs Act	O.J. of Bulgaria No. 15 of 6 February 1998	112
Decree of 14 July 1987, No. 2242	O.J. of Bulgaria No. 55 of 17 July 1987	22, 111, 112, 158
Law on Excises and Tax Warehouses Act	O.J. of Bulgaria No. 91 of 15 November 2005	112

Croatia Legislation

Document	Reported	Page Numbers
Act of Free Zones	O.J. of Croatia No. 44/96, 92/05, 85/08, 148/13	113
Customs Law	O.J. of Croatia No. 78/99, 94/99, 117/99, 92/01	113
Excise Duties Act	O.J. of Croatia No. 83/09	114

Czech Republic Legislation

Document	Reported	Page Numbers
VAT Act No. 235/2004	available at *https://www.mzv.cz/jnp/*	114
Excise Tax Act No. 353/2003	available at *https://www.mzv.cz/jnp/*	114

Estonian Legislation

Document	Reported	Page Numbers
VAT Act	O.J. of Estonia, I, 2003, 82, 554	115
Alcohol, Tobacco, Fuel and Electricity Excise Duty Act	O.J. of Estonia, I, 2003, 2, 17	116

Finnish Legislation

Document	Reported	Page Numbers
Act of 16 August 1991, No. 1144	Not published	117
VAT Act No. 1501 of 30 December 1993	available at *https://www.finlex.fi/*	116
Customs Act No. 1466 of 29 December 1994	available at *http://www.wipo.int/*	116
Act on Excise Duty No. 182/2010 of 19 March 2010	available at *https://www.alko.fi/*	116

French Legislation

Document	Reported	Page Numbers
Amending Finance Law of 29 December 2014, No. 1655	O.J of France of 30 December 2014	119, 120
Code General des Impotes	available at *www.legifrance.gouv.fr*	118
Code General des Impots de la Collectivite de Saint-Martin	available at *www.com-saint-martin.fr/*	122
French Customs Code	available at *www.legifrance.gouv.fr*	118
Law of 2 July 2004, No. 2004-639	available at *www.legifrance.gouv.fr*	121
Law of 21 July 2003, No. 2003-660, amending Article 199-*undecies* of the French Tax Code	available at *www.legifrance.gouv.fr*	121
Loi No. 96-987 du 14 novembre 1996 relative à la mise en oeuvre du pacte de relance pour la ville	available at *www.legifrance.gouv.fr*	119

German Legislation

Document	Reported	Page Numbers
Tobacco Tax Law (TabStG) of 15 July 2009,	O.J. of Germany, I S. 1870	123
Value Added Tax Act (UStG) of 26 November 1979	available at *http://www.gesetze-im-internet.de/*	123

Greek Legislation

Document	Reported	Page Numbers
Customs Code (Law No. 2960 of 22 November 2001)	O.J. of Greece No. 265/A/2001	124
VAT Code (Law No. 2859/2000)	O.J. of Greece No. 248/A/2000	124

Hungarian Legislation

Document	Reported	Page Numbers
Act CXXVII of 2007 on Value Added Tax,	available at *http://www.icnl.org/*	125

Italian Legislation

Document	Reported	Page Numbers
Circolare Italian Ministry of Economic Development No. 172230 of 9 April 2018	available at *http://www.sviluppoeconomico.gov.it/*	127
Decree-Law of 20 June 2017, No. 91	O.J. of Italy No. 141 of 20 June 2017	168
Decree of the President of the Council of Ministers of 25 January 2018, No. 12	O.J. of Italy No. 47 of 26 February 2018	129
Decreto del Commissario Generale del Governo italiano per il territorio di Trieste of 19 January 1955, No. 29	O.J. of Italy No. 3 of 21 January 1955	125
Decreto del Commissario Generale del Governo italiano per il territorio di Trieste of 21 December 1959, No. 53	O.J. No. 36 of 21 December 1959	125
Decreto del Presidente della Repubblica of 26 October 1972, No. 633 (Italian VAT Act)	O.J. of Italy No. 292 of 11 November 1972	130
Decreto del Presidente della Repubblica of 22 December 1986, No. 917 (Italian Income Tax Act)	O.J. of Italy No. 302 of 31 December 1986	131
Interministerial Decree April 10, 2013	O.J. of Italy No. 161 of 11 July 2013	127
Law Decree of 5 January 1948, No. 268	O.J. of Italy No. 91 of 17 April 1948	125

Document	Reported	Page Numbers
Law Decree of 26 October 1995, No. 504	O.J. of Italy No. 279 of 29 November 1995	126
Law Decree of 28 April 2009, No. 39	O.J. of Italy No. 97 of 28 April 2009	126
Law Decree of 24 January 2012, No. 1	O.J. of Italy No. 19 of 24 January 2012	126
Law Decree of 18 October 2012, No. 179	O.J. of Italy No. 245 of 19 October 2012	126
Law Decree of 19 June 2015, No. 78	O.J. of Italy No. 140 of 19 June 2015	127
Law Decree of 24 April 2017, No. 50	O.J. of Italy No. 95 of 24 April 2017	127
Law of 12 February 1955, No. 41	O.J. of Italy No. 51 of 3 March 1955	125
Law of 1 November 1973, No. 762	O.J. of Italy No. 310 of 1 December 1973	130
Law of 9 January 1991, No. 19	O.J. of Italy No. 17 of 21 January 1991	125
Law of 24 June 2009, No. 7	O.J. of Italy No. 147 of 27 June 2009	126
Law of 24 March 2012, No. 27	O.J. of Italy No. 71 of 24 March 2012	126
Law of 6 August 2015, No. 125	O.J. of Italy, No, 188 of 14 August 2015	
Law of 28 December 2015, No. 208	O.J. of Italy No. 302 of 20 December 2015	127
Law of 3 August 2017, No. 123	O.J. of Italy No. 188 of 12 August 2017	129
Law of 7 April 2017, No. 45	O.J. of Italy No. 84 of 10 April 2017	128
Regional Law of 11 May 2006, No. 4	O.J. of Region of Sardinia 2006, No. 15	61, 87

Latvian Legislation

Document	Reported	Page Numbers
Law on 'Tax Application in Free Ports and Special Economic Zones' of 27 July 2001	O.J. of Latvia No. 117 (2504) of 10 August 2001	131

Lithuanian Legislation

Document	Reported	Page Numbers
Law of 7 June 2005, No. X-233	O.J. of Lithuania, 2005, No. 76-2741	134
Law on Excise Duty of 30 October 2001, No. IX-569	O.J. of Lithuania, 2001, No. 98-3482	134
Law on the Fundamentals of Free Economic Zones of 28 June 1995, No. I-976	O.J. of Lithuania,1995, No. 59-1462	133, 134
Law on VAT of 5 March 2002, No. IX-751	O.J. of Lithuania, 2002, No. 35-1271	134

Luxembourg Legislation

Document	Reported	Page Numbers
VAT Act of 12 February 1979	O.J. of Luxembourg, 1979, Part A, No. 23	135

Malta Legislation

Document	Reported	Page Numbers
Act XXVI of 1989 (Malta Freeports Act), as amended by Legal Notice 103 of 1995	available at *http://www.maltafreeport.com.mt*	135
Act XXIII of 1998 (VAT Act)	available at *https://parlament.media*	136
Act XII of 1997 (Customs and Excise Tax Act)	available at *http://www.justiceservices.gov.mt/*	136

Polish Legislation

Document	Reported	Page Numbers
Act of 20 October 1994 on Special Economic Zones	O.J. of Poland No. 123/1994, item 600	25
Customs Code Act 1997	O.J. of Poland No. 1997/23/117	136
Customs Law of 28 December 1989	O.J. of Poland No. 75/1989	136

Document	Reported	Page Numbers
Excise Duty Act of 6 December 2008	O.J. of Poland 2009, No. 3, Item 11	137
Polish VAT Act	O.J. of Poland 2004,r. Nr 54, poz. No. 54, Item. 535.535	137

Portuguese Legislation

Document	Reported	Page Numbers
Decree Law of 20 October 1980, No. 500	O.J. of Portugal No. 243 of 20 October 1980	137
Decree Law of 26 June 1986, No. 165	O.J. of Portugal No. 144/1 of 26 June 1986	138
Decree of 21 June 2010, No. 73	O.J. of Portugal No. 118/1 of 21 June 2010	139
Law of 12 January 2009, No. 2	available at *http://www. alra.pt/*	140
Portuguese Tax Incentives Statute approved by Decree Law of 1 July 1989, No. 215	O.J. of Portugal No. 149/1 of 1 July 1989	138
Regional LegislativeDecree of 20 January 1999, No. 2/99/A	O.J. of Azores, I, No. 4 of 28 January 1999	55

Romanian Legislation

Document	Reported	Page Numbers
Government Urgency Ordinance of 16 June 1997, No. 31	O.J. of Romania, Part I, No. 125 of 19 June 1997	141
Law No. 571/2003	O.J. of Romania No. 927 of 23 December 2003	142
Law of 21 July 1992, No. 84	O.J. of Romania, Part I, No. 182 of 30 July 1992	141
Law of 29 June 2001, No. 332	O.J. of Romania, Part I, No. 356 of 3 July 2001	141
Romanian Fiscal Code of 2003	O.J. of Romania No. 688 of 10 September 2015	142

Slovenian Legislation

Document	Reported	Page Numbers
Economic Zones Act	O.J. of Slovenia No. 45 of 12 June 1998	143
VAT Act	O.J. of Slovenia No. 117/2006	143
Excise Duty Act	O.J. of Slovenia No. 97/2010	143

Spanish Legislation

Document	Reported	Page Numbers
Law of 25 March 1991, No. 8	O.J. of Spain No. 73 of 26 March 1991	151
Law of 7 June 1991, No. 20	O.J. of Spain No. 137 of 8 June 1991	145
Law of 28 December 1992, No. 37	O.J. of Spain No. 312 of 29 December 1992	144, 150
Law of 28 December 1992, No. 38	O.J. of Spain No. 312 of 29 December 1992, pp. 44305-44331	151
Law of 6 July 1994, No. 19	O.J. of Spain No. 161 of 7 July 1994	145
Law of 26 June 2014, No. 4	O.J. of Spain No. 168 of 11 July 2015 pp. 54383-54399	147
Ley Foral 26/2016 de 28 de diciembre, del Impuesto sobre Sociedades	O.J. of Spain No. 55, of 6 March 2017	149
Ley 12/2002 de 23 de mayo 2002, por la que se aprueba el Concierto Económico con la Comunidad Autónoma del País Vasco	O.J. of Spain No. 124 of 24 May 2002	58, 148
Norma Foral 2/2014 de 17 de enero, sobre el Impuesto de Sociedades del Territorio Histórico de Gipuzkoa	O.J. of Spain No. 13 of 22 January 2014	148, 149
Order HAP/1358 of 25 July 2014 which authorizes the establishment of the '*Consorcio de la Zona Franca de Sevilla*'	O.J. of Spain No. 182 of 28 July 2014, pp. 59873-59881	144
Order HAP/1412 of 29 August 2016 which authorizes the establishment of the '*Consorcio de la Zona Franca de Santander*'	O.J. of Spain No. 210 of 31 August 2016, pp. 62091-62100	144

Document	Reported	Page Numbers
Organic Law No. 1 of 13 March 1995 on the Statute of Autonomy of Ceuta	O.J. of Spain No. 62 of 14 March 1995	150
Organic Law No. 2 of 13 March 1995 on the Statute of Autonomy of Melilla	O.J. of Spain No. 62 of 14 March 1995	
Royal Decree of 5 March 2004, No. 3	O.J. of Spain No. 60 of 10 March 2004, pp. 10670-10721	150
Royal Decree of 5 March 2004, No. 4	O.J. of Spain No. 260 of 30 October 2013, pp. 87528 - 87568	150

United Kingdom Legislation

Document	Reported	Page Numbers
Finance Act 2014	available at *www.gibraltarlaws.gov.gi*	39
Imports and Exports Act, 1986 (Act. No. 1986-21)	available at *www.gibraltarlaws.gov.gi*	153
Income Tax Act	available at *www.gibraltarlaws.gov.gi*	152
Legal Notice No. 187 of 2010	O.J. of Gibraltar, II, No. 3827 of 23 December 2010	152

Index

A

Aland Islands, 16, 102, 111, 117, 182
Almunia package, 74–81, 171, 200, 207, 209, 254, 258
Altmark criteria, 72–74, 76, 77, 197, 199–207, 209, 210, 226, 227, 230, 236, 237, 254, 257, 258, 260
Asymmetrical autonomy, 160
Azores, 54–57, 103, 109, 111, 122, 140–141, 148, 159

B

Benefit principle, 244
Basque Country, 53, 57–59, 89, 103, 111, 148–149, 159, 162, 168, 180
Bulgaria, 22, 111–112, 158, 176
Busingen, 111, 123, 168, 182

C

Campione d'Italia, 111, 130–131, 182
Canary Islands, 15, 111, 144–147, 161, 172, 182
Capital gain tax, 110, 138, 152
Ceuta, 111, 150–151, 161, 168, 182
Classifications, 19, 27–28, 31, 40, 45, 143, 165–167, 257, 260
Code of Conduct for Business Taxation, 8, 13, 44, 100–106, 222–226, 228
Community Customs Code (CCC), 6
Concepts, 34–36, 95–98, 156–175
Corporate income tax (CIT), 57, 59, 102, 103, 122, 132, 134, 140, 145–150, 152, 212
Croatia, 113–114, 176
Customs duties, 4–6, 22–24, 27, 28, 82, 90–92, 95, 106, 111–116, 118, 122, 123, 125, 126, 130, 131, 133, 134–137, 139, 142, 143, 151, 152, 160, 164, 168, 176, 177, 183, 185, 188, 247
Customs warehouses, 28, 29, 92
Czech Republic, 114, 176

D

De minimis regulation, 64–65, 69, 74, 77–78, 209, 235, 248
Definitions, 16–17, 20–27, 174–175
Denmark, 111, 114–115, 176
Deufil, (ECJ), 53, 61–62
Duty-free shops, 28, 30

E

Economic and financial autonomy, 49, 56, 57, 180
Economic criteria, 68, 97, 98, 171
Economic tax incentives, 167–170, 172, 173, 183, 185, 234, 254, 257
Eligibility conditions, 246–247, 250
Eligible areas, 68, 220, 242, 249–251, 255, 259, 260

Eligible undertakings, 192–194, 223, 225, 227, 246, 249, 250, 254, 255, 258, 259
Estonia, 115–116, 176
EU cohesion policy, 18, 65–68, 233, 237–242, 251, 255, 260
European tax law, 3, 9–11, 13–15, 155–157, 175, 182, 184, 253, 256, 257, 259, 261–263
Excise duties, 82, 90, 106, 114–117, 123, 125, 126, 130, 131, 137, 139, 143, 144, 176, 185, 188, 247
Excise duty directive, 82, 91, 94, 112, 116–118, 126, 137, 160, 168
Exclusion regimes, 163, 164, 168, 174, 175, 181, 183, 189, 190, 256
Export Processing Zones (EPZs), 10, 17, 20, 26–27
Extra-Territorial Zone Model, 181–183

F

Finland, 111, 116–117, 176
Fiscal residue, 18, 220, 222, 228, 231, 234, 242–245, 249–251, 255, 258–262
France, 7, 22, 111, 118–122, 126, 128, 159, 161, 172, 176, 179, 186, 187, 197
Free Economic Zones (FEZs), 20, 111, 133–134, 168, 182
Free movement of capital, 82
Free movement of goods, 82, 93
Free movement of persons, 2, 9, 11–13, 82–84, 97, 211, 215–217, 219, 229, 234, 251, 255, 257, 258, 260
Free movement of services, 82, 89
Free movement of workers, 13, 83, 95, 211, 213–216, 221, 228
Free Port, 24–25, 114–115, 135–136, 143
Free Trade Zones, 10, 17, 22–24, 137–139, 144
Free Zone Model, 175–177, 182, 183
Free Zones, 23–23, 119–120, 126–128
Freedom of establishment, 83, 89, 162, 163, 188, 189, 211, 212, 221, 227–229
French Guyana, 118, 120
French Overseas Departments, 120–121, 122, 182
Functional dimension, 156, 157, 166–173, 175, 179, 180, 182, 183, 185–187, 189, 192–195, 197, 198, 226, 229, 231–232, 233, 254, 256, 257, 262
Fundamental freedoms, 3, 7, 9, 44, 79, 81–90, 106, 186, 196, 210–222, 226, 227

G

General Block Exemption Regulation (GBER), 52, 63–65, 69, 129, 178, 235, 236, 248
General legal theory, 11–14, 18, 19, 41, 155–184, 187–189, 192, 231–237, 251, 253, 254, 256–257, 261–263
Geographical delimitation, 29, 157–159, 174, 187–189, 196, 229
Germany, 4, 61, 111, 122–123, 168, 176
Gibraltar, 16, 52, 59–60, 103, 104, 111, 151–153, 159, 162, 168, 169, 180
Governance, 97, 171, 233, 240–242
Greece, 111, 124–125, 176
Guadeloupe, 15
Guidance on tax privileges related to SEZs, 104–105, 223, 225–226
Guidelines on Regional aid, 65–69, 145

H

Harmful tax competition, 13, 17, 43, 44, 99–105, 186, 196, 226, 257, 260
Harmonization, 5, 7, 22, 45, 65, 82, 90–99, 106, 107, 160, 168, 247
Helgoland, 111, 123, 168, 182
Hungary, 124–125, 176

Hybrid situations, 158, 182

I

Implementing models, 3, 11–14, 18, 19, 21, 156, 175–186, 188, 196, 229, 232, 233, 248, 251, 253, 254, 256, 257, 259
Infra-State body, 54, 55, 57, 58, 149, 152, 159, 177, 179–181, 183, 185, 236
Institutional autonomy, 56–59, 179
Italy, 7, 38, 68, 87, 111, 125–131, 158, 161, 168, 172, 176, 179, 186, 187, 197, 235

J

Juntas Generales, (ECJ), 53–54, 88–89

L

Latvia, 111, 131–134, 168, 176, 182
Lithuania, 111, 133–134, 168, 176, 182
Livigno, 111, 130, 181
Luxembourg, 111, 135, 176

M

Madeira, 7, 15, 103, 111, 137–139, 161, 172, 179, 197
Malta, 111, 135–136, 176
Martinique, 15, 120, 121
Material selectivity, 48, 52, 60
Mayotte, 15, 120, 121
Maximum aid intensity, 63, 129, 179, 235, 236, 248
Melilla, 111, 150–151, 161, 168, 182
Monitoring, 75, 191, 226, 228, 230, 242, 251, 261
Mount Athos, 111, 124, 181

N

Navarra, 103, 111, 148–149, 159, 168, 180
Notification requirement, 52, 63, 64, 73–75, 78, 129, 199, 206–209, 235

O

Obligations of the recipient undertaking, 194–195, 248–249
Organization for Economic Cooperation and Development (OECD), 38, 162, 246, 261

P

Permanent establishment, 84, 88, 89, 145, 162, 163, 183, 189, 211, 212, 215, 223, 227, 229, 246, 255, 258
Personal income tax (PIT), 53110, 145, 146, 148, 150
Poland, 25, 38, 104, 111, 136–137, 176
Polish Free Customs Duty Areas, 136
Portugal, 54, 103, 111, 137–141, 176, 179, 197
Primarolo report, 102, 103
Principle of proportionality, 218, 219, 222
Principle of tax non-discrimination, 8, 82–85, 87–89, 162, 212
Procedural aspects, 18, 245, 249–251
Procedural autonomy, 56–59, 180
Public interest, 38, 71, 90, 200, 202, 216–218, 222, 228, 231, 239, 240, 242, 245, 255, 258
Public Procurement procedure, 73, 76, 77, 79, 199, 205–207, 209, 210, 227, 250, 255, 258, 260

R

Real estate tax (RET), 110, 132, 134
Recast Vat Directive, 82, 91, 93–94, 112, 117, 118, 121, 126, 137, 143, 160, 168
Recipient undertaking, 194–195, 211–212, 194–195

Recommendations, 14, 18, 110, 253–263
Reference framework, 48, 49, 54, 55, 57–61, 109, 148, 149, 152, 157, 159–160, 163, 165, 174, 177, 179, 180, 182, 188, 191, 229
Regional autonomy, 54, 55
Regional fiscal aid, 30
Reunion, 15, 120, 121
Romania, 141–142
Rule of reason, 85, 86, 90

S

Saint-Martin, 15, 111, 121–122, 159, 168, 182
Sardinia, (ECJ), 60–61, 87–88
Scope of the tax measures, 172, 192, 194, 248
Services of general economic interest (SGEIs), 70–81, 198, 199, 209
Services of general interest (SGIs), 79, 198, 203
Slovenia, 111, 143, 176
Social advantages, 82, 91, 95–96, 107, 170, 171
Social Cohesion Zone, 201, 237–251, 257–259
Social criteria, 97, 98, 172, 193, 201
Social enterprises, 37–40, 96–99
Social services of general interest (SSGIs), 43, 44, 69–81, 89–90, 170, 171, 198, 200–202, 209, 226, 254, 257
Social tax incentives, 34–36, 170–173, 198
Spain, 53, 58, 59, 103, 111, 143–151, 159, 168, 176
Special Economic Zones (SEZs), 10, 17, 20, 25, 26, 104–105, 111, 129–133, 168, 174, 179, 182, 225–226
State aid case-law, 52–62
State aid exemptions, 50, 51, 70–72
State aid notion, 44–49, 199
State Aid Zone Model, 177–183, 197, 209, 235, 237
Structural dimension, 156, 163–166, 179, 181, 183, 189–192, 196, 229–230, 240
Subsidiarity, 240–242
Subsidies, 26, 28, 30–31, 56, 61, 72, 97, 146, 180
Substantial aspects, 28, 34, 246–249, 257
Subtractive regimes, 163–166, 174, 175, 179–181, 183, 189, 190, 196, 197, 230, 247, 256
Symmetrical autonomy, 160

T

Tax allowances, 165, 189–191, 196, 230, 247
Tax credits, 20, 31, 46, 47, 121, 128–130, 145, 146, 153, 165, 189–191, 196, 206, 230, 242, 247, 248, 250
Tax deferrals, 31, 166, 177, 190
Tax equity, 244
Tax exemption, 4, 25, 37, 45, 128, 165, 168, 190, 206
Tax-Free Zone, 7, 119–120, 126–128, 174
Tax havens, 28–29
Tax rebate, 31, 132, 166, 190
Tax relief, 17, 39, 40, 126, 149, 150, 166, 190
Tax replacement regime, 166, 190
Territorial connecting factor, 157, 160–163, 174, 175, 182, 183, 188–189, 212, 227, 229, 256, 258
Territorial dimension, 33, 41, 156–163, 166, 174, 176, 180, 182, 187–189, 196, 211, 229
Territorial selectivity, 48, 52–54, 59, 60, 148, 177, 179, 258
Territorial tax advantages, 2, 19, 43, 49, 55, 57, 109, 126, 159, 179
Theoretical concept, 33, 253

U

UGT-Rioja, (ECJ), 5, 57–59
Union Customs Code, 7, 9, 16, 29, 82, 91–94, 106, 109–118, 122–126, 130, 132–137, 139, 141–144, 151, 158, 160, 166, 168, 176, 177, 183, 185, 229
United Kingdom, 39, 59, 111, 151–153, 159, 216
United Nations, 20, 26
Urban Tax-Free Zones, 7, 119–120, 126–128

V

Value added tax (VAT). 5, 93–94

W

Withholding tax, 103, 110, 134, 138, 152, 168

EUCOTAX Series on European Taxation

(1) Peter HJ Essers, Guido JME de Bont & Eric CCM Kemmeren (eds), *The Compatibility of Anti-Abuse Provisions in Tax Treaties with EC Law,* 1998 (ISBN 90-411-9678-1).
(2) Gerard TK Meussen (ed.), *The Principle of Equality in European Taxation,* 1999 (ISBN 90-411-9693-5).
(3) Michael Lang (ed.), *Tax Treaty Interpretation,* 2001 (ISBN 90-411-9857-1).
(4) Pasquale Pistone, *The Impact of Community Law on Tax Treaties: Issues and Solutions,* 2002 (ISBN 90-411-9860-1).
(5) René Offermanns, *The Entrepreneurship Concept in a European Comparative Tax Law Perspective,* 2002 (ISBN 90-411-9887-3).
(6) Michael Lang & Mario Züger, *Settlement of Disputes in Tax Treaty Law,* 2002 (ISBN 90-411-9904-7).
(7) Carlo Pinto, *Tax Competition and EU Law,* 2003 (ISBN 90-411-9913-6).
(8) Michael Lang, Hans-Jörgen Aigner, Ulrich Scheuerle & Markus *Stefaner, CFC Legislation, Tax Treaties and EC Law,* 2004 (ISBN 90-411-2284-2).
(9) Mattias Dahlberg, *Direct Taxation in Relation to the Freedom of Establishment and the Free Movement of Capital,* 2005 (ISBN 90-411-2363-6).
(10) Michael Lang, Judith Herdin & Ines Hofbauer, *WTO and Direct Taxation,* 2005 (ISBN 90-411-2371-7).
(11) Dennis Weber, *Tax Avoidance and the EC Tray Freedoms: A Study of the Limitations under European Law for the Prevention of Tax Avoidance,* 2005 (ISBN 90-411-2402-0).
(12) Félix Alberto Vega Borrego, *Limitations on Benefits Clauses on Double Taxation Conventions,* 2005 (ISBN 90-411-2370-9).
(13) Michael Lang, Josef Schuch & Claus Staringer, *ECJ-Recent Developments in Direct Taxation,* 2006 (ISBN 90-411-2509-4).
(14) Reuven S. Avi-Yonah, James R. Hines Jr. & Michael Lang, *Comparative Fiscal Federalism. Comparing the European Court of Justice and the US Supreme Court's Tax Jurisprudence,* 2007 (ISBN 978-90-411-2552-1).
(15) Christiana HJI Panayi, *Double Taxation, Tax Treaties, Treaty-Shopping and the European Community,* 2007 (ISBN 978-90-411-2658-0).
(16) Dennis Weber, *The Influence of European Law on Direct Taxation: Recent and Future Developments,* 2007 (ISBN 978-90-411-2667-2).
(17) Michael Lang & Pasquale Pistone, *The EU and Third Countries: Direct Taxation,* 2007 (ISBN 978-90-411-2665-8).
(18) Oskar Henkow, *Financial Activities in European VAT: A Theoretical and Legal Research of the European VAT System and Preferred Treatment of Financial Activities,* 2007 (ISBN 978-90-411-2703-7).
(19) Michael Lang (ed.), *Tax Compliance Costs for Companies in an Enlarged European Community,* 2008 (ISBN 978-90-411-2666-5).

(20) Michael Lang (ed.), *Source versus Residence. Problems Arising from the Allocation of Taxing Rights in Tax Treaty Law and Possible Alternatives*, 2008 (ISBN 978-90-411-2763-1).
(21) Ioanna Mitroyanni, *Integration Approaches to Group Taxation in the European Internal Market*, 2008 (ISBN 978-90-411-2779-2).
(22) Rolf Eicke, *Tax Planning with Holding Companies. Repatriation of US Profits from Europe:Concepts, Strategies, Structures*, 2008 (ISBN978-90-411-2794-5).
(23) Peter Essers et al. (ed.), *The Influence of IAS/IFRS on the CCCTB, Tax Accounting, Disclosure and Corporate Law Accounting Concepts: 'A Clash of Cultures'*, 2008 (ISBN 978-90-411-2819-5).
(24) Tonny Schenk-Geers, *International Exchange of Information and the Protection of Taxpayers*, 2009 (ISBN 978-90-411-3142-3).
(25) Raymond Adema, *UCITS and Taxation: Towards Harmonization of the Taxation of UCITS*, 2009 (ISBN 978-90-411-2839-3).
(26) Michael Lang, Jianwen Liu & Gongliang Tang (eds), *Europe–China Tax Treaties*, 2010 (ISBN 978-90-411-3216-1).
(27) Michael Lang, Pasquale Pistone, Josef Schuch & Claus Staringer (eds), *Procedural Rules in Tax Law in the Context of European Union and Domestic Law*, 2010 (ISBN 978-90-411-3376-2).
(28) Sjaak J.J.M. Jansen, *Fiscal Sovereignty of the Member States in an Internal Market: Past and Future*, 2011 (ISBN 978-90-411-3403-5).
(29) Dennis Weber & Bruno da Silva, *From Marks & Spencer to X Holding: The Future of Cross-Border Group Taxation*, 2011 (ISBN 978-90-411-3399-1).
(30) Claus Bohn Jespersen, *Intermediation of Insurance and Financial Services in European VAT*, 2011 (ISBN 978-90-411-3732-6).
(31) Sabine Heidenbauer, *Charity Crossing Borders: The Fundamental Freedoms' Influence on Charity and Donor Taxation in Europe*, 2011 (ISBN 978-90-411-3813-2).
(32) Michael Lang, et al., *The Future of Indirect Taxation: Recent Trends in VAT and GST Systems around the World*, 2012 (ISBN 978-90-411-3797-5).
(33) Harm van den Broek, *Cross-Border Mergers within the EU: Proposals to Remove the Remaining Tax Obstacles*, 2012 (ISBN 978-90-411-3824-8).
(34) Michael Lang, et al. (eds), *Tax Treaty Case Law around the Globe – 2011*, 2012 (ISBN 978-90-411-3876-7).
(35) Dennis Weber (ed.), *CCCTB: Selected Issues*, 2012 (ISBN 978-90-411-3872-9).
(36) Daniël Smit, *EU Freedoms, Non-EU Countries and Company Taxation*, 2012 (ISBN 978-90-411-4041-8).
(37) Rita de la Feria, *VAT Exemptions: Consequences and Design Alternatives*, 2013 (ISBN 978-90-411-3276-5).
(38) Karin Simader, *Withholding Taxes and the Fundamental Freedoms*, 2013 (ISBN 978-90-411-4842-1).
(39) Madeleine Merkx, *Establishments in European VAT*, 2013 (ISBN 978-90-411-4554-3).
(40) Carla De Pietro, *Tax Treaty Override*, 2014 (ISBN 978-90-411-5406-4).

(41) G.K. Fibbe & A.J.A. Stevens (eds), *Hybrid Entities and the EU Direct Tax Directives*, 2015 (ISBN 978-90-411-5942-7).
(42) Gerard Staats, *Personal Pensions in the EU*, 2015 (ISBN 978-90-411-5953-3).
(43) Michael Lang & Ine Lejeune (eds), *VAT/GST in a Global Digital Economy*, 2015 (ISBN 978-90-411-5952-6).
(44) Massimo Basilavecchia, Lorenzo del Federico & Pietro Mastellone (eds), *Tax Implications of Environmental Disasters and Pollution*, 2015 (ISBN 978-90-411-5611-2).
(45) Cristina Trenta, *Rethinking EU VAT for P2P Distribution*, 2015 (ISBN 978-90-411-6137-6).
(46) Marie Lamensch, Edoardo Traversa & Servaas van Thiel (eds), *Value Added Tax and the Digital Economy: The 2015 EU Rules and Broader Issues*, 2016 (ISBN 978-90-411-6612-8).
(47) Raffaele Petruzzi, *Transfer Pricing Aspects of Intra-Group Financing*, 2016 (ISBN 978-90-411-6732-3).
(48) Mario Grandinetti (ed.), *Corporate Tax Base in the Light of the IAS/IFRS and EU Directive 2013/34: A Comparative Approach*, 2016 (ISBN 978-90-411-6745-3).
(49) Bruno da Silva, *The Impact of Tax Treaties and EU Law on Group Taxation Regimes*, 2016 (ISBN 978-90-411-6905-1).
(50) Michael Lang, Alfred Storck & Raffaele Petruzzi (eds), *Transfer Pricing in a Post-BEPS World*, 2016 (ISBN 978-90-411-6710-1).
(51) Marta Papis-Almansa, *Insurance in European VAT: Current and Preferred Treatment in the Light of the New Zealand and Australian GST Systems*, 2017 (ISBN 978-90-411-8360-6).
(52) Wolfgang Speckhahn, *Real Estate Investment Trusts In Europe: Europeanising Tax Regimes*, 2017 (ISBN 978-90-411-8360-6).
(53) Frank J.G. Nellen, *Information Asymmetries in EU VAT*, 2017 (ISBN 978-90-411-8837-3).
(54) Erik Ros, *EU Citizenship and Direct Taxation*, 2017 (ISBN 978-90-411-8584-6).
(55) Werner Haslehner, Georg Kofler & Alexander Rust (eds), *EU Tax Law and Policy in the 21st Century*, 2017 (ISBN 978-90-411-8815-1).
(56) Claudia Sanò, *National Legal Presumptions and European Tax Law*, 2018 (ISBN 978-90-411-6613-5).
(57) Christoph Marchgraber, *Double (Non-)Taxation and EU Law*, 2018 (ISBN 978-90-411-9410-7).
(58) Dennis Weber & Jan van de Streek (eds), *The EU Common Consolidated Corporate Tax Base: Critical Analysis*, 2018 (ISBN 978-90-411-9233-2).
(59) Werner Haslehner (ed.), *Investment Fund Taxation: Domestic Law, EU Law, and Double Taxation Treaties*, 2018 (ISBN 978-90-411-9669-9).
(60) Jérôme Monsenego, *Selectivity in State Aid Law and the Methods for the Allocation of the Corporate Tax Base*, 2018 (ISBN 978-90-411-9413-8).
(61) José Manuel Almudí Cid, Jorge A. Ferreras Gutiérrez & Pablo A. Hernández González-Barreda (eds), *Combating Tax Avoidance in the EU: Harmonization and Cooperation in Direct Taxation*, 2019 (ISBN 978-94-035-0154-3).

(62) Werner Haslehner, Georg Kofler & Alexander Rust (eds), *Time and Tax: Issues in International, EU, and Constitutional Law*, 2019 (ISBN 978-94-035-0354-7).

(63) Nathalie Wittock, *Sales Promotion Techniques and VAT in the EU*, 2019 (ISBN 978-94-035-0861-0).

(64) Carla De Pietro (ed.), *New Perspectives on Fiscal State Aid: Legitimacy and Effectiveness of Fiscal State Aid Control*, 2019 (ISBN 978-94-035-1415-4).

(65) Giorgio Beretta, *European VAT and the Sharing Economy*, 2019 (ISBN 978-94-035-1435-2).

(66) Claudio Cipollini, *Special Tax Zones and EU Law: Theory, Implementations, and Future Challenges*, 2020 (ISBN 978-94-035-1885-5).

www.ingramcontent.com/pod-product-compliance
Ingram Content Group UK Ltd.
Pitfield, Milton Keynes, MK11 3LW, UK
UKHW020241290926
15470UKWH00002B/658

9 789403 518855